Research & Education Association

The Best Teachers' Test Preparation for the

CSET®
Mathematics

Mel Friedman

Professor of Mathematics

And the Staff of
Research & Education Association

Visit our Educator Support Center at:
www.REA.com/teacher

The content specifications for the CSET®: Mathematics Test were created and implemented by the California Commission on Teacher Credentialing in conjunction with National Evaluation Systems, Inc., a unit of Pearson Education, Inc. For further information visit the CSET® website at *http://www.cset.nesinc.com*.

For all references in this book, CSET® and California Subject Examinations for Teachers® are trademarks of the California Commission on Teacher Credentialing and Pearson Education, Inc.

Research & Education Association
61 Ethel Road West
Piscataway, New Jersey 08854
E-mail: info@rea.com

The Best Teachers' Test Preparation for the California CSET®: Mathematics Test

Printed in the United States of America

Library of Congress Control Number 2007932692

ISBN-13: 978-0-7386-0180-9
ISBN-10: 0-7386-0180-2

REA® is a registered trademark of
Research & Education Association, Inc.

About Research & Education Association

Founded in 1959, Research & Education Association is dedicated to publishing the finest and most effective educational materials—including software, study guides, and test preps—for students in middle school, high school, college, graduate school, and beyond.

REA's Test Preparation series includes books and software for all academic levels in almost all disciplines. Research & Education Association publishes test preps for students who have not yet entered high school, as well as for high school students preparing to enter college. Students from countries around the world seeking to attend college in the United States will find the assistance they need in REA's publications. For college students seeking advanced degrees, REA publishes test preps for many major graduate school admission examinations in a wide variety of disciplines, including engineering, law, and medicine. Students at every level, in every field, with every ambition can find what they are looking for among REA's publications.

REA's practice tests are always based upon the most recently administered exams and include every type of question that you can expect on the actual exams.

REA's publications and educational materials are highly regarded and continually receive an unprecedented amount of praise from professionals, instructors, librarians, parents, and students. Our authors are as diverse as the fields represented in the books we publish. They are well-known in their respective disciplines and serve on the faculties of prestigious high schools, colleges, and universities throughout the United States and Canada.

Today, REA's wide-ranging catalog is a leading resource for teachers, students, and professionals.

We invite you to visit us at www.rea.com to find out how REA is making the world smarter.

Acknowledgments

We would like to thank REA's Carl Fuchs, President, for supervising development; Pam Weston, Vice President, Publishing, for setting the quality standards for production integrity and managing the publication to completion; Larry Kling, Vice President, Editorial, for his editorial direction; Alice Leonard, Senior Editor, for project management and preflight editorial review; Diane Goldschmidt, Senior Editor, for post-production quality assurance; Molly Solanki, Associate Editor, for her editorial contribution; Sandra Rush for her technical review and editorial contributions; Christine Saul, Senior Graphic Artist, for cover design; and Jeff LoBalbo, Senior Graphic Artist, for post-production file mapping.

We also gratefully acknowledge the team at Aquent Publishing Services for typesetting and Brooke Graves for indexing the manuscript.

CONTENTS

CHAPTER 3   73

REVIEW FOR SUBTEST II: DOMAIN 2: GEOMETRY; DOMAIN 4: PROBABILITY & STATISTICS

CHAPTER 4   151

REVIEW FOR SUBTEST III: DOMAIN 5: CALCULUS; DOMAIN 6: HISTORY OF MATHEMATICS

PRACTICE TEST 1 FOR SUBTEST I   205

CSET

Mathematics

Introduction

Passing the CSET: Mathematics Test

About This Book

REA's *The Best Teachers' Test Preparation for CSET: Mathematics* is a comprehensive guide designed to assist you in preparing for a mathematics educator license in California. To enhance your chances of success in this important step toward your career as a mathematics teacher, this test guide:

- Presents an accurate and complete overview of the three CSET subtests
- Identifies all of the important information and its representation on the test
- Provides a comprehensive review of every domain on the test
- Provides six full-length practice tests (two for each subtest)
- Suggests tips and strategies for successfully completing standardized tests
- Replicates the format of the official tests, including levels of difficulty
- Supplies the correct answer and detailed explanations for each question on the practice tests, which enable you to identify correct answers and understand why they are correct and, just as important, why the other answers are incorrect.

This guide is the result of studying many resources. The editors considered the most recent test administrations and professional standards. They also researched information from the California Commission on Teacher Credentialing (CCTC), professional journals, textbooks, and educators. This guide includes the best test preparation materials based on the latest information available.

About the Test

CSET: Mathematics consists of three separate subtests, each scored separately and composed of multiple-choice and constructed-response questions. The following chart is a clear representation of the subtests and their domains and approximate number of questions. This mathematics test represents the combined expertise of California educators, subject area specialists, and district-level educators who worked to develop and validate the test. This book contains a thorough review of each subtest, as well as the specific skills that demonstrate each content domain.

Who Administers the Test?

All the CSET tests are administered by National Evaluation Systems, Inc. (NES) and the CCTC. See contact information below.

Test Structure

CSET: Mathematics*			
Subtest	**Domains**	**Number of Multiple-Choice Questions**	**Number of Constructed-Response Questions**
I	Algebra	24	3
	Number Theory	6	1
	Subtest Total	30	4
II	Geometry	22	3
	Probability and Statistics	8	1
	Subtest Total	30	4
III	Calculus	26	3
	History of Mathematics	4	1
	Subtest Total	30	4

*Candidates verifying subject matter competence by examination for a credential in Foundational-Level Mathematics are required to take and pass Subtests I and II only.

Can I Retake the Test?

The CSET can be taken as many times as needed to achieve a passing score. Note: Once you pass a subtest, you do not have to take that subtest again, as long as you use the score toward certification within five years of the test date.

When Should the CSET Be Taken?

Candidates are typically nearing completion of or have completed their undergraduate work when they take CSET tests.

CSET tests are administered six times a year at 26 locations in California and five locations in other states. To receive information on upcoming administrations of the CSET, consult the CSET test date chart at the CSET website. For all information:

CSET Program

National Evaluation Systems

P.O. Box 340789

Sacramento, CA 95834-0789

Telephone: (916) 928-4003

Automated Information System: (800) 205-3334 (available 24 hours daily)

Website: *http://www.cset.nesinc.com*

Is There a Registration Fee?

To take any CSET test there is a fee. It is structured per subtest. A complete summary of the registration fees is included in the CSET Registration Bulletin at the website above.

Calculators

A calculator is needed and allowed **only** for Mathematics Subtest II: Geometry; Probability and Statistics. You must bring your own graphing calculator to the test site. Approved models of calculators appear in the Registration Bulletin available at the website above.

Test administration staff will clear the memory of your calculator before and after the test, so be certain to back up the memory of your calculator, including applications, to an external device before arriving at the test site.

How to Use This Book

How Do I Begin Studying?

Identify which CSET: Mathematics subtest you wish to prepare for, then review the organization of this test preparation guide.

1. To best utilize your study time, follow our CSET Independent Study Schedule. The schedule is based on a six-week program, but can be condensed if necessary.

2. Take the first practice test for each subtest, score it according to directions, then review the explanations to your answers carefully. Then, study the areas that your scores indicate need further review.

3. Review the format of the CSET.

4. Review the test-taking advice and suggestions presented later in this section.

5. Pay attention to the information about the objectives of the test.

6. Spend time reviewing topics that stand out as needing more study.

7. Take the second practice test for each subtest and follow the same procedure as #2 above.

8. Follow the suggestions at the end of this section for the day before and the day of the test.

When Should I Start Studying?

It is never too early to start studying for the CSET. The earlier you begin, the more time you will have to sharpen your skills. Do not procrastinate!

A six-week study schedule is provided at the end of this section to assist you in preparing for the CSET: Mathematics. This schedule can be adjusted to meet your unique needs. If your test date is only four weeks away, you can halve the time allotted to each section, but keep in mind that this is not the most effective way to study. If you have several months before your test date, you may wish to extend the time allotted to each section. Remember, the more time you spend studying, the better your chances of achieving your goal of a passing score.

Studying for CSET: Mathematics

It is very important for you to choose the time and place for studying that works best for you. Some students set aside a certain number of hours every morning to study, while some choose the night before going to sleep, and others study during the day, while waiting in line, or even while eating lunch. Choose a time when you can concentrate and your study will be most effective. Be consistent and use your time wisely. Work out a study routine and stick to it.

When you take a practice test, simulate the conditions of the actual test as closely as possible. Turn your television and radio off and sit down at a quiet table with your calculator, if allowed for that subtest. When you complete the practice test, score it and thoroughly review the explanations to the questions you answered incorrectly. Do not, however, review too much at any one time. Concentrate on one problem area at a time by examining the question and explanation, and by studying our review until you are confident that you have mastered the material. Keep track of your scores to discover areas of general weakness and to gauge your progress. Give extra attention to the review sections that cover your areas of difficulty, as this will build your skills and confidence on test day.

Format of CSET: Mathematics

CSET: Mathematics assesses the candidate's proficiency and depth of understanding of the foundations of the subject contained in the Mathematics Content Standards for California Public Schools.

Referring to the previous chart, CSET: Mathematics is composed of three subtests, which total 90 multiple-choice questions (30 for each subtest) and 12 constructed-response questions (4 for each subtest).

You are given five hours to complete the test, whether you take one, two, or all three subtests during one testing session. By monitoring your progress on the practice tests and adding one test at a time, you can reach your own comfort level and approach your testing session with confidence.

About the Review Sections

The subject review in this book is designed to help you sharpen the basic skills needed to approach the CSET: Mathematic test, as well as provide strategies for attacking the questions.

Each subtest is examined separately, clearly delineating the content domains. The skills required for all subtests fulfill the objectives of the CCTC and the Mathematics Content Standards for California Public Schools and are extensively discussed to optimize your understanding of what each specific CSET: Mathematics subtest covers.

Your schooling has taught you most of what you need to succeed on the test. Our review is designed to help you fit the information you have acquired into each specific subtest content domain. Reviewing your class notes and textbooks together with our reviews will give you an excellent springboard for passing the test.

Scoring CSET: Mathematics

Multiple-Choice Questions

A candidate's performance on CSET: Mathematics with multiple-choice questions is based strictly on the number of test questions answered correctly. Candidates do not lose any points for wrong answers. Each multiple-choice question counts the same toward the total score. These items are scored electronically and checked to verify accuracy.

Constructed-Response Questions

Constructed-response questions are short and focused responses that require a breadth of understanding of each subtest's content domain and the ability to relate concepts from different aspects of the field. Constructed-response questions are scored by at least two qualified California educators using standardized procedures.

Scorers focus on the extent to which a response fulfills the following performance characteristics:

Purpose: addressing the constructed-response assignment in relation to relevant CSET subject matter and/or content specifications

Subject Matter Knowledge: applying accurate subject matter knowledge as described in relevant CSET subject matter and/or content specifications

Support: using appropriate, quality supporting evidence in relation to relevant CSET subject matter and/or content specifications

Depth and Breadth of Understanding (not scored in all constructed-response questions): the degree to which the response demonstrates understanding of the relevant CSET subject matter requirements

Score Results

After you have taken the CSET, you will receive a score report for your records. Your results will also be sent to the CCTC and any institutions you indicated when you registered.

For each subtest taken on the CSET: Mathematics, your score report will include your passing status and, if you did not pass, your total subtest score. The reverse side of the score report contains diagnostic information about your performance.

Each CSET subtest is scored separately and a passing score on each subtest is required to pass the examination. For each CSET subtest, an individual's performance is evaluated against an established standard. The passing score for each subtest was established by the CCTC based on the professional judgments and recommendations of California educators.

Passing status is determined on the basis of total subtest performance. The total subtest score is based on the number of raw score points earned on each section (multiple-choice section and/or constructed-response section), the weighting of each section, and the scaling of that score. Raw scores are converted to a scale of 100 to 300, with the scaled score of 220 representing the minimum passing score.

Test-Taking Tips

Although some of you may not be familiar with tests like the CSET, this book will help acquaint you with this type of test and help alleviate your test-taking anxieties.

Tip 1. Become comfortable with the format of the CSET. When you are practicing, stay calm and pace yourself. After simulating the test only once, you will boost your chances of doing well, and you will be able to sit down for the actual test with much more confidence.

Tip 2. Read all of the possible answers. Just because you think you have found the correct response, do not automatically assume that it is the best answer. Read through each choice to be sure that you are not making a mistake by jumping to conclusions.

Tip 3. Use the process of elimination. Go through each answer to a question and eliminate as many of the answer choices as possible. By eliminating two answer choices, you have given yourself a better chance of getting the item correct since there will only be two choices left from which to make your guess. Answer all questions you can; you are not penalized for wrong answers, but you are rewarded for correct ones.

Tip 4. Place a question mark in your answer booklet next to answers you guessed, then recheck them later if you have time.

Tip 5. Work quickly and steadily. Avoid focusing on any one problem too long. Taking the practice tests in this book for your CSET test will help you learn to efficiently budget your time.

Tip 6. Learn the directions and format of the test. This will not only save time, but will also help you avoid anxiety (and the mistakes caused by getting anxious).

Tip 7. Be sure that the answer circle you are marking corresponds to the number of the question in the test booklet. The multiple-choice section is graded by machine and marking one answer in the wrong circle can throw off your answer key and your score. Be extremely careful.

The Day of the Test

Before the Test

On the day of the test, make sure to dress comfortably, so that you are not distracted by being too hot or too cold while taking the test. Plan to arrive at the test center early. This will allow you to collect your thoughts and relax before the test, and will also spare you the anguish that comes with being late.

You should check your CSET Registration Bulletin and other registration information to find out what time to arrive at the testing center.

Before you leave for the test center, make sure that you have your admission ticket and the following identification:

- one piece of current, government-issued identification, in the name in which you registered, bearing your photograph and signature
- one clear and legible photocopy of your original government-issued identification for each test session in which you are testing (i.e., one copy for the morning and/or one copy for the afternoon session)
- one additional piece of identification (with or without a photograph)

Note: If you do not have the required identification, you will be required to complete additional paperwork and have your photograph taken. This additional step will result in a reduction of your available testing time.

You must bring several sharpened No. 2 pencils with erasers, as none will be provided at the test center.

If you would like, you may wear a watch to the test center. However, you may not wear one that has a calculator, or one that makes noise. Dictionaries, textbooks, notebooks, briefcases, laptop computers, packages, and cell phones will not be permitted. Drinking, smoking, and eating are prohibited.

During the Test

You are given 5 hours to complete the CSET. Restroom breaks are allowed, but they count as testing time. Procedures will be followed to maintain test security. Once you enter the test center, follow all of the rules and instructions given by the test supervisor. If you do not, you risk being dismissed from the test and having your scores cancelled.

When all of the materials have been distributed, the test instructor will give you directions for filling out your answer sheet. Fill out this sheet carefully since this information will be printed on your score report. Once the test begins, mark only one answer per question, completely erase unwanted answers and marks, and fill in answers darkly and neatly.

After the Test

When you finish your test, hand in your materials and you will be dismissed. Then, go home and relax— you deserve it!

CSET Study Schedule

The following study schedule allows for thorough preparation to pass CSET: Mathematics. This is a suggested six-week course of study. This schedule can, however, be condensed if you have less time available to study, or expanded if you have more time. Whatever the length of your available study time, be sure to keep a structured schedule by setting aside ample time each day to study. Depending on your schedule, you may find it easier to study throughout the weekend. No matter which schedule works best for you, the more time you devote to studying, the more prepared and confident you will be on the day of the test.

Study Schedule	
Week	**Activity**
Week 1	Read and study Chapter 1, "Passing the CSET: Mathematics Test." This chapter will introduce you to the format of the exam and give you an overview of the subtests on each mathematics exam. Consult the website at *http://www.cset.nesinc.com* for any further information you may need.
Week 2	Take the first practice test for each of the three subtests. Use the answer key with explanations to identify your areas of strength and those areas where you need more study. Make a list of subject areas where you need additional aid.
Week 3	Study the review section of this book, taking notes, particularly on the sections you need to study most. Writing will aid in your retention of information. Textbooks for college mathematics will help in your preparation.
Week 4	Review and condense your notes. Develop a structured outline detailing specific acts. It may be helpful to use index cards to aid yourself in memorizing important facts and concepts.
Week 5	Take the second practice test for each of the three subtests in this book. Review the explanations for the questions you answered incorrectly.
Week 6	Re-study any areas you consider to be difficult by using your study materials, references, and notes. If you need a final confidence boost, take the tests again.

CSET

Mathematics

Review

Review for Subtest 1: Domain 1: Algebra; Domain 3: Number Theory

Integers and Real Numbers

Most of the numbers used in algebra belong to a set called the **real numbers** or **reals**. This set can be represented graphically by the real number line.

Given the number line below, we arbitrarily fix a point and label it with the number 0. In a similar manner, we can label any point on the line with one of the real numbers, depending on its position relative to 0. Numbers to the right of zero are positive, while those to the left are negative. Value increases from left to right, so that if a is to the right of b, it is said to be greater than b.

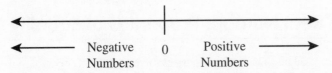

If we now divide the number line into equal segments, we can label the points on this line with real numbers. For example, the point 2 lengths to the left of zero is -2, while the point 3 lengths to the right of zero

is $+3$ (the $+$ sign is usually assumed, so $+3$ is written simply as 3). The number line now looks like this:

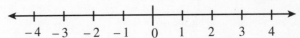

These boundary points represent the subset of the reals known as the **integers**. The set of integers is made up of both the positive and negative whole numbers: $\{\ldots -4, -3, -2, -1, 0, 1, 2, 3, 4,\ldots\}$. Some subsets of integers are:

Natural Numbers or Positive Numbers—the set of integers starting with 1 and increasing: $N = \{1, 2, 3, 4,\ldots\}$.

Whole Numbers—the set of integers starting with 0 and increasing: $W = \{0, 1, 2, 3,\ldots\}$.

Negative Numbers—the set of integers starting with -1 and decreasing: $Z = \{-1, -2, -3\ldots\}$.

Prime Numbers—the set of positive integers greater than 1 that are divisible only by 1 and themselves: $\{2, 3, 5, 7, 11, \ldots\}$.

Even Integers—the set of integers divisible by 2: $\{\ldots, -4, -2, 0, 2, 4, 6,\ldots\}$.

Odd Integers—the set of integers not divisible by 2: $\{\ldots, -3, -1, 1, 3, 5, 7,\ldots\}$.

Rational and Irrational Numbers

A rational number is any number that can be written in the form $\frac{a}{b}$ where a is any integer and b is any integer except zero. An irrational number is a number that cannot be written as a simple fraction. It is an infinite and nonrepeating decimal.

The tree diagram below shows the relationships among the different types of numbers.

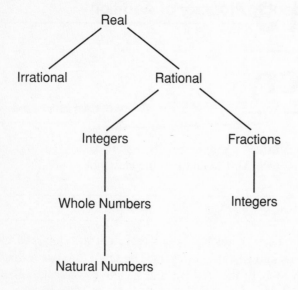

- **EXAMPLE**

  Here are some examples of some rational numbers.

2	3	5	10	32	−2	−4	−18	−25
$\frac{1}{4}$	$\frac{1}{2}$	$\frac{2}{3}$	$-\frac{1}{4}$	$\frac{4}{7}$	$-\frac{10}{55}$	$\frac{21}{9}$	$\frac{101}{635}$	

- **EXAMPLE**

  Here are some examples of irrational numbers.

  π — approximately equal to 3.14159

  e — approximately equal to 2.71828

  $\sqrt{2}$ — approximately equal to 1.41421

  $\sqrt{3}$ — approximately equal to 1.73205

  $\sqrt{5}$ — approximately equal to 2.23607

Real Numbers and Their Components

The set of all real numbers has various components. These components are the set of all natural numbers, N, the set of all whole numbers, W, the set of all integers, I, the set of all rational numbers, Q, and the set of all irrational numbers, S. Then,

$N = \{1, 2, 3, \ldots\},$

$W = \{0, 1, 2, 3, \ldots\},$

$I = \{\ldots, -3, -2, -1, 0, 1, 2, 3, \ldots\},$

$Q = \left\{ \frac{a}{b} \,\middle|\, a, b \in I \text{ and } b \neq 0 \right\};$

and $S = \{x \mid x$ has a decimal name which is nonterminating and does not have a repeating block$\}$.

It is obvious that $N \subseteq W$, $W \subseteq I$, and $I \subseteq Q$, but a similar relationship does not hold between Q and S. More specifically, the decimal names for elements of Q are

(1) terminating or

(2) nonterminating with a repeating block.

For example, $\frac{1}{2} = .5$ and $\frac{1}{3} = .333\ldots$ This means that Q and S have no common elements. Examples of irrational numbers include $.101001000\ldots$, π and $\sqrt{2}$.

All real numbers are normally represented by R and $R = Q \cup S$. This means that every real number is either rational or irrational. A nice way to visualize real numbers geometrically is that real numbers can be put in a one-to-one correspondence with the set of all points on a line.

Real Number Properties of Equality

The standard properties of equality involving real numbers are:

Reflexive Property of Equality

For each real number a,

$a = a.$

Symmetric Property of Equality

For each real number a, for each real number b,

if $a = b$, then $b = a$.

Transitive Property of Equality

For each real number a, for each real number b, for each real number c,

if $a = b$ and $b = c$, then $a = c$.

Real Number Operations and Their Properties

The operations of addition and multiplication are of particular importance. As a result, many properties concerning those operations have been determined and named. Here is a list of the most important of these properties.

Closure Property of Addition

For every real number a, for every real number b,

$a + b$

is a real number.

Closure Property of Multiplication

For every real number a, for every real number b,

ab

is a real number.

Commutative Property of Addition

For every real number a, for every real number b,

$a + b = b + a$.

Commutative Property of Multiplication

For every real number a, for every real number b,

$ab = ba$.

Associative Property of Addition

For every real number a, for every real number b, for every real number c,

$(a + b) + c = a + (b + c)$.

Associative Property of Multiplication

For every real number a, for every real number b, for every real number c,

$(ab)c = a(bc)$.

Identity Property of Addition

For every real number a,

$a + 0 = 0 + a = a$.

Identity Property of Multiplication

For every real number a,

$a \times 1 = 1 \times a = a$.

Inverse Property of Addition

For every real number a, there is a real number $-a$ such that

$a + -a = -a + a = 0$.

Inverse Property of Multiplication

For every real number a, $a \neq 0$, there is a real number a^{-1} such that

$a \times a^{-1} = a^{-1} \times a = 1$.

Distributive Property

For every real number a, for every real number b, for every real number c,

$a(b + c) = ab + ac$.

The operations of subtraction and division are also important, but less important than addition and multiplication. Here are the definitions for these operations.

For every real number a, for every real number b, for every real number c,

$$a - b = c \text{ if and only if } b + c = a.$$

For every real number a, for every real number b, for every real number c,

$$a \div b = c \text{ if and only if } c \text{ is the unique real number such that } bc = a.$$

The definition of division eliminates division *by* 0. Thus, for example, $4 \div 0$ is undefined, $0 \div 0$ is undefined, but $0 \div 4 = 0$.

In many instances, it is possible to perform subtraction by first converting a subtraction statement to an addition statement. This is illustrated below.

For every real number a, for every real number b,

$$\boxed{a - b = a + (-b).}$$

In a similar way, every division statement can be converted to a multiplication statement. Use the following model:

For every real number a, for every real number b, $b \neq 0$,

$$\boxed{a \div b = a \times b^{-1}}$$

Complex Numbers

A **complex number** is a number that can be written in the form $a + bi$, where a and b are real numbers and $i = \sqrt{-1}$. The number a is the **real part,** and the number b is the **imaginary part** of the complex number.

Returning momentarily to real numbers, the square of a real number cannot be negative. More specifically, the square of a positive real number is positive, the square of a negative real number is positive, and the square of 0 is 0. Then i is defined to be a number with a property that

$$i^2 = -1.$$

Obviously i is not a real number. C is then used to represent the set of all complex numbers and

$$C = \{a + bi \mid a \text{ and } b \text{ are real numbers}\}.$$

Here are the definitions of addition, subtraction, and multiplication of complex numbers.

To add, subtract, or multiply complex numbers, compute in the usual way, replace i^2 with -1, and simplify.

Suppose $x + yi$ and $z + wi$ are complex numbers. Then

$$(x + yi) + (z + wi) = (x + z) + (y + w)i$$
$$(x + yi) - (z + wi) = (x - z) + (y - w)i$$
$$(x + yi) \times (z + wi) = (xz - yw) + (xw + yz)i.$$

PROBLEM

Simplify the following: $(3 + i)(2 + i)$.

SOLUTION

$$\begin{aligned}(3 + i)(2 + i) &= 3(2 + i) + i(2 + i) \\ &= 6 + 3i + 2i + i^2 \\ &= 6 + (3 + 2)i + (-1) \\ &= 5 + 5i\end{aligned}$$

Division of two complex numbers is usually accomplished with a special procedure that involves the conjugate of a complex number. The conjugate of $a + bi$ is denoted by

$$\overline{a + bi} \text{ or } a - bi.$$

Also, $(a + bi)(a - bi) = a^2 + b^2$.

The usual procedure for division is illustrated below.

$$\begin{aligned}\frac{x + yi}{z + wi} &= \frac{x + yi}{z + wi} \times \frac{z - wi}{z - wi} \\ &= \frac{(xz + yw) + (-xw + yz)i}{z^2 + w^2} \\ &= \frac{xz + yw}{z^2 + w^2} + \frac{-xw + yz}{z^2 + w^2}i\end{aligned}$$

All the properties of real numbers described in the previous section carry over to complex numbers; however, those properties will not be stated again.

If a is a real number, then a can be expressed in the form $a = a + 0i$. Hence, every real number is a complex number and $R \subseteq C$.

Drill: Real and Complex Numbers

DIRECTIONS: For #1–7 and 10, simplify the expressions. For #8 and 9, solve the equations.

1. $3i^3 =$

   (A) $-3i$ (C) $9i$

   (B) $3i$ (D) $-i$

2. $2i^7 =$

   (A) $-128i$ (C) $14i$

   (B) $2i$ (D) $-2i$

3. $-4i^4 =$

   (A) 4 (C) $4i$

   (B) -4 (D) $-4i$

4. $-5i^6 =$

   (A) -5 (C) $-i$

   (B) $-5i$ (D) 5

5. $(3 + 2i)(2 + 3i) =$

   (A) $12 + 13i$ (C) $13i$

   (B) $-12 - 13i$ (D) $-13i$

6. $(2 - i)(2 + i) =$

   (A) -5 (C) $-5i$

   (B) $5i$ (D) 5

7. $(5 - 4i)^2 =$

   (A) $9 - 40i$ (C) $41 - 40i$

   (B) $-9 - 40i$ (D) $9 + 40i$

8. $x^2 + 16 = 0$

   (A) ± 4 (C) $4 \pm i$

   (B) $\pm 4i$ (D) $-4 \pm i$

9. $4y^2 + 1 = 0$

   (A) $\pm\dfrac{1}{2}$ (C) $-i \pm \dfrac{1}{2}$

   (B) $i \pm \dfrac{1}{2}$ (D) $\pm\dfrac{1}{2}i$

10. $\dfrac{2 + 6i}{1 - i} =$

    (A) 0 (C) $8i - 4$

    (B) $-2 - 4i$ (D) $-2 + 4i$

Algebra Terms

In algebra, letters or variables are used to represent numbers. A **variable** is defined as a placeholder, which can take on any of several values at a given time. A **constant**, on the other hand, is a symbol that takes on only one value at a given time. A **term** is a constant, a variable, or a combination of constants and variables. For example: 7.76, $3x$, xyz, $\dfrac{5z}{x}$, and $(0.99)x^2$ are terms. If a term is a combination of constants and variables, the constant part of the term is referred to as the **coefficient** of the variable. If a variable is written without a coefficient, the coefficient is assumed to be 1.

- **EXAMPLES**

  $3x^2$ y^3

  coefficient: 3   coefficient: 1

  variable: x variable: y

An **expression** is a collection of one or more terms. If the number of terms is greater than 1, the expression is said to be the sum of the terms.

- **EXAMPLES**

  $9, 9xy, 6x + \dfrac{x}{3}, 8yz - 2x$

An algebraic expression consisting of only one term is called a **monomial**; of two terms is called a **binomial**; of three terms is called a **trinomial**. In general, an algebraic expression consisting of two or more terms is called a **polynomial**.

Operations with Polynomials

A) **Addition of polynomials** is achieved by combining like terms, terms that differ only in their numerical coefficients. For example,

$$P(x) = (x^2 - 3x + 5) + (4x^2 + 6x - 3)$$

is the some of two polynomials. Note that the parentheses are used to distinguish the polynomials.

By using the commutative and associative properties, we can rewrite $P(x)$ as:

$$P(x) = (x^2 + 4x^2) + (6x - 3x) + (5 - 3)$$

By using the distributive property, we get:

$$(1 + 4)x^2 + (6 - 3)x + (5 - 3) = 5x^2 + 3x + 2$$

B) **Subtraction of two polynomials** is achieved by first changing the signs of all terms in the expression that is being subtracted and then adding this result to the other expression. For example,

$$(5x^2 + 4y^2 + 3z^2) - (4xy + 7y^2 - 3z^2 + 1)$$

$$= 5x^2 + 4y^2 + 3z^2 - 4xy - 7y^2 + 3z^2 - 1$$

$$= 5x^2 + (4y^2 - 7y^2) + (3z^2 + 3z^2) - 4xy - 1$$

$$= 5x^2 - 3y^2 + 6z^2 - 4xy - 1$$

C) **Multiplication of two or more monomials** is achieved by using the laws of exponents, the rules of signs, and the commutative and associative properties of multiplication. Multiply the coefficients and then multiply the variables according to the laws of exponents. For example,

$$(y^2)(5)(6y^2)(yz)(2z^2)$$

$$= (1)(5)(6)(1)(2)(y^2)(y^2)(yz)(z^2)$$

$$= 60[(y^2)(y^2)(y)][(z)(z^2)]$$

$$= 60(y^5)(z^3) = 60y^5z^3$$

D) **Multiplication of a polynomial by a monomial** is achieved by multiplying each term of the polynomial by the monomial and combining the results. For example,

$$(4x^2 + 3y)(6xz^2)$$

$$= (4x^2)(6xz^2) + (3y)(6xz^2)$$

$$= 24x^3z^2 + 18xyz^2$$

E) **Multiplication of a polynomial by a polynomial** is achieved by multiplying each of the terms of one polynomial by each of the terms of the other polynomial and combining the results. For example,

$$(5y + z + 1)(y^2 + 2y)$$

$$= [(5y)(y^2) + (5y)(2y)] + [(z)(y^2) + (z)(2y)] +$$

$$[(1)(y^2) + (1)(2y)]$$

$$= (5y^3 + 10y^2) + (y^2z + 2yz) + (y^2 + 2y)$$

$$= (5y^3) + (10y^2 + y^2) + (y^2z) + (2yz) + (2y)$$

$$= 5y^3 + 11y^2 + y^2z + 2yz + 2y$$

F) **Division of a monomial by a monomial** is achieved by first dividing the constant coefficients and the like variable factors separately, and then multiplying these quotients. For example,

$$6xyz^2 \div 2y^2z$$

$$= \left(\frac{6}{2}\right)\left(\frac{x}{1}\right)\left(\frac{y}{y^2}\right)\left(\frac{z^2}{z}\right)$$

$$= 3xy^{-1}z$$

$$= \frac{3xz}{y}$$

G) **Division of a polynomial by a polynomial** is achieved by following the given procedure, similar to long division of numbers.

Step 1: The terms of both the polynomials are arranged in order of descending powers of one variable.

Step 2: The first term of the dividend is divided by the first term of the divisor, which gives the first term of the quotient.

Step 3: This first term of the quotient is multiplied by the entire divisor and the result is subtracted from the dividend.

Step 4: Using the remainder obtained from Step 3 as the new dividend, Steps 2 and 3 are repeated until the remainder is zero or the degree of the remainder is less than the degree of the divisor.

Step 5: The result is written as follows:

$$\frac{dividend}{divisor} = quotient + \frac{remainder}{divisor}$$

Remember that the divisor cannot be zero.

For example, $(2x^2 + x + 6) \div (x + 1)$

$$
\begin{array}{r}
2x - 1 \\
(x+1) \overline{)2x^2 + x + 6} \\
\underline{-(2x^2 + 2x)} \\
-x + 6 \\
\underline{-(-x - 1)} \\
7
\end{array}
$$

The result is $(2x^2 + x + 6) \div (x + 1) = 2x - 1 + \dfrac{7}{x + 1}$

Drill: Operations with Polynomials

Addition

DIRECTIONS: Add the following polynomials.

1. $9a^2b + 3c + 2a^2b + 5c =$

    (A) $19a^2bc$ (C) $11a^4b^2 + 8c^2$

    (B) $11a^2b + 8c$ (D) $19a^4b^2c^2$

2. $14m^2n^3 + 6m^2n^3 + 3m^2n^3 =$

    (A) $20m^2n^3$ (C) $23m^2n^3$

    (B) $23m^6n^9$ (D) $32m^6n^9$

3. $3x + 2y + 16x + 3z + 6y =$

    (A) $19x + 8y$ (C) $19x + 8y + 3z$

    (B) $19x + 11yz$ (D) $11xy + 19xz$

4. $(4d^2 + 7e^3 + 12f) + (3d^2 + 6e^3 + 2f) =$

    (A) $23d^2e^3f$ (C) $33d^4e^6f^2$

    (B) $33d^2e^2f$ (D) $7d^2 + 13e^3 + 14f$

5. $3ac^2 + 2b^2c + 7ac^2 + 2ac^2 + b^2c =$

    (A) $12ac^2 + 3b^2c$ (C) $11ac^2 + 4ab^2c$

    (B) $14ab^2c^2$ (D) $15ab^2c^2$

Subtraction

DIRECTIONS: Subtract the following polynomials.

6. $14m^2n - 6m^2n =$

    (A) $20m^2n$ (C) $8m$

    (B) $8m^2n$ (D) 8

7. $3x^3y^2 - 4xz - 6x^3y^2 =$

    (A) $-7x^2y^2z$ (C) $-3x^3y^2 - 4xz$

    (B) $3x^3y^2 - 10x^4y^2z$ (D) $-x^2y^2z - 6x^3y^2$

8. $9g^2 + 6h - 2g^2 - 5h =$

    (A) $15g^2h - 7g^2h$ (C) $11g^2 + 7h$

    (B) $7g^4h^2$ (D) $7g^2 + h$

9. $7b^3 - 4c^2 - 6b^3 + 3c^2 =$

    (A) $b^3 - c^2$ (C) $13b^3 - c$

    (B) $-11b^2 - 3c^2$ (D) $7b - c$

10. $11q^2r - 4q^2r - 8q^2r =$

    (A) $22q^2r$ (C) $-2q^2r$

    (B) q^2r (D) $-q^2r$

Multiplication

DIRECTIONS: Multiply the following polynomials.

11. $5p^2t \times 3p^2t =$

    (A) $15p^2t$ (C) $15p^4t^2$

    (B) $15p^4t$ (D) $8p^2t$

12. $(2r + s)\,14r =$

    (A) $28rs$ (C) $16r^2 + 14rs$

    (B) $28r^2 + 14sr$ (D) $28r + 14sr$

13. $(4m + p)\,(3m - 2p) =$

    (A) $12m^2 + 5mp + 2p^2$

    (B) $12m^2 - 2mp + 2p^2$

    (C) $7m - p$

    (D) $12m^2 - 5mp - 2p^2$

14. $(2a + b)(3a^2 + ab + b^2) =$

    (A) $6a^3 + 5a^2b + 3ab^2 + b^3$

    (B) $5a^3 + 3ab + b^3$

    (C) $6a^3 + 2a^2b + 2ab^2$

    (D) $3a^2 + 2a + ab + b + b^2$

15. $(6t^2 + 2t + 1)\, 3t =$

    (A) $9t^2 + 5t + 3$ (C) $9t^3 + 6t^2 + 3t$

    (B) $18t^2 + 6t + 3$ (D) $18t^3 + 6t^2 + 3t$

Division

DIRECTIONS: Divide the following polynomials.

16. $(x^2 + x - 6) \div (x - 2) =$

    (A) $x - 3$ (C) $x + 3$

    (B) $x + 2$ (D) $x - 2$

17. $24b^4c^3 \div 6b^2c =$

    (A) $3b^2c^2$ (C) $4b^3c^2$

    (B) $4b^4c^3$ (D) $4b^2c^2$

18. $(3p^2 + pq - 2q^2) \div (p + q) =$

    (A) $3p + 2q$ (C) $3p - q$

    (B) $2q - 3p$ (D) $3p - 2q$

19. $(y^3 - 2y^2 - y + 2) \div (y - 2) =$

    (A) $(y - 1)^2$

    (B) $y^2 - 1$

    (C) $(y + 2)(y - 1)$

    (D) $(y + 1)^2$

20. $(m^2 + m - 14) \div (m + 4) =$

    (A) $m - 2$ (C) $m - 3 + \dfrac{4}{m + 4}$

    (B) $m - 3 - \dfrac{2}{m + 4}$ (D) $m - 3$

Simplifying and Factoring Algebraic Expressions

To factor a polynomial completely means to find the prime factors of the polynomial with respect to a specified set of numbers.

The following concepts are important while factoring or simplifying expressions.

A) The factors of an algebraic expression consist of two or more algebraic expressions which, when multiplied together, produce the given algebraic expression.

B) A **prime factor** is a polynomial with no factors other than itself and 1. The **least common multiple (LCM)** for a set of numbers is the smallest quantity divisible by every number of the set. For algebraic expressions, the least common numerical coefficients for each of the given expressions will be a factor.

C) The **greatest common factor (GCF)** for a set of numbers is the largest factor that is common to all members of the set.

D) For algebraic expressions, the greatest common factor is the polynomial of highest degree and the largest numerical coefficient which is a factor of all the given expressions.

Some important formulas, useful for the factoring of polynomials, are listed below.

$$ac + ad = a(c + d)$$

$$a^2 - b^2 = (a + b)(a - b)$$

$$(a + b)^2 = (a + b)(a + b) = a^2 + 2ab + b^2$$

$$(a - b)^2 = (a - b)(a - b) = a^2 - 2ab + b^2$$

$$x^2 + (a - b)x + ab = (x + a)(x + b)$$

$$acx^2 + (ab + bc)x + bd = (ax + b)(cx + d)$$

$$ac + bc + ad + bd = (a + b)(c + d)$$

$$(a + b)^3 = (a + b)(a + b)(a + b)$$

$$= a^3 + 3a^2b + 3ab^2 + b^3$$

$$(a - b)^3 = (a - b)(a - b)(a - b)$$

$$= a^3 - 3a^2b + 3ab^2 - b^3$$

$$a^3 - b^3 = (a - b)(a^2 + ab + b^2)$$

$a^3 + b^3 = (a + b)(a^2 - ab + b^2)$

$(a + b + c)^2 = a^2 + b^2 + c^2 + 2ab + 2ac + 2bc$

$a^4 - b^4 = (a - b)(a^3 + a^2b + ab^2 + b^3)$

$a^5 - b^5 = (a - b)(a^4 + a^3b + a^2b^2 + ab^3 + b^4)$

$a^6 - b^6 = (a - b)(a^5 + a^4b + a^3b^2 + a^2b^3 + ab^4 + b^5)$

$a^n - b^n = (a - b)(a^{n-1} + a^{n-2}b + a^{n-3}b^2 + \ldots + ab^{n-2} + b^{n-1})$

where n is any positive integer (1, 2, 3, 4, …)

$a^n + b^n = (a + b)(a^{n-1} - a^{n-2}b + a^{n-3}b^2 - \ldots - ab^{n-2} + b^{n-1})$

where n is any positive odd integer (1, 3, 5, 7, …).

A summary of the most useful of these formulas follows:

A) Difference of two squares: $a^2 - b^2 = (a + b)(a - b)$

If you can recognize the polynomial as the difference of two perfect squares, with no other terms, you can factor it into the product of the sum and difference of the square roots.

• **EXAMPLE**

Factor $x^2 - 4$

$x^2 - 4 = (x + 2)(x - 2)$

• **EXAMPLE**

Factor $9x^2 - 16$

$9x^2 - 16 = (3x + 4)(3x - 4)$

B) A trinomial of the form $x^2 + (a + b)x + ab$

If the coefficient of x^2 is 1, and you can recognize that the factors of the last term add up to the coefficient of the x term, you can factor the trinomial with just a few trials. Remember to pay attention to signs.

• **EXAMPLE**

Factor $x^2 + 6x + 8$

The possible factors of 8 are 2×4 and 1×8.

The sums of these factors are $2 + 4(= 6)$ and $1 + 8(= 9)$.

So the factors you would choose are 2 and 4.

$x^2 + 6x + 8 = (x + 2)(x + 4)$

• **EXAMPLE**

Factor $x^2 - x - 6$

The possible factors of -6 are $3 \times (-2)$, $2 \times (-3)$, $1 \times (-6)$, and $6 \times (-1)$.

The sums of these factors are $3 + (-2) = 1$, $2 + (-3) = -1$, $1 + (-6) = -5$, and $6 + (-1) = 5$.

You need factors that sum to -1, the coefficient of x.

These are 2 and -3. Therefore,

$x^2 - x - 6 = (x + 2)(x - 3)$

C) A trinomial of the form $acx^2 + (ab + bc)x + bd$.

Although this looks quite complicated, it is just a variation of the trinomial in (B) in which the coefficient of x^2 is not 1. For this type of trinomial, you are factoring not only the constant term, but also the coefficient of x^2. Then you must combine sums of combinations of these factors to see what combination yields the coefficient of x. This may involve more trials than (B), but it isn't as difficult as the explanation sounds. An example will show this.

• **EXAMPLE**

Factor $20x^2 + 47x + 21$

The possible factors of 20 are 4×5, 10×2, and 20×1

The possible factors of 21, the coefficient of x^2, are 3×7 and 21×1.

The sums of the combinations of these factors are:

$4 \times 3 + 5 \times 7$	$10 \times 3 + 2 \times 7$	$20 \times 3 + 1 \times 7$
$4 \times 7 + 5 \times 3$	$10 \times 7 + 2 \times 3$	$20 \times 7 + 1 \times 3$
$4 \times 21 + 5 \times 1$	$10 \times 21 + 2 \times 1$	$20 \times 21 + 1 \times 1$
$4 \times 1 + 5 \times 21$	$10 \times 1 + 2 \times 21$	$20 \times 1 + 1 \times 21$

This may look like a lot of work, but many combinations can be eliminated without even doing the math because their sum will obviously be more than 47, the coefficient of x. Also, once you find the right combination, you needn't check any others.

It turns out that the first combination

$4 \times 3 + 5 \times 7 = 12 + 35 = 47$ is the correct one.

So the factors for x^2 are 4 and 5 and those for the constant are 3 and 7, and the solution is:

$20x^2 + 47x + 21 = (4x + 7)(5x + 3)$

Note that the placement of the 7 and 3 are important because the x term has to have a coefficient of 47.

Always check your answer to make sure the factors will multiply together to give the original trinomial.

The procedure for factoring an algebraic expression completely is as follows:

Step 1: First find the greatest common factor if there is any. Then examine each factor remaining for greatest common factors.

Step 2: Continue factoring the factors obtained in Step 1 until all factors other than monomial factors are prime.

- **EXAMPLE**

Factoring $4 - 16x^2$,

$$4 - 16x^2 = 4(1 - 4x^2) = 4(1 + 2x)(1 - 2x)$$

PROBLEM

Express each of the following as a single term.

(1) $3x^2 + 2x^2 - 4x^2$

(2) $5axy^2 - 7axy^2 - 3xy^2$

SOLUTION

(1) Factor x^2 in the expression.

$3x^2 + 2x^2 - 4x^2 = (3 + 2 - 4)x^2 = 1x^2 = x^2$

(2) Factor xy^2 in the expression and then factor a.

$$5axy^2 - 7axy^2 - 3xy^2 = (5a - 7a - 3)xy^2$$
$$= [(5 - 7)a - 3]xy^2$$
$$= (-2a - 3)xy^2$$

PROBLEM

Simplify

$$\dfrac{\dfrac{1}{x-1} - \dfrac{1}{x-2}}{\dfrac{1}{x-2} - \dfrac{1}{x-3}}.$$

SOLUTION

Simplify the expression in the numerator by using the addition rule:

$$\frac{a}{b} + \frac{c}{d} = \frac{ad + bc}{bd}$$

Notice bd is the Least Common Denominator, LCD. We obtain

$$\frac{x - 2 - (x - 1)}{(x - 1)(x - 2)} = \frac{-1}{(x - 1)(x - 2)}$$

in the numerator.

Repeat this procedure for the expression in the denominator:

$$\frac{x - 3 - (x - 2)}{(x - 2)(x - 3)} = \frac{-1}{(x - 2)(x - 3)}$$

We now have

$$\frac{\dfrac{-1}{(x - 1)(x - 2)}}{\dfrac{-1}{(x - 2)(x - 3)}}$$

which is simplified by inverting the fraction in the denominator and multiplying it by the numerator and cancelling like terms

$$\frac{-1}{(x - 1)(x - 2)} \times \frac{(x - 2)(x - 3)}{-1} = \frac{x - 3}{x - 1}$$

PROBLEM

Factor $6ax^2 - 54a^3$

SOLUTION

Factor out the greatest common factor ($6a$):

$6ax^2 - 54a^3 = 6a(x^2 - 9a^2)$

Factor the difference of two squares:

$$= 6a(x + 3a)(x - 3a)$$

PROBLEM

Factor $x^2 + 5x + 6$

SOLUTION

The coefficient of x^2 is 1, so we are looking for two numbers whose product is 6 and sum is 5. They are 3 and 2.

Therefore $x^2 + 5x + 6 = (x + 3)(x + 2)$.

PROBLEM

Factor $2x^2 + 5x - 12$

SOLUTION

The factors of the coefficient of x^2 are 2×1

The factors of the constant term (-12) are $4 \times (-3)$, $3 \times (-4)$, $6 \times (-2)$, $2 \times (-6)$, $12 \times (-1)$, and $1 \times (-12)$

The combinations are:

$2(4) + 1(-3)$	$2(6) + 1(-2)$	$2(12) + 1(-1)$
$2(-3) + 1(4)$	$2(-2) + 1(6)$	$2(1) + 1(12)$
$2(3) + 1(-4)$	$2(2) + 1(-6)$	$2(1) + 1(-12)$
$2(-4) + 1(3)$	$2(-6) + 1(2)$	$2(-12) + 1(1)$

We need the one that adds up to $+5$, the coefficient of x.

It is the first combination $2(4) + 1(-3)$, so we need to go no further.

The answer is $2x^2 + 5x - 2 = (2x - 3)(x + 4)$

Drill: Simplifying Algebraic Expressions

DIRECTIONS: Simplify the following expressions.

1. $16b^2 - 25z^2 =$

   (A) $(4b - 5z)^2$ (C) $(4b - 5z)(4b + 5z)$

   (B) $(4b + 5z)^2$ (D) $(16b - 25z)^2$

2. $x^2 - 2x - 8 =$

   (A) $(x - 4)^2$ (C) $(x + 4)(x - 2)$

   (B) $(x - 6)(x - 2)$ (D) $(x - 4)(x + 2)$

3. $2c^2 + 5cd - 3d^2 =$

   (A) $(c - 3d)(c + 2d)$ (C) $(c - d)(2c + 3d)$

   (B) $(2c - d)(c + 3d)$ (D) $(2c + d)(c + 3d)$

4. $4t^3 - 20t =$

   (A) $4t(t^2 - 5)$ (C) $4t(t + 4)(t - 5)$

   (B) $4t^2(t - 20)$ (D) $2t(2t^2 - 10)$

5. $x^2 + xy - 2y^2 =$

   (A) $(x - 2y)(x + y)$ (C) $(x + 2y)(x + y)$

   (B) $(x - 2y)(x - y)$ (D) $(x + 2y)(x - y)$

Linear Equations

A linear equation with one unknown is one that can be put into the form $ax + b = 0$, where a and b are constants, $a \neq 0$.

To solve a linear equation means to transform it in the form $x = \dfrac{-b}{a}$.

A) If the equation has unknowns on both sides of the equality, it is convenient to put similar terms on the same sides. Refer to the following example.

$$4x + 3 = 2x + 9$$
$$4x + 3 - 2x = 2x + 9 - 2x$$
$$(4x - 2x) + 3 = (2x - 2x) + 9$$
$$2x + 3 = 0 + 9$$
$$2x + 3 - 3 = 0 + 9 - 3$$
$$2x = 6$$
$$\frac{2x}{2} = \frac{6}{2}$$
$$x = 3$$

B) If the equation appears in fractional form, it is necessary to transform it, using cross-multiplication, and then repeat the same procedure as in (A). For example, to solve

$$\frac{3x+4}{3} = \frac{7x+2}{5},$$

Use cross-multiplication to obtain:

$$\frac{3x+4}{3} \diagdown\kern-1em\diagup \frac{7x+2}{5}$$

$$3(7x + 2) = 5(3x + 4).$$

This is equivalent to:

$$21x + 6 = 15x + 20$$

$$21x - 15x + 6 = 15x - 15x + 20$$

$$6x + 6 - 6 = 20 - 6$$

$$6x = 14$$

$$x = \frac{14}{6}$$

$$x = \frac{7}{3}$$

C) If there are radicals in the equation, it is necessary to square both sides and then apply (A).

$$\sqrt{3x + 1} = 5$$

$$(\sqrt{3x + 1})^2 = 5^2$$

$$3x + 1 = 25$$

$$3x + 1 - 1 = 25 - 1$$

$$3x = 24$$

$$x = \frac{24}{3}$$

$$x = 8$$

Slope of the Line

The slope of the line containing two points (x_1, y_1) and (x_2, y_2) is given by:

$$\text{Slope} = m = \frac{y_2 - y_1}{x_2 - x_1}$$

Horizontal lines have a slope of zero, and the slope of vertical lines is undefined. Parallel lines have equal slopes and perpendicular lines have slopes that are negative reciprocals of each other.

The equation of a line with slope m passing through a point $Q(x_0, y_0)$ is of the form:

$$y - y_0 = m(x - x_0)$$

This is called the *point-slope form* of a linear equation.

The equation of a line passing through $Q(x_1, y_1)$ and $P(x_2, y_2)$ is given by:

$$\frac{y - y_1}{x - x_1} = \frac{y_2 - y_1}{x_2 - x_1}$$

This is the *two-point form* of a linear equation.

The equation of a line intersecting the x-axis at $(x_0, 0)$ and the y-axis at $(0, y_0)$ is given by:

$$\frac{x}{x_0} + \frac{y}{y_0} = 1$$

This is the *intercept form* of a linear equation.

The equation of a line with slope m intersecting the y-axis at $(0, b)$ is given by:

$$y = mx + b$$

This is the *slope-intercept* form of a linear equation.

PROBLEM

Find the slope, the y-intercept, and the x-intercept of the equation $2x - 3y - 18 = 0$.

SOLUTION

To find the slope and y-intercept, write the equation in the form of the general linear equation, $ax + by = c$. Then divide by b and solving for y, to obtain:

$$\frac{a}{b}x + y = \frac{c}{b}$$

$$y = \frac{c}{b} - \frac{a}{b}x$$

where $\frac{-a}{b} = $ slope and $\frac{c}{b} = y$-intercept

To find the x-intercept, solve for x and let $y = 0$:

$$x = \frac{c}{a} - \frac{b}{a}y$$

$$x = \frac{c}{a}$$

Thus, $2x - 3y - 18 = 0$

$$2x - 3y = 18$$

In this form we have $a = 2$, $b = -3$, and $c = 18$. Thus,

$$\text{slope} = -\frac{a}{b} = -\frac{2}{-3} = \frac{2}{3}$$

$$y\text{-intercept} = \frac{c}{b} = \frac{18}{-3} = -6$$

$$x\text{-intercept} = \frac{c}{a} = \frac{18}{2} = 9$$

PROBLEM

Find the equation for the line passing through (3, 5) and (–1, 2).

SOLUTIONS

A) Use the two-point form with $(x_1, y_1) = (3, 5)$ and $(x_2, y_2) = (-1, 2)$. Then

$$\frac{y - y_1}{x - x_1} = \frac{y_2 - y_1}{x_2 - x_1}$$

$$\frac{y_2 - y_1}{x_2 - x_1} = \frac{2 - 5}{-1 - 3} \quad \text{thus} \quad \frac{y - 5}{x - 3} = \frac{-3}{-4}$$

Cross multiply, $\quad -4(y - 5) = -3(x - 3)$.

Distribute, $\quad -4y + 20 = -3x + 9$

Place in general form, $\quad 3x - 4y = -11$.

B) Does the same equation result if we let $(x_1, y_1) = (-1, 2)$ and $(x_2, y_2) = (3, 5)$?

$$\frac{y_2 - y_1}{x_2 - x_1} = \frac{5 - 2}{3 - (-1)} \quad \text{thus} \quad \frac{y - 2}{x + 1} = \frac{3}{4}$$

Cross multiply, $\quad 4(y - 2) = 3(x + 1)$

Distribute $\quad 4y - 8 = 3x + 3$

Place in general form, $\quad 3x - 4y = -11$.

Hence, either replacement results in the same equation. Keep in mind that the coefficient of the x-term should always be positive.

PROBLEM

(a) Find the equation of the line passing through (2, 5) with slope 3.

(b) Suppose a line passes through the y-axis at (0, b). How can we write the equation if the point-slope form is used?

SOLUTION

(a) In the point-slope form, let $x_1 = 2$, $y_1 = 5$, $m = 3$.

The point-slope form of a line is:

$$y - y_1 = m(x - x_1)$$

$$y - 5 = 3(x - 2)$$

$$y - 5 = 3x - 6 \qquad \text{Distributive property}$$

$$y = 3x - 1 \qquad \text{Transposition}$$

(b) $y - b = m(x - 0)$

$$y = mx + b.$$

Notice that this is the slope-intercept form for the equation of a line.

PROBLEM

Construct the graph of the function defined by $y = 3x - 9$.

SOLUTION

This linear equation is in the slope-intercept form, $y = mx + b$.

A line can be determined by two points. Let us choose the intercepts. The x-intercept lies on the x-axis and the y-intercept is on the y-axis.

We can find the y-intercept by assigning 0 to x in the given equation and then find the x-intercept by assigning 0 to y. It is helpful to have a third point. We find a third point by assigning any value, say 4, to x and solving for y. Thus, we get the following table of corresponding numbers:

x	$y = 3x - 9$	y
0	$y = 3(0) - 9$	-9
3	$0 = 3x - 9, x = 9/3 = 3$	0
4	$y = 3(4) - 9$	3

The three points are (0, –9), (3, 0), and (4, 3). Draw a line through them as in the figure below.

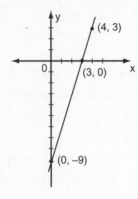

PROBLEM

Graph the function defined by $3x - 4y = 12$.

SOLUTION

Solve for y:

$$3x - 4y = 12$$
$$-4y = 12 - 3x$$
$$y = -3 + \frac{3}{4}x$$
$$y = \frac{3}{4}x - 3$$

The graph of this function is a straight line since it is of the form $y = mx + b$. The y-intercept crosses (intersects) the y-axis at the point (0, –3), since for $x = 0$, $y = b = -3$. The x-intercept crosses (intersects) the x-axis at the point (4, 0) since for $y = 0$, $3x = 12$, or $x = 4$.

These two points, (0, –3) and (4, 0) are sufficient to determine the graph (see Figure below). A third point, (8, 3), satisfying the equation of the function is plotted as a partial check of the intercepts. Note that the slope of

the line is $m = \frac{3}{4}$. This means that y increases three units as x increases four units anywhere along the line.

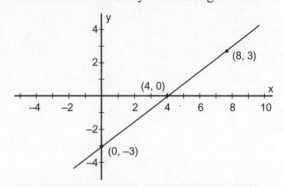

Two Linear Equations

Equations of the form $ax + by = c$, where a, b, c are constants and a, $b \neq 0$ are called **linear equations** with two unknown variables.

There are several ways to solve systems of linear equations with two variables.

Method 1: **Addition or subtraction**—If necessary, multiply the equations by numbers that will make the coefficients of one unknown in the resulting equations numerically equal. If the signs of equal coefficients are the same, subtract the equation; otherwise, add.

The result is one equation with one unknown; solve it and substitute the value into the other equations to find the unknown that was first eliminated.

Method 2: **Substitution**—Find the value of one unknown in terms of the other. Substitute this value into the other equation and solve.

Method 3: **Graph**—Graph both equations. The point of intersection of the drawn lines is a simultaneous solution for the equations, and its coordinates correspond to the answer that would be found analytically.

If the lines are parallel, they have no simultaneous solution.

Dependent equations are equations that represent the same line; therefore, every point on the line representing dependent equations represents a solution. Since there are an infinite number of points on a line, there are an infinite number of simultaneous solutions. For example,

$$\begin{cases} 2x + y = 8 \\ 4x + 2y = 16 \end{cases}$$

These equations are dependent. Since they represent the same line, all points that satisfy either of the equations are solutions of the system.

A system of linear equations is consistent if there is only one solution for the system.

A system of linear equations is inconsistent if it does not have any solutions.

• **EXAMPLE**

Find the point of intersection of the graphs of the equations as shown in the figure in the second column.

$$x + y = 3$$
$$3x - 2y = 14$$

To solve these linear equations, solve for y in terms of x. The equations will be in the form $y = mx + b$, where m is the slope and b is the intercept on the y-axis.

$$x + y = 3$$

Subtract x from both sides: $y = 3 - x$

$$3x - 2y = 14$$

Subtract $3x$ from both sides: $-2y = 14 - 3x$

Divide by -2: $y = -7 + \dfrac{3}{2}x$

The graphs of the linear functions, $y = 3 - x$ and $y = 7 + \dfrac{3}{2}x$ can be determined by plotting only two points. For example, for $y = 3 - x$, let $x = 0$, then $y = 3$. Let $x = 1$, then $y = 2$. The two points on this first line are $(0, 3)$ and $(1, 2)$. For $y = -7 + \dfrac{3}{2}x$ let $x = 0$, then $y = -7$. Let $x = 1$, then $y = -5\dfrac{1}{2}$. The two points on this second line are $(0, -7)$ and $(1, -5\dfrac{1}{2})$.

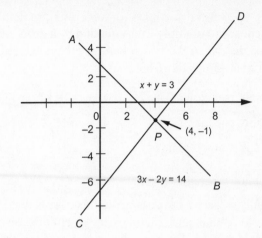

AB is the graph of the first equation, and CD is the graph of the second equation. The point of intersection P of the two graphs is the only point on both lines. The coordinates of P satisfy both equations and represent the desired solution of the problem. From the graph, P seems to be the point $(4, -1)$.

To find the point of intersection P of

$x + y = 3$ and $3x - 2y = 14$ algebraically, multiply the first equation by 2. Add these two equations to eliminate the variable y.

$$\begin{array}{r} 2x + 2y = 6 \\ 3x - 2y = 14 \\ \hline 5x = 20 \end{array}$$

Solve for x to obtain $x = 4$. Substitute this into $y = 3 - x$ to get $y = 3 - 4 = -1$. P is $(4, -1)$.

To show that $(4, -1)$ satisfies both equations, substitute this point into both equations.

$x + y = 3$	$3x - 2y = 14$
$4 + (-1) = 3$	$3(4) - 2(-1) = 14$
$4 - 1 = 3$	$12 + 2 = 14$
$3 = 3$	$14 = 14$

• **EXAMPLE**

Solve the equations.

$$2x + 3y = 6 \tag{1}$$

and

$$4x + 6y = 7 \tag{2}$$

There are several methods to solve this problem. We have chosen to multiply each equation by a different number so that when the two equations are added, one of the variables drops out. Thus,

Multiply equation (1) by 2: $4x + 6y = 12$ (3)

Multiply equation (2) by –1: $\underline{-4x - 6y = -7}$ (4)

Add equations (3) and (4): $0 = 5$

We obtain a peculiar result!

Actually, what we have shown in this case is that if there were a simultaneous solution to the given equations, then 0 would equal 5. But the conclusion is impossible; therefore, there can be no simultaneous solution to these two equations, and no point satisfies both.

The straight lines that are the graphs of these equations must be parallel if they never intersect, but not identical, which can be seen from the graph of these equations (see the figure).

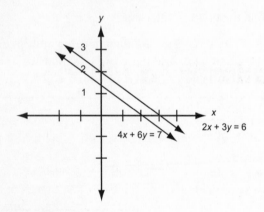

• **EXAMPLE**

Solve the system of equations.

$2x + 3y = 6$ (1)

and

$y = -\left(\dfrac{2x}{3}\right) + 2$.   (2)

There are several methods of solution for this problem. Since equation (2) already gives us an expression for y, we use the method of substitution.

Substitute $-\left(\dfrac{2x}{3}\right) + 2$ for y in the first equation:

$$2x + 3\left(-\frac{2x}{3} + 2\right) = 6$$

Distribute: $2x - 2x + 6 = 6$

$6 = 6$

The result $6 = 6$ is true, but indicates no solution. Actually, our work shows that no matter what real number x is, if y is determined by the second equation, then the first equation will always be satisfied.

The reason for this peculiarity may be seen if we take a closer look at the equation $y = -\left(\dfrac{2x}{3}\right) + 2$. It is equivalent to $3y = -2x + 6$, or $2x + 3y = 6$.

In other words, the two equations are equivalent. Any pair of values of x and y that satisfies one satisfies the other. Two systems of linear equations are said to be equivalent if and only if they have the same solution set.

It is hardly necessary to verify that in this case the graphs of the given equations are identical lines, and that there are an infinite number of simultaneous solutions to these equations.

A system of three linear equations in three unknowns is solved by eliminating one unknown from any two of the three equations and solving them. After finding two unknowns, substitute them in any of the equations to find the third unknown.

PROBLEM

Solve the system of equations

$2x + 3y - 4z = -8$ (1)

$x + y - 2z = -5$ (2)

$7x - 2y + 5z = 4$ (3)

SOLUTION

We cannot eliminate any variable from two pairs of equations by a single multiplication. However, both x and z may be eliminated from equations (1) and (2) by multiplying equation (2) by –2. Then

$$2x + 3y - 4z = -8 \qquad (1)$$
$$-2x - 2y + 4z = 10 \qquad (4)$$

By addition, we have $y = 2$. Although we may now eliminate either x or z from another pair of equations, we can more conveniently substitute $y = 2$ in equations (2) and (3) to get two equations in two variables. Thus, making the substitution $y = 2$ in equations (2) and (3), we have

$$x - 2z = -7 \qquad (5)$$
$$7x + 5z = 8 \qquad (6)$$

Multiply equation (5) by 5 and multiply (6) by 2. Then add the two new equations. Then $x = -1$. Substitute x in either equation (5) or (6) to find $z = 3$.

The solution of the system is $x = -1$, $y = 2$, and $z = 3$. Check by substitution.

A **homogeneous system** is a system of equations that has all constant terms equal to zero.

$$\begin{cases} a_{11}x_1 + a_{12}x_2 + \cdots + a_{1n}x_m = 0 \\ a_{21}x_1 + a_{22}x_2 + \cdots + a_{2n}x_m = 0 \\ \vdots \qquad \vdots \qquad \qquad \vdots \\ a_{n1}x_1 + a_{n2}x_2 + \cdots + a_{nn}x_m = 0 \end{cases}$$

A homogeneous system always has at least one solution which is called the trivial solution, that is $x_1 = 0$, $x_2 = 0, \ldots, x_m = 0$. For any given homogeneous system of equations, in which the number of variables is greater than or equal to the number of equations, there also are non-trivial solutions.

Drill: Two Linear Equations

DIRECTIONS: Find the solution set for each pair of equations.

1. $3x + 4y = -2$
   $x - 6y = -8$

   (A) $(2, -1)$ (C) $(-2, -1)$
   (B) $(1, -2)$ (D) $(-2, 1)$

2. $2x + y = -10$
   $-2x - 4y = 4$

   (A) $(6, -2)$ (C) $(-2, 6)$
   (B) $(-6, 2)$ (D) $(2, 6)$

3. $6x + 5y = -4$
   $3x - 3y = 9$

   (A) $(1, -2)$ (C) $(2, -1)$
   (B) $(1, 2)$ (D) $(-2, 1)$

4. $4x + 3y = 9$
   $2x - 2y = 8$

   (A) $(-3, 1)$ (C) $(3, 1)$
   (B) $(1, -3)$ (D) $(3, -1)$

5. $x + y = 7$
   $x = y - 3$

   (A) $(5, 2)$ (C) $(2, 5)$
   (B) $(-5, 2)$ (D) $(-2, 5)$

Quadratic Equations

A second-degree equation in x of the type $ax^2 + bx + c = 0$, $a \neq 0$, a, b, and c are real numbers, is called a quadratic equation.

To solve a quadratic equation is to find values of x that satisfy $ax^2 + bx + c = 0$. These values of x are called solutions, or roots, of the equation.

A quadratic equation has a maximum of two roots. Methods of solving quadratic equations:

A) Direct solution: Given $x^2 - 9 = 0$.

We can solve directly by isolating the variable x:

$$x^2 = 9$$
$$x = \pm 3$$

B) Factoring: Given a quadratic equation $ax^2 + bx + c = 0$, a, b, $c \neq 0$, to factor means to express it as the product $a(x - r_1)(x - r_2) = 0$, where r_1 and r_2 are the two roots.

Some helpful hints to remember are:

(a) $r_1 + r_2 = -\dfrac{b}{a}$.

(b) $r_1 \times r_2 = \dfrac{c}{a}$.

For example, solve for x:

$x^2 - 5x + 4 = 0$.

Since $r_1 + r_2 = \dfrac{-b}{a} = \dfrac{-(-5)}{1} = 5$, the possible solutions are $(3, 2)$, $(4, 1)$, and $(5, 0)$. Also $r_1 r_2 = \dfrac{c}{a} = \dfrac{4}{1} = 4$; this equation is satisfied only by the second pair, so $r_1 = 4$, $r_2 = 1$ and the factored form is $(x - 4)(x - 1) = 0$.

Take another example, $2x^2 - 12x + 16 = 0$.

Since $r_1 + r_2 = \dfrac{-b}{a} = \dfrac{-(-12)}{2} = 6$, the possible solutions are $(6, 0)$, $(5, 1)$, $(4, 2)$, $(3, 3)$. Also $r_1 r_2 = \dfrac{16}{2} = 8$, so the only possible answer is $(4, 2)$ and the expression $2x^2 - 12x + 16 = 0$ can be factored as $2(x - 4)(x - 2)$.

C) Completing the square: If it is difficult to factor the quadratic equation by using the previous method, we can try to complete the square.

For example, solve for x: $x^2 - 12x + 8 = 0$.

We know that the two roots added up should be 12 because $r_1 + r_2 = \dfrac{-b}{a} = \dfrac{-(-12)}{1} = 12$. The possible roots are $(12, 0)$, $(11, 1)$, $(10, 2)$, $(9, 3)$, $(8, 4)$, $(7, 5)$, $(6, 6)$.

But none of these satisfy $r_1 r_2 = 8$, so we cannot use factoring.

To complete the square, it is necessary to isolate the constant term,

$x^2 - 12x = -8$.

Then take $\dfrac{1}{2}$ coefficient of the x term, square it, and add to both sides

$$x^2 - 12x + \left(\dfrac{-12}{2}\right)^2 = -8 + \left(\dfrac{-12}{2}\right)^2$$
$$x^2 - 12x + 36 = -8 + 36 = 28$$

Now we can use the previous method to factor the left side: $r_1 + r_2 = 12$, $r_1 r_2 = 36$ is satisfied by the pair $(6, 6)$, so we have:

$$(x - 6)(x - 6) = (x - 6)^2 = 28.$$

Now take the square root of both sides and solve for x. Remember when taking a square root that the solution can be positive or negative.

$$(x - 6) = \pm\sqrt{28} = \pm 2\sqrt{7}$$
$$x = \pm 2\sqrt{7} + 6$$

So the roots are: $x = 2\sqrt{7} + 6$, $x = -2\sqrt{7} + 6$

Note that if the coefficient of x^2 is not 1, it is necessary to divide the equation by this coefficient and then proceed to solve by completing the square.

PROBLEM

Solve $2x^2 + 8x + 4 = 0$ by completing the square.

SOLUTION

Divide both sides by 2, the coefficient of x^2.

$x^2 + 4x + 2 = 0$

Subtract the constant term, 2, from both sides.

$x^2 + 4x = -2$

Add to each side the square of one-half the coefficient of the x-term.

$x^2 + 4x + 4 = -2 + 4$

Factor

$(x + 2)(x + 2) = (x + 2)^2 = 2$

Set the square root of the left member (a perfect square) equal to ± the square root of the right member and solve for x.

$$x + 2 = \sqrt{2} \quad \text{or} \quad x + 2 = -\sqrt{2}$$

The roots are $x = \sqrt{2} - 2$ and $x = -\sqrt{2} - 2$. Check each solution.

$$2\left(\sqrt{2} - 2\right)^2 + 8\left(\sqrt{2} - 2\right) + 4$$
$$= 2\left(2 - 4\sqrt{2} + 4\right) + 8\sqrt{2} - 16 + 4$$
$$= 4 - 8\sqrt{2} + 8 + 8\sqrt{2} - 16 + 4$$
$$= 0$$

$$2(-\sqrt{2} - 2)^2 + 8(-\sqrt{2} - 2) + 4$$
$$= 2\left(2 + 4\sqrt{2} + 4\right) - 8\sqrt{2} - 16 + 4$$
$$= 4 + 8\sqrt{2} + 8 - 8\sqrt{2} - 16 + 4$$
$$= 0$$

Quadratic Formula

Consider the polynomial:

$ax^2 + bx + c = 0$, where $a \neq 0$.

The roots of this equation can be determined in terms of the coefficients a, b, and c as shown below:

$$x = \frac{-b \pm \sqrt{b^2 - 4ac}}{2a}$$

where ± is read as "plus or minus" and $(b^2 - 4ac)$ is called the discriminant of the quadratic equation.

If the discriminant is equal to zero $(b^2 - 4ac = 0)$, both roots are rational and equal.

If the discriminant is greater than zero $(b^2 - 4ac > 0)$, then the roots are real and unequal. Further, the roots are rational if and only if a and b are rational and $(b^2 - 4ac)$ is a perfect square, otherwise the roots are irrational.

Note that if the discriminant is less than zero $(b^2 - 4ac < 0)$, the roots are complex numbers, since the discriminant appears under a radical and square roots of negatives are imaginary numbers. A real number added to an imaginary number yields a complex number.

• **EXAMPLE**

Compute the value of the discriminant and then determine the nature of the roots of each of the following four equations:

A) $4x^2 - 12x + 9 = 0$

B) $3x^2 - 7x - 6 = 0$

C) $5x^2 + 2x - 9 = 0$

D) $x^2 + 3x + 5 = 0$

A) $4x^2 - 12x + 9 = 0$,

Here a, b, and c are integers,

$a = 4$, $b = -12$, and $c = 9$.

Therefore,

$$b^2 - 4ac = (-12)^2 - 4(4)(9) = 144 - 144 = 0.$$

Since the discriminant is 0, the roots are rational and equal.

B) $3x^2 - 7x - 6 = 0$

Here a, b, and c are integers,

$a = 3$, $b = -7$, and $c = -6$.

Therefore,

$$b^2 - 4ac = (-7)^2 - 4(3)(-6) = 49 + 72 = 121 = 11^2.$$

Since the discriminant is a perfect square, the roots are rational and unequal.

C) $5x^2 + 2x - 9 = 0$

Here a, b, and c are integers,

$a = 5$, $b = 2$, and $c = -9$.

Therefore,

$$b^2 - 4ac = 2^2 - 4(5)(-9) = 4 + 180 = 184.$$

Since the discriminant is greater than zero, but not a perfect square, the roots are irrational and unequal.

D) $x^2 + 3x + 5 = 0$

Here a, b, and c are integers,

$$a = 1, \ b = 3, \text{ and } c = 5.$$

Therefore,

$$b^2 - 4ac = 3^2 - 4(1)(5) = 9 - 20 = -11.$$

Since the discriminant is negative, the roots are imaginary.

- **EXAMPLE**

Find the equation whose roots are $\dfrac{\alpha}{\beta}, \dfrac{\beta}{\alpha}$.

The roots of the equation are $x = \dfrac{\alpha}{\beta}$ and $x = \dfrac{\beta}{\alpha}$. Subtract $\dfrac{\alpha}{\beta}$ from both sides of the first equation:

$$x - \frac{\alpha}{\beta} = \frac{\alpha}{\beta} - \frac{\alpha}{\beta} = 0, \text{ or } x - \frac{\alpha}{\beta} = 0.$$

Subtract $\dfrac{\beta}{\alpha}$ from both sides of the second equation:

$$x - \frac{\beta}{\alpha} = \frac{\beta}{\alpha} - \frac{\beta}{\alpha} = 0, \text{ or } x - \frac{\beta}{\alpha} = 0.$$

Therefore:

$$\left(x - \frac{\alpha}{\beta}\right)\left(x - \frac{\beta}{\alpha}\right) = (0)(0),$$

or

$$\left(x - \frac{\alpha}{\beta}\right)\left(x - \frac{\beta}{\alpha}\right) = 0. \tag{1}$$

Equation (1) is of the form:

$$(x - c)(x - d) = 0, \text{ or}$$
$$x^2 - cx - dx + cd = 0, \text{ or}$$
$$x^2 - (c + d)x + cd = 0. \tag{2}$$

Note that c corresponds to the root $\dfrac{\alpha}{\beta}$ and d corresponds to the root $\dfrac{\beta}{\alpha}$. The sum of the roots is:

$$c + d = \frac{\alpha}{\beta} + \frac{\beta}{\alpha} = \frac{\alpha(\alpha)}{\alpha(\beta)} + \frac{\beta(\beta)}{\beta(\alpha)} = \frac{\alpha^2}{\alpha\beta} + \frac{\beta^2}{\alpha\beta}$$

$$= \frac{\alpha^2 + \beta^2}{\alpha\beta}$$

The product of the roots is:

$$c \times d = \frac{\alpha}{\beta} \times \frac{\beta}{\alpha} = \frac{\alpha\beta}{\beta\alpha} = \frac{\alpha\beta}{\alpha\beta} = 1$$

Using the form of Equation (2):

$$\left(x - \frac{\alpha}{\beta}\right)\left(x - \frac{\beta}{\alpha}\right)$$

$$= x^2 - \left(\frac{\alpha^2 + \beta^2}{\alpha\beta}\right)x + 1 = 0. \tag{3}$$

Multiply both sides of Equation (3) by $\alpha\beta$

$$\alpha\beta\left[x^2 - \left(\frac{\alpha^2 + \beta^2}{\alpha\beta}\right)x + 1\right] = \alpha\beta(0)$$

Distributing,

$$\alpha\beta x^2 - (\alpha^2 + \beta^2)x + \alpha\beta = 0,$$

which is the equation whose roots are $\dfrac{\alpha}{\beta}, \dfrac{\beta}{\alpha}$.

Radical Equation

An equation that has one or more unknowns under a radical is called a radical equation.

To solve a radical equation, isolate the radical term on one side of the equation and move all the other terms to the other side. Then both members of the equation are raised to a power equal to the index of the isolated radical.

After solving the resulting equation, the roots obtained must be checked, since this method often introduces extraneous roots. These introduced roots must be excluded if they are not solutions.

- **EXAMPLE**

Solve for x: $\sqrt{x^2 + 2} + 6x = x - 4$

$$\sqrt{x^2 + 2} = x - 4 - 6x = -5x - 4$$

$$\left(\sqrt{x^2 + 2}\right)^2 = (-(5x + 4))^2$$

$$x^2 + 2 = (5x + 4)^2$$

$x^2 + 2 = 25x^2 + 40x + 16$, or

$24x^2 + 40x + 14 = 0$

Applying the quadratic formula, we obtain:

$$x = \frac{-40 \pm \sqrt{1600 - 4(24)(14)}}{2(24)} = \frac{-40 \pm 16}{48}$$

$$x_1 = \frac{-7}{6}, x_2 = \frac{-1}{2}$$

Checking roots:

$$\sqrt{\left(\frac{-7}{6}\right)^2 + 2} + 6\left(\frac{-7}{6}\right) \overset{?}{=} \left(\frac{-7}{6}\right) - 4$$

$$\frac{11}{6} - 7 \overset{?}{=} \frac{-31}{6}$$

$$\frac{-31}{6} = \frac{-31}{6}$$

$$\sqrt{\left(\frac{-1}{2}\right)^2 + 2} + 6\left(\frac{-1}{2}\right) \overset{?}{=} \left(\frac{-1}{2}\right) - 4$$

$$\frac{3}{2} - 3 \overset{?}{=} \frac{-9}{2}$$

$$\frac{-3}{2} \neq \frac{-9}{2}$$

Hence, $-\frac{1}{2}$ is not a root of the equation, but $\frac{-7}{6}$ is a root.

PROBLEM

Solve for x: $4x^2 - 7 = 0$.

SOLUTION

This quadratic equation can be solved for x by using the quadratic formula, which applies to equations in the form $ax^2 + bx + c = 0$ (here, $b = 0$). There is, however, an easier method that we can use:

Adding 7 to both sides, $4x^2 = 7$

Dividing both sides by 4, $x^2 = \frac{7}{4}$

Taking the square root of both sides, $x = \pm\sqrt{\frac{7}{4}} = \pm\frac{\sqrt{7}}{2}$.

So, the two roots of the equation are $+\frac{\sqrt{7}}{2}$ and $-\frac{\sqrt{7}}{2}$.

PROBLEM

Solve the equation $2x^2 - 5x + 3 = 0$.

SOLUTION

$2x^2 - 5x + 3 = 0$

The equation is a quadratic equation of the form $ax^2 + bx + c = 0$ in which $a = 2$, $b = -5$, and $c = 3$. Therefore, the quadratic formula $x = \dfrac{-b \pm \sqrt{b^2 - 4ac}}{2a}$ may be used to find the solutions of the given equation. Substituting the values for a, b, and c in the quadratic formula:

$$x = \frac{-(-5) \pm \sqrt{(-5)^2 - 4(2)(3)}}{2(2)}$$

$$x = \frac{5 \pm \sqrt{1}}{4}$$

$$x = \frac{5 + 1}{4} = \frac{3}{2} \text{ and } x = \frac{5 - 1}{4} = 1$$

Check: Substituting $x = \frac{3}{2}$ in the given equation,

$$2\left(\frac{3}{2}\right)^2 - 5\left(\frac{3}{2}\right) + 3 = 0$$

$$0 = 0$$

Substituting $x = 1$ in the given equation,

$$2(1)^2 - 5(1) + 3 = 0$$

$$0 = 0$$

So the roots of $2x^2 - 5x + 3 = 0$ are $x = \frac{3}{2}$ and $x = 1$.

Quadratic Functions

The function $f(x) = ax^2 + bx + c$, $a \neq 0$, where a, b, and c are real numbers, is called a quadratic function (or a function of second degree) in one unknown.

The graph of $y = ax^2 + bx + c$ is a curve known as a parabola.

The vertex of the parabola is the point $\left(\dfrac{-b}{2a}, \dfrac{4ac - b^2}{4a} \right)$. The parabola's axis is the line $x = \dfrac{-b}{2a}$.

The graph of the parabola opens upward if $a > 0$ and downward if $a < 0$. If $a = 0$ the quadratic is reduced to a linear function whose graph is a straight line.

The figures below show parabolas with $a > 0$, and $a < 0$, respectively.

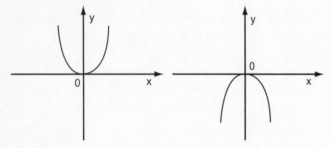

PROBLEM

> Solve the system
> $$y = -x^2 + 7x - 5 \qquad (1)$$
> $$y - 2x = 2 \qquad (2)$$

SOLUTION

Solving Equation (2) for y yields an expression for y in terms of x. Substituting this expression in Equation (1),

$$2x + 2 = -x^2 + 7x - 5 \qquad (3)$$

We have a single equation, in terms of a single variable, to be solved. Writing Equation (3) in standard quadratic form, we get

$$x^2 - 5x + 7 = 0 \qquad (4)$$

Since the equation is not factorable, the roots are not found in this manner. Evaluating the discriminant will indicate whether Equation (4) has real roots. The discriminant, $b^2 - 4ac$, of Equation (4) equals $(-5)^2 - 4(1)(7) = 25 - 28 = -3$. Since the discriminant is negative, equation (4) has no real roots, and therefore the system has no real solution. The graph of the equations shows that the parabola and the straight line have no point in common.

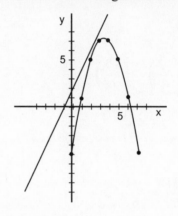

PROBLEM

> Solve the system
> $$y = 3x^2 - 2x + 5 \qquad (1)$$
> $$y = 4x + 2 \qquad (2)$$

SOLUTION

To obtain a single equation with one unknown variable, x, substitute the value of y from Equation (2) in Equation (1),

$$4x + 2 = 3x^2 - 2x + 5. \qquad (3)$$

Writing Equation (3) in standard quadratic form,

$$3x^2 - 6x + 3 = 0. \qquad (4)$$

We may simplify equation (4) by dividing both sides by 3, which is a factor common to each term:

$$x^2 - 2x + 1 = 0. \qquad (5)$$

To find the roots, factor and set each factor = 0. This may be done because whenever a product = 0, one or all of the factors must = 0.

$$(x - 1)(x - 1) = 0$$
$$x - 1 = 0 \quad x - 1 = 0$$
$$x = 1 \quad\quad x = 1$$

Equation (5) has two roots, each equal to 1. For $x = 1$, from Equation (2), we have $y = 4(1) + 2 = 6$. Therefore, the system has but one common solution:

$$x = 1, \quad y = 6.$$

We may check to see if our values satisfy Equation (1) as well:

Substituting:
$$y = 3x^2 - 2x + 5$$
$$6 \overset{?}{=} 3(1)^2 - 2(1) + 5$$
$$6 \overset{?}{=} 3 - 2 + 5$$
$$6 = 6$$

The figure below indicates that our solution is probably correct.

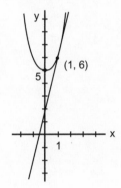

Quadratic Equations in Two Unknowns and Systems of Equations

A quadratic equation in two unknowns has the general form:

$$ax^2 + bxy + cy^2 + dx + ey + f = 0$$

where a, b, and c are not all zero and a, b, c, d, e, and f are constants.

Graphing: If $b^2 - 4ac < 0$, $b \neq 0$ and $a \neq c$, the graph of $ax^2 + bxy + cy^2 + dx + ey + f = 0$ is a closed curve called an ellipse. If $b = 0$ and $a = c$, the graph $ax^2 + bxy + cy^2 + dx + ey + f = 0$ is a point or a circle, or else it does not exist.

If $b^2 - 4ac > 0$, the graph of $ax^2 + bxy + cy^2 + dx + ey + f = 0$ is a curve called a hyperbola.

If $b^2 - 4ac = 0$, the graph of $ax^2 + bxy + cy^2 + dx + ey + f = 0$ is a parabola or a pair of parallel lines that may be coincident, or else it does not exist.

Solving Systems of Equations Involving Quadratics

Some methods for solving systems of equations involving quadratics are given below:

A) *One linear and one quadratic equation*
Solve the linear equation for one of the two unknowns, then substitute this value into the quadratic equation.

B) *Two quadratic equations*
Eliminate one of the unknowns by using the method given for solving systems of linear equations.

• **EXAMPLE**

$$\begin{cases} x^2 + y^2 = 9 & (1) \\ x^2 + 2y^2 = 18 & (2) \end{cases}$$

Subtracting Equation (1) from (2), we obtain:

$$y^2 = 9, \, y = \pm 3$$

By substituting the values of y into Equation (1) or (2), we obtain:

$$x_1 = 0 \text{ and } x_2 = 0$$

So the solutions are:

$$x = 0, y = 3 \text{ and } x = 0, y = -3$$

C) *Two quadratic equations, one homogeneous*
An equation is said to be homogeneous if it is of the form

$$ax^2 + bxy + cy^2 + dx + ey = 0.$$

Consider the system

$$\begin{cases} x^2 + 3xy + 2y^2 = 0 & (1) \\ x^2 - 3xy + 2y^2 = 12 & (2) \end{cases}$$

Equation (1) can be factored into the product of two linear equations:

$$x^2 + 3xy + 2y^2 = (x + 2y)(x + y) = 0$$

From this we determine that:

$$x + 2y = 0 \Rightarrow x = -2y \text{ or}$$
$$x + y = 0 \Rightarrow x = -y$$

Substituting $x = -2y$ into Equation (2), we find:

$$(-2y)^2 - 3(-2y)y + 2y^2 = 12$$
$$4y^2 + 6y^2 + 2y^2 = 12$$
$$12y^2 = 12$$
$$y^2 = 1$$
$$y = \pm 1, \text{ so } x = \pm 2$$

Substituting $x = -y$ into Equation (2) yields:

$$(-y)^2 - 3(-y)y + 2y^2 = 12$$
$$y^2 + 3y^2 + 2y^2 = 12$$
$$6y^2 = 12$$
$$y^2 = 2$$
$$y = \pm\sqrt{2}, \text{ so } x = \mp\sqrt{2}$$

So the solutions of Equations (1) and (2) are:

$$(2, -1), (-2, 1), (\sqrt{2}, -\sqrt{2}), \text{ and } (-\sqrt{2}, \sqrt{2})$$

D) *Two quadratic equations of the form*

$$ax^2 + bxy + cy^2 = d$$

Combine the two equations to obtain a homogeneous quadratic equation, then solve the equations by method (C).

E) *Two quadratic equations, each symmetrical in x and y*

Note: An equation is said to be symmetrical in x and y if by exchanging the coefficients of x and y we obtain the same equation.

Example: $x^2 + y^2 = 9$.

To solve systems involving this type of equations, substitute $u + v$ for x and $u - v$ for y and solve the resulting equations for u and v.

Example: Given the system below:

$$\begin{cases} x^2 + y^2 = 25 & (1) \\ x^2 + xy + y^2 = 37 & (2) \end{cases}$$

Substitute:

$$x = u + v$$
$$y = u - v$$

If we substitute the new values for x and y into Equation (2) we obtain:

$$(u + v)^2 + (u + v)(u - v) + (u - v)^2 = 37$$

$$u^2 + 2uv + v^2 + u^2 - v^2 + u^2 - 2uv + v^2 = 37$$
$$3u^2 + v^2 = 37$$

If we substitute the new values for x and y into Equation (1), we obtain:

$$(u + v)^2 + (u - v)^2 = 25$$
$$u^2 + 2uv + v^2 + u^2 - 2uv + v^2 = 25$$
$$2u^2 + 2v^2 = 25$$

The "new" system is:

$$3u^2 + v^2 = 37$$
$$2u^2 + 2v^2 = 25$$

By substituting $a = u^2$ and $b = v^2$, these equations become:

$$\begin{cases} 3a + b = 37 \\ 2a + 2b = 25 \end{cases}$$

and

$$a = \frac{49}{4}, \quad b = \frac{1}{4}$$

So

$$u^2 = \frac{49}{4} \quad \text{and} \quad v^2 = \frac{1}{4}$$
$$u = \pm\frac{7}{2}$$
$$v = \pm\frac{1}{2}$$
$$x = \frac{7}{2} + \frac{1}{2} = 4 \quad \text{or} \quad \frac{-7}{2} - \frac{1}{2} = -4$$
$$y = \frac{7}{2} - \frac{1}{2} = 3 \quad \text{or} \quad \frac{-7}{2} + \frac{1}{2} = -3$$

Since x and y are symmetrical, the possible solutions are $(4, 3), (-4, -3), (3, 4), (-3, -4)$.

Note that if the equation is symmetrical, it is possible to interchange the solutions, too. If $x = 3$, then $y = 4$ or vice versa.

PROBLEM

Solve the system.

$$2x^2 - 3xy - 4y^2 + x + y - 1 = 0$$
$$2x - y = 3.$$

SOLUTION

A system of equations consisting of one linear and one quadratic is solved by expressing one of the unknowns in the linear equation in terms of the other, and substituting the result in the quadratic equation. From the second equation, $y = 2x - 3$. Replacing y by this linear function of x in the first equation, we find

$$2x^2 - 3x(2x - 3) - 4(2x - 3)^2 + x + 2x - 3 - 1 = 0$$
$$2x^2 - 3x(2x - 3) - 4(4x^2 - 12x + 9) + x + 2x - 3 - 1 = 0$$

Using distribution, we get

$$2x^2 - 6x^2 + 9x - 16x^2 + 48x - 36 + x + 2x - 3 - 1 = 0$$

Combine terms, $\qquad -20x^2 + 60x - 40 = 0$

Divide both sides by -20, $\quad \dfrac{20x^2}{-20} + \dfrac{60x}{-20} - \dfrac{40}{-20} = \dfrac{0}{-20}$

$$x^2 - 3x + 2 = 0$$

Factor, $\qquad\qquad\qquad (x - 2)(x - 1) = 0$

Setting each factor equal to zero, we obtain:

$$x - 2 = 0 \qquad\qquad x - 1 = 0$$
$$x = 2 \qquad\qquad\quad x = 1$$

To find the corresponding y-values, substitute the x-values in $2x - y = 3$:

when $x = 1$, $\qquad\qquad$ when $x = 2$,
$$2(1) - y = 3 \qquad\qquad 2(2) - y = 3$$
$$2 - 3 = y \qquad\qquad\quad 4 - 3 = y$$
$$y = -1 \qquad\qquad\qquad y = 1$$

Therefore, the two solutions of the system are

$(1, -1)$ and $(2, 1)$,

and the solution set is $\{(1, -1), (2, 1)\}$.

PROBLEM

Solve the system.
$$2x^2 - 3xy + 4y^2 = 3 \qquad\qquad (1)$$
$$x^2 + xy - 8y^2 = -6 \qquad\qquad (2)$$

SOLUTION

Multiply both sides of the first equation by 2.

$$2\left(2x^2 - 3xy + 4y^2\right) = 2(3)$$
$$4x^2 - 6xy + 8y^2 = 6 \qquad\qquad (3)$$

Add Equation (3) to Equation (2):

$$\begin{array}{r} x^2 + xy - 8y^2 = -6 \\ 4x^2 - 6xy + 8y^2 = 6 \\ \hline 5x^2 - 5xy = 0 \end{array} \qquad (4)$$

Factoring out the common factor, $5x$, from the left side of Equation (4):

$$5x(x - y) = 0$$

Whenever a product $ab = 0$, where a and b are any two numbers, either $a = 0$ or $b = 0$ or both. Hence, either

$$5x = 0 \qquad \text{or} \qquad x - y = 0$$
$$x = 0/5 \qquad\qquad\qquad\quad x = y$$
$$x = 0$$

Substituting $x = 0$ in Equation (1):

$$2(0)^2 - 3(0)y + 4y^2 = 3$$
$$0 - 0 + 4y^2 = 3$$
$$4y^2 = 3$$
$$y^2 = \frac{3}{4}$$
$$y = \pm\sqrt{\frac{3}{4}}$$
$$= \pm\frac{\sqrt{3}}{\sqrt{4}}$$
$$= \pm\frac{\sqrt{3}}{2}$$

35

Hence, two solutions are: $\left(0, \dfrac{\sqrt{3}}{2}\right), \left(0, -\dfrac{\sqrt{3}}{2}\right)$

For the second solution ($x = y$), substitute x for y in Equation (1):

$$2x^2 - 3x(x) + 4(x)^2 = 3$$
$$2x^2 - 3x^2 + 4x^2 = 3$$
$$3x^2 = 3$$
$$x^2 = 3/3$$
$$x^2 = 1$$
$$x = \pm\sqrt{1} = \pm 1$$

Therefore, when $x = 1$, $y = x = 1$. Also, when $x = -1$, $y = x = -1$. Hence, two other solutions are: (1, 1) and (–1, –1). Thus the four solutions of the system are

$$\left(0, \dfrac{\sqrt{3}}{2}\right), \left(0, -\dfrac{\sqrt{3}}{2}\right), (1,1), \text{ and } (-1,-1)$$

Drill: Quadratic Equations

Solve for all values of x.

1. $x^2 - 2x - 8 = 0$

    (A) 4 and –2   (C) 4

    (B) 4 and 8   (D) –2 and 8

2. $x^2 + 2x - 3 = 0$

    (A) –3 and 2   (C) 3 and 1

    (B) 2 and 1   (D) –3 and 1

3. $x^2 - 7x = -10$

    (A) –3 and 5   (C) 2

    (B) 2 and 5   (D) –2 and –5

4. $x^2 - 8x + 16 = 0$

    (A) 8 and 2   (C) 4

    (B) 1 and 16   (D) –2 and 4

5. $3x^2 + 3x = 6$

    (A) 3 and –6   (C) –3 and 2

    (B) 2 and 3   (D) 1 and –2

6. $x^2 + 7x = 0$

    (A) 7   (C) –7

    (B) 0 and –7   (D) 0 and 7

7. $x^2 - 25 = 0$

    (A) 5   (C) 15 and 10

    (B) 5 and –5   (D) –5 and 10

8. $2x^2 + 4x = 16$

    (A) 2 and –2   (C) 4 and 8

    (B) 8 and –2   (D) 2 and –4

9. $2x^2 - 11x - 6 = 0$

    (A) 1 and –3   (C) 1

    (B) 0 and 4   (D) –½ and 6

10. $x^2 - 2x - 3 = 0$

    (A) 0   (C) 5 and –3

    (B) –1 and 3   (D) 2

Absolute Value Equations

The absolute value of a, $|a|$, is defined as

$|a| = a$ when $a > 0$,

$|a| = -a$ when $a < 0$,

$|a| = 0$ when $a = 0$.

When the definition of absolute value is applied to an equation, the quantity within the absolute value symbol is considered to have two values. This value can be either positive or negative before the absolute value is taken. As a result, each absolute value equation actually contains two separate equations.

When evaluating equations containing absolute values, proceed as follows:

- **EXAMPLE**

  $|5 - 3x| = 7$ is valid if either

$5 - 3x = 7$	or	$5 - 3x = -7$
$-3x = 2$		$-3x = -12$
$x = -\dfrac{2}{3}$		$x = 4$

  The solution set is therefore $x = \left(-\dfrac{2}{3}, 4\right)$.

Remember, the absolute value of a number cannot be negative. So, for the equation $|5x + 4| = -3$, there would be no solution.

Drill: Absolute Value Equations

DIRECTIONS: Find the appropriate solutions.

1. $|4x - 2| = 6$

   (A) -2 and -1　　(C) 2

   (B) -1 and 2　　(D) No solution

2. $\left|3 - \dfrac{1}{2}y\right| = -7$

   (A) -8 and 20　　(C) 2 and -5

   (B) 8 and -20　　(D) No solution

3. $2|x + 7| = 12$

   (A) -13 and -1　　(C) -1 and 13

   (B) -6 and 6　　(D) No solution

4. $|5x| - 7 = 3$

   (A) 2 and 4　　(C) -2 and 2

   (B) $\dfrac{4}{5}$ and 3　　(D) No solution

5. $\left|\dfrac{3}{4}m\right| = 9$

   (A) 24 and -16　　(C) -12 and 12

   (B) $\dfrac{4}{27}$ and $-\dfrac{4}{3}$　　(D) No solution

Inequalities

An inequality is a statement that the value of one quantity or expression is greater than (>), less than (<), greater than or equal to (≥), less than or equal to (≤), or not equal to (≠) that of another.

- **EXAMPLE**

  $5 > 4$

The expression above means that the value of 5 is greater than the value of 4.

A **conditional inequality** is an inequality whose validity depends on the values of the variables in the expression. That is, certain values of the variables will make the expression true, and others will make it false.

$3 - y > 3 + y$

is a conditional inequality for the set of real numbers, since it is true for any replacement less than zero and false for all others.

$x + 5 > x + 2$

is an **absolute inequality** for the set of real numbers, meaning that for any real value x, the expression on the left is greater than the expression on the right.

$5y < 2y + y$

is **inconsistent** for the set of non-negative real numbers. For any y greater than 0, the sentence is always false. An expression is inconsistent if it is always false when its variables assume allowable values.

The solution of a given inequality in one variable x consists of all values of x for which the inequality is true.

The graph of an inequality in one variable is represented by either a ray or a line segment on the real number line.

The endpoint is not a solution (shown by an open circle) if the variable is strictly less than or greater than a particular value.

- **EXAMPLE**

  $x > 2$

  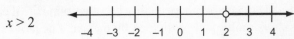

2 is not a solution and should be represented as shown.

The endpoint is a solution (shown by a filled circle) if the variable is either (1) less than or equal to or (2) greater than or equal to a particular value.

- **EXAMPLE**

$5 > x \geq 2$

In this case 2 is a solution and should be represented as shown.

Properties of Inequalities

If x and y are real numbers, then one and only one of the following statements is true.

$x > y$, $x = y$, or $x < y$.

This is the order property of real numbers.

If a, b, and c are real numbers, the following statements are true:

A) If $a < b$ and $b < c$ then $a < c$.

B) If $a > b$ and $b > c$, then $a > c$.

This is the transitive property of inequalities.

If a, b, and c are real numbers and $a > b$, then $a + c > b + c$ and $a - c > b - c$. This is the **addition property of inequality**.

Two inequalities are said to have the same **sense** if their signs of inequality point in the same direction.

The sense of an inequality remains the same if both sides are multiplied or divided by the same positive real number.

- **EXAMPLE**

$4 > 3$

If we multiply both sides by 5, we will obtain

$4 \times 5 > 3 \times 5$

$20 > 15$

The sense of the inequality does not change.

The sense of an inequality becomes opposite if each side is multiplied or divided by the same negative real number.

- **EXAMPLE**

$4 > 3$

If we multiply both sides by -5, we would obtain

$4 \times -5 < 3 \times -5$

$-20 < -15$

The sense of the inequality becomes opposite.

If $a > b$ and a, b, and n are positive real numbers, then

$a^n > b^n$ and $a^{-n} < b^{-n}$

If $x > y$ and $q > p$, then $x + q > y + p$.

If $x > y > 0$ and $q > p > 0$, then $xq > yp$.

Inequalities that have the same solution set are called **equivalent inequalities**.

PROBLEM

Solve the inequality $2x + 5 > 9$.

SOLUTION

Add -5 to both sides: $2x + 5 + (-5) > 9 + (-5)$

Additive inverse property: $2x + 0 > 9 + (-5)$

Additive identity property: $2x > 9 + (-5)$

Combine terms: $2x > 4$

Multiply both sides by $\frac{1}{2}$: $\frac{1}{2}(2x) > \frac{1}{2} \times 4$

$x > 2$

The solution set is

$X = \{x \mid 2x + 5 > 9\}$

$= \{x \mid x > 2\}$

(that is, all x such that x is greater than 2).

Drill: Inequalities

DIRECTIONS: Find the solution set for each inequality.

1. $3m + 2 < 7$

   (A) $m \geq \dfrac{5}{3}$ (C) $m < 2$

   (B) $m > 2$ (D) $m < \dfrac{5}{3}$

2. $\dfrac{1}{2}x - 3 \leq 1$

   (A) $-4 \leq x \leq 8$ (C) $x \leq 8$

   (B) $x \geq -8$ (D) $2 \leq x \leq 8$

3. $-3p + 1 \geq 16$

   (A) $p \geq -5$ (C) $p \leq \dfrac{-17}{3}$

   (B) $p \geq \dfrac{-17}{3}$ (D) $p \leq -5$

4. $-6 < \dfrac{2}{3}r + 6 \leq 2$

   (A) $-6 < r \leq -3$ (C) $r \geq -6$

   (B) $-18 < r \leq -6$ (D) $-2 < r \leq -\dfrac{4}{3}$

5. $0 < 2 - y < 6$

   (A) $-4 < y < 2$ (C) $-4 < y < -2$

   (B) $-4 < y < 0$ (D) $-2 < y < 4$

Vectors

Definition 1:

A scalar is a quantity that can be specified by a real number. It has only magnitude.

Definition 2:

A vector is a quantity that has both magnitude and direction. Velocity is an example of a vector quantity.

A vector (AB) is denoted by $\overrightarrow{AB}$, where B represents the head and A represents the tail. This is illustrated in the following figure.

The length of a line segment is the magnitude of a vector.

If the magnitude and direction of two vectors are the same, then they are equal.

Definition 3:

Vectors that can be translated from one position to another without any change in their magnitude or direction are called free vectors.

Definition 4:

The unit vector is a vector with a length (magnitude) of one.

Definition 5:

The zero vector has a magnitude of zero.

Definition 6:

The unit vector $\overrightarrow{i}$ is a vector with magnitude of one in the direction of the *x*-axis.

Definition 7:

The unit vector $\overrightarrow{j}$ is a vector with magnitude of one in the direction of the *y*-axis.

Vector Properties

When two vectors are added together, the resultant force of the two vectors produces the same effect as the two combined forces. This is illustrated in the following two figures.

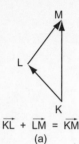

$\overrightarrow{KL} + \overrightarrow{LM} = \overrightarrow{KM}$
(a)

$\overrightarrow{NO} + \overrightarrow{NP} = \overrightarrow{NQ}$
(b)

In these diagrams, the vectors $\overrightarrow{KM}$ and $\overrightarrow{NQ}$ are the **resultant** forces.

Addition of Two Vectors

Let vector $\overrightarrow{A}$ be $<a_1, a_2>$ and vector $\overrightarrow{B}$ be $<b_1, b_2>$. Then

$$\overrightarrow{A} + \overrightarrow{B} = (a_1 + b_1)\overrightarrow{i} + (a_2 + b_2)\overrightarrow{j}$$

Multiplication of Vector by a Scalar

Let vector $\overrightarrow{A}$ be $a\overrightarrow{i} + b\overrightarrow{j}$ and let c be a constant. Then,

$$c\overrightarrow{A} = c(a\overrightarrow{i} + b\overrightarrow{j}) = ca\overrightarrow{i} + cb\overrightarrow{j}$$

Additive and Multiplicative Properties of Vectors

Let s, t and u represent vectors and d and c represent real constants. All of the following are true:

1. $s + t = t + s$

2. $(s + t) + u = s + (t + u)$

3. $s + 0 = s$

4. $s + (-s) = 0$

5. $(c+d)s = cs + sd$

6. $c(s+u) = cs + cu$

7. $c(st) = (cs)t$

8. $1 \cdot s = s$

9. $0 \cdot s = 0$

10. $\overrightarrow{s} \cdot \overrightarrow{s} = |\overrightarrow{s}|^2$

11. $c(d\overrightarrow{s}) = (cd)\overrightarrow{s}$

The magnitude $|s|$ of a vector $\overrightarrow{s} = a_1\overrightarrow{i} + a_2\overrightarrow{j}$ is

$$|s| = \sqrt{a_1^2 + a_2^2}$$

The difference between vectors $\overrightarrow{a}$ and $\overrightarrow{b}$ is given by the formula

$$\overrightarrow{a} - \overrightarrow{b} = \overrightarrow{a} + (-\overrightarrow{b})$$

Scalar (DOT) Product

Two vectors are parallel if (a) one is a scalar multiple of the other; and (b) neither is zero.

Definition:

If vector $\overrightarrow{A} = <a_1, a_2>$ and vector $\overrightarrow{B} = <b_1, b_2>$, then the scalar product of A and B is given by the formula

$$\overrightarrow{A} \cdot \overrightarrow{B} = a_1 b_1 + a_2 b_2$$

Theorem:

If θ is the angle between the vectors $\overrightarrow{A} = a_1\overrightarrow{i} + a_2\overrightarrow{j}$ and $\overrightarrow{B} = b_1\overrightarrow{i} + b_2\overrightarrow{j}$ then

$$\cos \theta = \frac{a_1 b_1 + a_2 b_2}{|A||B|}$$

Definition:

Let vector $\overrightarrow{A} = a_1\overrightarrow{i} + a_2\overrightarrow{j}$ and vector $\overrightarrow{B} = b_1\overrightarrow{i} + b_2\overrightarrow{j}$. The projection of vector $\overrightarrow{A}$ on $\overrightarrow{B}$ ($Proj_B A$) is given by the quantity $|A| \cos \theta$, where θ is the angle between the two vectors.

Therefore,

$$Proj_B\overrightarrow{A} = |A| \cos \theta = \frac{a_1 b_1 + a_2 b_2}{|B|} = \frac{\overrightarrow{A} \cdot \overrightarrow{B}}{|B|}$$

If the angle θ is acute, then $|A| \cos \theta$ is positive; if θ is obtuse, then $|A| \cos \theta$ is negative.

The scalar product of two non-zero vectors $\vec{A}$ and $\vec{B}$ is now redefined by the formula

$$\vec{A} \cdot \vec{B} = |A||B| \cos\theta = a_1 b_1 + a_2 b_2$$

PROBLEM

Which of the following vectors is equal to $\vec{MN}$ if $M = (2, 1)$ and $N = (3, -4)$?

(a) $\vec{AB}$, where $A = (1, -1)$ and $B = (2, 3)$

(b) $\vec{CD}$, where $C = (-4, 5)$ and $D = (-3, 10)$

(c) $\vec{EF}$, where $E = (3, -2)$ and $F = (4, -7)$.

SOLUTION

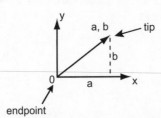

(a-0, b-0) represents the vector.

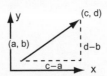

(c-a, d-b) represents the vector.

With each ordered pair in the plane there can be associated a vector from the origin to that point.

The vector is determined by subtracting the coordinates of the endpoint from the corresponding coordinates of the tip. As for $\vec{MN}$, the tip is the point corresponding to the second letter of the alphabetical notation, N, while the endpoint is the point corresponding to the first, M. In this problem, the vectors are of a general nature wherein their endpoints do not lie at the origin.

We first find the ordered pair that represents $\vec{MN}$.

$$\vec{MN} = (3 - 2, -4 - 1) = (1, -5)$$

Now, we find the ordered pair representing each vector.

(a) $\vec{AB} = (2 - 1, 3 - (-1)) = (1, 4)$

(b) $\vec{CD} = ((-3) - (-4), 10 - 5) = (1, 5)$

(c) $\vec{EF} = (4 - 3, -7 - (-2)) = (1, -5)$

Only $\vec{EF}$ and $\vec{MN}$ are equal.

Ratio, Proportion, and Variation

The **ratio** of two numbers x and y, written $x:y$, is the fraction $\dfrac{x}{y}$, where $y \neq 0$. A **proportion** is an equality of two ratios. The laws of proportion are listed below:

If $\dfrac{a}{b} = \dfrac{c}{d}$, then:

A) $ad = bc$ (called **cross-multiplication**)

B) $\dfrac{b}{a} = \dfrac{d}{c}$

C) $\dfrac{a}{c} = \dfrac{b}{d}$

D) $\dfrac{a+b}{b} = \dfrac{c+d}{d}$

E) $\dfrac{a-b}{b} = \dfrac{c-d}{d}$

Given a proportion $a:b = c:d$, then a and d are called the **extremes**, b and c are called the **means**, and d is called the **fourth proportional** to a, b, and c.

PROBLEM

Solve the proportion $\dfrac{x+1}{4} = \dfrac{15}{12}$.

SOLUTION

Cross-multiply to determine x; that is, multiply the numerator of the first fraction by the denominator of the second, and equate this to the product of the numerator of the second and the denominator of the first.

$$(x + 1)12 = 4 \times 15$$
$$12x + 12 = 60$$
$$x = 4$$

PROBLEM

If $a/b = c/d$, $a + b = 60$, $c = 3$, and $d = 2$, find b.

SOLUTION

We are given $\dfrac{a}{b} = \dfrac{c}{d}$. Cross multiplying,

we obtain $ad = bc$.

Adding bd to both sides, we have $ad + bd = bc + bd$, which is equivalent to $d(a + b) = b(c + d)$ or

$\dfrac{a + b}{b} = \dfrac{c + d}{d}$. This is law (D).

Replacing $(a + b)$ by 60, c by 3, and d by 2, we obtain

$$\frac{60}{b} = \frac{3 + 2}{2}$$
$$\frac{60}{b} = \frac{5}{2}$$

Cross multiplying, $5b = 120$

$$b = 24.$$

Variation

A) If x is directly proportional to y, written $x \propto y$, then $x = ky$ or $\dfrac{x}{y} = k$, where k is called the constant of proportionality or the constant of variation.

B) If x varies inversely as y, then $x = \dfrac{k}{y}$.

C) If x varies jointly as y and z, then $x = kyz$.

• EXAMPLE

If y varies jointly as x and z, and $3x:1 = y:z$, find the constant of variation.

The variable y varies jointly as x and z with k as the constant of variation, so

$$y = kxz.$$
$$3x:1 = y:z$$

Expressing this ratio as a fraction,

$$\frac{3x}{1} = \frac{y}{z}$$

Solving for y by cross-multiplying,

$$y = 3xz$$

Equating both relations for y, we have:

$$kxz = 3xz$$

Solving for the constant of variation, k, we divide both sides by xz to get

$$k = 3.$$

PROBLEM

If y varies directly with respect to x and $y = 3$ when $x = -2$, find y when $x = 8$.

SOLUTION

If y varies directly as x, then y is equal to some constant k times x; that is, $y = kx$ where k is a constant. We can now say $y_1 = kx_1$ and $y_2 = kx_2$ or $\dfrac{y_1}{x_1} = k$, $\dfrac{y_2}{x_2} = k$, which implies $\dfrac{y_1}{x_1} = \dfrac{y_2}{x_2}$ which is a proportion. Thus, $\dfrac{3}{-2} = \dfrac{y_2}{8}$.

Now solve for y_2:

By cross-multiplication,

$$3(8) = -2y_2$$
$$-12 = y_2$$

When $x = 8$, $y = -12$.

PROBLEM

> If y varies inversely as the cube of x, and $y = 7$ when $x = 2$, express y as a function of x.

SOLUTION

The relationship "y varies inversely with respect to x" is expressed as

$$y = \frac{k}{x}$$

The inverse variation is now with respect to the cube of x, x^3, and we have

$$y = \frac{k}{x^3}$$

Since $y = 7$ and $x = 2$ must satisfy this relation, we replace x and y by these values,

$$7 = \frac{k}{2^3} = \frac{k}{8}$$

and we find $k = 7 \times 8 = 56$. Substitution of this value of k in the general relation gives,

$$y = \frac{56}{x^3},$$

which expresses y as a function of x.

We may now, in addition, find the value of y corresponding to any value of x. If we had the added requirement to find the value of y when $x = 1.2$, $x = 1.2$ would be substituted in the function to give

$$y = \frac{56}{(1.2)^3} = \frac{56}{1.728} = 32.41$$

Other expressions in use are "is proportional to" for "varies directly," and "is inversely proportional to" for "varies inversely."

Drill: Ratios and Proportions

DIRECTIONS: Find the appropriate solutions.

1. Solve for n: $\dfrac{4}{n} = \dfrac{8}{5}$.

    (A) 10   (C) 6

    (B) 8   (D) 2.5

2. Solve for n: $\dfrac{2}{3} = \dfrac{n}{72}$.

    (A) 12   (C) 64

    (B) 48   (D) 56

3. Solve for n: $n{:}12 = 3{:}4$.

    (A) 8   (C) 9

    (B) 1   (D) 4

4. Four out of every five students at West High take a mathematics course. If the enrollment at West is 785, how many students take mathematics?

    (A) 628   (C) 705

    (B) 157   (D) 655

5. At a factory, three out of every 1,000 parts produced are defective. In a day, the factory can produce 25,000 parts. How many of these parts would be defective?

    (A) 7   (C) 750

    (B) 75   (D) 7,500

6. A summer league softball team won 28 out of the 32 games they played. What is the ratio of games won to games played?

    (A) 4:5   (C) 7:8

    (B) 3:4   (D) 2:3

Real-World Problems Involving Proportion

PROBLEM

> A chemist is preparing a chemical solution. She needs to add 3 parts sodium and 2 parts zinc to a flask of chlorine. If she has already placed 300 grams of sodium into the flask, how much zinc must she now add?

SOLUTION

1) Determine the ratio of sodium and zinc.

   3 parts sodium, 2 parts zinc = 3:2

2) Write the problem as a proportion.

   $$\frac{3}{2} = \frac{300}{?}$$

3) Cross-multiply to put the proportion in the following format:

   $AD = BC$ $3(?) = 2(300)$

4) Solve the right side of the proportion.

   $2(300) = 600$

5) Rewrite the proportion.

   $3(?) = 600$

6) Find the missing integer that solves the proportion. To do this, divide both sides by the known extreme, 3.

   $$\frac{3(?)}{3} = ?$$ $$\frac{600}{3} = 200$$

7) Rewrite the proportion.

   $? = 200$

   The solution is 200 grams of zinc.

PROBLEM

An automobile dealer has to sell 3.5 cars for every 1 truck to achieve the optimum profit. This year, it is estimated that 3,500 cars will be sold. How many trucks must he sell to achieve the optimum profit?

SOLUTION

1) Determine the ratio of cars to trucks.

   3.5 cars, 1 truck = 3.5:1

   Make both sides of the ratio an integer. To do this, multiply both sides of the ratio by 2.

   $2(3.5):2(1) = 7:2$

2) Write the problem as a proportion.

   $$\frac{7}{2} = \frac{3,500}{?}$$

3) Cross-multiply to put the proportion in the following format:

   $7(?) = 2(3,500)$

4) Solve the right side of the proportion.

   $2(3,500) = 7,000$

5) Rewrite the proportion.

   $7(?) = 7,000$

6) Find the missing integer that solves the proportion. To do this, divide both sides by the known extreme, 7.

   $$\frac{7(?)}{7} = ?$$ $$\frac{7,000}{7} = 1,000$$

7) Rewrite the proportion.

   $? = 1,000$

   The solution is 1,000 trucks.

PROBLEM

A baker is making a new recipe for chocolate chip cookies. He decides that for every 6 cups of flour, he needs to add 1 cup of sugar. He puts 30 cups of flour and 2 cups of sugar into the batter. How much more sugar does he need?

SOLUTION

1) Determine the ratio of flour to sugar.

   6 cups flour, 1 cup sugar = 6:1

2) Write the problem as a proportion.

   $$\frac{6}{1} = \frac{30}{?}$$

3) Cross-multiply to put the proportion in the following format:

   $6(?) = 1(30)$

4) Solve the right side of the proportion.

   $1(30) = 30$

5) Rewrite the proportion.

$6(?) = 30$

6) Find the missing integer that solves the proportion.

To do this, divide both sides by the known extreme, 6.

$$\frac{6(?)}{6} = ? \qquad\qquad \frac{30}{6} = 5$$

7) Rewrite the proportion.

$? = 5$

The solution is that 5 cups of sugar must be added to the batter.

8) Determine how many more cups of sugar are needed.

$5 - 2 = 3$

Since only 2 cups have been added so far, the baker must still add 3 cups.

Elementary Functions

A **function** is any process that assigns a single value of y to each number of x. Because the value of x determines the value of y, y is called the **dependent variable** and x is called the **independent variable**. The set of all the values of x by which the function is defined is called the **domain** of the function. The set of corresponding values of y is called the **range** of the function.

PROBLEM

Is $y^2 = x$ a function?

SOLUTION

Graph the equation. Note that x can have two values of y. Therefore, $y^2 = x$ is not a function.

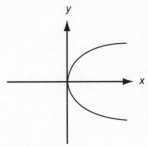

PROBLEM

Find the domain and range for $y = 5 - x^2$.

SOLUTION

First determine if there are any values that would make the function undefined (i.e., dividing by 0). There are none. The domain is the set of real numbers. The range can be found by putting some values in for x.

x	2	1	0	-1	-2
y	1	4	5	4	1

The range is the set of real numbers less than or equal to 5, or $R = \{y \mid y \le 5\}$.

PROBLEM

Evaluate $f(1)$ for $y = f(x) = 5x + 2$.

SOLUTION

$$f(x) = 5x + 2$$
$$f(1) = 5(1) + 2$$
$$= 5 + 2$$
$$= 7$$

Operations with Functions

Functions can be added, subtracted, multiplied, or divided to form new functions.

a. $(f + g)(x) = f(x) + g(x)$

b. $(f - g)(x) = f(x) - g(x)$

c. $(f \times g)(x) = f(x)\,g(x)$

d. $(f / g)(x) = f(x) / g(x)$

PROBLEM

Let $f(x) = 2x^2 - 1$ and $g(x) = 5x + 3$.
Determine the following functions:

(1) $f + g$ (2) $f - g$

(3) $f \times g$ (4) f / g

SOLUTION

(1) $(f + g)(x) = f(x) + g(x) = 2x^2 - 1 + 5x + 3$
$= 2x^2 + 5x + 2$

(2) $(f - g)(x) = f(x) - g(x) = 2x^2 - 1 - (5x + 3)$
$= 2x^2 - 1 - 5x - 3$
$= 2x^2 - 5x - 4$

(3) $(f \times g)(x) = f(x)\,g(x) = (2x^2 - 1)(5x + 3)$
$= 10x^3 + 6x^2 - 5x - 3$

(4) $(f / g)(x) = f(x) / g(x) = (2x^2 - 1) / (5x + 3)$

Note the domain of (4) is all real numbers except $-\dfrac{3}{5}$.

The **composite function** $f \circ g$ is defined as $(f \circ g)(x) = f(g(x))$.

PROBLEM

Given $f(x) = 3x$ and $g(x) = 4x + 2$.
Find $(f \circ g)(x)$ and $(g \circ f)(x)$.

SOLUTION

$(f \circ g)(x) = f(g(x)) = 3(4x + 2)$
$= 12x + 6$

$(g \circ f)(x) = g(f(x)) = 4(3x) + 2$
$= 12x + 2$

Note that $(f \circ g)(x) \neq (g \circ f)(x)$.

PROBLEM

Find $(f \circ g)(2)$ if
$f(x) = x^2 - 3$ and $g(x) = 3x + 1$

SOLUTION

$(f \circ g)(2) = f(g(2))$
$g(x) = 3x + 1$

Substitute the value of x.

$g(2) = 3(2) + 1$
$= 7$

$f(x) = x^2 - 3$

and $(f \circ g)(2) = f(g(2)) = f(7)$

$f(7) = (7)^2 - 3$
$= 49 - 3$
$= 46$

The **inverse** of a function, f^{-1}, is obtained from f by interchanging the x and y and then solving for y.

Two functions f and g are inverses of one another if $g \circ f = x$ and $f \circ g = x$. To find g when f is given, interchange x and y in the equation $y = f(x)$ and solve for $y = g(x)$. Then replace y with $f^{-1}(x)$.

The inverse of a function must be a function.

PROBLEM

Find the inverse of the functions

(1) $f(x) = 3x + 2$

(2) $f(x) = x^2 - 3$

SOLUTION

(1) $f(x) = y = 3x + 2$

To find $f^{-1}(x)$, interchange x and y.

$$x = 3y + 2$$

$$3y = x - 2$$

Solve for y, then replace y with $f^{-1}(x)$.

$$f^{-1}(x) = \frac{x - 2}{3}$$

(2) $f(x) = y = x^2 - 3$.

To find $f^{-1}(x)$, interchange x and y.

$$x = y^2 - 3$$

$$y^2 = x + 3$$

Solve for y, then replace y with $f^{-1}(x)$.

$$f^{-1}(x) = \sqrt{x + 3}$$

Logarithms and Exponential Functions and Equations

An equation

$$y = b^x$$

(with $b > 0$ and $b \neq 1$) is called an **exponential function**. The exponential function with base b can be written as

$$y = f(x) = b^x.$$

The inverse of an exponential function is the **logarithmic function**,

$$f^{-1}(x) = \log_b x.$$

PROBLEM

Write the following equations in logarithmic form:

$3^4 = 81$ and $M^k = 5$.

SOLUTION

The expression $y = b^x$ is equivalent to the logarithmic expression $\log_b y = x$. Therefore, $3^4 = 81$ is equivalent to the logarithmic expression

$$\log_3 81 = 4$$

and $M^k = 5$ is equivalent to the logarithmic expression

$$\log_M 5 = k.$$

PROBLEM

Find the value of $\log_5 25$ and $\log_4 x = 2$.

SOLUTION

$\log_5 25$ is equivalent to $5^x = 25$. Thus $x = 2$, since $5^2 = 25$.

$\log_4 x = 2$ is equivalent to $4^2 = x$, so $x = 16$.

Logarithm Properties

If M, N, p, and b are positive numbers, and $b = 1$, then

   a. $\log_b 1 = 0$

   b. $\log_b b = 1$

   c. $\log_b b^x = x$

   d. $\log_b M N = \log_b M + \log_b N$

   e. $\log_b M / N = \log_b M - \log_b N$

   f. $\log_b M^p = p \log_b M$

PROBLEM

If $\log_{10} 3 = .4771$ and $\log_{10} 4 = .6021$, find $\log_{10} 12$.

SOLUTION

Since $12 = 4(3)$, $\log_{10} 12 = \log_{10}(4)(3)$

Remember

$$\log_b M N = \log_b M + \log_b N.$$

Therefore,

$$\log_{10} 12 = \log_{10} 4 + \log_{10} 3$$

$$= .6021 + .4771$$

$$= 1.0792$$

Properties of Functions

A) A function F is **one to one** if for every range value there corresponds exactly one domain value of x.

B) A function is said to be **even** if $f(-x) = f(x)$ or

$$f(x) + f(-x) = 2f(x).$$

C) A function is said to be **odd** if $f(-x) = -f(x)$ or $f(x) + f(-x) = 0$.

D) Periodicity

A function f with domain X is **periodic** if there exists a positive real number p such that $f(x + p) = f(x)$ for all $x \in X$.

The smallest number p with this property is called the period of f.

Over any interval of length p, the behavior of a periodic function can be completely described.

E) The identity function $f(x) = x$ maps every x to itself.

Identity
function

F) The constant function $f(x) = c$ for all $x \in R$.

Constant
function

G) The "zeros" of an arbitrary function $f(x)$ are particular values of x for which $f(x) = 0$.

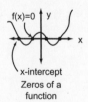

x-intercept
Zeros of a
function

PROBLEM

Find the domain D and range R of the function

$$\left(x, \frac{x}{|x|} \right).$$

SOLUTION

Note that the y-value of any coordinate pair (x,y) is $\frac{x}{|x|}$. We can replace x in the formula $\frac{x}{|x|}$ with any number except 0, since the denominator, $|x|$, cannot equal 0. This is because division by 0 is undefined. Therefore, the domain D is the set of all real numbers except 0. If x is negative, i.e., $x < 0$, then $|x| = -x$ by definition. Hence, if x is negative, then $\frac{x}{|x|} = \frac{x}{-x} = -1$. If x is positive, i.e. $x > 0$, then $|x| = x$ by definition. Hence, if x is positive, then $\frac{x}{|x|} = \frac{x}{x} = 1$. (The case where $x = 0$ has already been found to be undefined). Thus, there are only two numbers -1 and 1 in the range R of the function; that is, $R = \{-1, 1\}$.

PROBLEM

If $f(x) = 3x + 4$ and the domain $D = \{x \mid -1 \leq x \leq 3\}$, find the range of $f(x)$.

SOLUTION

We first prove that the value of $3x + 4$ increases when x increases. If for any value X, $X > x$, then we may multiply both sides of the inequality by a positive number to obtain an equivalent inequality. Thus, $3X > 3x$. We may also add a number to both sides of the inequality to obtain an equivalent inequality. Thus, $3X + 4 > 3x + 4$, so $3x + 4$ increases when x increases.

Hence, if x belongs to D, the function value $f(x) = 3x + 4$ is least when $x = -1$ and greatest when $x = 3$. Consequently, since $f(-1) = -3 + 4 = 1$ and $f(3) = 9 + 4 = 13$, the range is all y from 1 to 13; that is,

$$R = \{y \mid 1 \leq y \leq 13\}.$$

Graphing a Function

The Cartesian Coordinate System

Consider two lines, *x* and *y*, drawn on a plane region called *R*.

Let the intersection of *x* and *y* be the origin and let us impose a coordinate system on each of the lines.

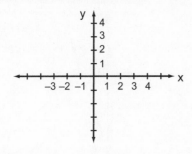

If (x, y) is a point or ordered pair on the coordinate plane *R* then *x* is the first coordinate and *y* is the second coordinate.

To locate an ordered pair on the coordinate plane simply measure the distance of *x* units along the *x*-axis, then measure vertically (parallel to the *y*-axis) *y* units.

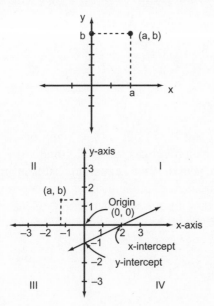

I, II, III, IV are called **quadrants** in the coordinate plane.

(a, b) is an **ordered pair** with *x*-coordinate *a* and *y*-coordinate *b*.

Drawing the Graph

There are several ways to plot the graph of a function. The process of computing and plotting points on the graph is always an aid in this endeavor. The more points we locate on the graph, the more accurate our drawing will be.

It is also helpful if we consider the symmetry of the function. That is,

a) A graph is symmetric with respect to the *x*-axis if whenever a point (x, y) is on the graph, then $(x, -y)$ is also on the graph.

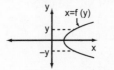

Symmetry about the *x*-axis
Note: This is not a function of *x*.

b) Symmetry with respect to the *y*-axis occurs when both points $(-x, y)$ and (x, y) appear on the graph for every *x* and *y* in the graph.

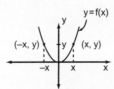

Symmetry about the *y*-axis

c) When the simultaneous substitution of $-x$ for *x* and $-y$ for *y* does not change the solution of the equation, the graph is said to be symmetric about the origin.

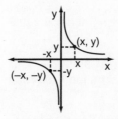

Symmetry about the origin

Another aid in drawing a graph is locating any vertical asymptotes. A **vertical asymptote** is a vertical line $x = a$, such that the functional value $|f(x)|$ grows indefinitely large as *x* approaches the fixed value *a*.

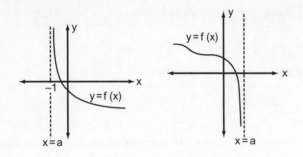

x	$y = 3x - 9$	y
0	$y = 3(0) - 9 = 0 - 9 =$	–9
4	$y = 3(4) - 9 = 12 - 9 =$	3
3	$0 = 3x - 9 = 3x = 9$	0

The three points are (0, –9), (4, 3), and (3, 0). Draw a line through them (see sketch).

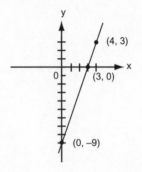

$x = a$ is a vertical asymptote for these functions

The following steps encapsulate the procedure for drawing a graph:

a) Determine the domain and range of the function.

b) Find the intercepts of the graph and plot them.

c) Determine the symmetries of the graph.

d) Locate the vertical asymptotes and plot a few points on the graph near each asymptote.

e) Plot additional points as needed.

PROBLEM

> Construct the graph of the function defined by $y = 3x - 9$.

SOLUTION

An equation of the form $y = mx + b$ is a linear equation; that is, the equation of a line.

A line can be determined by two points. Let us choose intercepts. The x-intercept lies on the x-axis and the y-intercept on the y-axis.

We find the intercepts by assigning 0 to x and solving for y and by assigning 0 to y and solving for x. It is helpful to have a third point when plotting a line. We find the third point by assigning an arbitrary value, say 4, to x and solving for y. Thus we get the following table of corresponding numbers:

PROBLEM

> Are the following points on the graph of the equation $3x - 2y = 0$?
>
> a) point (2, 3)?
>
> b) point (3, 2)?
>
> c) point (4, 6)?

SOLUTION

The point (a, b) lies on the graph of the equation $3x - 2y = 0$ if replacement of x and y by a and b, respectively, in the given equation results in an equation that is true.

a) Replacing (x, y) by (2, 3):

$$3x - 2y = 0$$

$$3(2) - 2(3) = 0$$

$$6 - 6 = 0$$

$$0 = 0, \text{ which is true.}$$

Therefore (2, 3) is a point on the graph.

b) Replacing (x, y) by $(3, 2)$:

$$3x - 2y = 0$$

$$3(3) - 2(2) = 0$$

$$9 - 4 = 0$$

$$5 = 0, \text{ which is not true.}$$

Therefore $(3, 2)$ is not a point on the graph.

c) Replacing (x, y) by $(4, 6)$:

$$3x - 2y = 0$$

$$3(4) - 2(6) = 0$$

$$12 - 12 = 0$$

$$0 = 0, \text{ which is true.}$$

Therefore $(4, 6)$ is a point on the graph.

This problem may also be solved geometrically as follows: draw the graph of the line $3x - 2 = 0$ on the coordinate axes. This can be done by solving for y and plotting the points shown in the following table:

x	$y = \dfrac{3}{2}x$
0	0
1	$\dfrac{3}{2} = 1\dfrac{1}{2}$
2	3
–2	–3

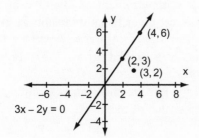

Observe that we obtain the same result as in our algebraic solution. The points $(2, 3)$ and $(4, 6)$ lie on the line $3x - 2y = 0$, whereas $(3, 2)$ does not.

Polynomial Functions and Their Graphs

A polynomial in x is an expression of the form

$$a_n x^n + a_{n-1} x^{n-1} + \ldots + a_1 x + a_0,$$

where $a_1, a_2, \ldots$ and a_n are real numbers and where all the exponents are positive integers. When $a_n \neq 0$, this polynomial is said to be of degree n. It is common to let $P(x)$ represent

$$a_n x^n + a_{n-1} x^{n-1} + \ldots + a_1 x + a_0.$$

Then $y = P(x)$ is a polynomial function. A function with the property that

$$P(-x) = P(x)$$

is an even function, while a function with the property

$$P(-x) = -P(x)$$

is an odd function. Even functions are symmetric with respect to the y-axis, while odd functions are symmetric with respect to the origin.

It would be possible to obtain the graph of a polynomial function $y = P(x)$ by simply setting up a table and plotting a large number of points; this is how a computer or a graphing calculator operates. However, it is often desirable to have some basic information about the graph prior to plotting points. The graph of the polynomial function, $y = a_0$ is a line parallel to the x-axis and $|a_0|$ units above or below the x-axis, depending on whether a_0 is positive or negative. A function of this type is called a constant function. The graph of the polynomial function

$$y = a_1 x + a_0$$

is a line with slope a_1 and with a_0 as the y-intercept. The graph of the polynomial function

$$y = a_2 x^2 + a_1 x + a_0$$

is a parabola.

It is much more difficult to graph a polynomial function with degree greater than two. However, here are three items that should be investigated.

(1) Find lines (x-axis and y-axis) of symmetry and find out whether the origin is a point of symmetry.

(2) Find out about intercepts. The y-intercept is easy to find, but the x-intercepts are usually much more difficult to identify. If possible, factor $P(x)$.

(3) Find out what happens to $P(x)$ when $|x|$ is large. This procedure is illustrated in the following example.

- **EXAMPLE**

  Graph

  $$y = x^4 - 5x^2 + 4$$

(1) The graph has symmetry with respect to the y-axis because $P(x) = P(-x)$.

(2) The y-intercept is at 4.

  Since

  $$x^4 - 5x^2 + 4 = (x^2 - 4)(x^2 - 1)$$
  $$= (x - 2)(x + 2)(x - 1)(x + 1),$$

  the x-intercepts are at 2, –2, 1, and –1.

(3) As $|x|$ gets large, $P(x)$ gets large.

  Here is a sketch of the graph.

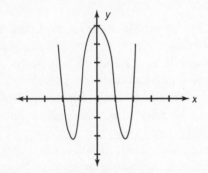

Rational Functions and Their Graphs

When $P(x)$ and $Q(x)$ are polynomials,

$$y = \frac{P(x)}{Q(x)}$$

is called a rational function. The domain of this function is the set of all real numbers x with the property that $Q(x) \neq 0$.

Graphing rational functions is rather difficult. As is the case for polynomial functions, it is desirable to have a general procedure for graphing rational functions. Here is the suggested method for graphing

$$y = \frac{P(x)}{Q(x)}$$

where $P(x) = a_n x^n + a_{n-1} x^{n-1} + \ldots + a_1 x + a_0$ and $Q(x) = b_m x^m + b_{m-1} x^{m-1} + \ldots + b_1 x + b_0$.

(1) Find lines (x-axis and y-axis) of symmetry and determine whether the origin is a point of symmetry.

(2) Find out about intercepts. The y-intercept is at $\dfrac{a_0}{b_0}$ and the x-intercepts will be at values of x where $P(x) = 0$.

(3) Find vertical asymptotes. A line $x = c$ is a vertical asymptote whenever $Q(c) = 0$ and $P(c) \neq 0$.

(4) Find horizontal asymptotes

    (a) If $m = n$, then $y = \dfrac{a_n}{b_m}$ is the horizontal asymptote.

    (b) If $m > n$, then $y = 0$ is the horizontal asymptote.

    (c) If $m < n$, then there is no horizontal asymptote.

This procedure is illustrated in the following example.

- **EXAMPLE**

  Graph

  $$y = \frac{x}{(x - 1)(x + 3)}$$

(1) The axes are not lines of symmetry, nor is the origin a point of symmetry.

(2) The x-intercept and the y-intercept are both at the origin.

(3) The lines $x = 1$ and $x = -3$ are both vertical asymptotes.

(4) The line $y = 0$ is the horizontal asymptote.

  Here is a sketch of the graph.

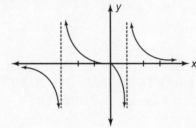

Special Functions and Their Graphs

It is possible to define a function by using different rules for different portions of the domain. The graphs of such functions are determined by graphing the different portions separately. Here is an example.

- **EXAMPLE**

Graph

$$f(x) = \begin{cases} x & \text{if } x \leq 1 \\ 2x & \text{if } x > 1 \end{cases}$$

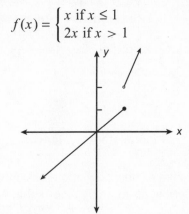

Notice that point $(1,1)$ is part of the graph, but $(1, 2)$ is not.

Functions that involve absolute value can often be completed by translating them to a two-rule form. Consider this example.

- **EXAMPLE**

Graph
$$f(x) = |x| - 1$$

Since $|x| = \begin{cases} x & \text{if } x \geq 0 \\ -x & \text{if } x < 0 \end{cases}$

$f(x)$ can be translated to the following form.
$$f(x) = \begin{cases} x - 1 & \text{if } x \geq 0 \\ -x - 1 & \text{if } x < 0 \end{cases}$$

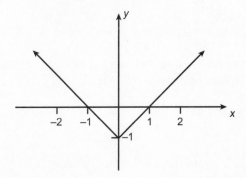

The greatest integer function, denoted by $f(x) = \big[|x|\big]$, is defined by $f(x) = j$, where j is the integer with the property that $j \leq x < j + 1$. The graph of this function follows.

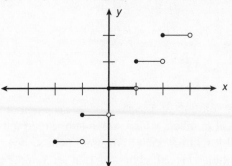

Linear Equations

A linear equation is an equation of the form $a_1x_1 + a_2x_2 + \ldots + a_nx_n = b$, where $a_1, \ldots, a_n$ and b are real constants.

- **EXAMPLES**

  a) $2x + 6y = 9$
  b) $x_1 + 3x_2 + 7x_3 = 5$
  c) $\alpha - 2 = 0$

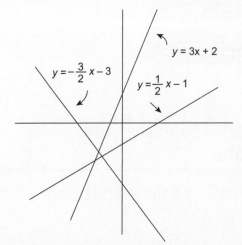

Linear equations in two variables are always straight lines.

A system of linear equations is a finite set of linear equations, all of which use the same set of variables.

- **EXAMPLES**

  a) $2x_1 + x_2 + 5x_3 = 4$

  $x_2 + 3x_3 = 0$

  $7x_1 + 3x_2 + x_3 = 9$

  b) $y - z = 5$

  $z = 1$

The solution of a system of linear equations is that set of real numbers which, when substituted into the set of variables, satisfies each equation in the system. The set of all solutions is called the solution set S of the system.

A consistent system of linear equations has at least one solution, while an inconsistent system has no solutions.

- **EXAMPLES**

  (a) $y + z = 9$ $S = \{5, 4\}$ (consistent system)

  $z = 4$

  (b) $x_1 + x_2 = 7$ $S = \varnothing$ (inconsistent system)

  $x_1 = 3$

  $x_1 - x_2 = 7$

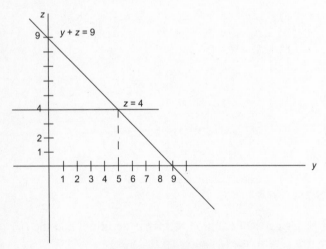

Consistent System

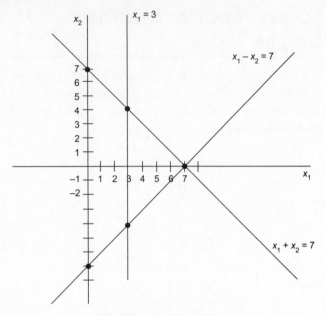

Inconsistent System

Every system of linear equations has either one solution, no solution, or infinitely many solutions.

A system of linear equations with infinitely many solutions is called a dependent system of linear equations.

Matrices

A matrix is a rectangular array of numbers, called entries.

- **EXAMPLES**

  a) $\begin{bmatrix} 6 & 2 \\ 3 & 1 \\ 0 & 0 \end{bmatrix}$

  b) $\begin{bmatrix} 3 \\ 1 \end{bmatrix}$

  c) $[1 \ \ 7 \ \ 2 \ \ 1]$

A matrix with n rows and n columns is called a square matrix of order n.

- **EXAMPLE**

  $\begin{bmatrix} 2 & 10 & 1 \\ 6 & 2 & 9 \\ 3 & 3 & 7 \end{bmatrix}$ is a square matrix of order 3.

Two matrices are called equal if they have the same size and entries in corresponding positions are the same.

Entries starting at the top left and proceeding to the bottom right of a square matrix are said to be on the main diagonal of that matrix.

- **EXAMPLE**

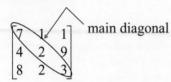 main diagonal

The sum $B + D$ is the matrix obtained when two matrices, B and D, are added together; they must both be of the same size. $B - D$ is obtained by subtracting the entries of D from the corresponding entries of B.

- **EXAMPLES**

a) $\begin{bmatrix} 1 & 2 \\ 2 & 6 \end{bmatrix} + \begin{bmatrix} -4 & 7 \\ 1 & 1 \end{bmatrix} = \begin{bmatrix} -3 & 9 \\ 3 & 7 \end{bmatrix}$

b) $\begin{bmatrix} 1 & 2 \\ 2 & 6 \end{bmatrix} - \begin{bmatrix} -4 & 7 \\ 1 & 1 \end{bmatrix} = \begin{bmatrix} 5 & -5 \\ 1 & 5 \end{bmatrix}$

The product of a matrix A by a scalar k is obtained by multiplying each entry of A by k.

- **EXAMPLE**

If $A = \begin{bmatrix} 4 & 7 \\ -1 & 2 \end{bmatrix}$ and $k = 3$, then $Ak = \begin{bmatrix} 12 & 21 \\ -3 & 6 \end{bmatrix}$.

When multiplying two matrices A and B, the matrices must be of the sizes $m \times n$ and $n \times p$ (the number of columns of A must equal the number of rows of B); to obtain the (ij) entry of AB, multiply the entries in row i of A by the corresponding entries in column j of B. Add up the resulting products; this sum is the (ij) entry of AB. If $AB = C$, then $C_{ij} = \sum_{k=1}^{n} a_{ik} b_{kj}$.

The size of C will be $m \times p$.

- **EXAMPLE**

If $A = \begin{bmatrix} 2 & 3 \\ 4 & 5 \end{bmatrix}$ and $B = \begin{bmatrix} 3 & 3 \\ 7 & 2 \end{bmatrix}$, then

$AB = \begin{bmatrix} (2 \cdot 3) + (3 \cdot 7) & (2 \cdot 3) + (3 \cdot 2) \\ (4 \cdot 3) + (5 \cdot 7) & (4 \cdot 3) + (5 \cdot 2) \end{bmatrix}$

$= \begin{bmatrix} 27 & 12 \\ 47 & 22 \end{bmatrix}$.

A matrix that contains entries corresponding to the coefficients of a system of linear equations, but excludes the constants of that system, is called a coefficient matrix.

- **EXAMPLE**

$\begin{array}{l} x_1 + 6x_2 - 2x_3 = 4 \\ 3x_1 + x_3 = 7 \\ 5x_1 - 3x_2 + x_3 = 0 \end{array} \begin{bmatrix} 1 & 6 & -2 \\ 3 & 0 & 1 \\ 5 & -3 & 1 \end{bmatrix}$

PROBLEM

Find $A + B$ where:

$A = \begin{bmatrix} 1 & -2 & 4 \\ 2 & -1 & 3 \end{bmatrix}, B = \begin{bmatrix} 0 & 2 & -4 \\ 1 & 3 & 1 \end{bmatrix}.$

SOLUTION

Using the definition of matrix addition, add the (ij) entry of A to the (ij) entry of B. Thus,

$A + B = \begin{bmatrix} 1+0 & -2+2 & 4-4 \\ 2+1 & -1+3 & 3+1 \end{bmatrix} = \begin{bmatrix} 1 & 0 & 0 \\ 3 & 2 & 4 \end{bmatrix}$

PROBLEM

Let $A = \begin{bmatrix} 2 & 3 & 7 \\ 4 & m & \sqrt{3} \\ 1 & 5 & a \end{bmatrix}$, $B = \begin{bmatrix} \alpha & \beta & \delta \\ \sqrt{5} & 3 & 1 \\ p & q & 4 \end{bmatrix}$.

Find $A + B$.

SOLUTION

Using the definition of matrix addition, add the (ij) entry of A to the (ij) entry of B. Thus,

$$A + B = \begin{bmatrix} 2 & 3 & 7 \\ 4 & m & \sqrt{3} \\ 1 & 5 & a \end{bmatrix} + \begin{bmatrix} \alpha & \beta & \delta \\ \sqrt{5} & 3 & 1 \\ p & q & 4 \end{bmatrix}$$

$$= \begin{bmatrix} 2+\alpha & 3+\beta & 7+\delta \\ 4+\sqrt{5} & m+3 & \sqrt{3}+1 \\ 1+p & 5+q & a+4 \end{bmatrix}$$

PROBLEM

If $A = \begin{bmatrix} 2 & 3 & 4 \\ 1 & 2 & 1 \end{bmatrix}$ and $B = \begin{bmatrix} 0 & 2 & 7 \\ 1 & -3 & 5 \end{bmatrix}$,

find $A - B$.

SOLUTION

$A - B$ is obtained by subtracting the entries of B from the corresponding entries of A.

$$A - B = \begin{bmatrix} 2 & 3 & 4 \\ 1 & 2 & 1 \end{bmatrix} - \begin{bmatrix} 0 & 2 & 7 \\ 1 & -3 & 5 \end{bmatrix}$$

$$= \begin{bmatrix} 2-0 & 3-2 & 4-7 \\ 1-1 & 2-(-3) & 1-5 \end{bmatrix}$$

$$= \begin{bmatrix} 2 & 1 & -3 \\ 0 & 5 & -4 \end{bmatrix}$$

PROBLEM

If $A = \begin{bmatrix} 2 & -2 & 4 \\ -1 & 1 & 1 \end{bmatrix}$ and $B = \begin{bmatrix} 0 & 1 & -3 \\ 1 & 3 & 1 \end{bmatrix}$,

find $2A + B$.

SOLUTION

$$2A = 2 \begin{bmatrix} 2 & -2 & 4 \\ -1 & 1 & 1 \end{bmatrix}$$

$$= \begin{bmatrix} 2 \times 2 & 2 \times (-2) & 2 \times 4 \\ 2 \times (-1) & 2 \times 1 & 2 \times 1 \end{bmatrix}$$

$$= \begin{bmatrix} 4 & -4 & 8 \\ -2 & 2 & 2 \end{bmatrix}$$

Then,

$$2A + B = \begin{bmatrix} 4 & -4 & 8 \\ -2 & 2 & 2 \end{bmatrix} + \begin{bmatrix} 0 & 1 & -3 \\ 1 & 3 & 1 \end{bmatrix}$$

$$= \begin{bmatrix} 4+0 & -4+1 & 8-3 \\ -2+1 & 2+3 & 2+1 \end{bmatrix}$$

$$2A + B = \begin{bmatrix} 4 & -3 & 5 \\ -1 & 5 & 3 \end{bmatrix}$$

PROBLEM

If $A = \begin{bmatrix} 1 & 2 & 4 \\ 2 & 6 & 0 \end{bmatrix}$ and $B = \begin{bmatrix} 4 & 1 & 4 & 3 \\ 0 & -1 & 3 & 1 \\ 2 & 7 & 5 & 2 \end{bmatrix}$,

find AB.

SOLUTION

Since A is a 2×3 matrix and B is a 3×4 matrix, the product AB is a 2×4 matrix.

$$AB = \begin{bmatrix} 1 & 2 & 4 \\ 2 & 6 & 0 \end{bmatrix} \begin{bmatrix} 4 & 1 & 4 & 3 \\ 0 & -1 & 3 & 1 \\ 2 & 7 & 5 & 2 \end{bmatrix}$$

$$= \begin{bmatrix} 1 \cdot 4 + 2 \cdot 0 + 4 \cdot 2 & 1 \cdot 1 + 2 \cdot (-1) + 4 \cdot 7 \\ 2 \cdot 4 + 6 \cdot 0 + 0 \cdot 2 & 2 \cdot 1 + 6 \cdot (-1) + 0 \cdot 7 \end{bmatrix}$$

$$\begin{bmatrix} 1 \cdot 4 + 2 \cdot 3 + 4 \cdot 5 & 1 \cdot 3 + 2 \cdot 1 + 4 \cdot 2 \\ 2 \cdot 4 + 6 \cdot 3 + 0 \cdot 5 & 2 \cdot 3 + 6 \cdot 1 + 0 \cdot 2 \end{bmatrix}$$

$$= \begin{bmatrix} 4 + 0 + 8 & 1 - 2 + 28 & 4 + 6 + 20 & 3 + 2 + 8 \\ 8 + 0 + 0 & 2 - 6 + 0 & 8 + 18 + 0 & 6 + 6 + 0 \end{bmatrix}$$

$$AB = \begin{bmatrix} 12 & 27 & 30 & 13 \\ 8 & -4 & 26 & 12 \end{bmatrix}$$

Matrices and Linear Equations

The augmented matrix for a system of linear equations is the matrix of the form:

$$\begin{bmatrix} a_{11} & a_{12} & \dots & a_{1n} & \Big| & b_1 \\ a_{21} & a_{22} & \dots & a_{2n} & \Big| & b_2 \\ \vdots & & & & & \\ a_{m1} & a_{m2} & \dots & a_{mn} & \Big| & b_m \end{bmatrix}$$

where a_{ij} represents each coefficient in the system and b_i represents each constant in the system.

• EXAMPLE

The augmented matrix for the system

$$\begin{aligned} x_1 + 6x_2 - 2x_3 &= 4 \\ 3x_1 \quad\quad + x_3 &= 7 \\ 5x_1 - 3x_2 + x_3 &= 0 \end{aligned}$$

is

$$\begin{bmatrix} 1 & 6 & -2 & \Big| & 4 \\ 3 & 0 & 1 & \Big| & 7 \\ 5 & -3 & 1 & \Big| & 0 \end{bmatrix}$$

Elementary row operations are operations on the rows of an augmented matrix, which are used to reduce that matrix to a more solvable form. (e.g., one with two zeros in one row). These operations are the following:

a)   Multiply a row by a non-zero constant.

b)   Interchange two rows.

c)   Add a multiple of one row to another row.

PROBLEM

By forming the augmented matrix and row reducing, determine the solutions of the following system:

$$\begin{aligned} 2x - y + 3z &= 4 \\ 3x \quad\quad + 2z &= 5 \\ -2x + y + 4z &= 6 \end{aligned}$$

SOLUTION

The augmented matrix of the system is:

$$\begin{bmatrix} 2 & -1 & 3 & \Big| & 4 \\ 3 & 0 & 2 & \Big| & 5 \\ -2 & 1 & 4 & \Big| & 6 \end{bmatrix} .$$

Add the first row to the third row:

$$\begin{bmatrix} 2 & -1 & 3 & \Big| & 4 \\ 3 & 0 & 2 & \Big| & 5 \\ 0 & 0 & 7 & \Big| & 10 \end{bmatrix}$$

This is the augmented matrix of:

$$\begin{aligned} 2x - y + 3z &= 4 \\ 3x \quad\quad + 2z &= 5 \\ 7z &= 10 \end{aligned}$$

The system has been sufficiently simplified now so that the solution can be found.

From the last equation we have $z = 10/7$. Substituting this value into the second equation and solving for x gives $x = 5/7$. Substituting $x = 5/7$ and $z = 10/7$ into the first equation and solving for y yields $y = 12/7$. The solution to the system is, therefore,

$$x = \frac{5}{7}, y = \frac{12}{7}, z = \frac{10}{7}.$$

PROBLEM

Solve the following linear system of equations:

$$2x + 3y - 4z = 5$$
$$-2x \quad + z = 7$$
$$3x + 2y + 2z = 3$$

SOLUTION

The augmented matrix for the system is:

$$\begin{bmatrix} 2 & 3 & -4 & | & 5 \\ -2 & 0 & 1 & | & 7 \\ 3 & 2 & 2 & | & 3 \end{bmatrix}$$

which can be reduced by using the following sequence of row operations:

Add the first row to the second row.

$$\begin{bmatrix} 2 & 3 & -4 & | & 5 \\ 0 & 3 & -3 & | & 12 \\ 3 & 2 & 2 & | & 3 \end{bmatrix}$$

Divide the first row by 2 and the second row by 3.

$$\begin{bmatrix} 1 & \frac{3}{2} & -2 & | & \frac{5}{2} \\ 0 & 1 & -1 & | & 4 \\ 3 & 2 & 2 & | & 3 \end{bmatrix}$$

Add –3 times the first row to the third row.

$$\begin{bmatrix} 1 & \frac{3}{2} & -2 & | & \frac{5}{2} \\ 0 & 1 & -1 & | & 4 \\ 0 & -\frac{5}{2} & 8 & | & -\frac{9}{2} \end{bmatrix}$$

Add 5/2 times the second row to the third row.

$$\begin{bmatrix} 1 & \frac{3}{2} & -2 & | & \frac{5}{2} \\ 0 & 1 & -1 & | & 4 \\ 0 & 0 & \frac{11}{2} & | & \frac{11}{2} \end{bmatrix}$$

This is the augmented matrix for the system:

$$x = \frac{3}{2y} - 2z = \frac{5}{2}$$
$$y - z = 4$$
$$\frac{11}{2z} = \frac{11}{2}$$

Now the solution to this system can be easily found. From the last equation we have $z = 1$. Substituting $z = 1$ in the second equation gives $y = 5$. Next, substitute $y = 5$ and $z = 1$ into the first equation. This gives $x = -3$. Therefore, the solution to the system is $x = -3$, $y = 5$, $z = 1$.

PROBLEM

Solve the following system:

$$x + y + 2z = 9$$
$$2x + 4y - 3z = 1$$
$$3x + 6y - 5z = 0$$

SOLUTION

The augmented matrix for the system is:

$$\begin{bmatrix} 1 & 1 & 2 & | & 9 \\ 2 & 4 & -3 & | & 1 \\ 3 & 6 & -5 & | & 0 \end{bmatrix} .$$

It can be reduced by elementary row operations.

Add –2 times the first row to the second row and –3 times the first row to the third row.

$$\begin{bmatrix} 1 & 1 & 2 & | & 9 \\ 0 & 2 & -7 & | & -17 \\ 0 & 3 & -11 & | & -27 \end{bmatrix}$$

Multiply the second row by ½.

$$\begin{bmatrix} 1 & 1 & 2 & | & 9 \\ 0 & 1 & -\frac{7}{2} & | & -\frac{17}{2} \\ 0 & 3 & -11 & | & -27 \end{bmatrix}$$

Add −3 times the second row to the third row.

$$\begin{bmatrix} 1 & 1 & 2 & | & 9 \\ 0 & 1 & -\frac{7}{2} & | & -\frac{17}{2} \\ 0 & 0 & -\frac{1}{2} & | & -\frac{3}{2} \end{bmatrix}$$

Multiply the third row by −2 to obtain

$$\begin{bmatrix} 1 & 1 & 2 & | & 9 \\ 0 & 1 & -\frac{7}{2} & | & -\frac{17}{2} \\ 0 & 0 & 1 & | & 3 \end{bmatrix}.$$

This is the augmented matrix for the system:

$$x + y + 2z = 9$$
$$y - \frac{7}{2}z = -\frac{17}{2}$$
$$z = 3$$

Solving this system gives $x = 1$, $y = 2$, and $z = 3$.

PROBLEM

For the following system, find the augmented matrix; then, by reducing, determine whether the system has a solution.

$$3x - y + z = 1$$
$$7x + y - z = 6 \qquad (1)$$
$$2x + y - z = 2$$

SOLUTION

The augmented matrix for the system is

$$\begin{bmatrix} 3 & -1 & 1 & | & 1 \\ 7 & 1 & -1 & | & 6 \\ 2 & 1 & -1 & | & 2 \end{bmatrix}.$$

This can be reduced by performing the following row operations. Divide the first row by 3.

$$\begin{bmatrix} 1 & -\frac{1}{3} & \frac{1}{3} & | & \frac{1}{3} \\ 7 & 1 & -1 & | & 6 \\ 2 & 1 & -1 & | & 2 \end{bmatrix}$$

Now add −7 times the first row to the second row and −2 times the first row to the third row.

$$\begin{bmatrix} 1 & -\frac{1}{3} & \frac{1}{3} & | & \frac{1}{3} \\ 0 & \frac{10}{3} & -\frac{10}{3} & | & \frac{11}{3} \\ 0 & \frac{5}{3} & -\frac{5}{3} & | & \frac{4}{3} \end{bmatrix}$$

Divide the second row by $10/3$, and add $-5/3$ times the second row to the third row.

The resultant matrix is

$$\begin{bmatrix} 1 & -\frac{1}{3} & \frac{1}{3} & | & \frac{1}{3} \\ 0 & 1 & -1 & | & \frac{11}{10} \\ 0 & 0 & 0 & | & -\frac{11}{6} \end{bmatrix}$$

The last row has three zeros, so the system has no solution.

Rules of Matrix Arithmetic

a) $A + B = B + A$ (Commutative Law of Addition)

b) $A + (B + C) = (A + B) + C$ (Associative Law of Addition)

c) $A(BC) = (AB)C$ (Associative Law of Multiplication)

d) $A(B \pm C) = AB \pm AC$ (Distributive Law)

e) $a(B + C) = aB + aC$

f) $(a \pm b)C = aC \pm bC$

g) $(ab)C = a(bC)$

h) $a(BC) = (aB)C = B(aC)$

A matrix whose entries are all zero is called a zero matrix, **0**.

- **EXAMPLES**

a) $$\begin{bmatrix} 0 & 0 \\ 0 & 0 \end{bmatrix}$$

b) $$\begin{bmatrix} 0 \\ 0 \\ 0 \end{bmatrix}$$

c) $$\begin{bmatrix} 0 & 0 & 0 \\ 0 & 0 & 0 \\ 0 & 0 & 0 \end{bmatrix}$$

Theorem

If the size of the matrices are such that the indicated operations can be performed, the following rules of matrix arithmetic are valid:

a) $A + 0 = 0 + A = A$

b) $A - A = 0$

c) $0 - A = -A$

d) $A0 = 0$

An identity matrix (I) is a square matrix with ones on the main diagonal and zeros everywhere else.

- **EXAMPLES**

a) $\begin{bmatrix} 1 & 0 \\ 0 & 1 \end{bmatrix}$

b) $\begin{bmatrix} 1 & 0 & 0 & 0 \\ 0 & 1 & 0 & 0 \\ 0 & 0 & 1 & 0 \\ 0 & 0 & 0 & 1 \end{bmatrix}$

If A is a square matrix and a matrix B exists such that $AB = BA = I$, then A is invertible and B is the inverse of A, denoted A^{-1}. An invertible matrix has one and only one inverse.

Theorem

If A and B are invertible matrices of the same size, then:

a) AB is invertible

b) $(AB)^{-1} = (B^{-1})(A^{-1})$

The formula for inverting a 2×2 matrix is

If $A = \begin{bmatrix} a & b \\ c & d \end{bmatrix}$, then $A^{-1} = \dfrac{1}{ad - bc} \begin{bmatrix} d & -b \\ -c & a \end{bmatrix}$.

- **EXAMPLE**

If $A = \begin{bmatrix} 1 & 2 \\ 3 & 4 \end{bmatrix}$, then $A^{-1} = \begin{bmatrix} -2 & 1 \\ \frac{3}{2} & -\frac{1}{2} \end{bmatrix}$.

Theorem

If A is an invertible matrix, then:

a) A^{-1} is invertible; $(A^{-1})^{-1} = A$

b) kA is invertible (where k is a non-zero scalar); $(kA)^{-1} = \dfrac{1}{k} A^{-1}$

c) A^n is invertible; $(A^n)^{-1} = (A^{-1})^n$

If A is a square matrix and x and y are positive integers, then:

a) $A^x A^y = A^{x+y}$

b) $(A^x)^y = A^{xy}$

PROBLEM

Show that

a) $A + B = B + A$ where:

$A = \begin{bmatrix} 3 & 1 & 1 \\ 2 & -1 & 1 \end{bmatrix}$ and $B = \begin{bmatrix} 4 & 2 & -1 \\ 0 & 0 & 2 \end{bmatrix}$.

b) $(A + B) + C = A + (B + C)$ where

$A = \begin{bmatrix} -2 & 6 \\ 2 & 1 \end{bmatrix}$, $B = \begin{bmatrix} 2 & 1 \\ 0 & 3 \end{bmatrix}$, and $C = \begin{bmatrix} -1 & 0 \\ 7 & 2 \end{bmatrix}$.

c)   If A and the zero matrix have the same size, then $A + 0 = A$ where:

$A = \begin{bmatrix} 2 & 1 \\ 1 & 2 \end{bmatrix}$.

d) $A + (-A) = 0$ where:

$A = \begin{bmatrix} 2 & 1 \\ 1 & 2 \end{bmatrix}$.

e) $(ab)A = a(bA)$ where $a = -5$, $b = 3$, and:

$$A = \begin{bmatrix} 6 & -1 & 0 \\ 1 & 2 & 1 \end{bmatrix}.$$

f) Find B if $2A - 3B + C = \mathbf{0}$ where:

$$A = \begin{bmatrix} -1 & 3 \\ 0 & 0 \end{bmatrix} \text{ and } C = \begin{bmatrix} -2 & -1 \\ -1 & 1 \end{bmatrix}.$$

SOLUTION

a) By the definition of matrix addition,

$$A + B = \begin{bmatrix} 3 & 1 & 1 \\ 2 & -1 & 1 \end{bmatrix} + \begin{bmatrix} 4 & 2 & -1 \\ 0 & 0 & 2 \end{bmatrix}$$

$$= \begin{bmatrix} 3+4 & 1+2 & 1+(-1) \\ 2+0 & -1+0 & 1+2 \end{bmatrix}$$

$$= \begin{bmatrix} 7 & 3 & 0 \\ 2 & -1 & 3 \end{bmatrix}$$

and

$$B + A = \begin{bmatrix} 4 & 2 & -1 \\ 0 & 0 & 2 \end{bmatrix} + \begin{bmatrix} 3 & 1 & 1 \\ 2 & -1 & 1 \end{bmatrix}$$

$$= \begin{bmatrix} 4+3 & 2+1 & -1+1 \\ 0+2 & 0+(-1) & 2+1 \end{bmatrix}$$

$$= \begin{bmatrix} 7 & 3 & 0 \\ 2 & -1 & 3 \end{bmatrix}$$

Thus, $A + B = B + A$.

b) $A + B = \begin{bmatrix} -2 & 6 \\ 2 & 1 \end{bmatrix} + \begin{bmatrix} 2 & 1 \\ 0 & 3 \end{bmatrix}$

$$= \begin{bmatrix} -2+2 & 6+1 \\ 2+0 & 1+3 \end{bmatrix}$$

$$= \begin{bmatrix} 0 & 7 \\ 2 & 4 \end{bmatrix}$$

and

$$(A + B) + C = \begin{bmatrix} 0 & 7 \\ 2 & 4 \end{bmatrix} + \begin{bmatrix} -1 & 0 \\ 7 & 2 \end{bmatrix}$$

$$= \begin{bmatrix} 0+(-1) & 7+0 \\ 2+7 & 4+2 \end{bmatrix}$$

$$= \begin{bmatrix} -1 & 7 \\ 9 & 6 \end{bmatrix}$$

$$B + C = \begin{bmatrix} 2 & 1 \\ 0 & 3 \end{bmatrix} + \begin{bmatrix} -1 & 0 \\ 7 & 2 \end{bmatrix}$$

$$= \begin{bmatrix} 2+(-1) & 1+0 \\ 0+7 & 3+2 \end{bmatrix}$$

$$= \begin{bmatrix} 1 & 1 \\ 7 & 5 \end{bmatrix}$$

and

$$A + (B + C) = \begin{bmatrix} -2 & 6 \\ 2 & 1 \end{bmatrix} + \begin{bmatrix} 1 & 1 \\ 7 & 5 \end{bmatrix}$$

$$= \begin{bmatrix} -2+1 & 6+1 \\ 2+7 & 1+5 \end{bmatrix}$$

$$= \begin{bmatrix} -1 & 7 \\ 9 & 6 \end{bmatrix}$$

Thus, $(A + B) + C = A + (B + C)$.

c) $A = \begin{bmatrix} 2 & 1 \\ 1 & 2 \end{bmatrix}$ $0 = \begin{bmatrix} 0 & 0 \\ 0 & 0 \end{bmatrix}.$

Thus,

$$A + 0 = \begin{bmatrix} 2 & 1 \\ 1 & 2 \end{bmatrix} + \begin{bmatrix} 0 & 0 \\ 0 & 0 \end{bmatrix}$$

$$= \begin{bmatrix} 2+0 & 1+0 \\ 1+0 & 2+0 \end{bmatrix}$$

$$= \begin{bmatrix} 2 & 1 \\ 1 & 2 \end{bmatrix}$$

Hence, $A + \mathbf{0} = A$.

d) $\quad -A = -1 \times \begin{bmatrix} 2 & 1 \\ 1 & 2 \end{bmatrix}$

$\quad = \begin{bmatrix} -1 \times 2 & -1 \times 1 \\ -1 \times 1 & -1 \times 2 \end{bmatrix}$

$\quad = \begin{bmatrix} -2 & -1 \\ -1 & -2 \end{bmatrix}$

Thus,

$A + (-A) = \begin{bmatrix} 2 & 1 \\ 1 & 2 \end{bmatrix} + \begin{bmatrix} -2 & -1 \\ -1 & -2 \end{bmatrix}$

$\quad = \begin{bmatrix} 2 + (-2) & 1 + (-1) \\ 1 + (-1) & 2 + (-2) \end{bmatrix}$

$\quad = \begin{bmatrix} 0 & 0 \\ 0 & 0 \end{bmatrix}$

Therefore, $A + (-A) = \mathbf{0}$.

$(ab)A = ((-5)(3)) \begin{bmatrix} 6 & -1 & 0 \\ 1 & 2 & 1 \end{bmatrix}$

$\quad = -15 \begin{bmatrix} 6 & -1 & 0 \\ 1 & 2 & 1 \end{bmatrix}$

$\quad = \begin{bmatrix} -90 & 15 & 0 \\ -15 & -30 & -15 \end{bmatrix}$

e) $bA = 3 \begin{bmatrix} 6 & -1 & 0 \\ 1 & 2 & 1 \end{bmatrix} = \begin{bmatrix} 3 \times 6 & 3 \times (-1) & 3 \times 0 \\ 3 \times 1 & 3 \times 2 & 3 \times 1 \end{bmatrix}$

$\quad = \begin{bmatrix} 18 & -3 & 0 \\ 3 & 6 & 3 \end{bmatrix}$

and

$a(bA) = -5 \begin{bmatrix} 18 & -3 & 0 \\ 3 & 6 & 3 \end{bmatrix}$

$\quad = \begin{bmatrix} -90 & 15 & 0 \\ -15 & -30 & -15 \end{bmatrix}$

Thus, $(ab)A = a(bA)$.

f) $\quad 2A - 3B + C = 2A + C - 3B = 0$ since matrix addition is commutative.

Now, add $3B$ to both sides of the equation to obtain $2A + C - 3B + 3B = 0 + 3B$.   (1)

Using the laws we exemplified in parts a) through d), Equation (1) becomes $2A + C = 3B$. Now,

$$\frac{1}{3}(2A + C) = \frac{1}{3}(3B),$$

which implies

$$B = \frac{1}{3}(2A + C).$$

$$2A + C = \begin{bmatrix} 2(-1) & 2(3) \\ 2(0) & 2(0) \end{bmatrix} + \begin{bmatrix} -2 & -1 \\ -1 & 1 \end{bmatrix} = \begin{bmatrix} -4 & 5 \\ -1 & 1 \end{bmatrix}$$

Thus,

$$B = \frac{1}{3}(2A + C) = \frac{1}{3}\begin{bmatrix} -4 & 5 \\ -1 & 1 \end{bmatrix} = \begin{bmatrix} -\frac{4}{3} & \frac{5}{3} \\ -\frac{1}{3} & \frac{1}{3} \end{bmatrix}$$

PROBLEM

Let $A = \begin{bmatrix} 1 & 1 \\ 3 & 7 \end{bmatrix}$ and $B = \begin{bmatrix} 2 & 5 \\ 4 & 0 \end{bmatrix}$.

Show $AB \neq BA$.

SOLUTION

$$AB = \begin{bmatrix} 1 & 1 \\ 3 & 7 \end{bmatrix}\begin{bmatrix} 2 & 5 \\ 4 & 0 \end{bmatrix} = \begin{bmatrix} 1 \cdot 2 + 1 \cdot 4 & 1 \cdot 5 + 1 \cdot 0 \\ 3 \cdot 2 + 7 \cdot 4 & 3 \cdot 5 + 7 \cdot 0 \end{bmatrix}$$

$$= \begin{bmatrix} 2 + 4 & 5 + 0 \\ 6 + 28 & 15 + 0 \end{bmatrix}$$

$$= \begin{bmatrix} 6 & 5 \\ 34 & 15 \end{bmatrix}$$

$$BA = \begin{bmatrix} 2 & 5 \\ 4 & 0 \end{bmatrix} \begin{bmatrix} 1 & 1 \\ 3 & 7 \end{bmatrix} = \begin{bmatrix} 2 \cdot 1 + 5 \cdot 3 & 2 \cdot 1 + 5 \cdot 7 \\ 4 \cdot 1 + 0 \cdot 3 & 4 \cdot 1 + 0 \cdot 7 \end{bmatrix}$$

$$= \begin{bmatrix} 2 + 15 & 2 + 35 \\ 4 + 0 & 4 + 0 \end{bmatrix}$$

$$= \begin{bmatrix} 17 & 37 \\ 4 & 4 \end{bmatrix}$$

Therefore, $AB \neq BA$.

Algebra Review Answer Key

Drill: Real and Complex Numbers

1. (A)	6. (D)
2. (D)	7. (A)
3. (B)	8. (B)
4. (D)	9. (D)
5. (C)	10. (D)

Drill: Operations with Polynomials

1. (B)	6. (B)	11. (C)	16. (C)
2. (C)	7. (C)	12. (B)	17. (D)
3. (C)	8. (D)	13. (D)	18. (D)
4. (D)	9. (A)	14. (A)	19. (B)
5. (A)	10. (D)	15. (D)	20. (B)

Drill: Simplifying Algebraic Expressions

1. (C)	3. (B)	5. (D)
2. (D)	4. (A)	

Drill: Two Linear Equations

1. (D)	3. (A)	5. (C)
2. (B)	4. (D)	

Drill: Quadratic Equations

1. (A)	6. (B)
2. (D)	7. (B)
3. (B)	8. (D)
4. (C)	9. (D)
5. (D)	10. (B)

Drill: Absolute Value Equations

1. (B)	3. (A)	5. (C)
2. (D)	4. (C)	

Drill: Inequalities

1. (D)	3. (D)	5. (A)
2. (C)	4. (B)	

Drill: Ratios and Proportions

1. (D)	3. (C)	5. (B)
2. (B)	4. (A)	6. (C)

Detailed Explanations of Answers

1. (A)

$3i^3 = 3i(i)^2 = 3i(-1) = -3i$

2. (D)

$2i^7 = 2i(i^2)(i^2)(i^2) = 2i(-1)(-1)(-1) = -2i$

3. (B)

$-4i^4 = -4(i^2)(i^2) = -4(-1)(-1) = -4$

4. (D)

$-5i^6 = -5(i^2)(i^2)(i^2) = -5(-1)(-1)(-1) = 5$

5. (C)

$$(3 + 2i)(2 + 3i) = 6 + \underbrace{9i + 4i} + 6i^2$$
$$= 6 + \quad 13i \quad - 6$$
$$= 13i$$

6. (D)

$$(2 - i)(2 + i) = 4 + 2i - 2i - i^2$$
$$= 4 + 0 - (-1)$$
$$= 5$$

7. (A)

$$(5 - 4i)^2 = (5 - 4i)(5 - 4i)$$
$$= (25 - 20i - 20i + 16i^2)$$
$$= 25 - 40i + 16(-1)$$
$$= 9 - 40i$$

8. (B)

$$x^2 + 16 = 0$$
$$x^2 = -16$$
$$x^2 = (16)(-1)$$
$$x = \pm 4i$$

9. (D)

$$4y^2 + 1 = 0$$
$$4y^2 = -1 \Rightarrow y^2 = -\frac{1}{4} \quad y = \pm\frac{1}{2}i$$

10. (D)

$$\frac{2 + bi}{1 - i} \times \frac{1 + i}{1 + i}$$
$$= \frac{2 + 8i + bi^2}{1 - i^2}$$
$$= \frac{2 + 8i + 6(-1)}{1 - (-1)}$$
$$= \frac{-4 + 8i}{2}$$
$$= -2 + 4i$$

1. (B)

$$9a^2b + 3c + 2a^2b + 5c = (9a^2b + 2a^2b) + (3c + 5c)$$
$$= 11a^2b + 8c$$

2. (C)

$$14m^2n^3 + 6m^2n^3 + 3m^2n^3 = (14 + 6 + 3)m^2n^3$$
$$= 23m^2n^3$$

3. **(C)**

$$3x + 2y + 16x + 3z + 6y = (3x + 16x) + (2y + 6y) + 3z$$
$$= 19x + 8y + 3z$$

4. **(D)**

$$(4d^2 + 7e^3 + 12f) + (3d^2 + 6e^3 + 2f) =$$
$$(4d^2 + 3d^2) + (7e^3 + 6e^3) + (12f + 2f) =$$
$$7d^2 + 13e^3 + 14f$$

5. **(A)**

$$3ac^2 + 2b^2c + 7ac^2 + 2ac^2 + b^2c =$$
$$(3ac^2 + 7ac^2 + 2ac^2) + (2b^2c + b^2c) =$$
$$12ac^2 + 3b^2c$$

6. **(B)**

$$14m^2n - 6m^2n = (14 - 6)m^2n = 8m^2n$$

7. **(C)**

$$3x^3y^2 - 4xz - 6x^3y^2 = (3x^3y^2 - 6x^3y^2) - 4xz$$
$$= -3x^3y^2 - 4xz$$

8. **(D)**

$$9g^2 + 6h - 2g^2 - 5h = (9g^2 - 2g^2) + (6h - 5h)$$
$$= 7g^2 + h$$

9. **(A)**

$$7b^3 - 4c^2 - 6b^3 + 3c^2 = (7b^3 - 6b^3) + (-4c^2 + 3c^2)$$
$$= b^3 - c^2$$

10. **(D)**

$$11q^2r - 4q^2r - 8q^2r = (11 - 4 - 8)q^2r = -q^2r$$

11. **(C)**

$$5p^2t \times 3p^2t = (5 \times 3)(p^2 \times p^2)(t \times t)$$
$$= 15p^4t^2$$

12. **(B)**

$$(2r + s)14r = (2r)(14r) + (s)(14r)$$
$$= 28r^2 + 14sr$$

13. **(D)**

$$(4m + p)(3m - 2p) = (4m)(3m) + (4m)(-2p)$$
$$+ (p)(3m) + (p)(-2p)$$
$$= 12m^2 + [(-8mp) + 3mp] +$$
$$(-2p^2)$$
$$= 12m^2 - 5mp - 2p^2$$

14. **(A)**

$$(2a + b)(3a^2 + ab + b^2) = (2a)(3a^2) + (2a)(ab) +$$
$$(2a)(b^2) + (b)(3a^2) + (b)(ab) + (b)(b^2)$$
$$= 6a^3 + 2a^2b + 2ab^2 + 3a^2b + ab^2 + b^3$$
$$= 6a^3 + 5a^2b + 3ab^2 + b^3$$

15. **(D)**

$$(6t^2 + 2t + 1)(3t) = (6t^2)(3t) + (2t)(3t) + (1)(3t)$$
$$= 18t^3 + 6t^2 + 3t$$

16. **(C)**

$$(x^2 + x - 6) \div (x - 2) = x - 2 \overline{)x^2 + x - 6}$$

$$\begin{array}{r} x + 3 \\ x - 2 \overline{)x^2 + x - 6} \\ -(x^2 - 2x) \\ \hline 3x - 6 \\ -(3x - 6) \\ \hline 0 \end{array}$$

17. **(D)**

$$24b^4c^3 \div 6b^2c = \frac{24}{6} \times \frac{b^4}{b^2} \times \frac{c^3}{c} = 4b^2c^2$$

18. (D)

$$(3p^2 + pq - 2q^2) \div (p + q)$$

$$= p + q \overline{)\begin{array}{l} 3p - 2q \\ 3p^2 + pq - 2q^2 \end{array}}$$
$$\underline{-(3p^2 + 3pq)}$$
$$-2pq - 2q^2$$
$$\underline{-(-2pq - 2q^2)}$$
$$0$$

19. (B)

$$(y^3 - 2y^2 - y + 2) \div (y - 2) = y - 2 \overline{)\begin{array}{l} y^2 - 1 \\ y^3 - 2y^2 - y + 2 \end{array}}$$
$$\underline{-(y^3 - 2y^2)}$$
$$0 - y + 2$$
$$\underline{-(-y + 2)}$$
$$0$$

20. (B)

$$(m^2 + m - 14) \div (m + 4)$$

$$m + 4 \overline{)\begin{array}{l} m - 3 - \frac{2}{m+4} \\ m^2 + m - 14 \end{array}}$$
$$\underline{-(m^2 + 4m)}$$
$$-3m - 14$$
$$\underline{-(-3m - 12)}$$
$$-2$$

Drill: Simplifying Algebraic Expressions

1. (C)

$$16b^2 - 25z^2 = (4b - 5z)(4b + 5z)$$

2. (D)

$$x^2 - 2x - 8 = (x - 4)(x + 2)$$

3. (B)

$$2c^2 + 5cd - 3d^2 = (2c - d)(c + 3d)$$

4. (A)

$$4t^3 - 20t = 4t(t^2 - 5)$$

5. (D)

$$x^2 + xy - 2y^2 = (x + 2y)(x - y)$$

Drill: Two Linear Equations

1. (D)

$$3x + 4y = -2 \quad = \quad 3x + 4y = -2$$
$$-3(x - 6y = -8) \quad = \quad \underline{+ -3x + 18y = 24}$$
$$0 + 22y = 22$$
$$y = 1$$

Substitute $y = 1$ in $x - 6y = -8$ to get

$$x - 6 = -8$$
$$\underline{+6 \quad +6}$$
$$x = -2$$

$$(-2, 1)$$

2. (B)

$$2x + y = -10$$
$$\underline{-2x - 4y = 4}$$
$$0 - 3y = -6$$
$$\frac{-3y}{-3} = \frac{-6}{-3}$$
$$y = 2$$

Substitute $y = 2$ in first equation to get

$$2x + 2 = -10$$
$$\underline{-2 = -2}$$
$$2x = -12$$
$$x = -6$$

$$(-6, 2)$$

3. **(A)**

$$6x + 5y = -4 = \quad 6x + 5y = -4$$
$$(3x - 3y = 9)(-2) = -6x + 6y = -18$$
$$\overline{\, 0 + 11y = -22}$$
$$y = -2$$

Substitute in the second equation to get

$$3x - 3\,(-2) = 9$$
$$3x + 6 \quad\;\; = 9$$
$$\underline{\;-6 \qquad\;\; -6\;}$$
$$3x \quad\;\; = 3$$
$$x \quad\;\; = 1$$

$$(1, -2)$$

4. **(D)**

$$4x + 3y = \qquad 9 = \quad 4x + 3y = \quad 9$$
$$(2x - 2y = 8)(-2) = -4x + 4y = -16$$
$$\overline{\, 0 + 7y = \;\; -7}$$
$$y = \quad -1$$

Substitute in the first equation to get

$$4x + 3(-1) = 9$$
$$4x - 3 = 9$$
$$\underline{\qquad +3 = +3\;}$$
$$4x = 12$$
$$x = 3$$

$$(3, -1)$$

5. **(C)**

$$x + y = 7 \;\; = \;\; x + y = \;\; 7$$
$$x = y - 3 \;\; = \;\; x - y = -3$$
$$\overline{\, 2x = \;\; 4}$$
$$x = \;\; 2$$

Substitute in the first equation to get

$$2 + y = 7$$
$$y = 5$$

$$(2, 5)$$

<hr>

Drill: Quadratic Equations

1. **(A)**

$$(x^2 - 2x - 8) = 0$$
$$(x - 4)(x + 2) = 0$$

The values of x are 4 and –2.

2. **(D)**

$$x^2 + 2x - 3 = 0$$
$$(x + 3)(x - 1) = 0$$

The values of x are –3 and 1.

3. **(B)**

$$x^2 - 7x = -10$$
$$x^2 - 7x + 10 = 0$$
$$(x - 5)(x - 2) = 0$$

The values of x are 2 and 5.

4. **(C)**

$$x^2 - 8x + 16 = 0$$
$$(x - 4)(x - 4) = 0$$
$$(x - 4)^2 = 0$$

The value of x is 4.

5. **(D)**

$$3x^2 + 3x = 6$$
$$3x^2 + 3x - 6 = 0$$
$$3(x^2 + x - 2) = 0$$
$$3(x + 2)(x - 1) = 0$$

The values of x are –2 and 1.

6. (B)

$x^2 + 7x = 0$

$x(x + 7) = 0$

The values of x are 0 and –7.

7. (B)

$x^2 - 25 = 0$

$(x - 5)(x + 5) = 0$

The values of x are 5 and –5.

8. (D)

$2x^2 + 4x = 16$

$2x^2 + 4x - 16 = 0$

$2(x^2 + 2x - 8) = 0$

$2(x - 2)(x + 4) = 0$

The values of x are 2 and –4.

9. (D)

$2x^2 - 11x - 6 = 0$

Using the quadratic formula with $a = 2$, $b = -11$, $c = -6$,

$x = \dfrac{-b \pm \sqrt{b^2 - 4ac}}{2a}$

$x = \dfrac{11 \pm \sqrt{121 + 48}}{4}$

$= \dfrac{11 \pm \sqrt{169}}{4}$

$= \dfrac{11 \pm 13}{4}$

The values of x are $\dfrac{11 - 13}{4} = -\dfrac{1}{2}$ and

$\dfrac{11 + 13}{4} = 6$

Alternate solution: $2x^2 - 11x - 6 = 0$

$(2x + 1)(x - 6) = 0$

The values of x are $-\dfrac{1}{2}$ and 6

10. (B)

$x^2 - 2x - 3 = 0$

$(x + 1)(x - 3) = 0$

The values of x are –1 and 3.

Drill: Absolute Value Equations

1. (B)

$|4x - 2| = 6$

$4x - 2 = 6$ or $4x - 2 = -6$

$4x = 8 4x = -4$

$x = 2$ or $x = -1$

2. (D)

$\left|3 - \dfrac{1}{2}y\right| = -7$

No solution. Absolute value must equal a positive number.

3. (A)

$2|x + 7| = 12$

$|x + 7| = 6 x + 7 = 6$ or $x + 7 = -6$

$ x = -1$ or $x = -13$

4. (C)

$|5x| - 7 = 3$

$|5x| = 10$

$5x = 10$ or $5x = -10$

$x = 2$ or $x = -2$

5. **(C)**

$$\left|\frac{3}{4}m\right| = 9$$

$$\frac{3}{4}m = 9 \qquad\qquad \frac{3}{4}m = -9$$

$$\frac{4}{3}\left(\frac{3}{4}m\right) = 9\left(\frac{4}{3}\right) \quad \frac{4}{3}\left(\frac{3}{4}m\right) = (-9)\left(\frac{4}{3}\right)$$

$$m = 12 \qquad\qquad m = -12$$

Drill: Inequalities

1. **(D)**

$$3m + 2 < 7$$
$$\underline{\quad -2 \quad -2\quad}$$
$$\left(\frac{1}{3}\right)3m < 5\left(\frac{1}{3}\right)$$
$$m < \frac{5}{3}$$

2. **(C)**

$$\frac{1}{2}x - 3 \le 1$$
$$\underline{\quad +3 \quad +3\quad}$$
$$\frac{1}{2}x \le 4$$
$$(2)\frac{1}{2}x \le 4(2)$$
$$x \le 8$$

3. **(D)**

$$-3p + 1 \ge 16$$
$$\underline{\quad -1 \quad -1\quad}$$
$$-3p \ge 15$$
$$\left(-\frac{1}{3}\right)-3p \ge 15\left(-\frac{1}{3}\right)$$
$$p \le -5$$

4. **(B)**

$$-6 < \frac{2}{3}r + 6 \le 2$$
$$\underline{-6 \qquad -6 \quad -6}$$
$$-12 < \frac{2}{3}r \le -4$$
$$\frac{3}{2}\left(-12 < \frac{2}{3}r \le -4\right)$$
$$-18 < r \le -6$$

5. **(A)**

$$0 < 2 - y < 6$$
$$\underline{-2 - 2 \quad -2}$$
$$-2 < -y < 4$$
$$-1(-2 < -y < 4)$$
$$2 > y > -4, \text{ or}$$
$$-4 < y < 2$$

Drill: Ratios and Proportions

1. **(D)**

$$\frac{4}{n} = \frac{8}{5} \qquad 5(4) = 8n$$
$$\left(\frac{1}{8}\right)20 = 8n\left(\frac{1}{8}\right)$$
$$\frac{20}{8} = n, \text{ or } 2.5 = n$$

2. **(B)**

$$\frac{2}{3} = \frac{n}{72} \qquad 2(72) = 3n$$
$$\frac{1}{3}(144) = (3n)\frac{1}{3}$$
$$48 = n$$

3. (C)

$$n:12 = 3:4 \Rightarrow \quad \frac{n}{12} = \frac{3}{4}$$
$$4n = (12)(3)$$
$$4n = 36$$
$$n = 9$$

4. (A)

$$4:5 = x:785 \Rightarrow \quad \frac{4}{5} = \frac{x}{785}$$
$$(785)(4) = 5x$$
$$\left(\frac{1}{5}\right)(785)(4) = (5x)\frac{1}{5}$$
$$(157)(4) = x$$
$$628 = x$$

5. (B)

$$3:1000 = y:25000 \Rightarrow$$

$$\frac{3}{1000} = \frac{y}{25000}$$
$$(3)(25000) = y(1000)$$
$$\frac{1}{1000}(3)(25000) = y(1000)\frac{1}{1000}$$
$$75 = y$$

6. (C)

$$28:32 \Rightarrow \frac{28}{32} = \frac{7}{8} \Rightarrow 7:8$$

REVIEW FOR SUBTEST II:
Domain 2: Geometry;
Domain 4: Probability
& Statistics

Points, Lines, and Angles

Geometry is built upon a series of undefined terms. These terms are those that we accept as known in order to define other undefined terms.

A) **Point:** Although we represent points on paper with small dots, a point has no size, thickness, or width.

B) **Line:** A line is a series of adjacent points that extends indefinitely. A line can be either curved or straight; however, unless otherwise stated, the term "line" refers to a straight line.

C) **Plane:** A plane is a collection of points lying on a flat surface that extends indefinitely in all directions.

Definitions

Definition 1

If A and B are two points on a line, then the **line segment** AB is the set of points on that line between A and B, including A and B, which are called the endpoints. This line segment is referred to as $\overline{AB}$. The whole line here is referred to as $\overleftrightarrow{AB}$.

Definition 2

Let A be a dividing point on a line. Then, a **ray**, or **half-line** is the set of all the points in one direction and the dividing point itself. The dividing point is called the endpoint or the vertex of the ray. The ray AB shown below is denoted by $\overrightarrow{AB}$.

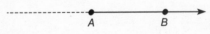

Definition 3

Three or more points are said to be **collinear** if and only if they lie on the same line.

Definition 4

Let X, Y, and Z be three collinear points. If Y is between X and Z, then $\overrightarrow{YX}$ and $\overrightarrow{YZ}$ are called **opposite rays**.

Definition 5

The **absolute value** of x, denoted by $|x|$, is defined as

$$|x| = \begin{cases} x & \text{if } x > 0 \\ 0 & \text{if } x = 0 \\ -x & \text{if } x < 0 \end{cases}$$

Definition 6

The absolute value of the difference of the coordinates of any two points on the real number line is the **distance** between those two points.

Definition 7

The **length** of a line segment is the distance between its endpoints.

Definition 8

Congruent segments are segments that have the same length. The sign for congruent is $\cong$.

Definition 9

The **midpoint** of a line segment is defined as the point of the segment that divides the segment into two congruent segments. (The midpoint is said to bisect the segment.)

PROBLEM

Solve for x when $|x - 7| = 3$.

SOLUTION

This equation, according to the definition of absolute value, expresses the conditions that $x - 7$ must be 3 or -3, since in either case the absolute value is 3. If $x - 7 = 3$, we have $x = 10$; if $x - 7 = -3$, we have $x = 4$. We see that two values of x solve the equation.

PROBLEM

Find point C between A and B in the figure below such that $\overline{AC} \cong \overline{CB}$.

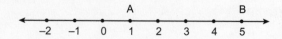

SOLUTION

We must determine point C in such a way that $\overline{AC} \cong \overline{CB}$, or $AC = CB$. We are first given that C is between A and B. Therefore, since the measure of the whole is equal to the sum of the measure of its parts:

$$AC + CB = AB \tag{1}$$

Using $AC = CB$, we can find the length of AC. From that we can find C.

First, we substitute AC for CB in Equation (1).

$$AC + AC = AB \tag{2}$$

$$2(AC) = AB \tag{3}$$

Dividing by 2 we have

$$AC = \left(\frac{1}{2}\right) AB \tag{4}$$

To find AC, we must know AB. We can find AB from the coordinates of A and B. They are 1 and 5, respectively. Accordingly,

$$AB = |5 - 1| \tag{5}$$

$$AB = 4 \tag{6}$$

We substitute 4 for AB in Equation (4)

$$AC = \left(\frac{1}{2}\right)(4) \tag{7}$$

$$AC = 2. \tag{8}$$

Therefore, C is 2 units from A. Since C is between A and B, the coordinate of C must be 3.

Definition 10

The **bisector** of a line segment is a line that divides the line segment into two congruent segments.

Definition 11

An **angle** is a collection of points that is the union of two rays having the same endpoint. An angle such as the one illustrated in the following figure can be referred to in any of the following ways:

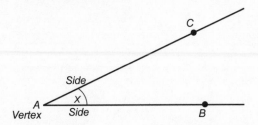

A) by a capital letter that names its vertex, $\angle A$;

B) by a lowercase letter or number placed inside the angle, $\angle x$

C) by three capital letters, where the middle letter is the vertex and the other two letters are not on the same ray, i.e., $\angle CAB$ or $\angle BAC$, both of which represent the angle illustrated in the above figure.

Definition 12

A set of points is **coplanar** if all the points lie in the same plane.

Definition 13

Two angles with a common vertex and a common side, but no common interior points, are called **adjacent angles**.

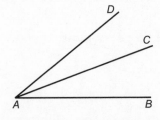

In the above figure, $\angle DAC$ and $\angle BAC$ are adjacent angles. Note: $\angle DAB$ and $\angle BAC$ are not adjacent angles because they have common interior points.

Definition 14

Vertical angles are two angles with a common vertex and with sides that are two pairs of opposite rays.

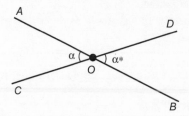

($\angle \alpha$ and $\angle \alpha^*$ are vertical angles.)

Definition 15

An **acute angle** is an angle whose measure is larger than 0° but smaller than 90°.

Definition 16

An angle whose measure is 90° is called a **right angle**.

Definition 17

An **obtuse angle** is an angle whose measure is larger than 90° but smaller than 180°.

Definition 18

An angle whose measure is 180° is called a **straight angle**. Note: Such an angle is, in fact, a straight line.

Definition 19

An angle whose measure is greater than 180° but less than 360° is called a **reflex angle**.

Definition 20

Complementary angles are two angles, whose measures sum to exactly 90°. Note: These angles do not have to be adjacent.

Definition 21

Supplementary angles are two angles who measures sum to exactly 180°. Note: These angles do not have to be adjacent.

Definition 22

Congruent angles are angles of equal measure.

Definition 23

A ray **bisects** (is the **bisector** of) an angle if the ray divides the angle into two angles that have equal measure.

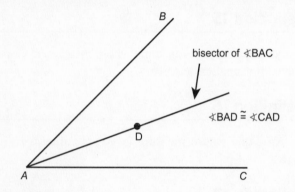

Definition 24

If the two non-common sides of adjacent angles form opposite rays, then the angles are called a **linear pair**. Note that ∡α and ∡β are supplementary.

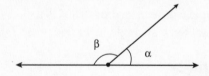

Definition 25

Two lines are said to be **perpendicular** if they intersect and form right angles. The symbol for perpendicular (or, is perpendicular to) is ⊥; $\overleftrightarrow{AB}$ is perpendicular to $\overleftrightarrow{CD}$ is written as $\overleftrightarrow{AB} \perp \overleftrightarrow{CD}$.

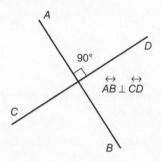

Definition 26

A line, a ray, or a line segment that bisects a line segment and is also perpendicular to that segment is called a **perpendicular bisector** of the line segment.

Definition 27

The **distance** from a point to a line is the measure of the perpendicular line segment from the point to that line. Note: The perpendicular is the shortest possible distance from the point to the line.

Definition 28

Two or more distinct lines are said to be **parallel** (∥) if and only if they are coplanar and they never intersect.

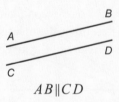

AB∥CD

Definition 29

The **projection of a given point** on a given line is the foot of the perpendicular drawn from the given point to the given line.

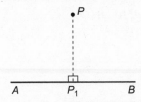

P_1 is the projection of P on $\overleftrightarrow{AB}$

The foot of a perpendicular from a point to a line is the point where the perpendicular meets the line.

Definition 30

The **projection of a segment** onto a given line (when the segment is not perpendicular to the line) is a segment with endpoints that are the projections of the endpoints of the given line segment onto the given line.

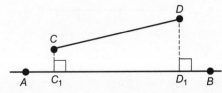

$\overline{C_1 D_1}$ is the projection of $\overline{CD}$ onto $\overleftrightarrow{AB}$

PROBLEM

The measure of the complement of a given angle is four times the measure of the angle. Find the measure of the given angle.

SOLUTION

By the definition of complementary angles, the sum of the measures of the two complements must equal 90°.

Accordingly,

(1) Let x = the measure of the angle

(2) Then $4x$ = the measure of the complement of this angle.

Therefore, from the discussion above,

$$x + 4x = 90°$$
$$5x = 90°$$
$$x = 18°$$

Therefore, the measure of the given angle is 18°.

PROBLEM

In the figure below, we are given $\overleftrightarrow{AB}$ and triangle ABC. We are told that the measure of $\sphericalangle 1$ is five times the measure of $\sphericalangle 2$. Determine the measures of $\sphericalangle 1$ and $\sphericalangle 2$.

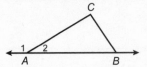

SOLUTION

Since $\sphericalangle 1$ and $\sphericalangle 2$ are adjacent angles whose non-common sides lie on a straight line, they are, by definition, supplementary. As supplements, their measures must sum to 180°.

If we let x = the measure of $\sphericalangle 2$,

then $5x$ = the measure of $\sphericalangle 1$.

To determine the respective angle measures, set $x + 5x = 180°$ and solve for x. $6x = 180°$. Therefore, $x = 30°$ and $5x = 150°$.

Therefore, the measure of $\sphericalangle 1 = 150°$ and the measure of $\sphericalangle 2 = 30°$.

Postulates

Postulate 1 (The Point Uniqueness Postulate)

Let n be any positive number.

Then there exists one and only one point N on $\overrightarrow{AB}$ such that $AN = n$. (AN is the length of n).

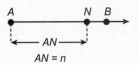

Postulate 2 (The Line Postulate)

Any two distinct points determine one and only one line that contains both points.

Postulate 3 (The Point Betweenness Postulate)

Let A and B be any two points. Then, there exists at least one point (and in fact an infinite number of such points) of $\overleftrightarrow{AB}$ such that P is between A and B, with $AP + PB = AB$.

Postulate 4

Two distinct straight lines can intersect at most at only one point.

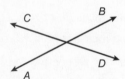

Postulate 5

The shortest line between any two points is a straight line.

Postulate 6

There is a one-to-one correspondence between the real numbers and the points of a line. That is, to every real number, there corresponds exactly one point of the line and to every point of the line there corresponds exactly one real number. (In other words, a line has an infinite number of points between any two distinct points.)

Postulate 7

One and only one perpendicular can be drawn to a given line through any point on that line. Given point O on line $\overleftrightarrow{AB}$, $\overleftrightarrow{OC}$ represents the only perpendicular to $\overleftrightarrow{AB}$ that passes through O.

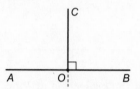

PROBLEM

In the figure below, point B is between points A and C, and point E is between points D and F. Given that $\overline{AB} \cong \overline{DE}$ and $\overline{BC} \cong \overline{EF}$. Prove that $\overline{AC} \cong \overline{DF}$.

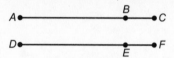

SOLUTION

Two important postulates will be employed in this proof. The Point Betweenness Postulate states that if point Y is between points X and Z, then $XY + YZ = XZ$. Furthermore, the Postulate states that the converse is also true—that is, if $XY + YZ = XZ$, then point Y is between points X and Z.

The Addition Postulate (a universal postulate not listed here) states that equal quantities added to equal quantities yield equal quantities. Thus, if $a = b$ and $c = d$, then $a + c = b + d$.

Given: Point B is between A and C; point E is between points D and F; $\overline{AB} \cong \overline{DE}$; $\overline{BC} \cong \overline{EF}$

Prove: $\overline{AC} \cong \overline{DF}$.

Statement	Reason
1. (For the given, see above)	1. Given.
2. $AB = DE$ $BC = EF$	2. Congruent segments have equal lengths.

3. $AB + BC = DE + EF$ 3. Addition Postulate.
4. $AC = DF$ 4. Point Between Postulate.
5. $\overline{AC} \cong \overline{DF}$ 5. Segments of equal length are congruent.

PROBLEM

Construct a line perpendicular to a given line through a given point on the given line.

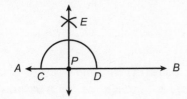

SOLUTION

Let line $\overleftrightarrow{AB}$ and point P be the given line and the given point, respectively.

We notice that $\angle APB$ is a straight angle. A line perpendicular to $\overleftrightarrow{AB}$ from point P will form adjacent congruent right angles with $\overleftrightarrow{AB}$, by the definition of a perpendicular. Since $\angle APB$ is a straight angle, the required perpendicular is the angle bisector of $\angle APB$.

We can complete our construction by bisecting $\angle APB$.

1. Using P as the center and any convenient radius, construct an arc that intersects $\overleftrightarrow{AB}$ at points C and D.

2. With C and D as centers and with a radius greater in length than the one used in Step 1, construct arcs that intersect. The intersection point of these two arcs is point E.

3. Draw $\overleftrightarrow{EP}$.

$\overleftrightarrow{EP}$ is the required angle bisector and, as such, $\overleftrightarrow{EP} \perp \overleftrightarrow{AB}$.

PROBLEM

Present a formal proof of the following conditional statement:

If $\overleftrightarrow{CE}$ bisects $\angle ADB$, and if $\overleftrightarrow{FDB}$ and $\overleftrightarrow{CDE}$ are straight lines, then $\angle a \cong \angle x$. (Refer to the following figure.)

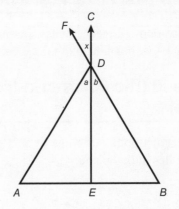

SOLUTION

In this problem, it will be necessary to recognize vertical angles and be knowledgeable of their key properties. Furthermore, we will need the definition of the bisector of an angle.

Vertical angles are two angles that have a common vertex, and whose sides are two pairs of opposite rays. Vertical angles are always congruent.

Lastly, the bisector of any angle divides the angle into two congruent angles.

Statement	**Reason**
1. $\overleftrightarrow{CE}$ bisects $\angle ADB$	1. Given.
2. $\angle a \cong \angle b$	2. A bisector of an angle divides the angle into two congruent angles.
3. $\overleftrightarrow{FDB}$ and $\overleftrightarrow{CDE}$ are straight lines	3. Given.
4. $\angle x$ and $\angle b$ are vertical angles	4. Definition of vertical angles.
5. $\angle b \cong \angle x$	5. Vertical angles are congruent.
6. $\angle a \cong \angle x$	6. Transitivity property of congruence of angles.

Note that Step 3 is essential because without $\overleftrightarrow{FDB}$ and $\overleftrightarrow{CDE}$ being straight lines, the definition of vertical angles would not be applicable to $\angle x$ and $\angle b$.

Postulate 8

The perpendicular bisector of a line segment is unique.

Postulate 9 (The Plane Postulate)

Any three non-collinear points determine one and only one plane that contains those three points.

Postulate 10 (The Points-in-a-Plane Postulate)

If two distinct points of a line lie in a given plane, then the line lies in that plane.

Postulate 11 (Plane Separation Postulate)

Any line in a plane separates the plane into two half planes.

Postulate 12

Given any angle, there exists one and only one real number between 0 and 180 corresponding to it. Note: $m\angle A$ refers to the measurement of angle A.

Postulate 13 (The Angle Sum Postulate)

If A is in the interior of $\angle XYZ$, then
$$m\angle XYZ = m\angle XYA + m\angle AYZ.$$

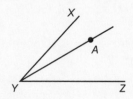

Postulate 14 (The Angle Difference Postulate)

If P is a point exterior to $\angle ABC$ but in the same half-plane (created by edge $\overleftrightarrow{BC}$) as A, then
$$m\angle ABP = m\angle PBC - m\angle ABC.$$

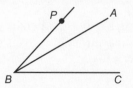

PROBLEM

To construct an angle whose measure is equal to the sum of the measures of two given angles.

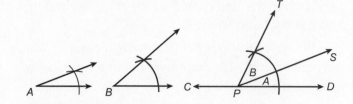

SOLUTION

To construct an angle equal to the sum of the measures of two given angles, we must invoke the theorem that states that the whole is equal to the sum of the parts. The construction, then, will duplicate the given angles in such a way as to form one larger angle equal in measure to the sum of the measures of the two given angles.

The two given angles, $\angle A$ and $\angle B$, are shown in the figure above.

1. Construct any line $\overleftrightarrow{CD}$, and mark a point P on it.

2. At P, using $\overrightarrow{PD}$ as the base, construct $\angle DPS \cong \angle A$.

3. Now, using $\overrightarrow{PS}$ as the base, construct $\angle SPT \cong \angle B$ at point P.

4. $\angle DPT$ is the desired angle, equal in measure to $m\angle A + m\angle B$. This follows because the measure of the whole, $\angle DPT$, is equal to the sum of the measure of the parts, $\angle A$ and $\angle B$.

Theorems

Theorem 1

All right angles are equal.

Theorem 2

All straight angles are equal.

Theorem 3

Supplements of the same or equal angles are themselves equal.

Theorem 4

Complements of the same or equal angles are themselves equal.

Theorem 5

Vertical angles are equal.

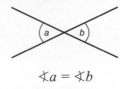

$$\not{a} = \not{b}$$

Theorem 6

Two supplementary angles are right angles if they have the same measure.

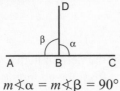

$$m\not\alpha = m\not\beta = 90°$$

Theorem 7

If two lines intersect and form one right angle, then the lines form four right angles.

PROBLEM

Find the measure of the angle whose measure is 40° more than the measure of its supplement.

SOLUTION

By the definition of supplementary angles, the sum of the measures of two supplements must equal 180°. Accordingly,

let x = the measure of the supplement of the angle.

Then $x + 40°$ = the measure of the angle.

Therefore, $x + (x + 40°) = 180°$

$$2x + 40° = 180°$$
$$2x = 140°$$
$$x = 70° \text{ and } x + 40° = 110°.$$

Therefore the measure of the angle is 110°.

PROBLEM

What is the measure of a given angle whose measure is half the measure of its complement?

SOLUTION

When two angles are said to be complementary we know that their measures must sum, by definition, to 90°.

If we let x = the measure of the given angle,

then $2x$ = the measure of its complement.

To determine the measure of the given angle, set the sum of the two angle measures equal to 90 and solve for x. Accordingly,

$$x + 2x = 90°$$
$$3x = 90°$$
$$x = 30°$$

Therefore, the measure of the given angle is 30° and its complement is 60°.

PROBLEM

Given that straight lines $\overleftrightarrow{AB}$ and $\overleftrightarrow{CD}$ intersect at point E, that $\angle BEC$ has measure 20° greater than 5 times a fixed quantity, and that $\angle AED$ has measure 60° greater than 3 times this same quantity: Find a) the unknown fixed quantity, b) the measure of $\angle BEC$, and c) the measure of $\angle CEA$. (For the actual angle placement, refer to the figure below.)

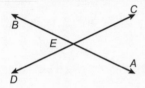

SOLUTION

a) Since $\overleftrightarrow{AB}$ and $\overleftrightarrow{CD}$ are straight lines intersecting at point E, $\angle BEC$ and $\angle AED$ are, by definition, vertical angles. As such, they are congruent and their measures are equal. Therefore, if we let x represent the fixed quantity, $\angle BEC = 5x + 20$ and $\angle AED = 3x + 60$; according to the information given. We can then set up the following equality, and solve for the unknown quantity.

$$5x + 20 = 3x + 60$$
$$5x - 3x = 60 - 20$$
$$2x = 40$$
$$x = 20$$

Therefore, the value of the unknown quantity is 20°.

b) From the information given about $\angle BEC$, we know that $m\angle BEC = (5x + 20)^{\circ}$. By substitution, we have

$$m\angle BEC = 5(20°) + 20° = 100° + 20° = 120°.$$

Therefore, the measure of $\angle BEC$ is 120°.

c) We know that $\overleftrightarrow{AB}$ is a straight line; therefore, $\angle CEA$ is the supplement of $\angle BEC$. Since the sum of the measure of two supplements is 180°, the following calculation can be made:

$$m\angle CEA + m\angle BEC = 180^{\circ}$$
$$m\angle CEA = 180^{\circ} - m\angle BEC,$$

Substituting in our value for $m\angle BEC$, we obtain:

$$m\angle CEA = 180^{\circ} - 120^{\circ} = 60^{\circ}$$

Therefore, the measure of $\angle CEA$ is 60°.

Theorem 8

Any point on the perpendicular bisector of a given line segment is equidistant from the ends of the segment.

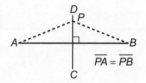

PROBLEM

In the accompanying figure $\overline{SM}$ is the perpendicular bisector of $\overline{QR}$, and $\overline{SN}$ is the perpendicular bisector of $\overline{QP}$. Prove that $SR = SP$.

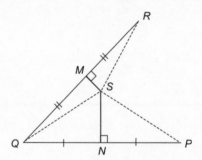

SOLUTION

Every point on the perpendicular bisector of a segment is equidistant from the endpoints of the segment.

Since point S is on the perpendicular bisector of $\overline{QR}$,

$$SR = SQ \qquad (1)$$

Also, since point S is on the perpendicular bisector of $\overline{QP}$,

$$SQ = SP \qquad (2)$$

By the transitive property (quantities equal to the same quantity are equal), we have:

$$SR = SP. \qquad (3)$$

Theorem 9

If a point is equidistant from the ends of a line segment, this point must lie on the perpendicular bisector of the segment.

Theorem 10

If two points are equidistant from the ends of a line segment, these points determine the perpendicular bisector of the segment.

Theorem 11

Every line segment has exactly one midpoint.

Theorem 12

There exists one and only one perpendicular to a line through a point outside the line. Take point C outside line $\overleftrightarrow{AB}$. $\overleftrightarrow{OC}$ represents the only perpendicular to $\overleftrightarrow{AB}$ that passes through C.

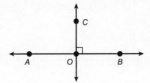

Theorem 13

If the exterior sides of adjacent angles are perpendicular to each other, then the adjacent angles are complementary.

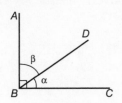

α and β are complementary

Theorem 14

Adjacent angles are supplementary if their exterior sides form a straight line.

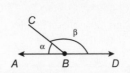

α and β are supplementary

Theorem 15

Two angles that are equal and supplementary to each other are right angles.

Congruent Angles and Congruent Line Segments

Definitions

Definition 1

Two or more geometric figures are congruent when they have the same shape and size. The symbol for congruence is $\cong$; hence, if triangle ABC is congruent to triangle DEF, we write $\triangle ABC \cong \triangle DEF$.

Definition 2

Two line segments are congruent if and only if they have the same measure.

Note: The expression "if and only if" can be used any time both a statement and the converse of that statement are true. Using definition 2, we can rewrite the statement as "two line segments have the same measure if and only if they are congruent." The two statements are identical.

Definition 3

Two angles are congruent if and only if they have the same measure.

PROBLEM

In the figure shown, $\triangle ABC$ is an isosceles triangle, such that $\overline{BA} \cong \overline{BC}$. Line segment $\overline{AD}$ bisects $\sphericalangle BAC$ and $\overline{CD}$ bisects $\sphericalangle BCA$. Prove that $\triangle ADC$ is an isosceles triangle.

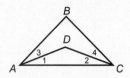

SOLUTION

In order to prove $\triangle ADC$ is isosceles, we must prove that two of its sides, $\overline{AD}$ and $\overline{CD}$, are congruent. To prove $\overline{AD} \cong \overline{CD}$ in $\triangle ADC$, we have to prove that the angles opposite $\overline{AD}$ and $\overline{CD}$, $\sphericalangle 1$ and $\sphericalangle 2$, are congruent.

Statement	Reason
1. $\overline{BA} \cong \overline{BC}$	1. Given.
2. $\sphericalangle BAC \cong \sphericalangle BCA$ or $m \sphericalangle BAC = m \sphericalangle BCA$	2. If two sides of a triangle are congruent, then the angles opposite them are congruent.
3. $\overline{AD} \sphericalangle$ bisects BAC $\overline{CD} \sphericalangle$ bisects BCA	3. Given.
4. $m \sphericalangle 1 = \left(\frac{1}{2}\right) m \sphericalangle BAC$ $m \sphericalangle 2 = \left(\frac{1}{2}\right) m \sphericalangle BCA$	4. The bisector of an angle divides the angle into two angles whose measures are equal.
5. $m \sphericalangle 1 = m \sphericalangle 2$	5. Division Postulate: Halves of equal quantities are equal.
6. $\sphericalangle 1 \cong \sphericalangle 2$	6. If the measure of two angles are equal, then the angles are congruent.
7. $\overline{CD} \cong \overline{AD}$	7. If two angles of a triangle are congruent, then the sides opposite these angles are congruent.
8. $\triangle ADC$ is an isosceles triangle.	8. If a triangle has two congruent sides, then it is an isosceles triangle.

Theorems

Theorem 1

Every line segment is congruent to itself.

Theorem 2

Every angle is congruent to itself.

Theorem 3

Given a line segment $\overline{AB}$ and a ray $\overrightarrow{XY}$, there exists one and only one point O on $\overrightarrow{XY}$ such that $\overline{AB} \cong \overline{XO}$.

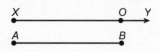

Theorem 4

If $\overline{AB} = \overline{CD}$, Q bisects $\overline{AB}$ and P bisects $\overline{CD}$, then $\overline{AQ} \cong \overline{CP}$ and $AQ = CP$.

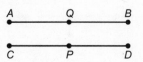

Theorem 5

If $m \sphericalangle ABC = m \sphericalangle DEF$, and $\overrightarrow{BX}$ and $\overrightarrow{EY}$ bisect $\sphericalangle ABC$ and $\sphericalangle DEF$, respectively, then $m \sphericalangle ABX = m \sphericalangle XBC = m \sphericalangle DEY = m \sphericalangle YEF$.

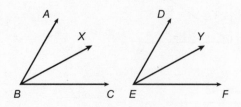

Theorem 6

Let P be in the interior of $\angle ABC$ and Q be in the interior of $\angle DEF$. If $m\angle ABP = m\angle DEQ$ and $m\angle PBC = m\angle QEF$, then $m\angle ABC = m\angle DEF$.

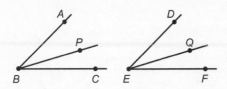

Theorem 7

Let P be in the interior of $\angle XYZ$ and Q be in the interior of $\angle ABC$. If $m\angle XYZ = m\angle ABC$ and $m\angle XYP = m\angle ABQ$ then $m\angle PYZ = m\angle QBC$.

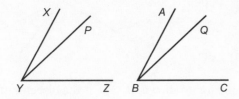

Postulates

By definition, a relation R is called an equivalence relation if relation R is reflexive, symmetric, and transitive.

Let R be a relation on a set A. Then:

R is reflexive if aRa for every a in A.

R is symmetric if aRb implies bRa.

R is transitive if aRb and bRc imply aRc.

Note: The term aRa means the relation R performed on a yields a. The term aRb means the relation R performed on a yields b.

Postulate 1

Congruence of segments is an equivalence relation.

(1) Congruence of segments is reflexive.

If $\overline{AB} \cong \overline{AB}$, $\overline{AB}$ is congruent to itself.

(2) Congruence of segments is symmetric.

If $\overline{AB} \cong \overline{CD}$, then $\overline{CD} \cong \overline{AB}$.

(3) Congruence of segments is transitive.

If $\overline{AB} \cong \overline{CD}$ and $\overline{CD} \cong \overline{EF}$, then $\overline{AB} \cong \overline{EF}$.

Postulate 2

Congruence of angles is an equivalence relation; that is, it is reflexive, symmetric, and transitive.

Postulate 3

Any geometric figure is congruent to itself.

Postulate 4

A geometric congruence may be reversed.

Postulate 5

Two geometric figures congruent to the same geometric figure are congruent to each other.

PROBLEM

Given triangle RST in the figure below, with $\overline{RT} \cong \overline{ST}$. Points A and B lie at the midpoint of $\overline{RT}$ and $\overline{ST}$, respectively. Prove that $\overline{RA} \cong \overline{SB}$.

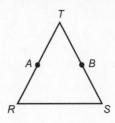

SOLUTION

This solution is best presented as a formal proof.

Statement		Reason
1. $\overline{RT} \cong \overline{ST}$ or $RT = ST$		1. Given.
2. A is the midpoint of $\overline{RT}$		2. Given.
3. $RA = \left(\dfrac{1}{2}\right)RT$		3. The midpoint of a line segment divides the line segment into two equal halves.
4. B is the midpoint of $\overline{ST}$		4. Given.
5. $SB = \left(\dfrac{1}{2}\right)ST$		5. The midpoint of a line segment divides the line segment into two equal halves.
6. $RA = SB$		6. Division Postulate: Halves of equal quantities are equal. (Statements 3 and 5.)
7. $\overline{RA} \cong \overline{SB}$		7. If two line segments are of equal length, then they are congruent.

Drill: Congruent Angles & Line Segments

DIRECTIONS:

Refer to the diagrams and find the appropriate solutions.

1. Find a.

    (A) 38°

    (B) 68°

    (C) 78°

    (D) 90°

2. Find c.

    (A) 32°

    (B) 48°

    (C) 58°

    (D) 82°

3. Determine x.

    (A) 21°

    (B) 23°

    (C) 51°

    (D) 102°

4. Find z.

    (A) 29°

    (B) 54°

    (C) 61°

    (D) 88°

5. In the figure shown, if $\overline{BD}$ is the bisector of angle ABC, and angle ABD is one-fourth the size of angle XYZ, what is the size of angle ABC?

    (A) 21°

    (B) 28°

    (C) 42°

    (D) 63°

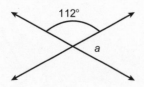

6. $\overrightarrow{BA} \perp \overrightarrow{BC}$ and $m \angle DBC = 53°$. Find $m \angle ABD$.

    (A) 27°

    (B) 33°

    (C) 37°

    (D) 53°

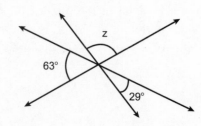

7. If $n \perp p$, which of the following statements is true?

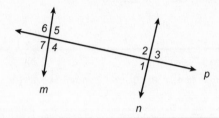

    (A) $\angle 1 \cong \angle 2$

    (B) $\angle 4 \cong \angle 5$

    (C) $m\angle 4 + m\angle 5 > m\angle 1 + m\angle 2$

    (D) $m\angle 3 > m\angle 2$

8. In the figure, if $p \perp t$ and $q \perp t$, which of the following statements is false?

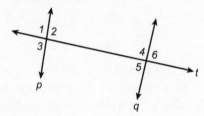

    (A) $\angle 1 \cong \angle 4$

    (B) $m\angle 2 + m\angle 3 = m\angle 4 + m\angle 6$

    (C) $m\angle 5 + m\angle 6 = 180°$

    (D) $m\angle 2 > m\angle 5$

9. If $a \| b$, find z.

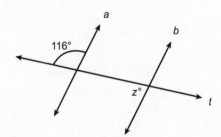

    (A)   26°   (C)   64°

    (B)   32°   (D)   86°

10. If $m \| n$, which of the following statements is not necessarily true?

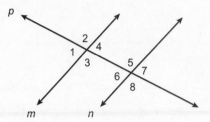

    (A) $\angle 2 \cong \angle 5$

    (B) $\angle 3 \cong \angle 6$

    (C) $m\angle 4 + m\angle 5 = 180°$

    (D) $\angle 1 \cong \angle 6$

Regular Polygons (Convex)

    A **polygon** is a figure with the same number of sides as angles.

    An **equilateral polygon** is a polygon all of whose sides are of equal measure.

    An **equiangular polygon** is a polygon all of whose angles are of equal measure.

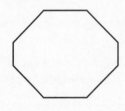

A **regular polygon** is a polygon that is both equilateral and equiangular.

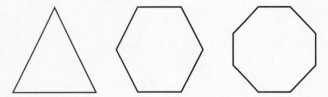

The **perimeter** of a regular polygon is the product of the length of a side(s) and the number of sides (*n*) $P = ns$.

The area of a regular polygon can be determined by using the **apothem** and **radius** of the polygon. The apothem (*a*) of a regular polygon is the segment from the center of the polygon perpendicular to a side of the polygon. The radius (*r*) of a regular polygon is the segment joining any vertex of a regular polygon with the center of that polygon.

(1) All radii of a regular polygon are congruent.

(2) The radius of a regular polygon is congruent to a side.

(3) All apothems of a regular polygon are congruent.

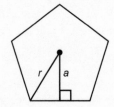

The **area** of a regular polygon equals one-half the product of the length of the apothem and the perimeter.

$$Area = \frac{1}{2}a \times p$$

An **exterior angle** of a regular polygon is formed by extending a side at an **interior angle**.

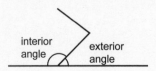

Since the exterior angles of a regular polygon would make one full rotation (360°) if they were all summed together, each exterior angle is

$$\frac{360°}{n}$$

where *n* is the number of sides (or angles) of the polygon.

Each interior angle is a supplement to its exterior angle. Therefore, each interior angle of a regular *n*-sided polygon is:

$$180° - \frac{360°}{n} = \frac{180°n - 360°}{n}$$
$$= \frac{180°(n - 2)}{n}$$

The length of the apothem of a regular hexagon is

$$a = \frac{s}{2}\sqrt{3}$$

where *s* is the length of a side or a radius. This comes from the Pythagorean Theorem and the following diagram, which is true for all regular hexagons.

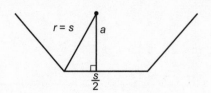

$$s^2 = a^2 + \left(\frac{s}{2}\right)^2$$

$$s^2 = a^2 + \frac{s^2}{4}$$

$$4s^2 = 4a^2 + s^2$$

$$4a^2 = 3s^2$$

$$a = \frac{s}{2}\sqrt{3}$$

PROBLEM

Each interior angle of a regular polygon contains 120°. How many sides does the polygon have?

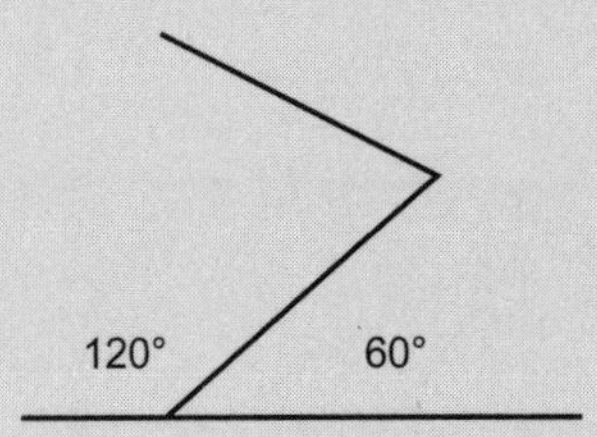

SOLUTION

At each vertex of a polygon, we can draw an exterior angle that is supplementary to the interior angle, as shown in the diagram.

Since we are told that the interior angle measures 120°, we can deduce that the exterior angle measures 60°.

Each exterior angle of a regular polygon of n sides measure $\dfrac{360°}{n}$ degrees. We know that each exterior angle measures 60°, and, therefore, by setting $\dfrac{360°}{n}$ equal to 60°, we can determine the number of sides in the polygon. The calculation is as follows:

$$\frac{360°}{n} = 60°$$

$$60°n = 360°$$

$$n = 6$$

Therefore, the regular polygon, with interior angles of 120°, has six sides and is called a hexagon.

PROBLEM

Find the area of a regular hexagon if one side has length 6.

SOLUTION

Since the length of a side equals 6, the radius also equals 6 and the perimeter equals 36. The base of the right triangle formed by the radius and apothem is half the length of a side, or 3. You can find the length of the apothem by using the Pythagorean Theorem.

$$a^2 + b^2 = c^2$$
$$a^2 + (3)^2 = (6)^2$$
$$a^2 = 36 - 9$$
$$a^2 = 27$$
$$a = 3\sqrt{3}$$

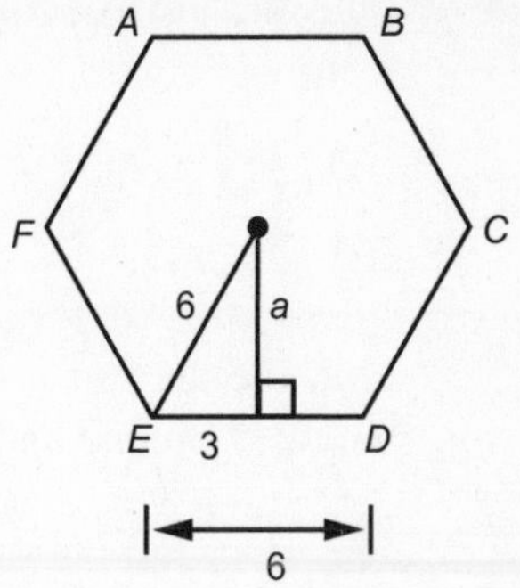

The apothem equals $3\sqrt{3}$. Therefore, the area of the hexagon

$$= \frac{1}{2}a \times p$$
$$= \frac{1}{2}(3\sqrt{3})(36)$$
$$= 54\sqrt{3}$$

Drill: Regular Polygons (Convex)

DIRECTIONS: Find the appropriate solutions.

1. Find the measure of an interior angle of a regular pentagon.

   (A) 55°   (C) 90°

   (B) 72°   (D) 108°

2. Find the sum of the measures of the exterior angles of a regular triangle.

   (A) 90°   (C) 180°

   (B) 115°   (D) 360°

3. A regular triangle has sides of 24 mm. If the apothem is $4\sqrt{3}$ mm, find the area of the triangle.

   (A) 72 mm^2 (C) 144 mm^2

   (B) $96\sqrt{3}$ mm^2 (D) $144\sqrt{3}$ mm^2

4. Find the area of a regular hexagon with sides of 4 cm.

   (A) $12\sqrt{3}$ cm^2 (C) $24\sqrt{3}$ cm^2

   (B) 24 cm^2 (D) 48 cm^2

5. Find the area of a regular decagon with sides of length 6 cm and an apothem of length 9.2 cm.

   (A) 55.2 cm^2 (C) 138 cm^2

   (B) 60 cm^2 (D) 276 cm^2

Similar Polygons

Definition

Two polygons are similar if there is a one-to-one correspondence between their vertices such that all pairs of corresponding angles are congruent and the ratios of the measures of all pairs of corresponding sides are equal. Note that although they must have the same shape, they may have different sizes.

Theorem 1

The perimeters of two similar polygons have the same ratio as the measure of any pair of corresponding line segments of the polygons.

Theorem 2

The ratio of the lengths of two corresponding diagonals of two similar polygons is equal to the ratio of the lengths of any two corresponding sides of the polygons.

Theorem 3

The perimeters of two similar polygons have the same ratio as the measures of any pair of corresponding sides of the polygons.

Theorem 4

Two polygons composed of the same number of triangles similar each to each, and similarly placed, are similar.

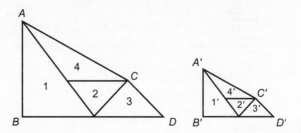

PROBLEM

Prove that any two regular polygons with the same number of sides are similar.

SOLUTION

For any two polygons to be similar, their corresponding angles must be congruent and their corresponding sides proportional. It is necessary to show that these conditions always exist between regular polygons with the same number of sides.

Let us examine the corresponding angles first. For a regular polygon with n sides. Each vertex (interior) angle is $\dfrac{(n-2)180}{n}$. Therefore, two regular polygons with the same number of sides will have corresponding vertex angles that are all of the same measure and, hence, are all congruent. This fulfills our first condition for similarity.

We must now determine whether the corresponding sides are proportional. It will suffice to show that the ratios of the lengths of every pair of corresponding sides are the same.

Since the polygons are regular, the sides of each one will be equal. Call the length of the sides of one polygon ℓ_1 and the length of the sides of the other polygon ℓ_2. Hence, the ratio of the lengths of corresponding sides will be ℓ_1/ℓ_2. This will be a constant for any pair of corresponding sides and, hence, the corresponding sides are proportional.

Thus, any two regular polygons with the same number of sides are similar.

PROBLEM

> The lengths of two corresponding sides of two similar polygons are 4 and 7. If the perimeter of the smaller polygon is 20, find the perimeter of the larger polygon.

SOLUTION

We know, by theorem, that the perimeters of two similar polygons have the same ratio as the measures of any pair of corresponding sides.

If we let s and p represent the side and perimeter of the smaller polygon and s' and p' represent the corresponding side and perimeter of the larger one, we can then write the proportion

$$p : p' = s : s'$$

By substituting the given values, we can solve for p'.

$$20 : p' = 4 : 7$$
$$\frac{20}{p'} = \frac{4}{7}$$
$$4p' = 140$$
$$p' = 35.$$

Therefore, the perimeter of the larger polygon is 35.

Triangles

A closed three-sided geometric figure is called a **triangle**. The points of the intersection of the sides of a triangle are called the **vertices** of the triangle. A side of a triangle is a line segment whose endpoints are the vertices of two angles of the triangle.

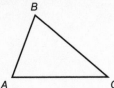

The **perimeter** of a triangle is the sum of the measures of the sides of the triangle.

A triangle with no equal sides is called a **scalene triangle**.

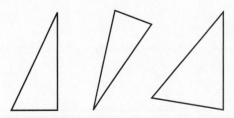

A triangle having at least two equal sides is called an **isosceles triangle**. The third side is called the **base** of the triangle, and the base angles (the angles opposite the equal sides) are equal.

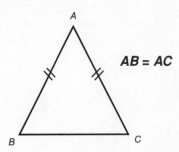

$AB = AC$

An **interior angle** of a triangle is an angle formed by two sides and includes the third side within its collection of points. The sum of the measures of the interior angles of a triangle is 180°.

An **equilateral triangle** is a triangle having three equal sides. $\overline{AB} = \overline{AC} = \overline{BC}$. An equilateral, triangle is also **equiangular**, with each angle equaling 60°.

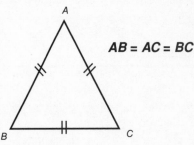

$AB = AC = BC$

A triangle with one obtuse angle (greater than 90°) is called an **obtuse triangle**.

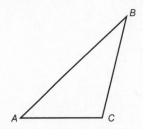

An **acute triangle** is a triangle with three acute angles (less than 90°).

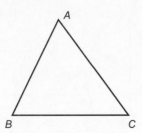

A triangle with a right angle is a **right triangle**. The side opposite the right angle in a right triangle is called the hypotenuse of the right triangle. The other two sides are called arms or legs of the right triangle. By the Pythagorean Theorem, the length of the three sides of a right triangle are related by the formula $c^2 = a^2 + b^2$ where c is the hypotenuse and a and b are the other sides (the legs).

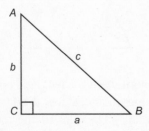

An **altitude** of a triangle is a line segment from a vertex of the triangle perpendicular to the opposite side.

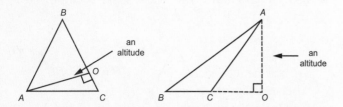

The **area** of a triangle is given by

$$A = \frac{1}{2}bh,$$

where h is the altitude and b is the base to which the altitude is drawn.

A line segment connecting a vertex of a triangle and the midpoint of the opposite side is called a **median** of the triangle.

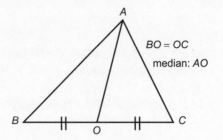

$BO = OC$

median: AO

A line that bisects and is perpendicular to a side of a triangle is called a **perpendicular bisector** of that side.

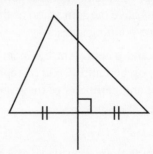

An **angle bisector** of a triangle is a line that bisects an angle and extends to the opposite side of the triangle.

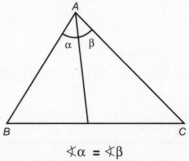

$$\measuredangle\alpha = \measuredangle\beta$$

The line segment that joins the midpoints of two sides of a triangle is called a **midline** of the triangle. The midline equals half of the third side.

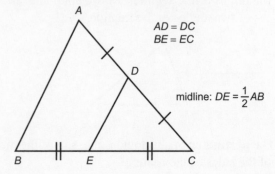

$AD = DC$
$BE = EC$

midline: $DE = \frac{1}{2}AB$

An **exterior angle** of a triangle is an angle formed outside a triangle by one side of the triangle and the extension of an adjacent side.

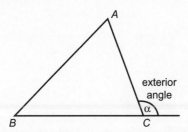

Three or more lines (or rays or segments) are **concurrent** if there exists one point common to all of them, that is, if they all intersect at the one point.

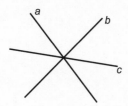

PROBLEM

Calculate the perimeter of the triangle below.

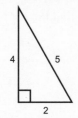

SOLUTION

1. Write the formula for the perimeter of a triangle.

perimeter = length of side 1 + length of side 2 + length of side 3

2. Substitute the known values into the formula.

perimeter = 4 + 2 + 5

3. Solve the equation.

perimeter = 11

The correct answer is that the perimeter of the triangle is 11.

PROBLEM

Calculate the area of the triangle below.

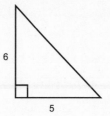

SOLUTION

1. Write the formula for the area of a triangle.

$$A = \frac{1}{2}bh$$

2. Substitute the known values into the formula. The base of the triangle is 5 and the height is 6.

$$A = \frac{1}{2}(5)(6)$$

3. Solve the equation.

$$A = 15$$

The correct answer is that the area of the triangle is 15.

PROBLEM

The measure of the vertex angle of an isosceles triangle exceeds the measurement of each base angle by 30°. Find the value of each angle of the triangle.

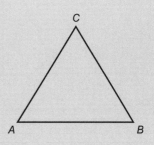

SOLUTION

We known that the sum of the values of the angles of a triangle is 180°. In an isosceles triangle, the angles opposite the congruent sides (the base angles) are, themselves, congruent and of equal value.

Therefore,

(1) Let x = the measure of each base angle.

(2) Then $x + 30$ = the measure of the vertex angle.

We can solve for x algebraically by keeping in mind the sum of all the measures will be 180°.

$$x + x + (x + 30) = 180$$
$$3x + 30 = 180$$
$$3x = 150$$
$$x = 50$$

Therefore, the base angles each measure 50°, and the vertex angle measures 80°.

PROBLEM

Calculate the area of the triangle below.

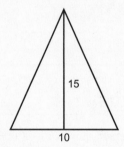

SOLUTION

1. Write the formula for the area of a triangle.

$$A = \frac{1}{2}bh$$

2. Substitute the known values into the formula. The base of the triangle is 10 and the height is 15.

$$A = \frac{1}{2}(10)(15)$$

3. Solve the equation.

$$A = 75$$

The correct answer is that the area of the triangle is 75.

Drill: Triangles

DIRECTIONS: Refer to the diagram and find the appropriate solution.

1. In $\triangle PQR$, $\measuredangle Q$ is a right angle. Find $m\measuredangle R$.

　　(A) 27°　　　　(C) 54°

　　(B) 33°　　　　(D) 67°

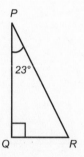

2. $\triangle MNO$ is isosceles. If the vertex angle, $\measuredangle N$, has a measure of 96°, find the measure of $\measuredangle M$.

　　(A) 21°

　　(B) 42°

　　(C) 64°

　　(D) 84°

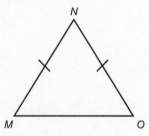

3. Find x.

　　(A) 15°

　　(B) 25°

　　(C) 30°

　　(D) 45°

4. The two triangles shown are similar. Find b.

   (A) $2\frac{2}{3}$

   (B) 3

   (C) 4

   (D) 16

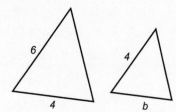

5. The two triangles shown are similar. Find a and b.

   (A) 5 and 10

   (B) 4 and 8

   (C) $4\frac{2}{3}$ and $7\frac{1}{3}$

   (D) $5\frac{1}{3}$ and 8

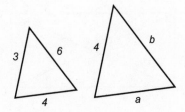

6. Find the area of $\triangle MNO$.

   (A) 22

   (B) 49

   (C) 56

   (D) 84

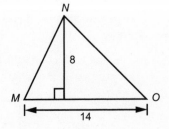

7. Find the area of $\triangle PQR$.

   (A) 31.5

   (B) 38.5

   (C) 53

   (D) 77

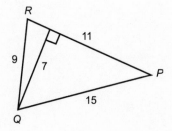

8. Find the area of $\triangle STU$.

   (A) $4\sqrt{2}$

   (B) $8\sqrt{2}$

   (C) $12\sqrt{2}$

   (D) $16\sqrt{2}$

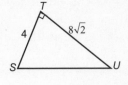

9. Find the area of $\triangle ABC$.

   (A) 54 cm²

   (B) 81 cm²

   (C) 108 cm²

   (D) 135 cm²

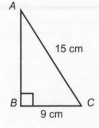

10. Find the area of $\triangle XYZ$.

   (A) 20 cm²

   (B) 50 cm²

   (C) $50\sqrt{2}$ cm²

   (D) 100 cm²

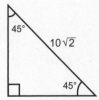

Quadrilaterals

A **quadrilateral** is a polygon with four sides.

Parallelograms

A **parallelogram** is a quadrilateral whose opposite sides are parallel.

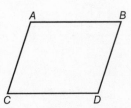

Two angles that have their vertices at the endpoints of the same side of a parallelogram are called **consecutive angles**.

The perpendicular segment connecting any point of a line containing one side of a parallelogram to the line containing the opposite side of the parallelogram is called the **altitude** of the parallelogram.

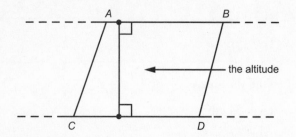

A **diagonal** of a polygon is a line segment joining any two nonconsecutive vertices.

The area of a parallelogram is given by the formula $A = bh$, where b is the base and h is the height drawn perpendicular to that base. Note that the height equals the altitude of the parallelogram.

$A = bh$

$A = (10)(3)$

$A = 30$

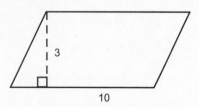

PROBLEM

Calculate the area of the parallelogram below.

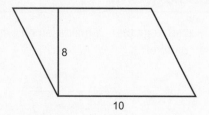

SOLUTION

1. Write the formula for the area of a parallelogram.

   $A = bh$, where b is the base and h is the height.

2. Substitute the known values into the formula.

   $A = 10(8)$

3. Solve the equation.

   $A = 80$

The correct answer is that the area of the parallelogram is 80.

Rectangles

A **rectangle** is a parallelogram with right angles.

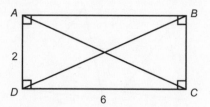

The diagonals of a rectangle are equal.

If the diagonals of a parallelogram are equal, the parallelogram is a rectangle.

If a quadrilateral has four right angles, then it is a rectangle.

The area of a rectangle is given by the formula $A = lw$, where l is the length and w is the width.

$A = lw$

$A = (3)(10)$

$A = 30$

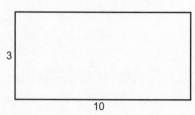

Rhombi

A **rhombus** is a parallelogram that has two adjacent sides that are equal.

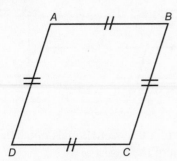

All sides of a rhombus are equal.

The diagonals of a rhombus are perpendicular to each other.

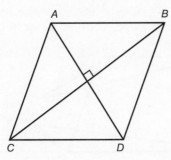

The area of a rhombus can be found by the formula $A = \frac{1}{2}(d_1 \times d_2)$ where d_1 and d_2 are the diagonals.

The diagonals of a rhombus bisect the angles of the rhombus.

If the diagonals of a parallelogram are perpendicular, the parallelogram is a rhombus.

If a quadrilateral has four equal sides, then it is a rhombus.

A parallelogram is a rhombus if either diagonal of the parallelogram bisects the angles of the vertices it joins.

PROBLEM

Calculate the area of the rhombus below.

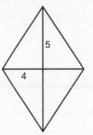

SOLUTION

1. Write the formula for the area of a rhombus.

$A = \frac{1}{2}(d_1 d_2)$, where d_1 and d_2 are the diagonals of the rhombus.

2. Substitute the known values into the formula.

$$A = \frac{1}{2}(5)(4)$$

3. Solve the equation.

$$A = 10$$

The correct answer is that the area of the rhombus is 10.

Squares

A **square** is a rhombus with a right angle.

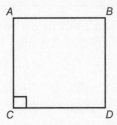

A square is an equilateral quadrilateral.

A square has all the properties of parallelograms and rectangles.

A rhombus is a square if one of its interior angles is a right angle.

In a square, the measure of either diagonal can be calculated by multiplying the length of any side by the square root of 2.

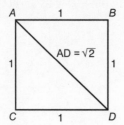

The area of a square is given by the formula $A = s^2$, where s is the side of the square. Since all sides of a square are equal, it does not matter which side is used.

$A = s^2$

$A = 6^2$

$A = 36$

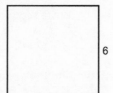

The area of a square can also be found by taking $\frac{1}{2}$ the product of the length of the diagonal squared.

$A = \frac{1}{2}d^2$

$A = \frac{1}{2}(8)^2$

$A = 32$

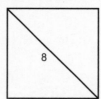

Trapezoids

A **trapezoid** is a quadrilateral with two and only two sides parallel. The parallel sides of a trapezoid are called **bases**.

The **median** of a trapezoid is the line joining the midpoints of the non-parallel sides.

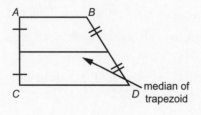

The perpendicular segment connecting any point in the line containing one base of the trapezoid to the line containing the other base is the **altitude** of the trapezoid.

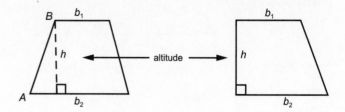

The area of a trapezoid equals one half the altitude times the sum of the bases, or

$$A = \frac{1}{2}h(b_1 + b_2).$$

An **isosceles trapezoid** is a trapezoid whose non-parallel sides are equal. A pair of angles including only one of the parallel sides is called a pair of base angles.

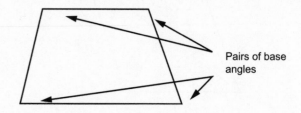

Pairs of base angles

The median of a trapezoid is parallel to the bases and equal to one-half their sum.

The base angles of an isosceles trapezoid are equal.

The diagonals of an isosceles trapezoid are equal.

The opposite angles of an isosceles trapezoid are supplementary.

PROBLEM

Calculate the area of the trapezoid below.

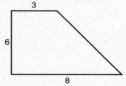

SOLUTION

1. Write the formula for the area of a trapezoid.

$A = \frac{1}{2}h(b_1 + b_2)$, where b_1 and b_2 are the bases and h is the height.

2. Substitute the known values into the formula.

$A = \frac{1}{2}(6)(3 + 8)$

3. Solve the equation.

$A = 33$

The correct answer is that the area of the trapezoid is 33.

Drill: Quadrilaterals

DIRECTIONS: Refer to the diagram and find the appropriate solution.

1. Quadrilateral *ABCD* is a parallelogram. If $m\angle B = (6x + 2)°$ and $m\angle D = 98°$, find *x*.

   (A) 12
   (B) 16
   (C) $16\frac{2}{3}$
   (D) 18

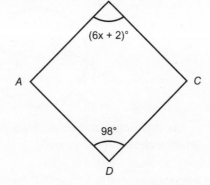

2. Find the area of parallelogram *STUV*.

   (A) 56
   (B) 90
   (C) 108
   (D) 162

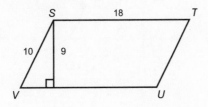

3. In rectangle *ABCD*, $\overline{AD} = 6$ cm and $\overline{DC} = 8$ cm. Find the length of the diagonal $\overline{AC}$.

   (A) 10 cm   (C) 20 cm
   (B) 12 cm   (D) 28 cm

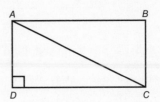

4. Find the area of rectangle *UVXY*.

   (A) 17 cm²
   (B) 34 cm²
   (C) 35 cm²
   (D) 70 cm²

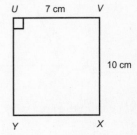

5. Find the length of $\overline{BO}$ in rectangle *BCDE* if the diagonal $\overline{EC}$ is 17 mm.

   (A) 6.55 mm
   (B) 8 mm
   (C) 8.5 mm
   (D) 17 mm

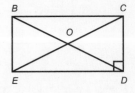

6. In rhombus *GHIJ*, $\overline{GI} = 6$ cm and $\overline{HJ} = 8$ cm. Find the length of $\overline{GH}$.

   (A) 3 cm
   (B) 4 cm
   (C) 5 cm
   (D) $4\sqrt{3}$ cm

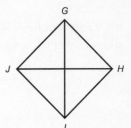

7. Find the area of the trapezoid *RSTU*.

(A) 80 cm²

(B) 87.5 cm²

(C) 140 cm²

(D) 175 cm²

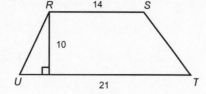

8. *ABCD* is an isosceles trapezoid. Find the perimeter.

(A) 21 cm (C) 30 cm

(B) 27 cm (D) 50 cm

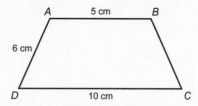

9. Find the area of trapezoid *MNOP*.

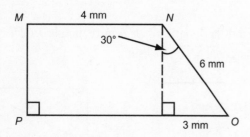

(A) $(17 + 3\sqrt{3})\,\text{mm}^2$ (C) $\dfrac{33\sqrt{3}}{2}\,\text{mm}^2$

(B) $\dfrac{33}{2}\,\text{mm}^2$ (D) 33 mm²

10. Trapezoid *XYZW* is isosceles. If $m\angle W = 58°$ and $m\angle Z = (4x - 6)°$, find *x*.

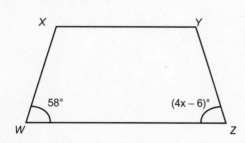

(A) 8 (C) 13

(B) 12 (D) 16

Circles

A **circle** is a set of points in the same plane equidistant from a fixed point, called its **center**. Circles are often named by their center point, such as circle *O*.

A **radius** of a circle is a line segment drawn from the center of the circle to any point on the circle.

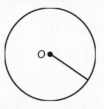

A portion of a circle is called an **arc** of the circle, designated $\overparen{AB}$.

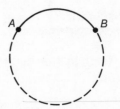

A line that intersects a circle in two points is called a **secant**.

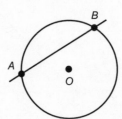

A line segment joining two points on a circle is called a **chord** of the circle.

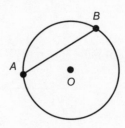

A chord that passes through the center of the circle is called a **diameter** of the circle.

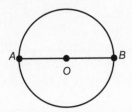

The line passing through the centers of two (or more) circles is called the **line of centers**.

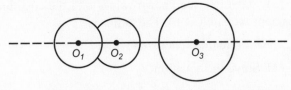

An angle whose vertex is on the circle and whose sides are chords of the circle is called an **inscribed angle** ($\angle$ BAC in the diagrams).

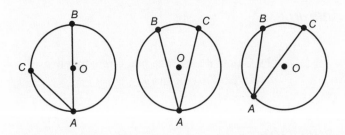

An angle whose vertex is at the center of a circle and whose sides are radii is called a **central angle**.

The measure of a minor arc is the measure of the central angle that intercepts that arc.

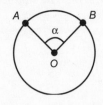

$$m\widehat{AB} = \alpha = m\angle AOB$$

The distance from a point P to a given circle is the distance from that point to the point where the circle intersects with a line segment with endpoints at the center of the circle and point P.

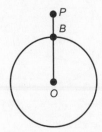

The distance of point P to the diagrammed circle with center O is the line segment $\overline{PB}$.

A line that has one and only one point of intersection with a circle is called a tangent to that circle. This point is called a **point of tangency**. In the diagram, Q and P are each points of tangency.

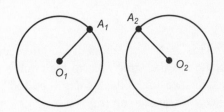

Congruent circles are circles whose radii are congruent.

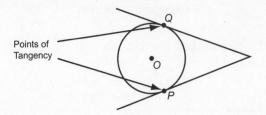

If $O_1A_1 \cong O_2A_2$, then $O_1 \cong O_2$.

The measure of a semicircle is 180°.

A **circumscribed circle** is a circle passing through all the vertices of a polygon. The polygon is said to be **inscribed** in the circle.

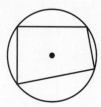

Circles that have the same center and unequal radii are called **concentric circles**.

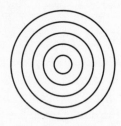

Concentric Circles

The **circumference** of a circle is the length of its outer edge, given by

$$C = \pi d = 2\pi r,$$

where r is the radius, d is the diameter, and π (pi) is a mathematical constant approximately equal to 3.14.

The **area** of a circle is given by

$$A = \pi r^2.$$

A full circle is 360°. The length of arc intercepted by a central angle has the same ratio to the circle's circumference as the measure of the arc has to be 360°, the full circle. Therefore, arc length is given by

$$\frac{n}{360} \times 2\pi r,$$

where n = measure of the central angle. The measure of an arc in degrees, however, is the same as the measure of its central angle.

A sector is the portion of a circle between two radii. Its area is given by

$$A = \frac{n}{360}(\pi r^2)$$

where n is the central angle formed by the radii.

PROBLEM

(1) Calculate the circumference of a circle that has a radius of 12 inches.

SOLUTION

(2) Write the formula for the circumference of a circle.

$$\text{circumference} = 2\pi r$$

(3) Substitute the known values into the equation. Pi is approximately 3.14. The radius is 12.

$$\text{circumference} = 2(3.14)12$$

(4) Solve the equation.

$$\text{circumference} = 75.4$$

The correct answer is that the circumference = 75.4 inches.

PROBLEM

(1) Calculate the area of a circle that has a diameter of 10 meters.

SOLUTION

(2) Write the formula for the area of a circle.

$$A = \pi r^2.$$

(3) Substitute the known values into the equation. Pi is approximately 3.14. The diameter of the circle is 10 meters, so the radius is 5 meters.

$$A = \pi(5)^2$$

(4) Solve the equation.

$$A = 78.5$$

The correct answer is that the area of the circle is 78.5 m^2.

PROBLEM

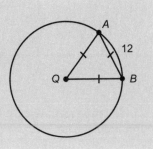

A and *B* are points on circle *Q* such that $\triangle AQB$ is equilateral. If the length of side $\overline{AB} = 12$, find the length of arc *AB*.

SOLUTION

To find the length of arc *AB*, we must find the measure of the central angle $\angle AQB$ and the measure of the radius $\overline{QA}$. $\angle AQB$ is an interior angle of the equilateral triangle $\triangle AQB$. Therefore,

$$m\angle AQB = 60°.$$

Similarly, in the equilateral $\triangle AQB$,

$$\overline{AQ} = \overline{AB} = \overline{QB} = 12.$$

Given the radius, *r*, and the central angle, *n*, the arc length is given by

$$\frac{n}{360} \times 2\pi r.$$

Therefore, by substitution,

$$\widehat{AB} = \frac{60}{360} \times 2\pi \times 12 = \frac{1}{6} \times 2\pi \times 12 = 4\pi.$$

Drill: Circles

DIRECTIONS: Determine the accurate measure.

1. Find the circumference of circle *A* if its radius is 3 mm.

    (A) 3π mm   (C) 9π mm

    (B) 6π mm   (D) 12π mm

2. Find the area of circle *I*.

    (A) 22 mm²

    (B) 121 mm²

    (C) 121π mm²

    (D) 132 mm²

3. The diameter of circle *Z* is 27 mm. Find the area of the circle.

    (A) 91.125 mm²   (C) 191.5π mm²

    (B) 182.25 mm²   (D) 182.25π mm²

4. The area of circle *B* is 225π cm². Find the length of the diameter of the circle.

    (A) 15 cm   (C) 30 cm

    (B) 20 cm   (D) 20π cm

5. The area of circle *X* is 144π mm² while the area of circle *Y* is 81π mm². Write the ratio of the radius of circle *X* to that of circle *Y*.

    (A) 3 : 4   (C) 9 : 12

    (B) 4 : 3   (D) 27 : 12

6. The radius of the smaller of two concentric circles is 5 cm while the radius of the larger circle is 7 cm. Determine the area of the shaded region.

    (A) 7π cm²

    (B) 24π cm²

    (C) 25π cm²

    (D) 36π cm²

    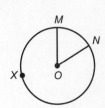

7. Find the measure of $\widehat{MN}$ if $m\angle MON = 62°$.

    (A) 16°

    (B) 32°

    (C) 59°

    (D) 62°

8. Find the measure of $\overset{\frown}{AXC}$.

    (A) 150°

    (B) 160°

    (C) 180°

    (D) 270°

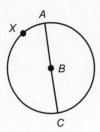

9. Find the measure of $\overset{\frown}{XY}$ in circle W.

    (A) 40°

    (B) 120°

    (C) 140°

    (D) 180°

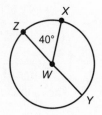

10. Find the area of the sector shown.

    (A) 4 cm²

    (B) 2π cm²

    (C) 16 cm²

    (D) 8π cm²

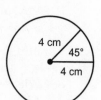

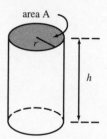

The volume of a right circular cylinder with radius r and height h is

$$V = \pi r^2 h.$$

The surface area of a right circular cylinder with radius r and height h is

$$A = 2\pi r^2 + 2\pi rh.$$

Intersecting Planes

If two different planes intersect, they intersect in a straight line.

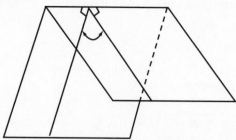

The angle between two planes is the angle between two rays on the two planes, each of which is perpendicular to the line of intersection of the planes.

Volume and Surface Area

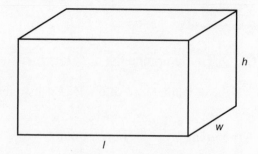

Rectangular solid

The volume of a rectangular solid with length l, width w, and height h is

$$V = lwh.$$

Solid Geometry

Cubes, Cylinders

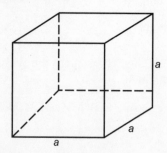

The volume of a cube with edge a is

$$V = a^3.$$

The surface area of a cube with edge a is

$$A = 6a^2.$$

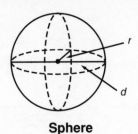

Sphere

The volume of a sphere with radius r is

$$V = \frac{4}{3}\pi r^3.$$

The surface area of a sphere with radius r is

$$A = 4\pi r^2.$$

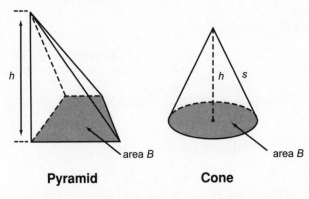

Pyramid   **Cone**

The volume of a pyramid or cone with base area B and height h is

$$V = \frac{1}{3}Bh.$$

If the base of the cone is a circle with radius r, then the base area is $A = \pi r^2$, so

$$V = \frac{1}{3}\pi r^2 h$$

The total area of a cone is the sum of the surface area of the conical part (πrs), where s is the slant height, plus the area of the circular base, so

$$A = \pi rs + \pi r^2.$$

PROBLEM

Calculate the volume of a sphere that has a radius of 2 meters.

SOLUTION

1. Write the formula for the volume of a sphere.

$$V = \frac{4}{3}\pi r^3$$

2. Substitute the known values into the equation. Pi is approximately 3.14 and the radius is 2 meters.

$$V = \frac{4}{3}\pi(2)^3 = \frac{4}{3}(3.14)(8)$$

3. Solve the equation.

$$V = 33.49 \text{ or } \sim 33.5$$

The correct answer is that the volume of the sphere is 33.5 m³.

PROBLEM

Calculate the volume of the rectangular solid that has a length of 5, a height of 1.5, and a width of 4.

SOLUTION

1. Write the formula for the volume of a rectangular solid.

$$V = l \times w \times h$$

2. Substitute the known values into the formula.

$$V = 5 \times 4 \times 1.5$$

3. Solve the equation.

$$V = 30$$

The correct answer is that the volume of the rectangular solid is 30.

PROBLEM

Calculate the volume of a pyramid that has a height of 3 feet. The area of the base of the pyramid was calculated to be 15 square feet.

SOLUTION

1. Write the formula for the volume of a pyramid.

$V = \frac{1}{3}Bh$, where B is the area of the base of the pyramid and h is the height.

2. Substitute the known values into the formula.

$$V = \frac{1}{3}(15)(3)$$

3. Solve the equation.

$$V = 15$$

The correct answer is that the volume of the pyramid is 15 cubic feet.

PROBLEM

Calculate the volume of the cone below.

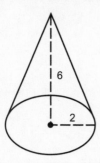

SOLUTION

1. Write the formula for the volume of a cone.

$$V = \frac{1}{3}\pi r^2 h$$

2. Substitute the known values into the equation.

$$V = \frac{1}{3}\pi(2)^2(6)$$

3. Solve the equation.

$$V = 25.12$$

The correct answer is that the volume of the cone is 25.12.

PROBLEM

Calculate the volume of the cylinder below.

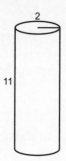

SOLUTION

1. Write the formula for the volume of a cylinder.

$$V = \pi r^2 h$$

2. Substitute the known values into the formula.

$$V = \pi(2)^2(11)$$

3. Solve the equation.

$$V = 138.16$$

The correct answer is that the volume is 138.16.

PROBLEM

Calculate the total area of the cone below. Round to the nearest meter.

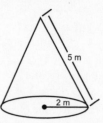

SOLUTION

1. Write the formula for the total area of a cone.

$A = \pi rs + \pi r^2$, where s is the slant height and r is the radius of the base.

2. Substitute the known values into the formula.

$$A = \pi(2)(5) + \pi(2)^2$$

3. Solve the equation.

$$A = 10\pi + 4\pi = 14\pi$$

$$A = 44$$

The correct answer is 44 m².

Coordinate Geometry

Coordinate geometry refers to the study of geometric figures using algebraic principles.

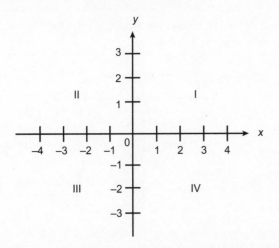

The graph shown is called the Cartesian coordinate plane. The graph consists of a pair of perpendicular lines called **coordinate axes**. The **vertical axis** is the *y*-axis and the **horizontal axis** is the *x*-axis. The point of intersection of these two axes is called the **origin**; it is the zero point of both axes. Furthermore, points to the right of the origin on the *x*-axis and above the origin on the *y*-axis represent positive real numbers. Points to the left of the origin on the *x*-axis or below the origin on the *y*-axis represent negative real numbers.

The four regions cut off by the coordinate axes are, in counterclockwise direction from the top right, called the first, second, third, and fourth quadrants, respectively. The first quadrant contains all points with two positive coordinates.

To plot a point on the graph when given the coordinates, draw perpendicular lines from the number-line coordinates to the point where the two lines intersect.

To find the coordinates of a given point on the graph, draw perpendicular lines from the point to the coordinates on the number line. The *x*-coordinate, or **abscissa**, is written before the *y*-coordinate or **ordinate**, and a comma is used to separate the two.

In the graph below, two points *A* and *B* are shown. In this case, point *A* has the coordinates (4, 2) and the coordinates of point *B* are (–3, –5).

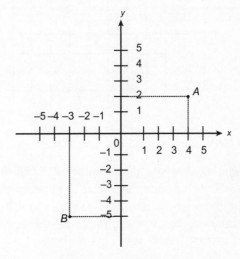

For any two points *A* and *B* with coordinates (x_A, y_A) and (x_B, y_B), respectively, the distance between *A* and *B* is represented by:

$$d = \sqrt{(x_A - x_B)^2 + (y_A - y_B)^2}$$

This is commonly known as the **distance formula**.

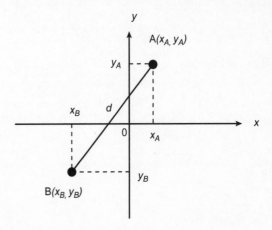

PROBLEM

Find the distance between points $A(1, 3)$ and $B(5, 3)$.

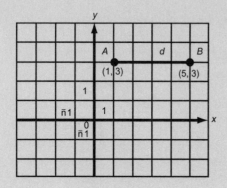

SOLUTION

In this case, where the ordinate (x coordinate) of both points is the same, the distance between the two points is given by the absolute value of the difference between the two abscissas. In fact, this case reduces to merely counting boxes, as the figure shows.

Let, x_1 = abscissa of A y_1 = ordinate of A

x_2 = abscissa of B y_2 = ordinate of B

d = the distance

Therefore, $d = |x_1 - x_2|$. By substitution, $d = |1 - 5| = |-4| = 4$. This answer can also be obtained by applying the general formula for distance between any two points.

$$d = \sqrt{(x_1 - x_2)^2 + (y_1 - y_2)^2}$$

By substitution,

$$d = \sqrt{(1 - 5)^2 + (3 - 3)^2}$$

$$= \sqrt{(-4)^2 + (0)^2}$$

$$= \sqrt{16}$$

$$= 4$$

The distance is 4.

To find the midpoint of a segment between the two given endpoints, use the formula

$$MP = \left(\frac{x_1 + x_2}{2}, \frac{y_1 + y_2}{2}\right)$$

where x_1 and y_1 are the coordinates of one point, and x_2 and y_2 are the coordinates of the other point.

Conic Sections

Conic sections are the curves formed when a plane intersects the surface of a right circular cone. As shown below, these curves are the circle, the ellipse, the parabola, and the hyperbola.

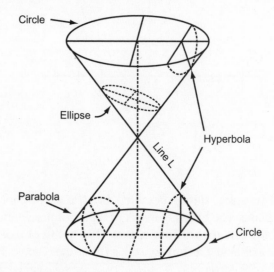

The Circle

As stated previously, a circle is defined to be the set of all points at a given distance from a given point. The given distance is called the radius, and the given point is called the center of the circle. Using the distance formula, we can establish that an equation of a circle with center of (h,k) and radius of r is

$$(x - h)^2 + (y - k)^2 = r^2$$

An equation of this kind is said to be in **standard form**. The following two examples illustrate the practicality of the standard form.

• **EXAMPLES**

1. Find an equation of the circle with center of (2,–3) with radius of 6.

$$(x - 2)^2 + [y - (-3)]^2 = 6^2$$
$$(x - 2)^2 + (y + 3)^2 = 36$$

2. Graph the equation listed below.

$$x^2 + y^2 - 6x + 10y + 30 = 0$$
$$(x^2 - 6x) + (y^2 + 10y) = -30$$

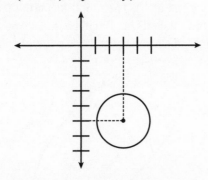

Use the method of completing the squares,

$$(x^2 - 6x + 9) + (y^2 + 10y + 25) = -30 + 9 + 25$$
$$(x - 3)^2 + (y + 5)^2 = 4$$

Notice, in the second example, how easy it is to graph

$$(x - 3)^2 + (y + 5)^2 = 4$$

because it is in standard form, which says it is a circle with center at (3, –5) and radius of 2, and how difficult it would be to graph

$$x^2 + y^2 - 6x + 10y + 30 = 0$$

in that form.

3. Write equations of the following circles:

(a) With center at (–1, 3) and radius 9.

(b) With center at (2, –3) and radius 5.

The equation of the circles with center at (a, b) and radius r is

$$(x - a)^2 + (y - b)^2 = r^2.$$

(a) Thus, the equation of the circle with center at (–1, 3) and radius 9 is

$$[x - (-1)]^2 + (y - 3)^2 = 9^2$$
$$(x + 1)^2 + (y - 3)^2 = 81$$

(b) Similarly the equation of the circle with center at (2,–3) and radius 5 is

$$(x - 2)^2 + [y - (-3)]^2 = 5^2$$
$$(x - 2)^2 + (y + 3)^2 = 25$$

PROBLEM

Find the center and radius of the circle.

$$x^2 - 4x + y^2 + 8y - 5 = 0 \qquad (1)$$

SOLUTION

We can find the radius and the coordinates of the center by completing the squares in both x and y. To complete the square in either variable, take half the coefficient of the variable term (i.e., the x term or the y term) and then square this value. The resulting number is then added to both sides of the equation. Completing the square in x:

$$\left[\frac{1}{2}(-4)\right]^2 = [-2]^2 = 4$$

Then equation (1) becomes:

$$(x^2 - 4x + 4) + y^2 + 8y = 5 + 4.$$

or

$$(x - 2)^2 + y^2 + 8y = 5 + 4 \qquad (2)$$

Note that we have also added 5 to both sides of equation (1):

$$(x - 2)^2 + y^2 + 8y = 9 \qquad (3)$$

Now, to complete the square in y:

$$\left[\frac{1}{2}(8)\right]^2 = [4]^2 = 16$$

Then equation (3) becomes:

$$(x - 2)^2 + (y^2 + 8y + 16) = 9 + 16,$$

or

$$(x - 2)^2 + (y + 4)^2 = 25 \qquad (4)$$

Note that the equation of a circle is:

$$(x - h)^2 + (y - k)^2 = r^2,$$

where (h, k) is the center of the circle and r is the radius of the circle. Equation (4) is in the form of the equation of a circle. Hence, equation (4) represents a circle with center $(2, -4)$ and radius = 5.

PROBLEM

> Find the equation of the circle of radius $r = 9$, with center on the line $y = x$ and tangent to both coordinate axes.

SOLUTION

As seen in the figure below, there are two such circles, O and O'. Let the centers of O and O' be (a, b) and (c, d), respectively.

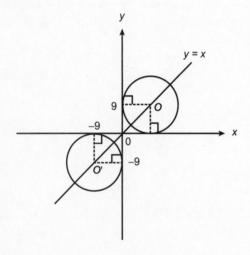

Since points (a, b) and (c, d) are on the line $y = x$, we have $a = b$ and $c = d$.

The equations will be

$$(x - a)^2 + (y - a)^2 = 9^2$$

and $(x - c)^2 + (y - c)^2 = 9^2$

Because the circles are tangent to both coordinate axes, we obtain $a = 9 = b$ and $c = -9 = d$ (see figure). Therefore, the equations are

$$(x - 9)^2 + (y - 9)^2 = 81 \text{ and}$$

$$(x + 9)^2 + (y + 9)^2 = 81.$$

The Ellipse

An **ellipse** is defined to be the set of all points in a plane, the sum of whose distance from two fixed points is a constant. Each of the fixed points is called a **focus**. The plural of the word focus is foci. A simple method of constructing an ellipse comes directly from this definition. Mark two of the foci and call them F_1 and F_2, then insert a thumb tack at each focus. Next, take a string that is longer than the distance between F_1 and F_2 and tie one end at F_1 and the other end at F_2. Then, pull the string taut with a pencil and trace the ellipse. It will be oval shaped and will have two lines of symmetry and one point of symmetry.

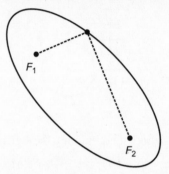

Using the distance formula, we can derive an equation of the ellipse with foci at $(c, 0)$ and $(-c, 0)$ with the sum of the distances of any point on the ellipse to the two foci being of $2a$. The standard equation of such an ellipse is

$$\frac{x^2}{a^2} + \frac{y^2}{b^2} = 1,$$

where $b^2 = a^2 - c^2$. Therefore, $a^2 > b^2$. Here is a graph of such an ellipse.

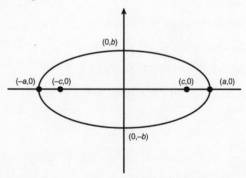

The center of the ellipse is the point midway between the foci. In this case, the center is at the origin. The segment from $(-a, 0)$ to $(a, 0)$ is called the major axis, and its length is $2a$. The segment from

(0,–b) to (0, b) is called the minor axis, and its length is 2b. In the ellipse, the x-axis and the y-axis are lines of symmetry, and the origin is a point of symmetry. The **eccentricity** e of an ellipse is defined to be $\frac{c}{a}$. When this ratio is close to 0, the ellipse resembles a circle, but when this ratio is close to 1, the ellipse is elongated.

We can graph an ellipse when the standard equation is given. In most cases, it is desirable to convert the equation to that form. This process is illustrated in the example below.

• **EXAMPLE**

Graph

$$9x^2 + 16y^2 = 144$$

To convert this equation to the standard form, divide all terms by the constant.

$$9x^2 + 16y^2 = 144$$

$$\frac{9x^2}{144} + \frac{16y^2}{144} = \frac{144}{144}$$

$$\frac{x^2}{16} + \frac{y^2}{9} = 1$$

$$\frac{x^2}{4^2} + \frac{y^2}{3^2} = 1$$

The graph is shown below

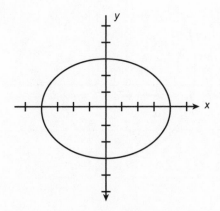

For an ellipse with foci at (0, c) and (0, –c), which means the major axis is vertical, and with the sum of distances as 2a, the standard equation is

$$\frac{y^2}{a^2} + \frac{x^2}{b^2} = 1$$

The following table illustrates what happens when the center of the ellipse is not at the origin.

Center of ellipse	Sum of distances	Foci	Standard equation
(h, k)	$2a$	$(h+c, k)$ and $(h-c, k)$	$\dfrac{(x-h)^2}{a^2} + \dfrac{(y-k)^2}{b^2} = 1$
(h, k)	$2a$	$(h, k+c)$ and $(h, k-c)$	$\dfrac{(y-k)^2}{a^2} + \dfrac{(x-h)^2}{b^2} = 1$

In both cases, $b^2 = a^2 - c^2$.

PROBLEM

Discuss the graph of $\dfrac{x^2}{25} + \dfrac{y^2}{9} = 1$.

SOLUTION

Since this is an equation of the form $\dfrac{x^2}{a^2} + \dfrac{y^2}{b^2} = 1$, with $a = 5$ and $b = 3$, it represents an ellipse. The simplest way to sketch the curve is to find its intercepts.

If we set $x = 0$, then

$$y = \sqrt{\left(1 - \frac{x^2}{25}\right)9} = \sqrt{\left(1 - \frac{0^2}{25}\right)9} = \pm3$$

so that the y-intercepts are at (0,3) and (0,–3). Similarly the x-intercepts are found by setting $y = 0$:

$$x = \sqrt{\left(1 - \frac{y^2}{9}\right)25}$$

$$= \sqrt{\left(1 - \frac{0^2}{9}\right)25}$$

$$= \pm5$$

so that the x-intercepts are at $(5, 0)$ and $(-5, 0)$.

We can now sketch the ellipse.

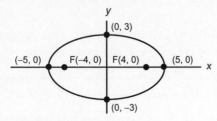

To locate the foci we note that

$$c^2 = a^2 - b^2 = 5^2 - 3^2$$

$$c^2 = 25 - 9 = 16$$

$$c = \pm 4.$$

The foci lie on the major axis of the ellipse. In this case it is the x-axis since $a = 5$ is greater than $b = 3$. Therefore, the foci are $(\pm c, 0)$, that is, at $(-4, 0)$ and $(4, 0)$. The sum of the distances from any point on the curve to the foci is $2a = 2(5) = 10$.

PROBLEM

In the equation of an ellipse,
$$4x^2 + 9y^2 - 16x + 18y - 11 = 0,$$
determine the standard form of the equation, and find the values of a, b, c, and e.

SOLUTION

By completing the squares, we can arrive at the standard form of the equation, from which the values of the parameters can be determined. Thus,

$$4(x^2 - 4x + 4) + 9(y^2 + 2y + 1) = 36.$$

or

$$4(x - 2)^2 + 9(y + 1)^2 = 36. \text{ Dividing by 36,}$$

$$\frac{(x - 2)^2}{9} + \frac{(y + 1)^2}{4} = 1.$$

Thus, the center of the ellipse is at $(2, -1)$. Comparing this equation with the general form,

$$\frac{x^2}{a^2} + \frac{y^2}{b^2} = 1, \text{ where } a > b, \text{ we see that}$$

$$a = 3, b = 2, \text{ and}$$

$$c = \sqrt{a^2 - b^2} = \sqrt{5}.$$

Finally, $e = \dfrac{c}{a} = \dfrac{\sqrt{5}}{3} \approx 0.745$.

A sketch of this ellipse is shown below.

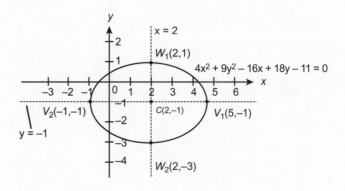

PROBLEM

Find the equation of the ellipse that has vertices V_1 $(-2, 6)$, V_2 $(-2, -4)$, and foci F_1 $(-2, 4)$, F_2 $(-2, -2)$. (See figure.)

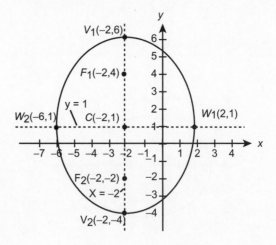

SOLUTION

Since the vertices and foci are on the line $x = -2$, the major axis is on the line $x = -2$. The center has $x = -2$, and the y value is half the difference between the vertices, or $\frac{1}{2}(|6| - |-4|) = \frac{1}{2}(10) = 5$ units from either vertex, so the center is at $(-2, 1)$. a, the length of the semimajor axis, equals the difference between the y-coordinates of V_1 (say) and the center, so $a = 5$. From the coordinates of the foci, $c = 3$. Since $b^2 = a^2 - c^2$, $b = \sqrt{25 - 9} = 4$, and the ends of the minor axis, on $y = 1$, are at $W_1 (2, 1)$ and $W_2 (-6, 1)$. The equation can now be written, in the form

$$\frac{(y - k)^2}{a^2} + \frac{(x - h)^2}{b^2} = 1$$

as $\quad \dfrac{(y - 1)^2}{25} + \dfrac{(x + 2)^2}{16} = 1.$

Geometry Review Answer Key

**Drill: Congruent Angles &
Line Segments**

1. (B) 6. (C)
2. (A) 7. (A)
3. (C) 8. (D)
4. (D) 9. (C)
5. (C) 10. (B)

Drill: Regular Polygons (Convex)

1. (D) 4. (C)
2. (D) 5. (D)
3. (D)

Drill: Triangles

1. (D) 6. (C)
2. (B) 7. (B)
3. (C) 8. (D)
4. (A) 9. (A)
5. (D) 10. (B)

Drill: Quadrilaterals

1. (B) 6. (C)
2. (D) 7. (D)
3. (A) 8. (B)
4. (D) 9. (C)
5. (C) 10. (D)

Drill: Circles

1. (B) 6. (B)
2. (C) 7. (D)
3. (D) 8. (C)
4. (C) 9. (C)
5. (B) 10. (B)

Detailed Explanations of Answers

1. (B)

The two marked angles are adjacent and form a straight line. Therefore, they are supplementary, which means they total 180°.

$$112° + a = 180°$$
$$a = 68°$$

2. (A)

The two marked angles are vertical angles formed when two lines intersect. Vertical angles are congruent. Therefore $c = 32°$.

3. (C)

The three marked angles are adjacent and form a straight angle. A straight angle = 180°.

$$27° + 2x + x = 180°$$
$$3x = 180° - 27°$$
$$3x = 153°$$
$$x = 51°$$

4. (D)

The angle between the 63° angle and $\angle z$ is a vertical angle to the 29° angle, so it equals 29° as well. The three angles are adjacent and form a straight angle. A straight angle =180°.

$$63° + 29° + z = 180°$$
$$92° + z = 180°$$
$$z = 180° - 92°$$
$$z = 88°$$

5. (C)

If $\overline{BD}$ bisects $\angle ABC$, $m\angle ABD = \frac{1}{2}m\angle ABC$. $m\angle ABD = \frac{1}{4}m\angle XYZ$, and $\angle XYZ = 84°$ are given.

Then $m\angle ABD = \frac{1}{4}(84°) = 21°$

$$21° = \frac{1}{2}m\angle ABC$$

So $m\angle ABC = 42°$

6. (C)

If $\overrightarrow{BA} \perp \overrightarrow{BC}$, $\angle ABC$ is a right angle, and $m\angle ABC = 90°$

$$m\angle ABC = m\angle ABD + m\angle DBC$$
$$90° = m\angle ABD + 53°$$
$$m\angle ABD = 90° - 53° = 37°$$

7. (A)

If $n \perp p$, the lines form four congruent right angles, so $\angle 1 \cong \angle 2$. Also $m\angle 3 = m\angle 2$, so (D) is false. Nothing is known about line m with respect to line p, so all that can be said is that the vertical angles are equal. Answers (B) and (C) are not necessarily true.

8. (D)

If $p \perp t$ and $q \perp t$ all of the angles formed are congruent right (90°) angles. Therefore only $m\angle 2 > m\angle 5$ is false.

9. (C)

If $a \parallel b$, the corresponding angles are equal. The $116°$ angle forms a straight angle with the angle that corresponds to z. Therefore $116° + z = 180°$

$$z = 180° - 116°$$
$$z = 64°$$

10. (B)

If $m \parallel n$, the vertical and corresponding angles are congruent, or $\angle 2 \cong \angle 3 \cong \angle 5 \cong \angle 8$, and $\angle 1 \cong \angle 4 \cong \angle 6 \cong \angle 7$. In addition, each pair of adjacent angles forms a straight angle, so, for example, $m \angle 4 + m \angle 2 = 180°$, or by substitution, $m \angle 4 + m \angle 5 = 180°$. The only statement that is not necessarily true, then, is (B).

Drill: Regular Polygons (Convex)

1. (D)

A regular pentagon is five-sided. Therefore, each interior angle is

$$\frac{180°(n-2)}{n} = \frac{180°(5-2)}{5} = \frac{540°}{5} = 108°$$

2. (D)

Each exterior angle is $\dfrac{360°}{n} = \dfrac{360°}{3} = 120°$
The sum is therefore $3(120°) = 360°$.

3. (D)

$$a = 4\sqrt{3} \text{ mm} \qquad P = \text{perimeter} = 3(24) = 72 \text{ mm}$$
$$A = \frac{1}{2}ap = \frac{1}{2}(4\sqrt{3})(72) = 144\sqrt{3} \text{ mm}^2$$

4. (C)

$s = 4$ cm, which makes the apothem

$$a = \frac{s}{2}\sqrt{3} = \frac{4}{2}\sqrt{3} = 2\sqrt{3} \text{ cm}$$
$$A = \frac{1}{2}ap = \frac{1}{2}(2\sqrt{3})(6)(4) = 24\sqrt{3} \text{ cm}^2$$

5. (D)

$$A = \frac{1}{2}ap = \frac{1}{2}a(s)(10) = \frac{1}{2}(9.2)(6)(10) = 276 \text{ cm}^2$$

Drill: Triangles

1. (D)

Since $\angle Q$ is a right angle, $m \angle Q = 90°$. Therefore, since the sum of the angles of a triangle is $180°$,

$$90° + 23° + m \angle R = 180°$$
$$m \angle R = 67°$$

2. (B)

$$96° + m < \text{M} + m < \text{O} = 180°$$

But $m < \text{O} = m < \text{M}$

so $96° + 2m < \text{M} = 180°$

$$2m < \text{M} = 84°$$
$$m < \text{M} = 42°$$

3. (C)

$$3x + 2x + x = 180°$$
$$6x = 180°$$
$$x = 30°$$

4. (A)

$$6 : 4 = 4 : b \Rightarrow \frac{6}{4} = \frac{4}{b} \Rightarrow 6b = 16$$

$$b = \frac{16}{6} = 2\frac{4}{6} = 2\frac{2}{3}$$

5. (D)

$$3 : 4 = 6 : b \qquad b = 8$$

$$3 : 4 = 4 : a$$

$$\frac{3}{4} = \frac{4}{a}$$

$$3a = 16 \quad a = 16\left(\frac{1}{3}\right) = 5\frac{1}{3}$$

6. (C)

$$A = \frac{1}{2}bh = \frac{1}{2}(14)(8) = 56$$

7. (B)

$$A = \frac{1}{2}bh = \frac{1}{2}(11)(7) = 38\frac{1}{2}, \text{ or } 38.5$$

8. (D)

$$A = \frac{1}{2}bh = \frac{1}{2}(4)(8\sqrt{2}) = 16\sqrt{2}$$

9. (A)

Using the Pythagorean Theorem,

$$\overline{AB} = \sqrt{(\overline{AC})^2 - (\overline{BC})^2} = \sqrt{(15)^2 - (9)^2} = \sqrt{144}$$

$$= 12 \text{ cm.}$$

Then $A = \frac{1}{2}bh = \frac{1}{2}(9)(12) = 54 \text{ cm}^2$

10. (B)

This is an isosceles right triangle, so the legs are equal. Using the Pythagorean Theorem,

$$(10\sqrt{2})^2 = a^2 + a^2$$

$$200 = 2a^2$$

$$a^2 = 100$$

$$a = 10$$

so the sides are 10 cm each.

$$A = \frac{1}{2}bh = \frac{1}{2}(10)(10) = 50 \text{ cm}^2$$

Drill: Quadrilaterals

1. (B)

$\measuredangle B$ and $\measuredangle D$ are opposite angles in the parallelogram and are equal. Therefore,

$$6x + 2 = 98$$

$$6x = 96$$

$$x = 16$$

2. (D)

$$A = bh = (18)(9) = 162$$

3. (A)

Using the Pythagorean Theorem,

$$\overline{AC} = \sqrt{(\overline{AD})^2 + (\overline{DC})^2}$$

$$= \sqrt{(6)^2 + (8)^2}$$

$$= \sqrt{36 + 64}$$

$$= \sqrt{100}$$

$$= 10 \text{ cm}$$

4. (D)

$$A = bh = (7)(10) = 70 \text{ cm}^2$$

5. (C)

The diagonals of a rectangle are equal, so

$$\overline{EC} = \overline{BD} = 17$$
$$\overline{BO} = \frac{1}{2}\overline{BD} = \frac{1}{2}(17) = 8.5$$

6. (C)

Using the Pythagorean Theorem,

$$\overline{GH} = \sqrt{\left(\frac{1}{2}\overline{GI}\right)^2 + \left(\frac{1}{2}\overline{HJ}\right)^2}$$
$$= \sqrt{\left[\left(\frac{1}{2}\right)(6)\right]^2 + \left[\left(\frac{1}{2}\right)(8)\right]^2}$$
$$= \sqrt{(3)^2 + (4)^2}$$
$$= \sqrt{25} = 5$$

7. (D)

$$A = \frac{1}{2}(b_1 + b_2)h$$
$$= \frac{1}{2}(14 + 21)(10)$$
$$= \frac{1}{2}(35)(10)$$
$$= 175$$

8. (B)

The nonparallel sides of an isosceles trapezoid are equal, so

$$\overline{BC} = \overline{AD} = 6$$
$$P = 6 + 6 + 5 + 10 = 27$$

9. (C)

Use the Pythagorean Theorem to find the height.

$$6^2 = h^2 + 3^2$$
$$h^2 = 27$$
$$h = 3\sqrt{3} .$$

The area of this trapezoid is the area of the rectangle plus the area of the triangle, or

$$A = \underset{\text{rectangle}}{bh} + \frac{1}{2}\underset{\text{triangle}}{bh} = (4)\left(3\sqrt{3}\right) + \frac{1}{2}(3)\left(3\sqrt{3}\right)$$
$$= 12\sqrt{3} + \frac{9}{2}\sqrt{3} = \frac{33}{2}\sqrt{3}$$

10. (D)

The base angles of an isosceles trapezoid are equal.

Therefore, $\angle W = \angle Z$ so

$$58 = 4x - 6$$
$$64 = 4x$$
$$16 = x$$

Drill: Circles

1. (B)

$$C = 2\pi r = 2(\pi)(3) = 6\pi$$

2. (C)

$$A = \pi r^2 = \pi(11)^2 = 121\pi$$

3. (D)

$$A = \pi r^2 \quad r = \frac{1}{2}d = \frac{1}{2}(27) = 13.5$$
$$A = \pi(13.5)^2 = 182.25\pi$$

4. (C)

$$A = 225\pi = \pi r^2 \text{ so } r = \sqrt{225} = 15$$
$$d = 2r = 2(15) = 30$$

5. (B)

$$A_X = \pi r^2 = 144\pi \quad r_X = 12$$
$$A_Y = \pi r^2 = 81\pi \quad r_Y = 9$$
$$r_X : r_Y = 12 : 9 = 4 : 3$$

6. (B)

Shaded Area = Larger Area − Smaller Area

$$= \pi r_1^{\,2} - \pi r_2^{\,2}$$
$$= \pi(7)^2 - \pi(5)^5$$
$$= 49\pi - 25\pi$$
$$= 24\pi$$

7. (D)

Measure of arc = measure of central angle.
Therefore, $\overset{\frown}{MN} = \measuredangle MON = 62°$.

8. (C)

The measure of a semicircle is 180°. Therefore, $\overset{\frown}{AXC} = 180°$.

9. (C)

Since $\overset{\frown}{ZXY}$ is semicircle, $180° - 40° = 140°$.

10. (B)

$$A = \frac{n}{360}(\pi r^2) = \frac{45}{360}(4^2\pi) = \frac{1}{8}(16\pi) = 2\pi.$$

Probability

Probability is defined as the likelihood of the occurrence of an event or as the chance that some particular event will occur.

- **EXAMPLE**

A weather report might indicate the chance of rain to be 70%, which could be interpreted as the probability of rain = .70.

a) Objective Probability (Calculated)

In most instances, the probability that an event will occur is determined by a mathematical formula and is based on empirical evidence.

$$P(X) = \frac{\text{No. of outcomes corresponding to event } X}{\text{Total no. of possible outcomes}}$$

- **EXAMPLE**

The probability of drawing a queen from a deck of cards is defined as:

$$P(\text{Queen}) = \frac{\text{No. of queens in the deck}}{\text{Total no. of cards in the deck}}$$

$$= \frac{4}{52} = \frac{1}{13}, \text{ or } .077.$$

b) Subjective Probability

When the probability of an event occurring is based on the personal (or professional) judgment of an individual or group of individuals, the probability is referred to as "subjective."

- **EXAMPLE**

The probability that sales will increase by $500,000 next year if we increase our advertising expenditure by $10,000 is .25.

Properties of Probabilities

The following three properties are characteristics of all probabilities:

1. $0 \leq P(X) \leq 1$; every probability is contained within the range 0 to 1, inclusive, where 0 represents absolute certainty that the event will not occur and 1 represents absolute certainty that the event will occur.

- **EXAMPLE**

$P(\text{Head on Coin}) = \dfrac{1}{2}$

$P(\text{6 on Die}) = \dfrac{1}{6}$

$P(\text{Ace of Spades}) = \dfrac{1}{52}$

2. $\displaystyle\sum_{i=1}^{n} P_i(X) = 1$; the probabilities of all possible simple events that can occur within a given experiment will sum to 1.

- **EXAMPLE**

coin: $P(\text{Head}) + P(\text{Tail}) = \dfrac{1}{2} + \dfrac{1}{2} = 1$

die: $P(1) + P(2) + P(3) + P(4) + P(5) + P(6) =$
$\dfrac{1}{6} + \dfrac{1}{6} + \dfrac{1}{6} + \dfrac{1}{6} + \dfrac{1}{6} + \dfrac{1}{6} = 1$

cards: $P(\text{Club}) + P(\text{Heart}) + P(\text{Spade}) + P(\text{Diamond})$
$= \dfrac{1}{4} + \dfrac{1}{4} + \dfrac{1}{4} + \dfrac{1}{4} = 1$

3. $P(X) + P(\text{Not } X) = 1$; the probability that event X occurs plus the probability that event X does not occur sums to 1.

- **EXAMPLE**

coin: $P(\text{Head}) + P(\text{Not a Head}) = \dfrac{1}{2} + \dfrac{1}{2} = 1$

die: $P(6) + P(\text{Not a 6}) = \dfrac{1}{6} + \dfrac{5}{6} = 1$

cards: $P(\text{Spade}) + P(\text{Not a Spade}) = \dfrac{13}{52} + \dfrac{39}{52} = 1,$
or $\dfrac{1}{4} + \dfrac{3}{4} = 1$

Methods of Computing Probabilities

a) Addition

1. Mutually Exclusive Events

   Mutually exclusive events cannot occur simultaneously. In order to determine the probability that either event X occurs or event Y occurs, the individual probabilities of event X and event Y are added.

   $P(X \text{ or } Y) = P(X) + P(Y)$

• **EXAMPLE**

   The probability that either a club or a spade is drawn from a deck of cards in a single draw is defined as:

   $$P(\text{Club or Spade}) = P(\text{Club}) + P(\text{Spade})$$
   $$= \frac{13}{52} + \frac{13}{52}$$
   $$= \frac{26}{52}$$
   $$= \frac{1}{2} \text{ or } .5$$

   Note: This concept applies to more than two events as well.

2. Non-Mutually Exclusive Events

   Non-mutually exclusive events can occur simultaneously. In order to determine the probability that either event X occurs or event Y occurs, the individual probabilities of event X and event Y are added and the probability that the two occur simultaneously is subtracted from the total.

   $$\boxed{P(X \text{ or } Y) = P(X) + P(Y) - P(X \, \& \, Y)}$$

• **EXAMPLE**

   The probability that either a Queen or a Spade is drawn from a deck of cards in a single draw is defined as:

   $$P(\text{Queen or Spade}) = P(\text{Queen}) + P(\text{Spade}) - $$
   $$P(\text{Queen \& Spade})$$
   $$= \frac{4}{52} + \frac{13}{52} - \frac{1}{52}$$
   $$= \frac{16}{52}$$
   $$= \frac{4}{13}.$$

   Notice in this example that we must subtract $\frac{1}{52}$ from the total since the Queen of Spades is counted in the total number of Queens and it is also counted in the total number of Spades. If we do not subtract $P(\text{Queen \& Spade})$, we are counting that one card twice.

b) Multiplication

1. Independent Events

   Two (or more) events are independent if the occurrence of one event has no effect upon whether or not the other event occurs. In order to determine the probability that event X occurs and event Y occurs, the individual probability of event X and event Y are multiplied together.

   $$\boxed{P(X \text{ and } Y) = P(X) \times P(Y)}$$

• **EXAMPLES**

a) The probability of tossing a 6 on a single die followed by the toss of a 3 is:

   $$P(6 \text{ and } 3) = P(6) \times P(3)$$
   $$= \frac{1}{6} \times \frac{1}{6}$$
   $$= \frac{1}{36}.$$

b) The probability of tossing three heads in 3 tosses of a coin:

   $$P(H, H, H) = P(H) \times P(H) \times P(H)$$
   $$= \frac{1}{2} \times \frac{1}{2} \times \frac{1}{2}$$
   $$= \frac{1}{8}.$$

c) The probability of drawing a heart from a deck of cards, replacing the first card, and drawing a club on the second draw:

$$P(H \text{ and } C) = P(H) \times P(C)$$
$$= \frac{13}{52} \times \frac{13}{52}$$
$$= \frac{1}{4} \times \frac{1}{4}$$
$$= \frac{1}{16}.$$

2. Dependent Events

Two (or more) events are dependent if the occurrence of one event has some effect upon whether or not the other event occurs. In order to determine the probability that event X occurs and event Y occurs, when X and Y are dependent, the formula is:

$$\boxed{P(X \text{ and } Y) = P(X) \times P(Y \mid X)}$$

or

$$\boxed{P(X \text{ and } Y) = P(Y) \times P(X \mid Y)}$$

where $P(Y \mid X)$ is read as the probability that event Y will occur, given that event X has already occurred, and $P(X \mid Y)$ is read as the probability that event X will occur given that event Y has already occurred.

$P(X \mid Y)$ may be calculated using the following formula:

$$\boxed{P(X \mid Y) = \frac{P(X \text{ and } Y)}{P(Y)}}$$

This formula is frequently "broken down" further and written this way:

$$\boxed{P(X \mid Y) = \frac{P(X) \times P(Y \mid X)}{P(X) \times P(Y \mid X) + P(Not\,X)P(Y \mid Not\,X)}}$$

This latter version is called **Bayes Theorem** and the use of it is called Bayesian Analysis.

• **EXAMPLES**

a) A box contains 6 red balls, 4 green balls, and 5 purple balls. What is the probability that a red ball is drawn on the first draw and a purple ball is drawn on the second draw, if the first ball is not replaced prior to the second ball being drawn

$$P(\text{Red and Purple}) = P(R) \times P(P \mid R)$$
$$= \frac{6}{15} \times \frac{5}{14}$$
$$= \frac{30}{210}$$
$$= \frac{1}{7}$$

b) Three cards are drawn from a deck. What is the probability that the first is a Queen, the second is a Queen, and the third is a King? Assume that each card is **not** replaced prior to the next one being drawn.

$$P(Q1, Q2, K) = P(Q1) \times P(Q2 \mid Q1) \times$$
$$P(K \mid Q1 \,\&\, Q2)$$
$$= \frac{4}{52} \times \frac{3}{51} \times \frac{4}{50}$$
$$= \frac{48}{132,600}$$
$$= .0004$$

c) Two workers assemble parts from a production process. The probability that worker A makes a mistake in assembling a part is .02 and the probability that worker B makes a mistake is .03. However, worker A assembles 55% of the parts while worker B assembles the remaining 45%. If an assembled part is randomly selected from all of those produced during a given time period and it is determined to be defective, what is the probability that worker A assembled this part?

Let A = Assembled by worker A

B = Assembled by worker B (Same as "not A")

D = Defective

$$P(A \mid D)$$
$$= \frac{P(A)P(D \mid A)}{P(A) \times P(D \mid A) + P(B) \times P(D \mid B)}$$
$$= \frac{.55 \times .02}{(.55)(.02) + (.45)(.03)} = \frac{.011}{.025} = .449$$

Probability Tables

A tabular approach is often easier to understand when calculating probabilities.

- **EXAMPLE**

For the last example, the probability table is as follows:

ASSEMBLED PARTS

		GOOD	DEFECTIVE	TOTAL
Worker	A	.5390	.0110	.55
	B	.4365	.0135	.45
TOTAL		.9755	.0245	1.00

The **cell** probabilities are referred to as **joint probabilities**, which represent the combined probability of the two events (row and column) occurring; for example, the probability that worker A assembled the part and it is good is .5390. The **total** row and column probabilities are referred to as **marginal probabilities**, which are the sums of the joint probabilities over the rows or columns. For example, .45 is a marginal probability representing the probability that worker B assembled the part. It is the sum of .4365 (probability that worker B assembled it and it is good) plus .0135 (the probability that B assembled it and it is defective).

Counting Methods

Sampling and Counting

There are many instances in the application of probability theory where it is desirable and necessary to count the outcomes in the sample space and the outcomes in an event. For example, in the special instance of a uniform probability function, the probability of an event is known when the number of outcomes that comprises the event is known; that is, as soon as the number of outcomes in the subset that defines the event is known.

If a sample space $S = \{e_1, e_2, \ldots, e_n\}$ contains n simple events, $E_i = \{e_i\}$, $i = 1, 2, \ldots, n$, then using a uniform probability model, we assign probability $1/n$ for each point in S; that is, $P(E_i) = 1/n$. To determine the probability of an event A, we need,

1. The number of possible outcomes in S.

2. The number of outcomes in the event A.

Then,

$$P(A) = \frac{\text{number of outcomes corresponding to } A}{\text{number of possible outcomes in } S}$$

Frequently, it may be possible to enumerate fully all the sample space points in S and then count how many of these correspond to the event A. For example, if a class consists of just three students, and the instructor always calls on each student once and only once during each class, then if we label the students 1, 2, and 3, we can easily enumerate the points in S as

$$S = \{(1, 2, 3), (1, 3, 2), (2, 1, 3), (2, 3, 1), (3, 1, 2), (3, 2, 1)\}$$

Assume that the instructor chooses a student at random. It would seem reasonable to adopt a uniform probability model and assign probability $\frac{1}{6}$ to each point in S. If A is the event that John is selected last, then

John = 3

$A = \{(1, 2, 3), (2, 1, 3)\}$

$P(A) = \frac{2}{6} = \frac{1}{3}$

It would be most unusual for a class to consist of only three students. The total enumeration of the sample space becomes even more complicated if we increase the class size to only 6 students. To deal with these situations in which the sample space contains a large number of points, we need to have an understanding of basic counting or combinatorial procedures.

The Fundamental Principle of Counting

Suppose a man has four ways to travel from New York to Chicago, three ways to travel from Chicago to Denver, and six ways to travel from Denver to San Francisco, how many ways can he go from New York to San Francisco via Chicago and Denver?

If we let A_1 be the event "going from New York to Chicago," A_2 be the event "going from Chicago to Denver," and A_3 be the event "going from Denver to San Francisco," then because there are 4 ways to accomplish A_1, 3 ways to accomplish A_2, and 6 ways to accomplish A_3, the number of routes the man can follow is

$$(4) \times (3) \times (6) = 72$$

We can now generalize these results and state them formally as the fundamental principle or multiplication rule of counting.

Fundamental Principle of Counting

If an operation consists of a sequence of k separate steps of which the first can be performed in n_1 ways, followed by the second in n_2 ways, and so on until the kth can be performed in n_k ways, then the operation consisting of k steps can be performed in

$$n_1 \times n_2 \times n_3 \ldots \ldots n_k$$

ways.

Tree Diagrams

A tree diagram is a device that can be used to list all possible outcomes of a sequence of experiments where each experiment can occur only in a finite number of ways.

The following tree diagram lists the different ways three different flavors of ice cream, chocolate (c), vanilla (v), and strawberry (s), can be arranged on a cone, with no flavor used more than once.

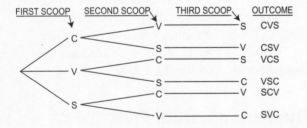

The tree starts with three branches in the first stage, representing the three possibilities for the first stage. For each outcome at the first stage, there are two possibilities at the second stage. Then, for each outcome in the second stage, there is only one possibility at the third stage. Consequently, there are $3 \times 2 \times 1$, or 6, different arrangements.

Using a tree diagram, we can develop the sample space for an experiment consisting of tossing a fair coin and then rolling a die as follows:

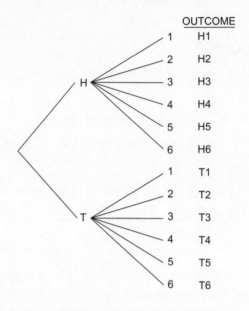

Factorial Notation

Consider how many ways the owner of an ice cream parlor can display ten ice cream flavors in a row along the front of the display case. The first position can be filled in ten ways, the second position in 9 ways, and the third position in 8 ways, and so on. By the fundamental counting principle, there are

$$(10) \times (9) \times (8) \times (7) \times \ldots \times (2) \times (1)$$

or 3,628,800 ways to display the flavor. If there were 16 flavors, there would be $(16) \times (15) \times (14) \times \ldots \times (3) \times (2) \times (1)$ ways to arrange them.

In general, if n is a natural number, then the product from 1 to n inclusive is denoted by the symbol $n!$ (read as "n factorial" or as "factorial n") and is defined as

$$n! = n(n-1)(n-2) \ldots (3)(2)(1),$$

where n is a positive natural number.

There are two fundamental properties of factorials:

1. By definition, $0! = 1$

2. $n(n-1)! = n!$

    For example, $(6)(5!) = 6!$

Counting Procedures Involving Order Restrictions (Permutations)

Suppose a class consists of 5 students. The instructor calls on exactly three students out of the 5 students during each class period to answer three different questions. To apply the uniform probability model, we need to know how many points there are in the sample space S. Note that each point in S is an ordered triplet; that is, the point $(3, 5, 1)$ is different from the point $(5, 3, 1)$. The same three people were called upon to respond, but the order of response is different. Such an arrangement is referred to as a permutation.

A **permutation** of a number of objects is any arrangement of these objects in a definite order.

For example, if a class consists of 3 students, then there are $3 \times 2 \times 1 = 6$ ways in which the students might be called upon.

In general, if the class had consisted of n students and all of them had been called upon, then the responses could have taken place in

$$n(n-1)(n-2) \ldots (3)(2)(1)$$

ways. Hence,

The number of permutations of a set of n distinct objects, taken all together, is $n!$

In our example of the class consisting of 5 students, only 3 students were to be called on to respond; that is, we are interested in an ordered subset.

An arrangement of r distinct objects taken from a set of n distinct objects, $r \leq n$, is called a permutation of n objects taken r at a time. The total number of such orderings is denoted by nPr, and defined as

$$nPr = \frac{n!}{(n-r)!}$$

In our example, $n = 5$, $r = 3$,

$$5P3 = \frac{5!}{(5-3)!} = 5 \times 4 \times 3 = 60$$

If we have n items with r objects alike, then the number of distinct permutations taking all n at a time is

$$\frac{n!}{r!}$$

In general,

In a set of n elements having r_1 elements of one type, r_2 elements of a second type, and so on to r_k element of a kth type, then the number of distinct permutations of the n elements, taken all together, is given by

$$nPn = \frac{n!}{r_1! r_2! r_3! \ldots r_k!}$$

where $\sum_{i=1}^{k} r_i = n$

For example, the number of ways a group of 10 people of which 6 are females and 4 are males can line up for theatre tickets, if we are interested only in distinguishing between sexes, is given by

$$10P10 = \frac{10!}{6!4!} = 210$$

Counting Procedures Not Involving Order Restrictions (Combinations)

Suppose that a class of 12 students selects a committee of 3 to plan a party. A possible committee is John, Sally, and Joe. In this situation, the order of the three is not important because the committee of John, Sally, and Joe, is the same as the committee of Sally, Joe, and John.

When choosing committee members and in other cases of selection where order is not important, we are interested in combinations, not permutations.

A subset of r objects selected without regard to order from a set of n different objects, $r \leq n$, is called a combination of n objects taken r at a time. The total number of combinations of n things taken r at a time is denoted by nCr or $\binom{n}{r}$ and is defined as

$$nCr = \binom{n}{r} = \frac{n!}{r!(n-r)!}$$

In our example, the number of possible committees that could plan the party can be calculated by

$$12C3 = \binom{12}{3} = \frac{12!}{3!(12-3)!} = 220$$

PROBLEM

> A deck of playing cards is thoroughly shuffled, and a card is drawn from the deck. What is the probability that the card drawn is the ace of diamonds?

SOLUTION

The probability of an event occurring is

$$\frac{\text{the number of ways the event can occur}}{\text{the number of possible outcomes}}$$

In our case there is one way the event can occur, for there is only one ace of diamonds and there are 52 possible outcomes (for there are 52 cards in the deck). Hence, the probability that the card drawn is the ace of diamonds is $\frac{1}{52}$.

PROBLEM

> A bag contains four black and five blue marbles. A marble is drawn and then replaced, after which a second marble is drawn. What is the probability that the first is black and the second blue?

SOLUTION

Let C = event that the first marble drawn is black.

D = event that the second marble drawn is blue.

The probability that the first is black and the second is blue can be expressed symbolically:

$P(C \text{ and } D) = P(CD)$.

We can apply the following theorem. If two events, A and B, are independent, then the probability that A and B will occur is

$P(A \text{ and } B) = P(AB) = P(A) \times P(B)$.

Note that two or more events are said to be independent if the occurrence of one event has no effect upon the occurrence or non-occurrence of the other. In this case, the occurrence of choosing a black marble has no effect on the selection of a blue marble and vice versa; since, when a marble is drawn it is then replaced before the next marble is drawn. Therefore, C and D are two independent events.

$P(CD) = P(C) \times P(D)$

$$P(C) = \frac{\text{number of ways to choose a black marble}}{\text{number of ways to choose a marble}}$$

$$= \frac{4}{9}$$

$$P(D) = \frac{\text{number of ways to choose a blue marble}}{\text{number of ways to choose a marble}}$$

$$= \frac{5}{9}$$

$$P(CD) = P(C) \times P(D) = \frac{4}{9} \times \frac{5}{9} = \frac{20}{81}$$

PROBLEM

> A traffic count at a highway junction revealed that out of 5,000 cars that passed through the junction in one week, 3,000 turned to the right. Find the probability that a car will turn (A) to the right and (B) to the left. Assume that the cars cannot go straight or turn around.

SOLUTION

(A) If an event can happen in s ways and fail to happen in f ways, and if all these ways ($s + f$) are assumed to be equally likely, then the probability (p) that the event will happen is

$$p = \frac{s}{s + f} = \frac{\text{successful ways}}{\text{total ways}}.$$

In this case $s = 3,000$ and $s + f = 5,000$. Hence,

$$p = \frac{3,000}{5,000} = \frac{3}{5}.$$

(B) If the probability that an event will happen is $\frac{a}{b}$, then the probability that this event will not happen is $1 - \dfrac{a}{b}$. Thus, the probability that a car will not turn

right, but left, is $1 - \dfrac{3}{5} = \dfrac{2}{5}$. This same conclusion can also

be arrived at using the following reasoning:

Since 3,000 cars turned to the right, $5,000 - 3,000 =$ 2,000 cars turned to the left. Hence, the probability that a car will turn to the left is

$$\frac{2,000}{5,000} = \frac{2}{5}.$$

Drill: Permutations, Combinations, and Probability

1. How many games would it take a baseball coach to try every possible batting order with his nine players?

    (A) 9   (C) 81

    (B) 45   (D) 362,880

2. What is the probability of drawing an ace from a well-shuffled deck of 52 cards?

    (A) 0.0769   (C) 0.0196

    (B) 0.0192   (D) 0.0385

3. In how many different ways can the letters a, b, c, and d be arranged if they are selected three at a time?

    (A) 8   (C) 24

    (B) 12   (D) 4

4. What is the probability that in a single throw of two dice the sum of 10 will appear?

    (A) $\dfrac{10}{36}$ (C) $\dfrac{1}{12}$

    (B) $\dfrac{1}{6}$ (D) $\dfrac{2}{10}$

5. A bag contains four white balls, six black balls, three red balls, and eight green balls. If one ball is drawn from the bag, find the probability that it will be either white or green.

    (A) $\dfrac{1}{3}$ (C) $\dfrac{4}{7}$

    (B) $\dfrac{2}{3}$ (D) $\dfrac{4}{13}$

6. A box contains 30 blue balls, 40 green balls, and 15 red balls. What is the probability of choosing a red ball first followed by a blue ball?

    (A) 0.3571   (C) 0.0620

    (B) 0.1765   (D) 0.0630

7. When rolling a six-sided die, what is the probability of getting either a four or five?

    (A) 0.5000   (C) 0.2500

    (B) 0.3333   (D) 0.1670

8. What is the probability of getting at most one head in three coin tosses?

    (A) 0   (C) $\dfrac{1}{2}$

    (B) $\dfrac{1}{4}$ (D) $\dfrac{3}{4}$

9. In how many ways can we arrange four letters (a, b, c, and d) in different orders?

    (A) 4   (C) 16

    (B) 8   (D) 24

10. Six dice are thrown. What is the probability of getting six ones?

    (A) 0.0000214 (C) 0.00001

    (B) 0.0278   (D) 0.1667

Permutation, Combination, and Probability Drill Answer Key

1.	(D)	6.	(D)
2.	(A)	7.	(B)
3.	(C)	8.	(C)
4.	(C)	9.	(D)
5.	(C)	10.	(A)

Detailed Explanations of Answers

Drill: Permutations, Combinations and Probability

1. (D)

The coach has 9 choices for the first position, 8 for the second, 7 for the third, etc., or 9! choices. 9! = 362,880.

2. (A)

$$\text{Probability} = \frac{\text{Number of favorable outcomes}}{\text{Number of possible outcomes}}$$

There are 4 aces and 52 cards, so

$$P = \frac{4}{52} = \frac{1}{13} = 0.0769$$

3. (C)

This is a permutation since order (arrangement) is to be considered.

$$4P_3 = \frac{4!}{(4-3)!} = 4 \times 3 \times 2 = 24$$

4. (C)

There are only 3 ways a sum of 10 will appear, (6, 4), (5, 5), and (4, 6). There are $6 \times 6 = 36$ ways the dice can land. The probability of a sum of 10 is therefore $\frac{3}{36} = \frac{1}{12}$.

5. (C)

$$P(X \text{ or } Y) = P(X) + P(Y)$$

There are 21 balls altogether, of which 4 are white and 8 are green.

$$P(\text{white or green}) = P(\text{white}) + P(\text{green})$$
$$= \frac{4}{21} + \frac{8}{21} = \frac{12}{21} = \frac{4}{7}$$

6. (D)

$$P(X \text{ and } Y) = P(X) \times P(Y)$$

There are 85 balls for the first pick, of which 15 are red, so $P(\text{red}_1) = \frac{15}{85}$.

There are then 84 balls for the second pick, of which 30 are blue, so $P(\text{blue}_2) = \frac{30}{84}$.

So $P(\text{red}_1 \text{ and } \text{blue}_2) = \frac{15}{85} \times \frac{30}{84} = \frac{3}{17} \times \frac{15}{42}$

$$= \frac{45}{714} = .0630 .$$

7. (B)

$$P(4 \text{ or } 5) = P(4) + P(5) = \frac{1}{6} + \frac{1}{6} = \frac{2}{6} = \frac{1}{3} = 0.3333 .$$

8. (C)

Use a tree diagram to solve this problem:

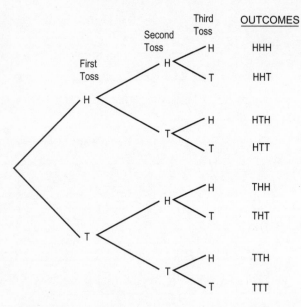

There are 8 possible outcomes, and 4 have at most one head.

So $P = \dfrac{4}{8} = \dfrac{1}{2}$.

9. (D)

Order makes a difference, so we are talking about permutations.

$$4P_4 = \frac{4!}{(4-4)!} = \frac{4 \times 3 \times 2 \times 1}{0!} = \frac{24}{1} = 24$$

10. (A)

These are independent events, so

$P(1_1 \text{ and } 1_2 \text{ and } 1_3 \text{ and } 1_4 \text{ and } 1_5 \text{ and } 1_6)$

$= P(1_1) \times P(1_2) \times P(1_3) \times P(1_4) \times P(1_5) \times P(1_6)$

$= \dfrac{1}{6} \times \dfrac{1}{6} \times \dfrac{1}{6} \times \dfrac{1}{6} \times \dfrac{1}{6} \times \dfrac{1}{6} = \dfrac{1}{46656} = 0.0000214$.

Statistics

Data Description: Graphs

Repeated measurements yield data, which must be organized according to some principle. The data should be arranged in such a way that each observation can fall into one, and only one, category. A simple graphical method of presenting data is the pie chart, which is a circle divided into parts that represent categories.

• **EXAMPLE**

2006 Budget

38% came from individual income taxes

28% from social insurance receipts

13% from corporate income taxes

12% from borrowing

5% from excise taxes

4% other

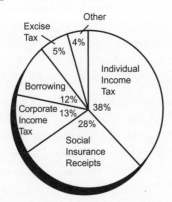

This data can also be presented in the form of a bar chart or bar graph.

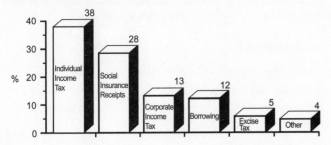

• **EXAMPLE**

The population of the United States for the years 1860 through 1960 is shown in the table below,

Year	Population in millions
1860	31.4
1870	39.8
1880	50.2
1890	62.9
1900	76.0
1910	92.0
1920	105.7
1930	122.8
1940	131.7
1950	151.1
1960	179.3

in this graph,

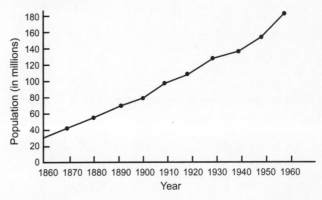

and in this bar chart.

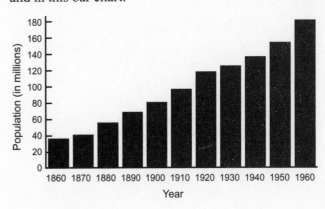

• **EXAMPLE**

A quadratic function is given by

$$y = x^2 + x - 2$$

We compute the values of y corresponding to various values of x.

x	-3	-2	-1	0	1	2	3
y	4	0	-2	-2	0	4	10

From this table, the points shown on the graph below are obtained:

$(-3, 4)\ (-2, 0)\ (-1, -2)\ (0, -2)\ (1, 0)\ (2, 4)\ (3, 10)$

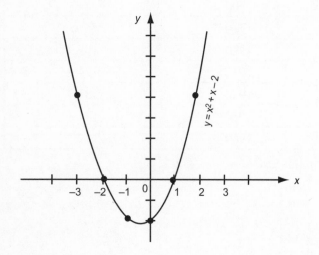

The curve shown is called a parabola. The general equation for a parabola is

$$y = ax^2 + bx + c, \quad a \neq 0$$

where a, b, and c are constants.

PROBLEM

Twenty students are enrolled in the foreign language department, and their major fields are as follows: Spanish, Spanish, French, Italian, French, Spanish, German, German, Russian, Russian, French, German, German, German, Spanish, Russian, German, Italian, German, and Spanish.

(a) Make a frequency distribution table.

(b) Make a frequency bar graph.

SOLUTION

(a) The frequency distribution table is constructed by writing down the major field and next to it the number of students.

Major Field	Number of Students
German	7
Russian	3
Spanish	5
French	3
Italian	2
Total	20

(b) A bar graph follows:

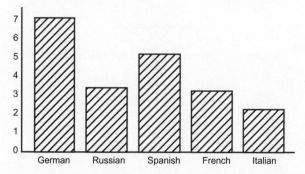

In the bar graph, the fields are listed and spaced evenly along the horizontal axis. Each specified field is represented by a rectangle, and all have the same width. The height of each, identified by a number on the vertical axis, corresponds to the frequency of that field.

A **box-and-whiskers** plot is a graph that displays five statistics. A minimum score, a maximum score, and three percentiles. A percentile value for a score tells you the percentage of scores lower than it. The beginning of the box is the score at the 25th percentile. The end of the box represents the 75th percentile. The score inside of the box is the median, or the score at the 50th percentile. Attached to the box you will find two whiskers. The score at the end of the left whisker is the minimum score. The score at the end of the right whisker is the maximum score.

• EXAMPLE

In the box-and-whiskers plot below, the minimum score is 70, the score at the 25th percentile is 78, the median score is 82, the score at the 75th percentile is 90, and the maximum score is 94.

Scores on a Test

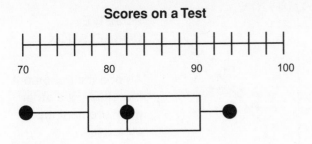

PROBLEM

Using the box-and-whiskers plot below, what was the median score on the geography test?

Scores on a Geography Test

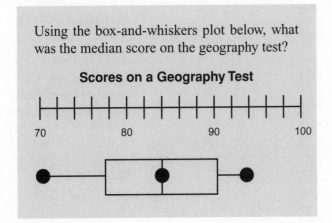

SOLUTION

The median score is 84. On a box-and-whiskers plot, the median score (50th percentile) is the score on the inside of the box.

A **stem-and-leaf plot** is a way of displaying scores in groups. A stem-and-leaf plot gives you a picture of the scores, as well as the actual numbers themselves in a compact form. In this type of plot, a score is broken into a stem and a leaf. The leaf consists of the smallest digit and the stem consists of the remaining larger digits.

• EXAMPLE

Task: Create a stem and leaf plot using the following scores.

Scores: 64, 48, 61, 81, 63, 59, 70, 54, 76, 61, 55, 31

Solution: The first step is to take these scores and create a set of "ranked ordered scores," ordering the scores from smallest to largest. Notice that the minimum score is 31, and the maximum score is 81.

Ranked Ordered Scores: 31, 48, 54, 55, 59, 61, 61, 63, 64, 70, 76, 81

The second step is to list the range of scores for the stems in a column. The stem of our smallest score (31) is 3, and that of our largest score (81) is 8. List all of the whole numbers between 3 and 8.

The third step is to put the leaves on the stems. Take each score, one at a time and put the last digit in a column next to its stem. For example, the last digit of 31 is 1, so put a 1 next to its stem of 3. The last digit of 48 is 8, so put an 8 next to its stem of 4. Do this for the remaining scores.

Stems	Leaves
8	1
7	0 6
6	1 1 3 4
5	4 5 9
4	8
3	1

A stem-and-leaf plot gives you a picture of how the scores are grouped so that you can begin to understand their meaning. In this example, you can see that 4 people got a score in the 60s. You can also see that the high score was 81, and the low score war 31.

PROBLEM

Stems	Leaves
6	5
5	3 6
4	0 1 7
3	2 9
2	4

The stem-and-leaf plot above was created using what set of scores?

SOLUTION

In this stem-and-leaf plot, the stems are the first digit, and the leaves are the remaining digits. Starting from the bottom, the first score is 24, the second score is 32, then comes 39, 40, 41, 47, 53, 56, and 65.

A **scatter-plot** is a graph that shows the relationship between two variables. A scatter-plot is a set of (x, y) coordinates. Each coordinate is a point on the graph. x represents a value of one variable, while y represents the value of another variable. Remember, a variable is just a measurement that can take on more than one value. A scatter-plot is useful because in one picture you can see if there is a relationship between two variables. It has been said that, "A picture is worth a thousand words." Likewise, "A graph is worth a thousand numbers."

- **EXAMPLE**

Given: Variable *x* represents Grade level. Variable *y* represents Hours of Homework each week.

Task: Using the data below, construct a scatter-plot.

Question: What is the relationship between these two variables?

x	Grade Level	1	2	3	4	5	6	7	8	9	10	11	12
y	Hours of Homework	2	3	3	6	4	10	7	10	12	9	14	15

Answer: You can think of these two variables as one set of (*x*, *y*) coordinates on a graph. Remember, a coordinate is just a point. Graph the following points: (1, 2), (2, 3), (3, 3), (4, 6), (5, 4), (6, 10), (7, 7), (8, 10), (9, 12), (10, 9), (11, 14), and (12, 15). This graph shows that as grade level increases, the number of homework hours per week tends to increase.

Scatterplot

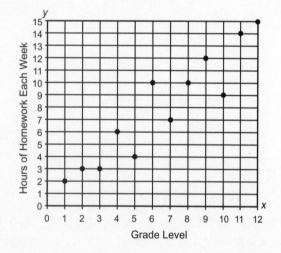

A statistic called **correlation** tells you if two measurements go together along a straight line. A scatter-plot is one way of looking at correlation. There are three different types of correlation.

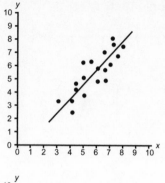

POSITIVE CORRELATION

As one measurement increases, the other measurement also increases.

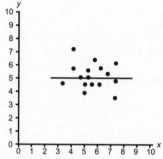

ZERO CORRELATION

The two measurements are not related to each other along a straight line.

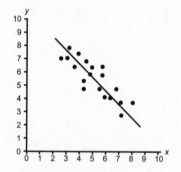

NEGATIVE CORRELATION

As one measurement increases, the other measurement decreases.

Types of Frequency Curves

In applications we find that most of the frequency curves fall within one of the categories listed.

1. One of the most popular is the bell-shaped or symmetrical frequency curve.

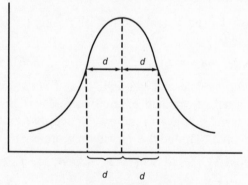

Bell-shaped or Symmetrical

Note that observations equally distant from the maximum have the same frequency. The normal distribution has a symmetrical frequency curve.

2. The U-shaped curve has maxima at both ends.

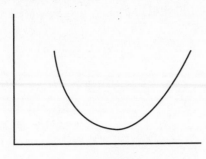

U-shaped

3. A curve can also be skewed to one side. A skew to the left occurs when the slope to the right of the maximum is steeper than the slope to the left. The opposite holds for the frequency curve skewed to the right.

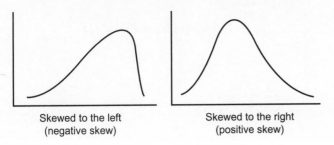

Skewed to the left   Skewed to the right
(negative skew)   (positive skew)

4. A J-shaped curve has a maximum at one end.

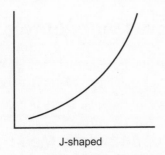

J-shaped

5. A multimodal frequency curve has two or more maxima. If it has two maxima, it is called bimodal.

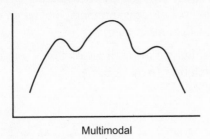

Multimodal

PROBLEM

What are two ways to describe the form of a frequency distribution? How would the following distributions be described?

(a)   (b)

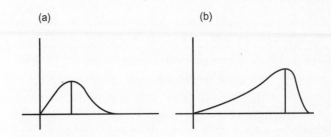

SOLUTION

The form of a frequency distribution can be described by its departure from symmetry or skewness and its degree of peakedness (kurtosis).

If the few extreme values are higher than most of the others, we say that the distribution is "positively skewed" or "skewed to the right."

If the few extreme values are lower than most of the others, we say that the distribution is "negatively skewed" or "skewed to the left."

(a) This distribution has extreme values in the upper half of the curve and is skewed to the right or positively skewed.

(b) The extreme values of this distribution are in the lower half of the curve. Thus, the distribution is negatively skewed or skewed to the left.

Numerical Methods of Describing Data

Introduction

Once we have a sufficient number of measurements, it is easy to find the frequency distribution. Graphic methods, however, are very often impractical or difficult to convey.

To remedy the situation, one can use a few numbers that describe the frequency distribution without drawing a real graph. Such numbers are called numerical descriptive measures, and each one describes a certain aspect of the frequency distribution. None of them yields the exact shape of the frequency distribution. Rather, they give us some notion of the general shape of the whole graph or parts of it.

For example, saying that somebody is 6'4" and weighs 250 lbs. does not describe the person in detail, but it does give us the general idea of a tall, stout man.

It is important to describe the center of the distribution of measurements as well as how the measurements behave about the center of the distribution. For that purpose, we define central tendency and variability. In practical applications, we deal with one of two essentially different situations:

1. The measurements are gathered about the whole population. Numerical descriptive measures for a population are called **parameters**.

2. The measurements are gathered about the sample. Numerical descriptive measures for a sample are called **statistics**.

If we have only statistics, we are not able to calculate the values of parameters. But, by using statistics, we can make reasonable estimates of parameters that describe the whole population. The most popular mathematical means of describing frequency distribution is an average. An **average** is a value that is representative or typical of a set of measurements.

Usually, averages are called measures of central tendency. We will be using different kinds of averages, such as the arithmetic mean, the geometric mean, and the harmonic mean. Different averages should be applied depending on the data, the purpose, and the required accuracy.

Notation and Definitions of Means

By

$$x_1, x_2, \ldots, x_n$$

we denote the measurements observed in a sample of size n. The subscript i in x_i is called an index. It stands for any of the numbers $1, 2, \ldots, n$.

We will be using the summation notation. The symbol

$$\sum_{i=1}^{n} x_i$$

denotes the sum of all x_i's, that is,

$$\sum_{i=1}^{n} x_i = x_1 + x_2 + \ldots + x_{n-1} + x_n$$

*   **EXAMPLE**

$$\sum_{i=1}^{4} x_i y_i = x_1 y_1 + x_2 y_2 + x_3 y_3 + x_4 y_4$$

*   **EXAMPLE**

Let a be a constant. Then

$$\sum_{k=1}^{n} a x_k = a x_1 + a x_2 + \ldots + a x_n$$

$$= a(x_1 + x_2 + \ldots + x_n)$$

$$= a \sum_{k=1}^{n} x_k$$

In general,

$$\sum a x_k = a \sum x_k$$

and

$$\sum (ax + by) = a \sum x + b \sum y$$

Often, when no confusion can arise, we write

$$\sum_k = x_k \text{ instead of } \sum_{k=1}^{n} x_k.$$

Definition of Arithmetic Mean

The **arithmetic mean**, or mean, of a set of measurements is the sum of the measurements divided by the total number of measurements. It plays an important role in statistical inference.

The arithmetic mean of a set of numbers $x_1, x_2, \ldots, x_n$ is denoted by $\bar{x}$ (read "x bar").

$$\bar{x} = \frac{\sum_{i=1}^{n} x_i}{n} = \frac{x_1 + x_2 + \cdots + x_n}{n}$$

- **EXAMPLE**

  The arithmetic mean of the numbers 3, 7, 1, 24, 11, and 32 is

  $$\bar{x} = \frac{3+7+1+24+11+32}{6} = 13$$

- **EXAMPLE**

  Let $f_1, f_2, \ldots, f_n$ be the frequencies of the numbers $x_1, x_2, \ldots, x_n$ (i.e., number x_i occurs f_i times). The arithmetic mean is

  $$\bar{x} = \frac{f_1 x_1 + f_2 x_2 + \ldots + f_n x_n}{f_1 + f_2 + \ldots + f_n} = \frac{\sum_{i=1}^{n} f_i x_i}{\sum_{i=1}^{n} f_i}$$

  $$= \frac{\sum f x}{\sum f}$$

  Note that the total frequency, that is, the total number of cases, is $\sum_{i=1}^{n} f_i$.

- **EXAMPLE**

  If the measurements 3, 7, 2, 8, 0, and 4 occur with frequencies 3, 2, 1, 5, 10, and 6, respectively, then the arithmetic mean is

  $$\bar{x} = \frac{3 \times 3 + 7 \times 2 + 2 \times 1 + 8 \times 5 + 0 \times 10 + 4 \times 6}{3 + 2 + 1 + 5 + 10 + 6} \approx 3.3$$

  Keep in mind that the arithmetic mean is strongly affected by extreme values.

- **EXAMPLE**

  Consider four workers whose annual salaries are $2,500, $3,200, $3,700, and $48,000. The arithmetic mean of their salaries is

  $$\frac{\$57,400}{4} = \$14,350$$

  The figure $14,350, however, can hardly represent the typical annual salary of the four workers.

The **deviation** d_i of x_i from its mean $\bar{x}$ is defined to be

$$d_i = x_i - \bar{x}$$

The sum of the deviations of $x_1, x_2, \ldots, x_n$ from their mean $\bar{x}$ is equal to zero. Indeed,

$$\sum_{i=1}^{n} d_i = \sum_{i=1}^{n} (x_i - \bar{x}) = 0$$

Thus,

$$\sum_{i=1}^{n} (x_i - \bar{x}) = \sum_{i=1}^{n} x_i - n\bar{x} = \sum x_i - n\frac{\sum x_i}{n}$$

$$= \sum x_i - \sum x_i = 0$$

- **EXAMPLE**

  If $z_1 = x_1 + y_1, \ldots, z_n = x_n + y_n$, then $\bar{z} = \bar{x} + \bar{y}$. Indeed,

  $$\bar{x} = \frac{\sum x}{n}, \bar{y} = \frac{\sum y}{n}, \text{ and } \bar{z} = \frac{\sum z}{n}$$

  We have

  $$\bar{z} = \frac{\sum z}{n} = \frac{\sum (x+y)}{n} = \frac{\sum x}{n} + \frac{\sum y}{n} = \bar{x} + \bar{y}$$

  We will be using different symbols for the sample mean and the population mean. The population mean is denoted by μ, and the sample mean is denoted by $\bar{x}$. The sample mean $\bar{x}$ will be used to make inferences about the corresponding population mean μ.

- **EXAMPLE**

  Suppose a bank has 500 savings accounts. We pick a sample of 12 accounts. The balance on each account in dollars is

657	284	51
215	73	327
65	412	218
539	225	195

The sample mean $\bar{x}$ is

$$\bar{x} = \frac{\sum_{i=1}^{12} x_i}{12} = \$271.75$$

The average amount of money for the 12 sampled accounts is $271.75. Using this information, we estimate the total amount of money in the bank to be

$$\$271.75 \times 500 = \$135,875.$$

PROBLEM

The following measurements were taken by an antique dealer as he weighed to the nearest pound his prized collection of anvils. The weights were 84, 92, 37, 50, 50, 84, 40, and 98. What was the mean weight of the anvils?

SOLUTION

The average or mean weight of the anvils is

$$\bar{x} = \frac{\text{sum of observations}}{\text{number of observations}}$$

$$= \frac{84 + 92 + 37 + 50 + 50 + 84 + 40 + 98}{8}$$

$$= \frac{535}{8} = 66.88 \cong 67 \text{ pounds}$$

An alternate way to compute the sample mean is to rearrange the terms in the numerator, grouping the numbers that are the same. Thus,

$$\bar{x} = \frac{(84 + 84) + (50 + 50) + 37 + 40 + 90 + 98}{8}$$

We see that we can express the mean in terms of the frequency of observations. The frequency of an observation is the number of times a number appears in a sample.

$$\bar{x} = \frac{2(84) + 2(50) + 37 + 40 + 90 + 98}{8}$$

The observations 84 and 50 appear in the sample twice, and thus each observation has frequency 2.

PROBLEM

The numbers 4, 2, 7, and 9 occur with frequencies 2, 3, 11, and 4, respectively. Find the arithmetic mean.

SOLUTION

To find the arithmetic mean, $\bar{x}$, multiply each different number by its associated frequency. Add these products, then divide by the total number of numbers.

$$\bar{x} = [(4)(2) + (2)(3) + (7)(11) + (9)(4)] \div 20$$

$$= (8 + 6 + 77 + 36) \div 20$$

$$= 127 \div 20 = 6.35$$

All means can also be computed for the grouped data, that is, when data are presented in a frequency distribution. Then, all values within a given class interval are considered to be equal to the class mark, or midpoint, of the interval.

Measures of Central Tendency

Definition of the Mode

The **mode** of a set of numbers is the value that occurs most often (with the highest frequency).

Observe that the mode may not exist. Also, if the mode exists, it may not be unique. For example, for the numbers 1, 1, 2, and 2, the mode is not unique.

- **EXAMPLE**

The set of numbers 2, 2, 4, 7, 9, 9, 13, 13, 13, 26, and 29 has mode 13.

The set of numbers that has two or more modes is called **bimodal**.

For grouped data – data presented in the form of a frequency table – we do not know the actual measurements, only how many measurements fall into each interval. In such a case, the mode is the midpoint of the class interval with the highest frequency.

Note that the mode can also measure popularity. In this sense, we can determine the most popular model of car or the most popular actor.

- **EXAMPLE**

One can compute the mode from a histogram or frequency distribution.

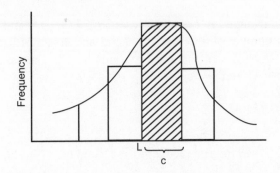

The shaded area indicates the modal class, that is, the class containing the mode.

$$Mode = L + c \left[\frac{\Delta_1}{\Delta_1 + \Delta_2} \right]$$

where

L is the lower class boundary of the modal class

c is the size of the modal class interval

Δ_1 is the excess of the modal frequency over the frequency of the next lower class

Δ_2 is the excess of the modal frequency over the frequency of the next higher class

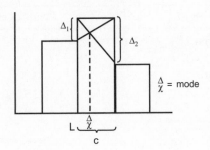

PROBLEM

Find the mode of the sample 14, 19, 16, 21, 18, 19, 24, 15, and 19.

SOLUTION

The number 19 is observed three times in this sample, and no other observation appears as frequently. The mode of this sample is therefore 19.

PROBLEM

Find the mode or modes of the sample 6, 7, 7, 3, 8, 5, 3, and 9.

SOLUTION

In this sample the numbers 7 and 3 both appear twice. There are no other observations that appear as frequently as these two. Therefore, 3 and 7 are the modes of this sample. The sample is called "bimodal."

PROBLEM

Find the mode of the sample 14, 16, 21, 19, 18, 24, and 17.

SOLUTION

In this sample all the numbers occur with the same frequency. There is no single number that is observed more frequently than any other. Thus, there is no mode or all observations are modes. The mode is not a useful concept here.

Definition of Median

The **median** of a set of numbers is defined as the middle value when the numbers are arranged in order of magnitude. The number of observations that lie above the median is the same as the number of observations that lie below it.

Usually, the median is used to measure the midpoint of a large set of numbers. For example, we can talk about the median age of people getting married. Here, the median reflects the central value of the data for a large set of measurements. For small sets of numbers, we use the following conventions:

- For an odd number of measurements, the median is the middle value.

- For an even number of measurements, the median is the average of the two middle values.

In both cases, the numbers have to be arranged in order of magnitude.

- **EXAMPLE**

The scores of a test are 78, 79, 83, 83, 87, 92, and 95. Hence, the median is 83.

- **EXAMPLE**

The median of the set of numbers 21, 25, 29, 33, 44, and 47 is $\dfrac{29+33}{2} = 31$. Note that the median of an even number of measurements need not be one of the measurements.

It is more difficult to compute the median for grouped data. The exact value of the measurements is not known; hence, we know only that the median is located in a particular class interval. The problem is where to place the median within this interval.

For grouped data, the median obtained by interpolation is given by

$$\text{Median} = L + \frac{c}{f_{\text{median}}} \left(\frac{n}{2} - \left(\sum f \right)_{\text{cum}} \right)$$

where

L = the lower class limit of the interval that contains the median

c = the size of the median class interval

f_{median} = frequency of the median class

n = the total frequency

$\left(\sum f \right)_{\text{cum}}$ = the sum of frequencies (cumulative frequency) for all classes before the median class

PROBLEM

Find the median of the sample 34, 29, 26, 37, and 31.

SOLUTION

Arranged in order, we have 26, 29, 31, 34, and 37. The number of observations is odd, and thus the median is 31. Note that there are two numbers in the sample above 31 and two below 31.

PROBLEM

Find the median of the sample 34, 29, 26, 37, 31, and 34.

SOLUTION

The sample arranged in order is 26, 29, 31, 34, 34, and 37. The number of observations is even, and thus the median, or middle number, is chosen halfway between the third and fourth numbers. In this case, the median is

$$\frac{31+34}{2} = 32.5$$

- **EXAMPLE**

The weight of 50 men is depicted in the table below in the form of a frequency distribution.

Weight	Frequency
115 – 121	2
122 – 128	3
129 – 135	13
136 – 142	15
143 – 149	9
150 – 156	5
157 – 163	3
TOTAL	50

Class 136 – 142 has the highest frequency.

The mode is the midpoint of the class interval with the highest frequency.

$$\text{Mode} = \frac{135.5 + 142.5}{2} = 139$$

We can also use the formula

$$\text{Mode} = L + c\left(\frac{\Delta_1}{\Delta_1 + \Delta_2}\right)$$

where
$$L = 135.5$$
$$c = 7$$
$$\Delta_1 = 15 - 13 = 2$$
$$\Delta_2 = 15 - 9 = 6$$
$$\text{Mode} = 135.5 + 7 \times \frac{2}{2+6} = 137.25$$

The median is located in class $136 - 142$.

We have

$$\text{Median} = L + \frac{c}{f_{\text{median}}}\left(\frac{n}{2} - \left(\sum f\right)_{\text{cum}}\right)$$

where
$$L = 135.5$$
$$c = 7$$
$$f_{\text{median}} = 15$$
$$n = 50$$
$$\left(\sum f\right)_{\text{cum}} = 2 + 3 + 13 = 18$$

Hence,

$$\text{Median} = 135.5 + \frac{7}{15}\left[\frac{50}{2} - 18\right] = 138.77$$

To compute the arithmetic mean for grouped data, we compute the midpoint x_i of each of the intervals and use the formula

$$\bar{x} = \frac{\displaystyle\sum_{i=1}^{n} f_i x_i}{\displaystyle\sum_{i=1}^{n} f_i}$$

We have

$$\bar{x} = \frac{118 \times 2 + 125 \times 3 + 132 \times 13 + 139 \times 15 + 146 \times 9 + 153 \times 5 + 160 \times 3}{50}$$

$$= 139.42$$

For symmetrical curves, the mean, mode, and median all coincide.

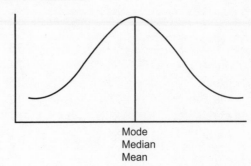

Mode
Median
Mean

For a distribution, skewed to the left, we have the following:

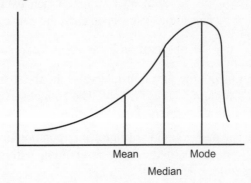

Mean   Mode
       Median

For a distribution skewed to the right, we have the following:

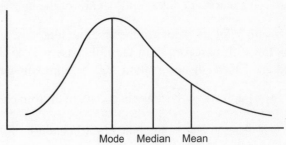

Mode   Median   Mean

PROBLEM

> Find the median weight from the following table.

Class Boundaries	Class Weights	Frequencies
58.5 – 61.5	60	4
61.5 – 64.5	63	8
64.5 – 67.5	66	12
67.5 – 70.5	69	13
70.5 – 73.5	72	21
73.5 – 76.5	75	15
76.5 – 79.5	78	12
79.5 – 82.5	81	9
82.5 – 85.5	84	4
85.5 – 88.5	87	2

SOLUTION

There are 100 observations in the sample. The median will be the 50th observation. When using an even-numbered sample of grouped data, the convention is to call the $\frac{n}{2}$th observation the median. There are 37 observations in the first four intervals, and the first five intervals contain 58 observations. The 50th observation is in the fifth class interval.

We use the technique of linear interpolation to estimate the position of the 50th observation within the class interval.

The width of the fifth class is three, and there are 21 observations in the class. To interpolate, we imagine that each observation takes up $\frac{3}{21}$ units of the interval. There are 37 observations in the first four intervals, and thus the 13th observation in the fifth class will be the median. This 13th observation will be approximately $13\left(\frac{3}{21}\right)$ units from the lower boundary of the fifth class interval. The median is thus the lower boundary of the fifth class plus $13\left(\frac{3}{21}\right)$, or

$$\text{median} = 70.5 + \frac{13}{7} = 72.36$$

PROBLEM

> A sample of drivers involved in motor vehicle accidents was categorized by age. The results appear as:
>
> | Age | Number of Accidents |
> |---|---|
> | 16 – 25 | 28 |
> | 26 – 35 | 13 |
> | 36 – 45 | 12 |
> | 46 – 55 | 8 |
> | 56 – 65 | 19 |
> | 66 – 75 | 20 |
>
> What is the value of the median?

SOLUTION

The total number of accidents is 100. The median is the $\frac{100}{2} = $ 50th number when the numbers are arranged in ascending order. (In this case, we have intervals of numbers instead of just numbers.) The two intervals 16 – 25 and 26 – 35 consist of 41 count. We need nine numbers from the interval 36 – 45. Use the lower boundary of this interval 36 – 45, which is 35.5, and add $\frac{9}{12}$ of the width of the interval (10).

Then

$$35.5 + \frac{9}{12}(10) = 43$$

Measures of Variability

Range and Percentiles

The degree to which numerical data tend to spread about an average value is called the **variation** or **dispersion** of the data. We shall define various measures of dispersion.

The simplest measure of data variation is the range.

Definition of Range

The **range** of a set of numbers is defined to be the difference between the largest and the smallest number of the set. For grouped data, the range is the difference between the upper limit of the last interval and the lower limit of the first interval. The range is not a very satisfactory measure of dispersion as it involves only two of the observations in the sample.

• **EXAMPLE**

The range of the numbers 3, 6, 21, 24, and 38 is $38 - 3 = 35$.

PROBLEM

Find the range of the sample composed of the observations 33, 53, 35, 37, and 49.

SOLUTION

In this sample, the largest observation is 53 and the smallest is 33. The difference is $53 - 33 = 20$, and the range is 20.

Definition of Percentiles

The nth percentile of a set of numbers arranged in order of magnitude is the value that has $n\%$ of the numbers below it and $(100 - n)\%$ above it.

• **EXAMPLE**

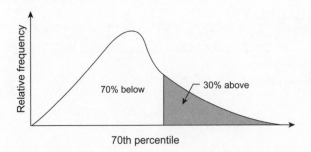

Percentiles are often used to describe the results of achievement tests. For example, someone graduates in the top 10% of the class. Frequently used percentiles

are the 25th, 50th and 75th percentiles, which are called the lower quartile, the middle quartile (median), and the upper quartile, respectively.

Definition of Interquartile Range

The interquartile range, abbreviated IQR, of a set of numbers is the difference between the upper and lower quartiles, as shown on the graph below.

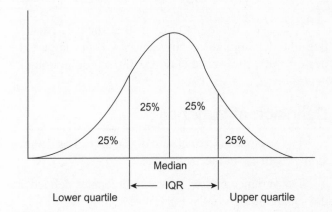

PROBLEM

In a sample of data, the 75th percentile is the number 23. If the interquartile range is 10, what number represents the 25th percentile?

SOLUTION

The interquartile range = the difference between the 75th percentile and the 25th percentile. If $x = $ 25th percentile, we have $23 - x = 10$, so $x = 13$.

Definition of Standard Deviation

The standard deviation of a set $x_1, x_2, \ldots, x_n$ of n numbers is defined by

$$s = \sqrt{\frac{\sum_{i=1}^{n}(x_i - \bar{x})^2}{n}} = \sqrt{\overline{(x - \bar{x})^2}}$$

The sample standard deviation is denoted by s, while the corresponding population standard deviation is denoted by σ.

For grouped data, we use the modified formula for standard deviation. Let the frequencies of the numbers $x_1, x_2, \ldots, x_n$ be $f_1, f_2, \ldots, f_n$, respectively. Then,

$$s = \sqrt{\frac{\sum f_i (x_i - \bar{x})^2}{\sum f_i}} = \sqrt{\frac{\sum f(x - \bar{x})^2}{\sum f}}$$

Often, in the definition of the standard deviation, the denominator is not n but $n - 1$. For large values of n, the difference between the two definitions is negligible.

Definition of Variance

The **variance** is a measure of the spread or dispersion of data about the sample mean.

The variance of a set of measurements is defined as the square of the standard deviation. Thus,

$$s^2 = \frac{\sum_{i=1}^{n} (x_i - \bar{x})^2}{n - 1}$$

or

$$s^2 = \frac{\sum_{i=1}^{n} f_i (x_i - \bar{x})^2}{\sum_{i=1}^{n} f_i}$$

Usually, the variance of the sample is denoted by s^2, and the corresponding population variance is denoted by σ^2.

• EXAMPLE

A simple manual task was given to six children, and the time each child took to complete the task was measured. Results are shown in the following table.

x_i	$x_i - \bar{x}$	$(x_i - \bar{x})^2$
12	2.5	6.25
9	−0.5	0.25
11	1.5	2.25
6	−3.5	12.25
10	0.5	0.25
9	−0.5	0.25
Total 57	0	21.5

For this sample, we shall find the standard deviation and variance.

The average $\bar{x}$ is 9.5.

$$\bar{x} = 9.5$$

The standard deviation is

$$s^2 = \sqrt{\frac{21.5}{5}} = 2.07$$

and the variance is

$$s^2 = 4.3$$

PROBLEM

A couple has six children whose ages are 6, 8, 10, 12, 14, and 16. Find the variance in ages.

SOLUTION

To compute the variance, we first calculate the sample mean.

$$\bar{x} = \frac{\sum x_i}{n} = \frac{\text{sum of observations}}{\text{number of observations}}$$

$$= \frac{6 + 8 + 10 + 12 + 14 + 16}{6} = \frac{66}{6} = 11$$

The variance is defined to be

$$s^2 = \frac{\sum\limits_{i=1}^{n}(x_i - \bar{x})^2}{n-1}$$

$$= \frac{(6-11)^2 + (8-11)^2 + (10-11)^2 + (12-11)^2 + (14-11)^2 + (16-11)^2}{5}$$

$$= \frac{25 + 9 + 1 + 1 + 9 + 25}{5} = \frac{70}{5} = 14$$

Sampling

Sample quantities, such as sample mean, or deviation, are called **sample statistics** or **statistics**. Based on these quantities, we estimate the corresponding quantities for the entire population, which are called **population parameters** or **parameters**. For two different samples, the difference between sample statistics can be due to chance variation or some significant factor. The latter case should be investigated, and possible mistakes corrected. Statistical inference is a study of inferences made concerning a population and based on the samples drawn from it.

Probability theory evaluates the accuracy of such inferences. The most important initial step is the choice of samples that are representative of a population. The methods of sampling are called the **design** of the experiment. One of the most widely used methods is random sampling.

Random Sampling

A sample of n measurements chosen from a population N ($N > n$) is said to be a random sample if every different sample of the same size n from the population has an equal probability of being selected.

A sample must meet the following conditions in order to be random:

(1) Equal Chance. A sample meets the condition of equal chance if it is selected in such a way that every observation in the entire population has an equal chance of being included in the sample.

(2) Independence. A sample meets this condition when the selection of any single observation does not affect the chances for selection of any other.

Samples that are not random are called biased.

One way of obtaining a random sample is to assign a number to each member of the population. The population thus becomes a set of numbers. Then, using the random number table, we can choose a sample of any desired size.

- **EXAMPLE**

Suppose 1,000 voters are registered and eligible to vote in an upcoming election. To conduct a poll, you need a sample of 50 persons, so you assign a number between one and 1,000 to each voter. Then, using the random number table or a computer program, you choose at random 50 numbers, which are 50 voters. This is your required sample.

Sampling With and Without Replacement

From a bag containing ten numbers from 1 to 10, we have to draw three numbers. As the first step, we draw a number. Now, we have the choice of replacing or not replacing the number in the bag. If we replace the number, then this number can come up again. If the number is not replaced, then it can come up only once.

Sampling in which each element of a population may be chosen more than once (i.e., where the chosen element is replaced) is called **sampling with replacement**. Sampling without replacement takes place when each element of a population can be chosen only once.

Remember that populations can be finite or infinite.

- **EXAMPLE**

A bag contains ten numbers. We choose two numbers without replacement. This is sampling from a finite population.

- **EXAMPLE**

A coin is tossed ten times and the number of tails is counted. This is sampling from an infinite population.

PROBLEM

> The following sampling procedure is to be classified as producing a random sample or as producing a biased sample. Decide whether the procedure is random or biased.
>
> In order to solve a particular problem, an investigator selects 100 people, each of which will provide 5 scores. The investigator will then take the average of each set of scores. This will yield 100 averages. Is this sample of average scores a random sample?

SOLUTION

The 100 elements are now independent. When repeated measures can be converted to a single score, so that each individual that is observed contributes just one summary observation (such as an average), the independence condition is met. Use of an average often helps to reduce the effects of chance variation within an individual's performance. Also, any observation would have an equal chance of being chosen. The sample is random.

PROBLEM

> A wheat researcher is studying the yield of a certain variety of wheat in the state of Colorado. She has at her disposal five farms scattered throughout the state on which she can plant the wheat and observe the yield. Describe the sample and the target population. Under what conditions will this be a random sample?

SOLUTION

The sample consists of the wheat yields on the five farms. The target population consists of the yields of wheat on every farm in the state. This sample will be random if (1) every farm in the state has an equal chance of being selected and (2) the selection of any particular farm is independent of the selection of any other farm.

Sampling Distributions

A population is given from which we draw samples of size n, with or without replacement. For each sample, we compute a statistic, such as the mean, standard deviation, or variance. These numbers will depend on the sample, and they will vary from sample to sample. In this way, we obtain a distribution of the statistic, which is called the **sampling distribution**.

For example, if for each sample we measure its mean, then the distribution obtained is the sampling distribution of means. We can obtain the sampling distributions of variances, standard deviations, medians, and so forth in the same way.

Correlation

Regression or estimation enables us to estimate one variable (the dependent variable) from one or more independent variables.

Correlation establishes the degree of the relationship between variables. It answers the question: how well does a given equation describe or explain the relationship between independent and dependent variables?

Perfect Correlation

If all values of the variables fit the equation without errors, we say that the variables are perfectly correlated.

The area of a square S is in perfect correlation to its side d:

$$S = d^2.$$

When tossing two coins, we record the result for each coin. Assuming that the coins are fair, there is no relationship between the results for each coin; that is, they are uncorrelated.

Between perfectly correlated and uncorrelated situations, there are situations with some degree of correlation. The heights and weights of people show some correlation. We let x represent one variable (height) and let y represent the other variable (weight). We then try to determine the correlation between x and y.

Simple correlation and simple regression occur when only two variables are involved. When more than two variables are involved, we speak of multiple correlation.

Correlation Coefficient

The degree of the relationship between two variables, x and y, is described by the **correlation coefficient**. It is actually a measure of how close to a straight line the data points are. If n observations are given

$$(x_i, y_i) \; i = 1, 2, \ldots, n$$

we can compute the sample correlation coefficient r.

$$r = \frac{\sum (x - \bar{x})(y - \bar{y})}{\sqrt{\sum (x - \bar{x})^2 \sum (y - \bar{y})^2}}$$

The following list states some properties of r:

1. $-1 \le r \le 1$

2. $r > 0$ indicates a positive linear relationship, and $r < 0$ indicates a negative linear relationship.

3. $r = 0$ indicates no linear relationship.

If y tends to increase as x increases, the correlation is positive.

Similarly, if y tends to decrease as x increases, the correlation is negative.

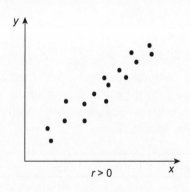

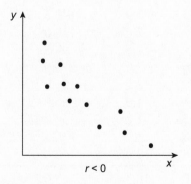

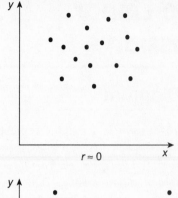

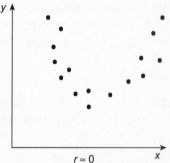

In addition, the **variability** in the data measures how much the data are spread out from the mean. Measures of variability include the range, variance, and standard deviation.

• **EXAMPLE**

Compare the data on the following two bar graphs, each of which has a mean of 20:

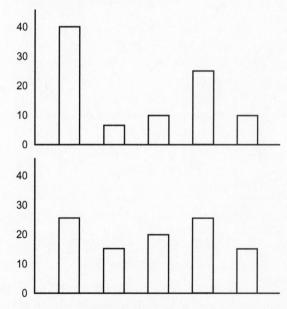

The data in the first graph are clearly more variable than the data in the second graph.

147

Simple Linear Regression

Scatter Diagram

A *scatter diagram* is a graphic representation of the relationship between two variables. It consists of an *x*-axis for coding the *independent variable* and a *y*-axis for coding the *dependent variable*. The data values are represented by points or dots within the grid and are plotted as they relate to both the *x* and *y* variables.

• **EXAMPLE**

x = Speed of Machine (rpm)	*y* = % Defectives Produced by Machine
50	1.5
75	1.9
60	2.0
65	1.5
90	3.0
70	2.5
55	1.0
45	1.2
80	1.7
70	2.0

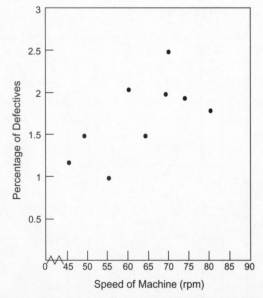

Speed of Machine (rpm)

The purpose of a scatter diagram is to allow for the comparison of the independent variable (*x*) with the dependent variable (*y*) so that we may get a feel for how they are related. We can observe both the direction of the

relationship, i.e., whether they are both changing in the same direction or in opposite directions, as well as the apparent strength of the relationship between the two variables. If we imagine a straight line through the middle of the points and then look at how close the points are to this imaginary line, we can get some idea about the strength of the relationship. The closer the points are to the line, and the sharper the slope of the line, the stronger the relationship between *x* and *y*.

Regression Equation

Simple linear regression is a technique by which one dependent variable (*y*) is regressed against one independent variable (*x*) and the relationship between the two is in the form of a straight line. The equation for calculating of the regression line is:

$$y_i = a + bx_i$$

where: y_i = the ith value of the dependent variable,

      x_i = the ith value of the independent variable.

$$b = \frac{\sum xy - n\bar{x}\bar{y}}{\sum x^2 - n\bar{x}^2} \qquad a = \frac{\sum y - b\sum x}{n}$$

• **EXAMPLE**

Assume that we use the data from the previous example and compute the regression equation, where *x* = speed of machine measured in revolutions per minute and *y* = percentage of defective items produced by the machine at the specified rates.

x (rpm)	y (%)	xy	x²
50	1.5	75.0	2,500
75	1.9	142.5	5,625
60	2.0	120.0	3,600
65	1.5	97.5	4,225
90	3.0	270.0	8,100
70	2.5	175.0	4,900
55	1.0	55.0	3,025
45	1.2	54.0	2,025
80	1.7	136.0	6,400
70	2.0	140.0	4,900
TOTAL 660	**18.3**	**1,265.0**	**45,300**

$$\bar{x} = \sum x/n \qquad \bar{y} = \sum y/n$$
$$= 660/10 \qquad = 18.3/10$$
$$= 66 \qquad = 1.83$$
$$= 66 \qquad = 1.83$$

$$b = \frac{\sum xy - n\bar{x}\bar{y}}{\sum x^2 - n\bar{x}^2}$$

$$= \frac{1265 - 10(66)(1.83)}{45,300 - 10(66)^2}$$

$$= \frac{1265 - 1207.8}{45,300 - 43,560}$$

$$= \frac{57.2}{1740}$$

$$= .033$$

$$a = \frac{\sum y - b\sum x}{n}$$

$$= \frac{18.3 - .033(660)}{10}$$

$$= \frac{18.3 - 21.78}{10}$$

$$= \frac{-3.48}{10}$$

$$= -.348$$

Therefore: $y = a + bx$, i.e.,

$$y = -.348 + .033x.$$

The value of "b" is the slope of the line. In this equation, $b = .033$ tells us that for every unit increase in rpm, the percentage of defective units produced increases by .033 percent. This is an indication of a positive relationship between x and y; i.e., as x increases, y also increases, which is evident as well from the scatter diagram.

SCATTER DIAGRAM WITH REGRESSION LINE

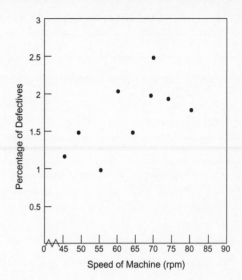

The value of "a", which is the y-intercept, indicates that at the point where $x = 0$, the regression line would cross the y-axis at $-.348$. A strict interpretation of this value would be that if we operate the machine at 0 rpm, we would produce $-.348$ defectives. Obviously, if we were operating the machine at 0 rpm, it would not be producing any items and, consequently, the percentage of defectives would be 0 also. We must keep in mind that the regression equation is valid only for a relevant range of x values.

Once we have plotted the data in a scatter diagram and calculated the regression equation, it is generally useful to plot a regression line. Since we know that this will be a straight line, we may substitute two values for x into the equation, solve for y, and plot the straight line from these points. Using the previous example, we can illustrate this.

• **EXAMPLE**

SCATTER DIAGRAM WITH REGRESSION LINE

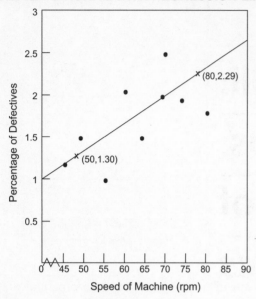

If $x = 50$; $y = -.348 + .033(50) = 1.30$
If $x = 80$; $y = -.348 + .033(80) = 2.29$

Now we have a "real" line through the data points and we can observe that the points fall "relatively" close to the line, which implies that the relationship between the speed at which the machine operates and the percentage of defectives it produces is "relatively" strong. Also, we note that the relationship is positive in that the line has an upward slope. If the relationship is inverse or negative, the sign of "*b*" will be negative and the regression line will therefore slope downward.

Once we have measured the relationship between x and y, of what value is this knowledge? If we are satisfied that the relationship is strong enough, we may use the regression equation x to predict the value of y from predetermined values of x. For example, what percentages of defective items should we expect if we set the rpm rate at some prespecified value? We can answer this question by substituting this prespecified value into the equation for x and solving for y.

• **EXAMPLE**

What percentage of defectives would we expect if we set the rpm rate at 95?

$$y = a + bx$$
$$y = -.348 + .033(95)$$
$$y = 2.787, \text{ or } 2.79\%$$

What percentage of defectives would we expect if we set the rpm rate at 40?

$$y = -.348 + .033(40)$$
$$= .972, \text{ or } .97\%$$

Note that when we use a regression equation to predict values of y from x, we should not use x values that are extremely different from those used to build the equation. That is, we cannot expect the same linear relationship to hold indefinitely over all values of x.

Review for Subtest III: Domain 5: Calculus; Domain 6: History of Mathematics

Trigonometry

Trigonometry is a field of mathematics that basically is used to find the missing measures (lengths of sides and angles) in a triangle if you have some information about the triangle. Extensions of the use of trigonometry include astronomy, geography, and even medical imaging. The values of trigonometric functions for any angle are available in "trig" tables or on most calculators.

Angles and Trigonometric Functions

The basic trigonometric functions are based on the right triangle, such as $\triangle ABC$, shown in the figure below:

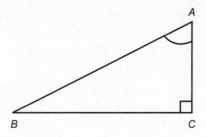

Definition 1: Sine

$$\sin \angle A = \frac{BC}{AB}$$
$$= \frac{\text{measure of side opposite } \angle A}{\text{measure of hypotenuse}}$$

Definition 2: Cosine

$$\cos \angle A = \frac{AC}{AB}$$
$$= \frac{\text{measure of side adjacent to } \angle A}{\text{measure of hypotenuse}}$$

Definition 3: Tangent

$$\tan \angle A = \frac{BC}{AC}$$
$$= \frac{\text{measure of side opposite } \angle A}{\text{measure of side adjacent to } \angle A}$$

Definition 4: Cotangent

$$\cot \angle A = \frac{AC}{BC}$$
$$= \frac{\text{measure of side adjacent to } \angle A}{\text{measure of side opposite } \angle A}$$

Definition 5: Secant

$$\sec \angle A = \frac{AB}{AC}$$

$$= \frac{\text{measure of hypotenuse}}{\text{measure of side adjacent to } \angle A}$$

Definition 6: Cosecant

$$\csc \angle A = \frac{AB}{BC}$$

$$= \frac{\text{measure of hypotenuse}}{\text{measure of side opposite to } \angle A}$$

The following table gives the values of sine, cosine, tangent, and cotangent for some special angles. The angles are given in radians and in degrees. A **radian** is a measure of the central angle in a circle and is usually expressed in terms of π. A full circle has 360°, or 2π radians.

α	Sin α	Cos α	Tan α	Cot α
$0°$	0	1	0	∞
$\frac{\pi}{6} = 30°$	$\frac{1}{2}$	$\frac{\sqrt{3}}{2}$	$\frac{1}{\sqrt{3}}$	$\sqrt{3}$
$\frac{\pi}{4} = 45°$	$\frac{1}{\sqrt{2}}$	$\frac{1}{\sqrt{2}}$	1	1
$\frac{\pi}{3} = 60°$	$\frac{\sqrt{3}}{2}$	$\frac{1}{2}$	$\sqrt{3}$	$\frac{1}{\sqrt{3}}$
$\frac{\pi}{2} = 90°$	1	0	∞	0

A circle with center located at the origin of the rectangular coordinate axes with radius equal to one unit length is called a unit circle. Its equation is $x^2 + y^2 = 1$.

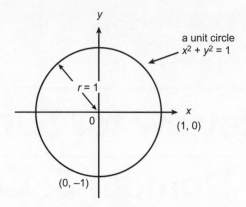

An angle whose vertex is at the origin of a rectangular coordinate system and whose initial side coincides with the positive x-axis is said to be in standard position with respect to the coordinate system. See $\angle \theta$ in the figure below.

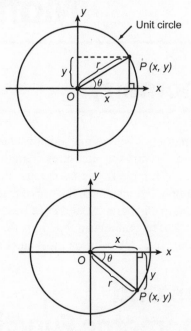

A quadrant angle is an angle in standard position whose terminal side lies on one of the axes of a Cartesian coordinate system.

An angle in standard position with respect to a Cartesian coordinate system whose terminal side lies in the first (or second or third or fourth) quadrant is called a first (or second or third or fourth) quadrant angle.

If θ is a non-quadrantal angle in standard position and $P(x, y)$ is any point, distinct from the origin, on the terminal side of θ, then the six trigonometric functions of θ are defined in terms of the abscissa (x-coordinate), ordinate (y-coordinate), and distance $\overline{OP}$ as follows:

$$\text{sine } \theta = \sin \theta = \frac{\text{ordinate}}{\text{distance}} = \frac{y}{r}$$

$$\text{cosine } \theta = \cos \theta = \frac{\text{abscissa}}{\text{distance}} = \frac{x}{r}$$

$$\text{tangent } \theta = \tan \theta = \frac{\text{ordinate}}{\text{abscissa}} = \frac{y}{x}$$

$$\text{cotangent } \theta = \cot \theta = \frac{\text{abscissa}}{\text{ordinate}} = \frac{x}{y}$$

$$\text{secant } \theta = \sec \theta = \frac{\text{distance}}{\text{abscissa}} = \frac{r}{x}$$

$$\text{cosecant } \theta = \csc \theta = \frac{\text{distance}}{\text{ordinate}} = \frac{r}{y}$$

The signs of the functions in the quadrants depend on whether the ordinate or abscissa is positive or negative in that quadrant (the distance r is always taken as positive). Thus, for $x < 90°$, if $\sin x = A$, $\sin (x + 180) = -A$, or $\sin x = -\sin (x + 180)$.

The value of trigonometric functions of quadrantal angles are given in the table below.

θ	$\sin \theta$	$\cos \theta$	$\tan \theta$	$\cot \theta$	$\sec \theta$	$\csc \theta$
0°	0	1	0	$\pm\infty$	1	$\pm\infty$
90°	1	0	$\pm\infty$	0	$\pm\infty$	1
180°	0	−1	0	$\pm\infty$	−1	$\pm\infty$
270°	−1	0	$\pm\infty$	0	$\pm\infty$	−1

• **EXAMPLES**

1. Find $\sin \theta$ given $A = 30°$.

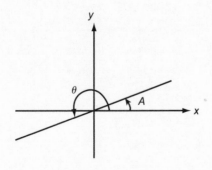

Obviously, $\theta = 180° + A = 210°$. Since sine is negative in the third quadrant, we have

$$\sin \theta = \sin 210° = -|\sin(210° - 180°)| = -\sin 30°$$

$$= -\frac{1}{2}.$$

2. If $\sin 2x = -\sin(-x + 9°)$, find x.
    Since $\sin x = -\sin (x + 180)$,

    $$\sin 2x = -\sin(-x + 9°) = \sin(-x + 9° + 180°)$$

    So $2x = -x + 9° + 180°$ and $x = 63°$

Basic Identities

$$\sin^2\alpha + \cos^2\alpha = 1$$

$$\tan \alpha = \frac{\sin \alpha}{\cos \alpha}$$

$$\cot \alpha = \frac{\cos \alpha}{\sin \alpha} = \frac{1}{\tan \alpha}$$

$$\csc \alpha = \frac{1}{\sin \alpha}$$

$$\sec \alpha = \frac{1}{\cos \alpha}$$

$$1 + \tan^2\alpha = \sec^2\alpha$$

$$1 + \cot^2\alpha = \csc^2\alpha$$

One can find all the trigonometric functions of an acute angle when the value of any one of them is known.

• **EXAMPLES**

Given α is an acute angle and $\csc \alpha = 2$, then

$$\sin \alpha = \frac{1}{\csc \alpha} = \frac{1}{2}, \text{ and since } \cos^2 \alpha + \sin^2 \alpha = 1,$$

$$\cos \alpha = \sqrt{1 - \sin^2 \alpha}$$

$$= \sqrt{1 - \left(\frac{1}{2}\right)^2}$$

$$= \sqrt{1 - \frac{1}{4}}$$

$$= \frac{\sqrt{3}}{2}$$

$$\tan \alpha = \frac{\sin \alpha}{\cos \alpha} = \frac{\frac{1}{2}}{\frac{\sqrt{3}}{2}} = \frac{1}{\sqrt{3}} = \frac{\sqrt{3}}{3}$$

$$\cot \alpha = \frac{1}{\tan \alpha} = \sqrt{3}$$

$$\sec \alpha = \frac{1}{\cos \alpha} = \frac{1}{\frac{\sqrt{3}}{2}} = \frac{2}{\sqrt{3}} = \frac{2\sqrt{3}}{3}$$

If ϕ is an acute angle in standard position, and θ is related to ϕ in each quadrant, as shown by the dashed lines in the following figure,

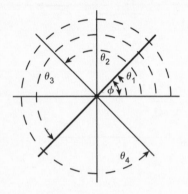

i) If θ is a first quadrant angle, and ϕ is in standard position, then

    a) $\sin \theta = \sin \phi$ d) $\cot \theta = \cot \phi$

    b) $\cos \theta = \cos \phi$ e) $\sec \theta = \sec \phi$

    c) $\tan \theta = \tan \phi$ f) $\csc \theta = \csc \phi$

ii) If θ is a second quadrant angle:

    a) $\sin \theta = \sin \phi$ d) $\cot \theta = -\cot \phi$

    b) $\cos \theta = -\cos \phi$ e) $\sec \theta = -\sec \phi$

    c) $\tan \theta = -\tan \phi$ f) $\csc \theta = \csc \phi$

iii) If θ is a third quadrant angle, then

    a) $\sin \theta = -\sin \phi$ d) $\cot \theta = \cot \phi$

    b) $\cos \theta = -\cos \phi$ e) $\sec \theta = -\sec \phi$

    c) $\tan \theta = \tan \phi$ f) $\csc \theta = -\csc \phi$

iv) If θ is a fourth quadrant angle, then

    a) $\sin \theta = -\sin \phi$ d) $\cot \theta = -\cot \phi$

    b) $\cos \theta = \cos \phi$ e) $\sec \theta = \sec \phi$

    c) $\tan \theta = -\tan \phi$ f) $\csc \theta = -\csc \phi$

Addition and Subtraction Formulas

$$\sin (A \pm B) = \sin A \cos B \pm \cos A \sin B$$
$$\cos (A \pm B) = \cos A \cos B \mp \sin A \sin B$$
$$\tan(A \pm B) = \frac{\tan A \pm \tan B}{1 \mp \tan A \tan B}$$

Double-Angle Formulas

$$\sin 2A = 2 \sin A \cos A$$
$$\cos 2A = 2 \cos^2 A - 1$$
$$= 1 - 2 \sin^2 A$$
$$= \cos^2 A - \sin^2 A$$
$$\tan 2A = \frac{2 \tan A}{1 - \tan^2 A}$$

Half-Angle Formulas

$$\sin \frac{A}{2} = \pm \frac{\sqrt{1 - \cos A}}{2}$$
$$\cos \frac{A}{2} = \pm \frac{\sqrt{1 + \cos A}}{2}$$

$$\tan \frac{A}{2} = \pm \sqrt{\frac{1 - \cos A}{1 + \cos A}}$$
$$= \frac{1 - \cos A}{\sin A}$$
$$= \frac{\sin A}{1 + \cos A}$$

$$\cot \frac{A}{2} = \sqrt{\frac{1 + \cos A}{1 - \cos A}} = \frac{1 + \cos A}{\sin A} = \frac{\sin A}{1 - \cos A}$$

Sum and Difference Formulas

$$\sin A + \sin B = 2\sin\left(\frac{A+B}{2}\right)\cos\left(\frac{A-B}{2}\right)$$

$$\sin A - \sin B = 2\cos\left(\frac{A+B}{2}\right)\sin\left(\frac{A-B}{2}\right)$$

$$\cos A + \cos B = 2\cos\left(\frac{A+B}{2}\right)\cos\left(\frac{A-B}{2}\right)$$

$$\cos A - \cos B = 2\sin\left(\frac{A+B}{2}\right)\sin\left(\frac{A-B}{2}\right)$$

$$\tan A + \tan B = \frac{\sin(A+B)}{\cos A \cos B}$$

$$\tan A - \tan B = \frac{\sin(A-B)}{\cos A \cos B}$$

Product Formulas of Sines and Cosines

$$\sin A \sin B = \frac{1}{2}[\cos(A-B) - \cos(A+B)]$$

$$\cos A \cos B = \frac{1}{2}[\cos(A+B) + \cos(A-B)]$$

$$\sin A \cos B = \frac{1}{2}[\sin(A+B) + \sin(A-B)]$$

$$\cos A \sin B = \frac{1}{2}[\sin(A+B) - \sin(A-B)]$$

- **EXAMPLE**

If $\sin\alpha = \frac{3}{5}$ and $\cos\beta = \frac{3}{5}$, find $\cos(\alpha+\beta)$.

Since $\cos(\alpha+\beta) = \cos\alpha\cos\beta - \sin\alpha\sin\beta$, we need to find $\cos\alpha$ and $\sin\beta$.

$$\cos\alpha = \sqrt{1 - \sin^2\alpha} = \sqrt{1 - \frac{9}{25}} = \sqrt{\frac{16}{25}} = \frac{4}{5}$$

$$\sin\beta = \sqrt{1 - \cos^2\beta} = \sqrt{1 - \frac{9}{25}} = \sqrt{\frac{16}{25}} = \frac{4}{5}$$

So,

$$\cos(\alpha+\beta) = \frac{4}{5} \times \frac{3}{5} - \frac{3}{5} \times \frac{4}{5} = 0$$

Properties and Graphs of Trigonometric Functions

The **sine function** is the graph of $y = \sin x$. Other trigonometric functions are defined similarly.

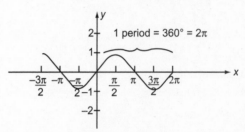

Sine Function

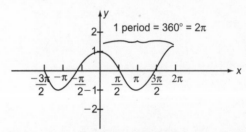

Cosine Function

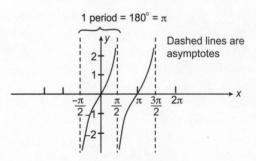

Tangent Function

- **EXAMPLE**

Draw one period of the graph for the function $y = 0.5\sin(4x + \frac{\pi}{6})$ and indicate its amplitude, period, and phase shift.

$$x = 0, y = 0.5 \sin \frac{\pi}{6}$$

$$x = \frac{\pi}{4}, y = 0.5 \sin(\pi + \frac{\pi}{6}) = -0.5 \sin \frac{\pi}{6}$$

$$x = \frac{\pi}{2}, y = 0.5 \sin(2\pi + \frac{\pi}{6}) = 0.5 \sin \frac{\pi}{6}$$

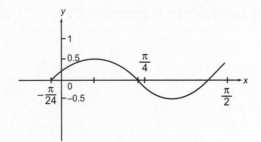

So, amplitude $= \dfrac{1}{2}$

period $= \dfrac{\pi}{2}$

At $y = 0$, $\sin\left(4x + \dfrac{\pi}{6}\right) = 0$

Therefore, $4x = -\dfrac{\pi}{6}$ and $x = -\dfrac{\pi}{24}$, so

phase shift $= -\dfrac{\pi}{24}$

Inverse Trigonometric Functions

If $-1 < x < 1$, then there are infinitely many angles whose sine is x, as we can see by looking at the graph of the sine function. Therefore, it is common to restrict the range of inverse trigonometric functions as follows:

arcsin $x =$ the angle between $-\dfrac{\pi}{2}$ and $\dfrac{\pi}{2}$ whose sine is x.

arccsc $x =$ the angle between $-\dfrac{\pi}{2}$ and $\dfrac{\pi}{2}$ whose cosecant is x.

arctan $x =$ the angle between $-\dfrac{\pi}{2}$ and $\dfrac{\pi}{2}$ whose tangent is x.

arccos $x =$ the angle between 0 and π whose cosine is x.

arcsec $x =$ the angle between 0 and π whose secant is x.

arccot $x =$ the angle between 0 and π whose cotangent is x.

PROBLEM

Evaluate arcsin $\dfrac{1}{2}$.

SOLUTION

Since $\sin \dfrac{\pi}{6} = \dfrac{1}{2}$, $\arcsin \dfrac{1}{2} = \dfrac{\pi}{6}$. The sine function and the arcsine function (abbreviated arcsin or $\sin^{-1}$) are inverses of each other in the sense that the composition of the two functions is the identity function (that is the function that takes x back to x).

$$\sin(\arcsin x) = x$$
$$\arcsin(\sin x) = x$$

Periodicity

The **period** of a (repeating) function, f, is the smallest positive number p such that $f(x) = f(x + p)$ for all x.

The period of the tangent and cotangent function is π. This fact is clear from the graphs of the tangent and cotangent functions. Pick any angle, x, on the x-axis, and notice $x + \pi$ has the same tangent as x. The period of the other trigonometric functions is 2π.

If the period of a function f is p, and $g(x) = f(nx)$, then the period of g is p/n.

PROBLEM

What is the period of sin $3x$?

SOLUTION

Since the period of sin x is 2π, the period of sin $3x$ is $\dfrac{2\pi}{3}$.

Use Trigonometry to Solve Right-Triangle Problems

PROBLEM

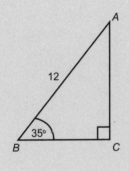

Determine length of side $\overline{AC}$ in the figure below.

SOLUTION

1. Determine if sine, cosine, or tangent is needed.

Since the angle and hypotenuse are known, and the opposite side needs to be determined, use sine.

2. Write the ratio for sine.

$$\sin \measuredangle B = \frac{\text{opposite side}}{\text{hypotenuse}}$$

3. Using a calculator, find the sine of $\measuredangle B$.

$$\sin \measuredangle B = \sin(35°) = 0.574$$

4. Rewrite the ratio.

$$0.574 = \frac{\text{opposite side}}{12}$$

5. Multiply both sides of the equation by 12 to determine the length of the opposite side.

$$6.88 = \text{length of } \overline{AC}$$

The correct answer is that the length of $\overline{AC}$ is 6.88.

PROBLEM

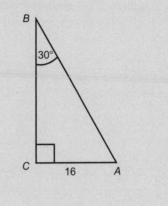

Determine the length of side $\overline{AB}$ in the figure below.

SOLUTION

1. Determine if sine, cosine, or tangent is needed. Since the angle and opposite side are known, and the hypotenuse needs to be determined, use sine.

2. Write the ratio for sine.

$$\sin \measuredangle B = \frac{\text{opposite side}}{\text{hypotenuse}}$$

3. Using a calculator, find the sine of $\measuredangle B$.

$$\sin \measuredangle B = \sin(30) = 0.50$$

4. Rewrite the ratio.

$$0.50 = \frac{16}{\text{hypotenuse}}$$

5. Multiply both sides of the equation by the hypotenuse.

$$\text{hypotenuse}(0.50) = 16$$

6. Divide both sides of the equation by 0.50 to determine the length of the hypotenuse.

$$\text{hypotenuse} = 32$$

The correct answer is that the length of $\overline{AB}$ is 32.

PROBLEM

A carpenter is trying to determine the height of a flagpole so she can build a new flagpole. The distance from the flagpole to the carpenter is 30 feet. The angle of inclination (the line of sight from where the carpenter is standing to the top of the flagpole) is 30°. See the figure below.

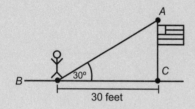

What is the height of the flagpole?

SOLUTION

1. Determine if sine, cosine, or tangent is needed. Since the angle and adjacent side are known, and the opposite side needs to be determined, use tangent.

2. Write the ratio for tangent.

$$\tan ∢B = \frac{\text{opposite side}}{\text{adjacent side}}$$

3. Using a calculator, find the tangent of ∢B.

$$\tan ∢B = \tan(30) = 0.577$$

4. Rewrite the ratio. $0.577 = \dfrac{\text{opposite side}}{30 \text{ feet}}$

5. Multiply both sides of the equation by 30 to determine the length of $\overline{AC}$.

$$17.31 = \text{length of } \overline{AC}.$$

The correct answer is that the height of the flagpole is 17.31 feet.

PROBLEM

A man is playing billiards with his friend. The cue ball hits the 7 ball at point C. The ball travels to point B and is deflected toward point A (the pocket). If the distance of $\overline{CB}$ is 14 inches, angle C is 60°, and ∢B is 90°, what is the length of $\overline{AB}$? See the figure below.

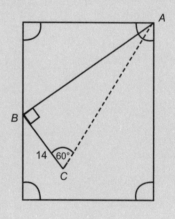

SOLUTION

1. Determine if sine, cosine, or tangent is needed. Since the angle and adjacent side are known, and the opposite side needs to be determined, use tangent.

2. Write the ratio for tangent.

$$\tan ∢C = \frac{\text{opposite side}}{\text{adjacent side}}$$

3. Using a calculator, find the tangent of ∢C.

$$\tan ∢C = \tan(60) = 1.73$$

4. Rewrite the ratio.

$$1.73 = \frac{\text{opposite side}}{14 \text{ inches}}$$

5. Multiply both sides of the equation by 14 to determine the length of $\overline{AB}$.

$$24.22 = \text{length of } \overline{AB}$$

The correct answer is that the distance to the pocket is 24.22 inches.

Drill: Trigonometry

1. $\tan^{-1}(-\sqrt{3}) =$

    (A) −60°   (C) 30°

    (B) 60°   (D) −30°

2. Calculate $\dfrac{\sin^{-1}\frac{1}{2}}{\tan^{-1}1}$.

    (A) $\dfrac{1}{2}$ (C) 45°

    (B) 30°   (D) $\dfrac{2}{3}$

3. Find cos[arc sin(−1)].

    (A) $\dfrac{1}{2}$ (C) 0

    (B) $\dfrac{\sqrt{3}}{2}$ (D) $-\dfrac{\sqrt{3}}{2}$

4. If x is inside $[0, \pi]$, one solution for the equation $\sqrt{1 + \sin^2 x} = \sqrt{2}\,\sin x$ is

    (A) $\dfrac{5}{2}\pi$ (C) $\dfrac{3}{2}\pi$

    (B) $\dfrac{\pi}{6}$ (D) $\dfrac{\pi}{2}$

5. $\sec^2\theta - \tan^2\theta =$

    (A) $\dfrac{4}{5}$ (C) −1

    (B) $\dfrac{1}{2}$ (D) 1

6. $\dfrac{\sin(45° + x) + \sin(45° - x)}{\cos x} =$

    (A) $\sqrt{2}$ (C) $\dfrac{\sqrt{2}}{2}$

    (B) $\tan x$ (D) $\dfrac{\sqrt{2}}{2}\cos x$

7. The amplitude of $y = \dfrac{\sqrt{3}}{3}\sin x + \cos x$ is

    (A) $\dfrac{\sqrt{3}}{2}$ (C) $\dfrac{\sqrt{3}}{4}$

    (B) $\dfrac{\sqrt{2}}{2}$ (D) $\dfrac{2\sqrt{3}}{3}$

8. $\dfrac{\csc x}{2\cos x} =$

    (A) $\cos 3x$ (C) $\sin 2x$

    (B) $\tan 2x$ (D) $\csc 2x$

Trigonometry Drill
Answer Key

1. (A)	5. (D)
2. (D)	6. (A)
3. (C)	7. (D)
4. (D)	8. (D)

Detailed Explanations of Answers

1. (A)

Using the table, you will find $\tan^{-1}(-\sqrt{3}) = -60°$ in the 4th quadrant.

2. (D)

$$\frac{\sin^{-1}\frac{1}{2}}{\tan^{-1}1} = \frac{30}{45} = \frac{2}{3}$$

3. (C)

$$\cos[\arcsin(-1)] = \cos(-90) = 0$$

4. (D)

$$\left[\sqrt{1+\sin^2 x}\right]^2 = \left[\sqrt{2}\sin x\right]^2 \Rightarrow 1+\sin^2 x = 2\sin^2 x$$

Subtract $2\sin^2 x$:

$$\frac{-2\sin^2 x}{1-\sin^2 x} = \frac{-2\sin^2 x}{0}$$
$$\cos^2 x = 0$$

$\cos x = 0$ at $\dfrac{\pi}{2}$ or $\dfrac{3}{2}\pi$

$\dfrac{3}{2}\pi$ won't satisfy the original domain for x

So $\dfrac{\pi}{2}$ is the answer.

5. (D)

$$\sec^2\theta - \tan^2\theta = (\tan^2\theta + 1) - \tan^2\theta = 1$$

6. (A)

$$\frac{\sin(45° + x) + \sin(45° - x)}{\cos x}$$

$$= \frac{\sin 45\cos x + \cos 45\sin x + \sin 45\cos x - \cos 45\sin x}{\cos x}$$

$$= \frac{2\sin 45\cos x}{\cos x}$$

$$= 2\sin 45$$

$$= 2\left(\frac{\sqrt{2}}{2}\right)$$

$$= \sqrt{2}$$

7. (D)

$$y = \frac{\sqrt{3}}{3}\sin x + \cos x$$

Test reference angles 0, 30, 45, 60, and 90 to determine that 30 is the greatest

$$\frac{\sqrt{3}}{3}\sin(30) + \cos(30) = \frac{\sqrt{3}}{3}\left(\frac{1}{2}\right) + \left(\frac{\sqrt{3}}{2}\right)$$

$$= \frac{\sqrt{3}}{6} + \frac{\sqrt{3}}{2}$$

$$= \frac{\sqrt{3}}{6} + \frac{3\sqrt{3}}{6}$$

$$= \frac{4\sqrt{3}}{6}$$

$$= \frac{2\sqrt{3}}{3}$$

8. (D)

$$\frac{\csc x}{2\cos x} = \frac{\frac{1}{\sin x}}{2\cos x} = \frac{1}{2\sin x\cos x} = \frac{1}{\sin 2x} = \csc 2x$$

Calculus

Limits

Definition

Let f be a function that is defined on an open interval containing a, but possibly not defined at a itself. Let L be a real number. The statement

$$\lim_{x \to a} f(x) = L$$

defines the limit of the function $f(x)$ at the point a. Very simply, L is the value that the function has as the point a is approached.

PROBLEM

$$\lim_{x \to 2} f(x) = 2x + 1$$

SOLUTION

As $x \to 2$, $f(x) \to 5$. Therefore, $\lim_{x \to 2}(2x + 1) = 5$

PROBLEM

$$\text{Find } \lim_{x \to 3} f(x) = \frac{x^2 - 9}{x + 1}$$

SOLUTION

$$\lim_{x \to 3} = \frac{x^2 - 9}{x + 1} = \frac{0}{4} = 0.$$

Theorems on Limits

The following are important properties of limits:

Consider $\lim_{x \to a} f(x) = L$ and $\lim_{x \to a} g(x) = K$, then

A) Uniqueness – If $\lim_{x \to a} f(x)$ exists, then it is unique.

B) $\lim_{x \to a}[f(x) + g(x)] = \lim_{x \to a} f(x) + \lim_{x \to a} g(x) = L + K$

C) $\lim_{x \to a}[f(x) - g(x)] = \lim_{x \to a} f(x) - \lim_{x \to a} g(x) = L - K$

D) $\lim_{x \to a}[f(x) \cdot g(x)] = \lim_{x \to a} f(x) \cdot \lim_{x \to a} g(x) = L \cdot K$

E) $\lim_{x \to a} \dfrac{f(x)}{g(x)} = \dfrac{\lim_{x \to a} f(x)}{\lim_{x \to a} g(x)} = \dfrac{L}{K}$ provided $K \neq 0$

F) $\lim_{x \to a} \dfrac{1}{g(x)} = \dfrac{1}{K}, K \neq 0$

G) $\lim_{x \to a}[f(x)]^n = [\lim_{x \to a} f(x)]^n$ for $n > 0$

H) $\lim_{x \to a}[cf(x)] = c[\lim_{x \to a} f(x)], c \in R$

I) $\lim_{x \to a} cx^n = c \lim_{x \to a} x^n = ca^n, c \in R$

J) If f is a polynomial function then $\lim_{x \to a} f(x) = f(a)$ for all $a \in R$.

K) $\lim_{x \to a} \sqrt[n]{x} = \sqrt[n]{a}$ when $a \geq 0$ and n is a positive integer or when $a \leq 0$ and n is an odd positive integer.

L) $\lim_{x \to a} \sqrt[n]{f(x)} = \sqrt[n]{\lim_{x \to a} f(x)}$ when n is a positive integer

M) If $f(x) \leq h(x) \leq g(x)$ for all x in an open interval containing a, except possibly at a, and if $\lim_{x \to a} f(x) = L = \lim_{x \to a} g(x)$ then $\lim_{x \to a} h(x) = L$.

PROBLEM

$$\text{Find } \lim_{x \to 0}(x\sqrt{x - 3})$$

SOLUTION

In checking the function by simple substitution, we see that:

$$x\sqrt{x - 3} = 0$$

if $x = 0$.

However, this function does not have real values for values of x less than 3. Therefore, since x cannot approach 0, $f(x)$ does not approach 0 and the limit does not exist. This example illustrates that we cannot properly find

$$\lim_{x \to a} f(x)$$

by finding $f(a)$, even though they are equal in many cases. We must consider values of x near a, but not equal to a.

One-Sided Limits

Suppose f is a function such that it is not defined for all values of x. Rather, it is defined in such a way that it "jumps" from one y value to the next instead of smoothly going from one y value to the next. Examples are shown in the figures below.

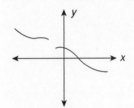

$y = f(x)$ is not defined for all x values.

$y = f(x)$ "jumps" from a positive value to a negative one.

The statement $\lim_{x \to a^+} f(x) = R$ tells us that as x approaches "a" from the right or from positive infinity, the function f has the limit R.

Similarly, the statement $\lim_{x \to a^-} f(x) = L$ says that as x approaches "a" from the left-hand side or from negative infinity, the function f has the limit L.

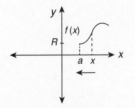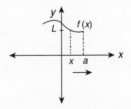

Right-hand limit   **Left-hand limit**

If f is defined in an open interval containing a, except possibly at a, then

$$\lim_{x \to a} f(x) = L \text{ if and only if}$$

$$\lim_{x \to a^+} f(x) = \lim_{x \to a^-} f(x) = L$$

Notice that in the figure below, the right-hand limit is not the same as the left-hand limit,

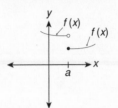

PROBLEM

Let $f(x)$ and $g(x)$ be defined by:

$$f(x) = \begin{cases} x^2 + 2x, & x \le 1, \\ 2x, & x > 1, \end{cases}$$

$$g(x) = \begin{cases} 2x^3, & x \le 1, \\ 3, & x > 1. \end{cases}$$

Find $\lim_{x \to 1}[f(x) \cdot g(x)]$ if it exists.

SOLUTION

Neither $f(x)$ nor $g(x)$ have limits as $x \to 1$, but one-sided limits exist for both functions. It is possible that the product of two functions may have a limit, even though the two functions do not have limits individually.

$$\lim_{x \to 1^-} f(x) = 3, \quad \lim_{x \to 1^+} f(x) = 2,$$
$$\lim_{x \to 1^-} g(x) = 2, \quad \lim_{x \to 1^+} g(x) = 3.$$

Therefore,

$$\lim_{x \to 1^-}[f(x) \cdot g(x)] = 6$$

and

$$\lim_{x \to 1^+}[f(x) \cdot g(x)] = 6.$$

Consequently,

$$\lim_{x \to 1}[f(x) \cdot g(x)] = 6.$$

PROBLEM

Given that *f* is the function defined by:

$$f(x) = \begin{cases} x - 3 & \text{if } x \neq 4 \\ 5 & \text{if } x = 4, \end{cases}$$

Find $\lim\limits_{x \to 4} f(x)$.

SOLUTION

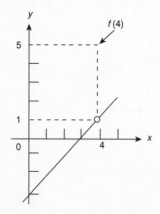

When plotting $f(x)$ to obtain a visual representation, it is seen that $f(x) = x - 3$ is a straight line that has a break or discontinuity at the point $x = 4$. At $x = 4$, the value of $f(x)$ is given as 5, and not as 1, the value that $f(x)$ would assume if the line were continuous. However, when evaluating $\lim\limits_{x \to 4} f(x)$, we are considering values of x close to 4 but not equal to 4. Thus we have

$$\lim_{x \to 4} f(x) = \lim_{x \to 4}(x - 3)$$
$$= 1.$$

In this example,

$$\lim_{x \to 4} f(x) = 1.$$

But $f(4) = 5$; therefore,

$$\lim_{x \to 4} f(x) \neq f(4)$$

Special Limits

A) $\lim\limits_{x \to 0} \dfrac{\sin x}{x} = 1, \quad \lim\limits_{x \to 0} \dfrac{1 - \cos x}{x} = 0$

B) $\lim\limits_{x \to \infty}(1 + \dfrac{1}{n})^n = e, \quad \lim\limits_{x \to 0}(1 + n)^{1/n} = e$

C) For $a > 1$ $\lim\limits_{x \to +\infty} a^x = +\infty, \; \lim\limits_{x \to -\infty} a^x = 0$

$\qquad \lim\limits_{x \to +\infty} \log_a x = +\infty, \lim\limits_{x \to 0} \log_a x = -\infty$

D) For $0 < a < 1$, $\lim\limits_{x \to +\infty} a^x = 0, \; \lim\limits_{x \to -\infty} a^x = +\infty$

$\qquad \lim\limits_{x \to +\infty} \log_a x = -\infty, \lim\limits_{x \to 0} \log_a x = +\infty$

Some nonexistent limits that are frequently encountered are:

A) $\lim\limits_{x \to 0} \dfrac{1}{x^2}$, as x approaches zero, x^2 gets very small and also becomes zero therefore $\dfrac{1}{0}$ is undefined and the limit does not exist.

B) $\lim\limits_{x \to 0} \dfrac{|x|}{x}$ does not exist.

Proof:

If $x > 0$, then $\dfrac{|x|}{x} = \dfrac{x}{x} = 1$ and hence lies to the right of the y-axis, the graph of f coincides with the line $y = 1$. If $x < 0$ then $\dfrac{-x}{x} = -1$ and the graph of f coincides with the line $y = -1$ to the left of the y-axis.

If it were true that $\lim\limits_{x \to 0} \dfrac{|x|}{x} = L$ for some L, then the preceding remarks imply that $-1 \leq L \leq 1$.

If we consider any pair of horizontal lines $y = L \pm \theta$, where $0 < \theta < 1$, then there exists points on the graph that are not between these lines for some non-zero x in every interval $(-\theta, \theta)$ containing 0. It follows that the limit does not exist.

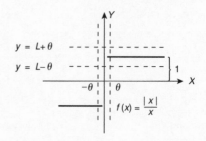

PROBLEM

Find $\lim\limits_{x \to 3} f(x) = \dfrac{1}{(x-3)^2}$, $x \neq 3$

SOLUTION

Sketching the graph of this function about $x = 3$, we see that it increases without bound as x tends to 3.

Using the method of simple substitution, we find that $\lim\limits_{x \to 3} f(x) = \infty$. There is no limit.

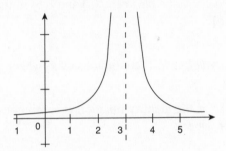

PROBLEM

Find $\lim\limits_{x \to 3} \dfrac{5x}{6 - 2x}$.

SOLUTION

$$\lim_{x \to 3} 5x = 15$$

and

$$\lim_{x \to 3} [6 - 2x] = 0$$

Therefore,

$$\lim_{x \to 3} \frac{5x}{6 - 2x} = \frac{15}{0} = \infty.$$

The function has no limit.

Continuity

A function f is continuous at a point a if $\lim\limits_{x \to a} f(x) = f(a)$.
This implies that three conditions are satisfied:

a) $f(a)$ exists; that is, f is defined at a

b) $\lim\limits_{x \to a} f(x)$ exists, and

c) the two numbers are equal.

To test continuity at a point $x = a$ we test whether

$$\lim_{x \to a^+} f(x) = \lim_{x \to a^-} f(x) = f(a)$$

PROBLEM

Investigate the continuity of the function:

$$h(x) = \begin{cases} 3 + x & \text{if } x \leq 1 \\ 3 - x & \text{if } 1 < x. \end{cases}$$

SOLUTION

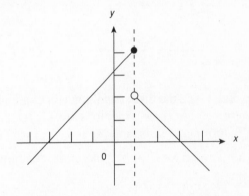

Because there is a break in the graph at the point $x = 1$, we investigate the three conditions for continuity at the point $x = 1$. The three conditions are: (1) $f(x_0)$ is defined, (2) $\lim\limits_{x \to x_0} f(x)$ exists, (3) $\lim\limits_{x \to x_0} f(x) = f(x_0)$. At $x = 1$, $h(1) = 4$; therefore, condition (1) is satisfied.

$$\lim_{x \to 1^-} h(x) = \lim_{x \to 1^-} (3 + x) = 4$$
$$\lim_{x \to 1^+} h(x) = \lim_{x \to 1^+} (3 - x) = 2.$$

Because $\lim\limits_{x \to 1^-} h(x) \neq \lim\limits_{x \to 1^+} h(x)$, we conclude that $\lim\limits_{x \to 1} h(x)$ does not exist. Therefore, condition (2) fails to hold at 1.

Hence, h is discontinuous at 1.

PROBLEM

Investigate the continuity of:

$$F(x) = \begin{cases} |x - 3| & \text{if } x \neq 3 \\ 2 & \text{if } x = 3. \end{cases}$$

SOLUTION

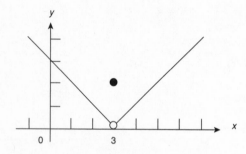

We investigate the three conditions for continuity at the point $x = 3$. The three conditions are: (1) $f(x_0)$ is defined, (2) $\lim\limits_{x \to x_0} f(x)$ exists, and (3) $\lim\limits_{x \to x_0} f(x) = f(x_0)$.

At $x = 3$, we have $F(3) = 2$; therefore, condition (1) is satisfied.

$\lim\limits_{x \to 3^-} F(x) = 0$ and $\lim\limits_{x \to 3^+} F(x) = 0$. Therefore, $\lim\limits_{x \to 3} F(x)$ exists and is 0; therefore, condition (2) is satisfied.

$\lim\limits_{x \to 3} F(x) = 0$, but $F(3) = 2$. Therefore, condition (3) is not satisfied. F is thus discontinuous at 3.

Theorems of Continuity

A) A function defined in a closed interval $[a, b]$ is continuous in $[a, b]$ if and only if it is continuous in the open interval (a, b), as well as continuous from the right at "a" and from the left at "b".

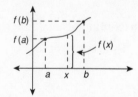

B) If f and g are continuous functions at a, then so are the functions $f + g, f - g, fg$ and f / g, where $g(a) \neq 0$.

C) If $\lim\limits_{x \to a} g(x) = b$ and f is continuous at b, then $\lim\limits_{x \to a} f(g(x)) = f(b) = f[\lim\limits_{x \to a} g(x)]$.

D) If g is continuous at a and f is continuous at $b = g(a)$, then
$$\lim\limits_{x \to a} f(g(x)) = f[\lim\limits_{x \to a} g(x)] = f(g(a)).$$

E) Intermediate Value Theorem. If f is continuous on a closed interval $[a, b]$ and if $f(a) \neq f(b)$, then f takes on every value between $f(a)$ and $f(b)$ in the interval $[a, b]$.

F) $f(x) = k, k \in R$, is continuous everywhere.

G) $f(x) = x$, the identity function is continuous everywhere.

H) If f is continuous at a, then $\lim\limits_{n \to \infty} f(a + \frac{1}{n}) = f(a)$.

I) If f is continuous on an interval containing a and b, $a < b$, and if $f(a) \cdot f(b) < 0$ then there exists at least one point c, $a < c < b$ such that $f(c) = 0$.

PROBLEM

Let h be defined by:

$$h(x) = \begin{cases} 4 - x^2 & \text{if } x \leq 1 \\ 2 + x^2 & \text{if } 1 < x. \end{cases}$$

Find each of the following limits if they exist:

$$\lim\limits_{x \to 1^-} h(x), \lim\limits_{x \to 1^+} h(x), \lim\limits_{x \to 1} h(x).$$

SOLUTION

It is desirable to sketch the given function to aid in visualizing the problem.

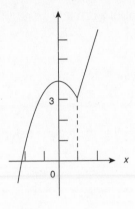

The Derivative

The Definition and Δ-Method

The derivative of a function expresses its rate of change with respect to an independent variable. The derivative is also the slope of the tangent line to the curve.

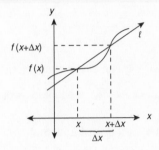

Now,

$$\lim_{x \to 1^-} h(x) = \lim_{x \to 1^-} -(4 - x^2) = 3$$

$$\lim_{x \to 1^+} h(x) = \lim_{x \to 1^+} +(2 + x^2) = 3$$

Therefore, $\lim_{x \to 1} h(x)$ exists and is equal to 3. Note that $h(1) = 3$. This holds because the function is continuous.

PROBLEM

If $h(x) = \sqrt{4 - x^2}$, prove that $h(x)$ is continuous in the closed interval $[-2, 2]$.

SOLUTION

To prove continuity we employ the following definition: A function defined in the closed interval $[a, b]$ is said to be continuous in $[a, b]$ if and only if it is continuous in the open interval (a, b), as well as continuous from the right at a and continuous from the left at b. The function h is continuous in the open interval $(-2, 2)$. We must show that the function is continuous from the right at -2 and from the left at 2. Therefore, we must show that $f(-2)$ is defined and $\lim_{x \to -2^+} f(x)$ exists and that these are equal. Also, we must show that $f(2) = \lim_{x \to 2^-} f(x)$.

We have:

$$\lim_{x \to -2^+} \sqrt{4 - x^2} = 0 = h(-2),$$

and

$$\lim_{x \to -2^-} \sqrt{4 - x^2} = 0 = h(2).$$

Thus, h is continuous in the closed interval $[-2, 2]$.

Consider the graph of the function f in the figure. Choosing a point x and a point $x + \Delta x$ (where Δx denotes a small distance on the x-axis) we can obtain both, $f(x)$ and $f(x + \Delta x)$. Drawing a tangent line, l, of the curve through the points $f(x)$ and $f(x + \Delta x)$, we can measure the rate of change of this line. As we let the distance, Δx, approach zero, then

$$\lim_{\Delta x \to 0} \frac{f(x + \Delta x) - f(x)}{\Delta x}$$

becomes the instantaneous rate of change of the function or the derivative.

We denote the derivative of the function f to be f'. So we have

$$f'(x) = \lim_{\Delta x \to 0} \frac{f(x + \Delta x) - f(x)}{\Delta x}$$

If $y = f(x)$, some common notations for the derivative are

$$y' = f'(x)$$

$$\frac{dy}{dx} = f'(x)$$

$$D_x y = f'(x) \text{ or } Df = f'$$

PROBLEM

> Find the slope of each of the following curves at the given point, using the Δ-method.
>
> a) $y = 3x^2 - 2x + 4$ at $(1, 5)$
>
> b) $y = x^3 - 3x + 5$ at $(-2, 3)$.

SOLUTION

The slope of a given curve at a specified point is the derivative, in this case $\dfrac{\Delta y}{\Delta x}$, evaluated at that point.

a)   From the Δ-method we know that:

$$\frac{\Delta y}{\Delta x} = \frac{f(x + \Delta x) - f(x)}{\Delta x}.$$

For the curve $y = 3x^2 - 2x + 4$, we find:

$$\frac{\Delta y}{\Delta x} = \frac{3(x + \Delta x)^2 - 2(x + \Delta x) + 4 - (3x^2 - 2x + 4)}{\Delta x}$$

$$= \frac{3x^2 + 6x\Delta x + 3(\Delta x)^2 - 2x - 2\Delta x + 4 - 3x^2 + 2x - 4}{\Delta x}$$

$$= \frac{6x\Delta x + 3(\Delta x)^2 - 2\Delta x}{\Delta x}$$

$$= 6x + 3\Delta x - 2.$$

$$\lim_{\Delta x \to 0} \frac{\Delta y}{\Delta x} = \lim_{\Delta x \to 0} 6x + 3\Delta x - 2 = 6x - 2.$$

At $(1, 5)$, $\dfrac{\Delta y}{\Delta x} = 4$ is the required slope.

b)   Again using the Δ-method, $\dfrac{\Delta y}{\Delta x}$ for the curve:

$y = x^3 - 3x + 5$, can be found as follows:

$$\frac{\Delta y}{\Delta x} = \frac{f(x + \Delta x) - f(x)}{\Delta x}$$

$$\frac{\Delta y}{\Delta x} = \frac{(x + \Delta x)^3 - 3(x + \Delta x) + 5 - (x^3 - 3x + 5)}{\Delta x}$$

$$= \frac{x^3 + 3x^2\Delta x + 3x(\Delta x)^2 + (\Delta x)^3 - 3x - 3\Delta x + 5 - x^3 + 3x - 5}{\Delta x}$$

$$= \frac{3x^2\Delta x + 3x(\Delta x)^2 + (\Delta x)^3 - 3\Delta x}{\Delta x}$$

$$= 3x^2 + 3x\Delta x + (\Delta x)^2 - 3.$$

$$\lim_{\Delta x \to 0} \frac{\Delta y}{\Delta x} = \lim_{\Delta x \to 0} 3x^2 + 3x\Delta x + (\Delta x)^2 - 3 = 3x^2 - 3.$$

At $(-2, 3)$, $\dfrac{\Delta y}{\Delta x} = 9$ is the required slope.

PROBLEM

> Find the average rate of change, by the Δ process, for:
>
> $$y = \frac{1}{x}.$$

SOLUTION

$$y = f(x) = \frac{1}{x}$$

The average rate of change is defined to be

$$\frac{\Delta y}{\Delta x} \text{ with } \Delta y = f(x + \Delta x) - f(x).$$

Since

$$f(x) = \frac{1}{x}, \; f(x + \Delta x) = \frac{1}{x + \Delta x},$$

and

$$\Delta y = \frac{1}{x + \Delta x} - \frac{1}{x} = \frac{x - (x + \Delta x)}{x(x + \Delta x)}$$

$$= \frac{-\Delta x}{x(x + \Delta x)}.$$

Now,

$$\frac{\Delta y}{\Delta x} = \frac{-\Delta x}{x(x + \Delta x)\Delta x} = \frac{-1}{x(x + \Delta x)}$$

Therefore, the average rate of change is $\dfrac{-1}{x(x + \Delta x)}$.

The Derivative at a Point

If f is defined on an open interval containing "a", then

$$f'(a) = \lim_{x \to a} \frac{f(x) - f(a)}{x - a},$$

provided the limit exists.

PROBLEM

Find the instantaneous rate of the function:

$$y = \frac{2x}{x + 1}$$

for any value of x and for $x = 2$.

SOLUTION

The instantaneous rate of change of a function is defined as,

$$\lim_{\Delta x \to 0} \frac{\Delta y}{\Delta x} = \lim_{\Delta x \to 0} \frac{f(x + \Delta x) - f(x)}{\Delta x}$$

Therefore,

$$\Delta y = f(x + \Delta x) - f(x).$$

In this case,

$$f(x) = \frac{2x}{x + 1}$$

$$f(x + \Delta x) = \frac{2(x + \Delta x)}{x + \Delta x + 1}$$

Substituting, we have:

$$\Delta y = \frac{2x + 2 \cdot \Delta x}{x + \Delta x + 1} - \frac{2x}{x + 1}$$

$$= \frac{(2x + 2 \cdot \Delta x)(x + 1) - 2x(x + \Delta x + 1)}{(x + \Delta x + 1)(x + 1)}$$

$$\frac{2x^2 + 2x \cdot \Delta x + 2x + 2 \cdot \Delta x - 2x^2 - 2x \cdot \Delta x - 2x}{(x + \Delta x + 1)(x + 1)}$$

$$= \frac{2 \cdot \Delta x}{(x + \Delta x + 1)(x + 1)}.$$

$$\frac{\Delta y}{\Delta x} = \frac{2 \cdot \Delta x}{(x + \Delta x + 1)(x + 1)(\Delta x)}$$

$$= \frac{2}{(x + \Delta x + 1)(x + 1)}$$

Now,

$$\lim_{\Delta x \to 0} \frac{\Delta y}{\Delta x} = \lim_{\Delta x \to 0} \frac{2}{(x + \Delta x + 1)(x + 1)}.$$

Substituting 0 for Δx we have,

$$\lim_{\Delta x \to 0} \frac{\Delta y}{\Delta x} = \frac{2}{(x + 1)^2},$$

the instantaneous rate of change for any value of x.

For $x = 2$, we have,

$$\frac{2}{(x + 1)^2} = \frac{2}{(2 + 1)^2} = \frac{2}{9}.$$

PROBLEM

Find the rate of change of y with respect to x at the point $x = 5$, if

$$2y = x^2 + 3x - 1.$$

SOLUTION

Rate of change is defined as

$$\lim_{\Delta x \to 0} \frac{\Delta y}{\Delta x}, \text{ with}$$

$$\Delta y = f(x + \Delta x) - f(x).$$

We have:

$$2\Delta y = (x + \Delta x)^2 + 3(x + \Delta x) - 1 - (x^2 + 3x - 1)$$

$$= x^2 + 2x \cdot \Delta x + (\Delta x)^2 + 3x + 3\Delta x - 1 - x^2 - 3x + 1$$

$$= 2x \cdot \Delta x + (\Delta x)^2 + 3\Delta x.$$

Dividing by Δx,

$$\frac{2\Delta y}{\Delta x} = \frac{2x \cdot \Delta x}{\Delta x} + \frac{(\Delta x)^2}{\Delta x} + \frac{3\Delta x}{\Delta x}$$

$$= 2x + \Delta x + 3$$

and

$$\frac{\Delta y}{\Delta x} = x + \frac{\Delta x}{2} + \frac{3}{2}.$$

Now,

$$\lim_{\Delta x \to 0} \frac{\Delta y}{\Delta x} = \lim_{\Delta x \to 0} x + \frac{\Delta x}{2} + \frac{3}{2} = x + \frac{3}{2}.$$

For $x = 5$,

$$\lim_{\Delta x \to 0} \frac{\Delta y}{\Delta x} = 5 + \frac{3}{2} = 6\frac{1}{2}.$$

Rules for Finding the Derivatives

General rule:

A) If f is a constant function, $f(x) = c$, then $f'(x) = 0$.

B) If $\boxed{f(x) = x, \text{ then } f'(x) = 1.}$

C) If f is differentiable, then $\boxed{(cf(x))' = cf'(x)}$

D) Power Rule: If $f(x) = x^n$, $n \in z$, then
$f'(x) = nx^{n-1}$; if $n < 0$ then x^n is not defined at $x = 0$.

E) If f and g are differentiable on the interval (a, b) then:

   a) $\boxed{(f + g)'(x) = f'(x) + g'(x)}$

   b) Product Rule: $\boxed{(fg)'(x) = f(x)g'(x) + g(x)f'(x)}$

     Example: Find $f'(x)$ if $f(x) = (x^3 + 1)(2x^2 + 8x - 5)$.
$$f'(x) = (x^3 + 1)(4x + 8) + (2x^2 + 8x - 5)(3x^2)$$
$$= 4x^4 + 8x^3 + 4x + 8 + 6x^4 + 24x^3 - 15x^2$$
$$= 10x^4 + 32x^3 - 15x^2 + 4x + 8$$

   c) Quotient Rule:

$$\boxed{\left(\frac{f}{g}\right)'(x) = \frac{g(x)f'(x) - f(x)g'(x)}{[g(x)]^2}}$$

Example: Find $f'(x)$ if $f(x) = \dfrac{3x^2 - x + 2}{4x^2 + 5}$

$$f'(x) = \frac{(4x^2 + 5)(6x - 1) - (3x^2 - x + 2)(8x)}{(4x^2 + 5)^2}$$

$$= \frac{(24x^3 - 4x^2 + 30x - 5) - (24x^3 - 8x^2 + 16x)}{(4x^2 + 5)^2}$$

$$= \frac{(4x^2 + 14x - 5)}{(4x^2 + 5)^2}$$

F) If $f(x) = x^{m/n}$, then $f'(x) = \dfrac{m}{n} x^{\frac{m}{n} - 1}$
where $m, n \in z$ and $n \neq 0$

G) Polynomials: If $f(x) = (a_0 + a_1 x + a_2 x^2 + \ldots + a_m x)$,
then $f'(x) = a_1 + 2a_2 x + 3a_3 x^2 + \ldots + na_m x^{-1}$.
This employs the power rule and rules concerning constants.

H) Chain Rule: Let $f(u)$ be a composite function, where $u = g(x)$.
Then $f'(u) = f'(u)g'(x)$, or if $y = f(u)$ and $u = g(x)$ then $D_x y = (D_u y)(D_x u) = f'(u)g'(x)$

PROBLEM

Find the derivative of: $y = x^{3b}$.

SOLUTION

Applying the theorem for $d(u^n)$,

$$\frac{\Delta y}{\Delta x} = 3b \cdot x^{3b-1}.$$

PROBLEM

Find the derivative of: $y = (x^2 + 2)^3$.

SOLUTION

Method 1. We may expand the cube and write:

$$\frac{dy}{dx} = \frac{d}{dx}[(x^2 + 2)^3] = \frac{d}{dx}(x^6 + 6x^4 + 12x^2 + 8)$$

$$= 6x^5 + 24x^3 + 24x.$$

Method 2. Let $u = x^2 + 2$, then $y = (x^2 + 2)^3 = u^3$;

Using the chain rule we have:

$$\frac{dy}{dx} = \frac{dy}{du} \cdot \frac{du}{dx} = \frac{d(u^3)}{du} \cdot \frac{d(x^2+2)}{dx} = 3u^2(2x)$$
$$= 3(x^2+2)^2 \cdot (2x) = 3(x^4 + 4x^2 + 4) \cdot (2x)$$
$$= 6x^5 + 24x^3 + 24x.$$

Implicit Differentiation

An implicit function of x and y is a function in which one of the variables is not directly expressed in terms of the other. If these variables are not easily or practically separable, we can still differentiate the expression.

Apply the normal rules of differentiation such as the product rule, the power rule, etc. Remember also the chain rule, which states $\frac{du}{dx} \times \frac{dx}{dt} = \frac{du}{dt}$.

Once the rules have been properly applied, we will be left with, as in the example of x and y, some factors of $\frac{dy}{dx}$.

We can then algebraically solve for the derivative $\frac{dy}{dx}$ and obtain the desired result.

PROBLEM

If $x^2 + y^2 = 16$, find $\frac{dy}{dx}$ as an implicit function of x and y.

SOLUTION

Since y is a function of x, we differentiate the equation implicitly in terms of x and y. We have:

$$2x + 2y \cdot \frac{dy}{dx} = 0 \text{ or } 2y\frac{dy}{dx} = -2x.$$
$$\frac{dy}{dx} = -\frac{x}{y}.$$

PROBLEM

Find $\frac{dy}{dx}$ for the expression:
$2x^4 - 3x^2y^2 + y^4 = 0$.

SOLUTION

The equation $2x^4 - 3x^2y^2 + y^4 = 0$, could be solved for y and then differentiated to obtain $\frac{dy}{dx}$, but an easier method is to differentiate implicitly and then solve for $\frac{dy}{dx}$.

Hence, from $2x^4 - 3x^2y^2 + y^4 = 0$ we obtain:

$$8x^3 - 6x^2y\frac{dy}{dx} - 6xy^2 + 4y^3\frac{dy}{dx} = 0.$$

Solving for $\frac{dy}{dx}$,

$$4y^3\frac{dy}{dx} - 6x^2y\frac{dy}{dx} = 6xy^2 - 8x^3.$$
$$(4y^3 - 6x^2y)\frac{dy}{dx} = 6xy^2 - 8x^3.$$

$$\frac{dy}{dx} = \frac{6xy^2 - 8x^3}{4y^3 - 6x^2y}$$
$$= \frac{3xy^2 - 4x^3}{2y^3 - 3x^2y}.$$

Trigonometric Differentiation

The three most basic trigonometric derivatives are:

$$\frac{d}{dx}(\sin x) = \cos x,$$
$$\frac{d}{dx}(\cos x) = -\sin x,$$
$$\frac{d}{dx}(\tan x) = \sec^2 x,$$

Any trigonometric function can be differentiated by applying these basics in combination with the general rules for differentiating algebraic expressions.

The following will be most useful if committed to memory:

$$D_x \sin u = \cos u \, D_x u$$

$$D_x \cos u = -\sin u \, D_x u$$

$$D_x \tan u = \sec^2 u \, D_x u$$

$$D_x \cot u = -\csc^2 u \, D_x u$$

$$D_x \sec u = \tan u \sec u \, D_x u$$

$$D_x \csc u = -\csc u \cot u \, D_x u$$

PROBLEM

Find the derivative of: $y = \sin ax^2$.

SOLUTION

Applying the theorem for the derivative of the sine of a function,

$$\frac{dy}{dx} = \cos ax^2 \cdot \frac{d}{dx}(ax^2)$$

$$= 2ax \cos ax^2.$$

PROBLEM

Find the derivative of: $y \tan 3\theta$.

SOLUTION

Let $u = 3\theta$

Then, $y = \tan u$, and

$$\frac{dy}{d\theta} = \frac{dy}{du} \cdot \frac{du}{d\theta}$$

$$\frac{du}{d\theta} = 3,$$

and $\dfrac{dy}{du} = \sec^2 u.$

Therefore,

$$\frac{dy}{d\theta} = \frac{dy}{du} \cdot \frac{du}{d\theta} = \sec^2 u \cdot 3 = 3 \sec^2(3\theta).$$

Inverse Trigonometric Differentiation

Here are the derivatives for the inverse trigonometric functions. If u is a differentiable function of x, then:

$$D_x \sin^{-1} u = \frac{1}{\sqrt{1-u^2}} D_x u, \quad |u| < 1$$

$$D_x \cos^{-1} u = \frac{-1}{\sqrt{1-u^2}} D_x u, \quad |u| < 1$$

$$D_x \tan^{-1} u = \frac{1}{1+u^2} D_x u,$$

$$D_x \cot^{-1} u = \frac{-1}{1+u^2} D_x u,$$

$$D_x \sec^{-1} u = \frac{1}{|u|\sqrt{u^2-1}} D_x u, u = f(x), |f(x)| > 1$$

$$D_x \csc^{-1} u = \frac{-1}{|u|\sqrt{u^2-1}} D_x u, u = f(x), |f(x)| > 1$$

PROBLEM

Find the derivative of $y = \arcsin 4x$.

SOLUTION

We use the formula for differentiation of the $\sin^{-1}$ or arc sin function, which states:

$$\frac{d}{dx} \sin^{-1} u = \frac{1}{\sqrt{1-u^2}} \frac{du}{dx}$$

with $u = 4x$, $du = 4$.

Hence

$$\frac{dy}{dx} = \frac{1}{\sqrt{1-16x^2}}(4) = \frac{4}{\sqrt{1-16x^2}}$$

PROBLEM

> Given: $y = \arctan \dfrac{3}{x}$, find $\dfrac{dy}{dx}$.

SOLUTION

In this example, we use the formula:

$$\frac{d(\arctan u)}{dx} = \frac{1}{1+u^2} \cdot \frac{du}{dx}.$$

For

$$y = \arctan \frac{3}{x},\, u = \frac{3}{x},\, \text{and } du = \frac{-3}{x^2}.$$

Therefore,

$$\frac{dy}{dx} = \frac{1\left(\frac{-3}{x^2}\right)}{1+\left(\frac{3}{x}\right)^2} = \frac{\frac{-3}{x^2}}{\frac{x^2+9}{x^2}} = \frac{-3}{x^2+9}.$$

Exponential and Logarithmic Differentiation

The exponential function e^x has a simple derivative. Its derivative is itself.

$$\frac{d}{dx}e^x = e^x$$

and

$$\frac{d}{dx}e^u = e^u\frac{du}{dx}$$

Since the natural logarithmic function is the inverse of $y = e^x$ and $\ln e = 1$, it follows that

$$\frac{d}{dx}\ln y = \frac{1}{y}\frac{dy}{dx}$$

and

$$\frac{d}{dx}\ln u = \frac{1}{u}\frac{du}{dx}$$

$\ln x \equiv \log_e x$ is called the logarithm of base e where $e \equiv 2.7182818 \,\text{---}$

If x is any real number and a is any positive real number, then

$$a^x = e^{x \ln a.}$$

From this definition we can obtain the following:

a) $\dfrac{d}{dx}a^x = a^x \ln a$

and $\dfrac{d}{dx}a^u = a^u \ln a \dfrac{du}{dx}$

where $a > 0$, $a \neq 1$

b) $\dfrac{d}{dx}(\log_a x) = \dfrac{1}{x \ln a}$, and $\dfrac{d}{dx}(\log_a |u|) = \dfrac{1}{u \ln a}\dfrac{du}{dx}$

where $u \neq 0$

Sometimes it is useful to take the logs of a function and then differentiate since the computation becomes easier (as in the case of a product).

PROBLEM

> If $y = e^{\frac{1}{x^2}}$, find $D_x y$.

SOLUTION

To find $D_x y = \dfrac{dy}{dx}$, we use the differentiation formula:

$$\frac{d}{dx}e^u = e^u\frac{du}{dx},\, \text{with } u = \frac{1}{x^2}.\, \text{We obtain:}$$

$$D_x y = e^{\frac{1}{x^2}}\left(-\frac{2}{x^3}\right) = -\frac{2e^{\frac{1}{x^2}}}{x^3}.$$

PROBLEM

Find the derivative of:

$$y = \left(e^{\frac{1}{x}}\right)^2.$$

SOLUTION

We can first rewrite the function as:

$$y = e^{\frac{2}{x}}.$$

Now we use the formula:

$$\frac{d}{dx}e^u = e^u \frac{du}{dx},$$

letting $u = \dfrac{2}{x}$. Then,

$$\frac{du}{dx} = \frac{(x)(0) - (2)(1)}{x^2} = -\frac{2}{x^2}.$$

Applying the formula, we obtain:

$$\frac{dy}{dx} = e^{\frac{2}{x}} \cdot \left(-\frac{2}{x}\right)$$

$$= -\frac{2e^{\frac{2}{x}}}{x^2}.$$

Steps in Logarithmic Differentiation

1. $y = f(x)$ given

2. $\ln y = \ln f(x)$ take logs and simplify

3. $D_x (\ln y) = D_x (\ln f(x))$ differentiate implicitly

4. $\dfrac{1}{y} D_x y = D_x(\ln f(x))$

5. $D_x y = f(x) D_x(\ln f(x))$ multiply by $y = f(x)$

To complete the solution, it is necessary to differentiate $\ln f(x)$. If $f(x) < 0$ for some x, then step 2 is invalid and we should replace step 1 by $|y| = |f(x)|$, and then proceed.

Example: $y = (x+5)(x^4+1)$

$$\ln y = \ln[(x+5)(x^4+1)] = \ln(x+5) + \ln(x^4+1)$$

$$\frac{d}{dx}\ln y = \frac{d}{dx}\ln(x+5) + \frac{d}{dx}\ln(x^4+1)$$

$$\frac{1}{y}\frac{dy}{dx} = \frac{1}{x+5} + \frac{4x^3}{x^4+1}$$

$$\frac{dy}{dx} = (x+5)(x^4+1)\left[\frac{1}{x+5} + \frac{4x^3}{x^4+1}\right]$$

$$= (x^4+1) + 4x^3(x+5)$$

This is the same result as obtained by using the product rule.

PROBLEM

Find the derivative of $y = \ln(1-2x)^3$

SOLUTION

It is best to rewrite the equation as:

$$y = 3\ln(1-2x).$$

Then we apply the formula:

$$\frac{d}{dx}\ln u = \frac{1}{u}\frac{du}{dx},$$

letting $u = (1-2x)$. Then $\dfrac{du}{dx} = -2$. We obtain:

$$\frac{dy}{dx} = 3\left(\frac{1}{1-2x}\right)(-2) = \frac{-6}{1-2x}.$$

High-Order Derivatives

The derivative of any function is also a legitimate function that we can differentiate. The second derivative can be obtained by:

$$\frac{d}{dx}\left[\frac{d}{dx}u\right] = \frac{d^2}{dx^2}u = u'' = D^2 u,$$

where $u = g(x)$ is differentiable.

The general formula for higher orders and the *n*th derivative of *u* is,

$$\underbrace{\frac{d}{dx}\frac{d}{dx}\cdots\frac{d}{dx}}_{n \text{ times}}u = \frac{d^{(n)}}{dx^n}u = u^{(n)} = D_x^{(n)}u.$$

The rules for first-order derivatives (e.g., sums, products, chain rule) apply at each stage of higher-order differentiation.

A function that satisfies the condition that its nth derivative is zero is the general polynomial

$$p_{n-1}(x) = a_{n-1}x^{n-1} + a_{n-2}x^{n-2} + \ldots + a_0.$$

PROBLEM

Find the sixth derivative of $y = x^6$.

SOLUTION

First derivative $= 6x^{6-1} = 6x^5$

Second derivative $= 5 \cdot 6x^{5-1} = 30x^4$

Third derivative $= 4 \cdot 30x^{4-1} = 120x^3$

Fourth derivative $= 3 \cdot 120x^{3-1} = 360x^2$

Fifth derivative $= 2 \cdot 360x^{2-1} = 720x^1 = 720x$

Sixth derivative $= 1 \cdot 720x^{1-1} = 720x^0 = 720$

The seventh derivative is seen to be zero, and therefore the function $y = x^6$ has seven derivatives.

PROBLEM

Find y'' for the expression $xy^3 = 1$.

SOLUTION

To find the second derivative, y'', we must first find the first derivative and then differentiate that. We could solve for *y* and then differentiate to obtain y', but an alternative is implicit differentiation,

$$xy^3 = 1.$$

Differentiating implicitly,

$$3xy^2 \cdot y' + y^3 = 0.$$
$$3xy^2 \cdot y' = -y^3.$$
$$y' = \frac{-y^3}{3xy^2}.$$
$$= -\frac{y}{3x}.$$

Now we take the derivative of y' to find y''.

$$y'' = \frac{d}{dx}\left(\frac{-y}{3x}\right)$$
$$= \frac{3xy' - 3y}{9x^2}$$
$$= -\frac{1}{3}\left[\frac{x \cdot y' - y}{x^2}\right].$$

Substituting $y' = -\dfrac{y}{3x}$ in the expression for y'' and simplifying, we get

$$y'' = -\frac{1}{3}\left[\frac{x\left(\frac{-y}{3x}\right) - y}{x^2}\right]$$
$$= -\frac{1}{3}\left[\frac{-\frac{y}{3} - y}{x^2}\right]$$
$$= -\frac{1}{3}\left[\frac{-\frac{4}{3}y}{x^2}\right]$$
$$= \frac{4y}{9x^2}.$$

Application of the Derivative

Rolle's Theorem

Let *f* be continuous on a closed interval $[a, b]$. Assume $f'(x)$ exists at each point in the open interval (a, b).

If $f(a) = f(b) = 0$ then there is at least one point (x_0) in (a, b) such that $f'(x_0) = 0$.

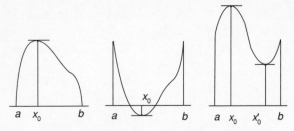

Three functions that satisfy the hypotheses, hence the conclusion, of Rolle's theorem.

The Mean Value Theorem

If f is continuous on $[a, b]$ and has a derivative at every point in the interval (a, b), then there is at least one number c in (a, b) such that

$$f'(c) = \frac{f(b) - f(a)}{b - a}$$

Notice in the figure below that the secant has slope

$$\frac{f(b) - f(a)}{b - a}$$

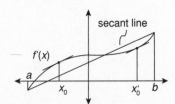

and $f'(x)$ has slope of the tangent to the point $(x, f(x))$. For some x_0 in (a, b) these slopes are equal.

PROBLEM

  a) State and prove the Mean Value Theorem for the derivative of a real-valued function of a single real variable.

  b) Give a geometrical interpretation to this result.

SOLUTION

a) Let f be a real-valued function of a real variable, x, that is continuous on a closed interval $[a, b]$ and

has a derivative in the open interval (a, b). Then the Mean Value Theorem states that there exists a point c in (a, b) such that

$$f(b) - f(a) = f'(c)(b - a).$$

To prove this theorem, consider the function

$$\phi(x) = f'(x) - \left(f(a) + \frac{f(b) - f(a)}{b - a}(x - a) \right).$$

As can be seen from the figure below, θ is the difference of f and the linear function whose graph consists of the line segment passing through the points $(a, f(a))$ and $(b, f(b))$. Since f is continuous on $[a, b]$, so is θ and since f has a derivative at all points in (a, b), so does θ. Furthermore, $\theta(a) = \theta(b) = 0$ so that all the conditions of Rolle's Theorem are satisfied for the function $\theta(x)$. Hence the conclusion of that theorem holds: There is a point $c \in (a, b)$ such that

$$\phi(c) = f'(c) - \frac{f(b) - f(a)}{b - a} = 0$$

or

$$f'(c) = \frac{f(b) - f(a)}{b - a}.$$

Thus, the theorem is proved.

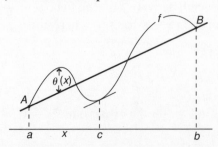

b) The geometrical interpretation of the equation can be seen in the figure. The equation states that there is a point c whose tangent line has the same slope as (i.e., is parallel to) the line connecting A and B.

PROBLEM

If $f(x) = 3x^2 - x + 1$, find the point x_0 at which $f'(x)$ assumes its mean value in the interval [2, 4].

SOLUTION

Recall the Mean Value Theorem. Given a function $f(x)$ which is continuous in $[a, b]$ and differentiable in (a, b), there exists a point x_0 where $a < x_0 < b$ such that:

$$\frac{f(b) - f(a)}{b - a} = f'(x_0),$$

where x_0 is the mean point in the interval.

In our problem, $3x^2 - x + 1$ is continuous, and the derivative exists in the interval (2, 4). We have:

$$\frac{f(4) - f(2)}{4 - 2} = \frac{[3(4)^2 - 4 + 1] - [3(2^2) - 2 + 1]}{4 - 2}$$
$$= f'(x_0),$$

or

$$\frac{45 - 11}{2} = 17 = f'(x_0) = 6x_0 - 1.$$
$$6x_0 = 18$$
$$x_0 = 3.$$

$x_0 = 3$ is the point where $f'(x)$ assumes its mean value.

Consequences of the Mean Value Theorem

A) If f is defined on an interval (a, b) and if $f'(x) = 0$ for each point in the interval, then $f(x)$ is constant over the interval.

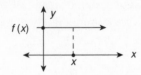

B) Let f and g be differentiable on an interval (a, b). If, for each point x in the interval, $f'(x)$ and $g'(x)$ are equal, then there is a constant, c, such that

$$f(x) + c = g(x) \text{ for all } x.$$

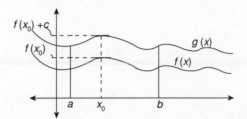

C) The Extended Mean Value Theorem. Assume that the function f and its derivative f' are continuous on $[a, b]$ and that f'' exists at each point x in (a, b). Then there exists at least one point x_0, $a < x_0 < b$, such that

$$f(b) = f(a) + (b - a)f'(a) + \frac{1}{2}(b - a)^2 f''(x_0).$$

PROBLEM

Show: $e^x \geq 1 + x$ for all real numbers x.

SOLUTION

Divide the problem into 3 cases; $x = 0$, $x > 0$, $x < 0$.

Case 1. $x = 0$

For $x = 0$, we have $e^0 \geq 1 + 0$, or $1 = 1$.

Case 2. $x > 0$

For this case, we apply the Mean Value Theorem. We let

$$f(x) = e^x$$

and let the interval be $[0, x]$. Applying the theorem, we have

$$\frac{f(x) - f(0)}{x - 0} = \frac{e^x - e^0}{x - 0} = f'(x_0) = e^{x_0},$$

where $0 < x_0 < x$.

Simplifying, we have:

$$e^x = e^{x_0} \cdot x + e^0 = xe^{x_0} + 1$$

since $x_0 > 0, e^{x_0} > 1$. Therefore,

$$e^x > x + 1$$

Case 3. $x < 0$

Solution is similar to Case 2 and will be left to the reader as an exercise.

Combining the three results, we have the desired inequality.

L'Hôpital's Rule

An application of the Mean Value Theorem is in the evaluation of

$$\lim_{x \to a} \frac{f(x)}{g(x)} \text{ where } f(a) = 0 \text{ and } g(a) = 0.$$

L'Hôpital's rule states that if the $\lim_{x \to a} \dfrac{f(x)}{g(x)}$ is an indeterminate form (i.e., $\frac{0}{0}$ or $\frac{\infty}{\infty}$), then we can differentiate the numerator and the denominator separately and arrive at an expression that has the same limit as the original problem.

Thus, $\lim_{x \to a} \dfrac{f(x)}{g(x)} = \lim_{x \to a} \dfrac{f'(x)}{g'(x)}$

In general, if $f(x)$ and $g(x)$ have properties

1) $f(a) = g(a) = 0$

2) $f^{(k)}(a) = g^{(k)}(a) = 0$ for $k = 1, 2, \ldots n$

but 3) $f^{(n+1)}(a)$ or $g^{(n+1)}(a)$ is not equal to zero, then

$$\lim_{x \to a} \frac{f(x)}{g(x)} = \frac{f^{(n+1)}(x)}{g^{(n+1)}(x)}$$

PROBLEM

Evaluate $\lim_{x \to 2} \dfrac{(2x^2 - 4x)}{x - 2}$.

SOLUTION

The function takes the form $\frac{0}{0}$ at $x = 2$, and therefore we can apply L'Hôpital's rule to obtain:

$$\lim_{x \to 2} \frac{4x - 4}{1} = 4$$

We can also solve the problem in a different way by noting that the numerator can be factored.

$$\lim_{x \to 2} \frac{(2x^2 - 4x)}{x - 2} = \lim_{x \to 2} \frac{2x(x - 2)}{x - 2}$$
$$= \lim_{x \to 2} 2x$$
$$= 4.$$

PROBLEM

Find $\lim_{x \to 3} \dfrac{x^2 - x - 6}{x - 3}$

SOLUTION

This limit may be found by writing

$$\frac{x^2 - x - 6}{x - 3} = \frac{(x + 2)(x - 3)}{x - 3} = x + 2.$$

Hence $\lim_{x \to 3} (x + 2) = 5$.

Since $\frac{0}{0}$ (indeterminate) is obtained by substitution of $x = 3$ in the original function, the limit may also be obtained by L'Hôpital's rule by differentiating separately the numerator and denominator. Thus

$$\lim_{x \to 3} \frac{x^2 - x - 6}{x - 3} = \lim_{x \to 3} \frac{2x - 1}{1} = 5.$$

The application of L'Hôpital's rule is the more systematic approach and should generally be tried first, if another method is not immediately apparent.

Tangents and Normals

Tangents

A line that is tangent to a curve at a point a, must have the same slope as the curve. That is, the slope of the tangent is simply

$$m = \lim_{h \to 0} \frac{f(a+h) - f(a)}{h}$$

Therefore, if we find the derivative of a curve and evaluate for a specific point, we obtain the slope of the curve and the tangent line to the curve at that point.

A curve is said to have a vertical tangent at a point $(a, f(a))$ if f is continuous at a and $\lim_{x \to a} |f'(x)| = \infty$.

PROBLEM

> Using the Δ-method, find the points on the curve $y = \dfrac{x}{3} + \dfrac{3}{x}$, at which the tangent line is horizontal.

SOLUTION

When the slope of a curve equals zero, the curve has a horizontal tangent. We can find the points at which the tangent line is horizontal by calculating the slope $\dfrac{dy}{dx}$, setting it equal to zero and solving for x. By the Δ-method,

$$\frac{\Delta y}{\Delta x} = \frac{f(x + \Delta x) - f(x)}{\Delta x}$$

$$\frac{\Delta y}{\Delta x} = \frac{\frac{(x+\Delta x)}{3} + \frac{3}{(x+\Delta x)} - \left(\frac{x}{3} + \frac{3}{x}\right)}{\Delta x}$$

$$= \frac{\frac{x}{3} + \frac{\Delta x}{3} + \frac{3}{x+\Delta x} - \frac{x}{3} - \frac{3}{x}}{\Delta x}$$

$$= \frac{\frac{\Delta x}{3} + \frac{3}{x+\Delta x} - \frac{3}{x}}{\Delta x}.$$

$$\frac{\Delta y}{\Delta x} = \frac{\frac{x^2 \Delta x + x(\Delta x)^2 - 9\Delta x}{3(x+\Delta x)x}}{\Delta x}$$

$$= \frac{x^2 + x\Delta x - 9}{3x^2 + 3x\Delta x}.$$

$$\frac{dy}{dx} = \lim_{\Delta x \to 0} \frac{\Delta y}{\Delta x} = \lim_{\Delta x \to 0} \frac{x^2 + x\Delta x - 9}{3x^2 + 3x\Delta x} = \frac{x^2 - 9}{3x^2}.$$

We can set this value, which is the slope, equal to zero and solve for x.

$$\frac{x^2 - 9}{3x^2} = 0$$

$$\frac{(x-3)(x+3)}{x(3x)} = 0$$

$$x = 3, x = -3.$$

(Remember that x cannot be zero, for that would give an infinite slope.)

Substituting these values for x back into $y = \dfrac{x}{3} + \dfrac{3}{x}$, we can obtain the y coordinates. We find $(3, 2)$ and $(-3, -2)$ to be the required points.

Normals

A line normal to a curve at a point must have a slope perpendicular to the slope of the tangent line. If $f'(x) \neq 0$, then the equation for the normal line at a point (x_0, y_0) is

$$\boxed{y - y_0 = \frac{-1}{f'(x_0)}(x - x_0).}$$

PROBLEM

> Find the equations of the tangent line and the normal to the curve $y = x^2 - x + 3$ at the point $(2, 5)$.

SOLUTION

Since the equation of a straight line passing through a given point can be expressed in the form: $y - y_1 = m(x - x_1)$, this is appropriate for finding the equations of the tangent and normal. Here $x_1 = 2$ and $y_1 = 5$. The slope, m, of the tangent line is found by taking the derivative, $\frac{dy}{dx}$, of the curve: $y = x^2 - x + 3$.

$$\frac{dy}{dx} = 2x - 1.$$

At $(2, 5)$, $\frac{dy}{dx} = 2(2) - 1 = 3$, therefore the slope, m, of the tangent line is 3. Substituting x_1, y_1 and m into the equation $y - y_1 = m(x - x_1)$ we obtain:

$$y - 5 = 3(x - 2),$$

as the equation of the tangent line, or

$$3x - y - 1 = 0.$$

Since the slope of the normal is given by: $m' = -\frac{1}{m}$,

and since $m = 3$, the slope of the normal is $m' = -\frac{1}{3}$. Substituting $x_1 = 2$, $y_1 = 5$ and the slope of the normal, $m' = -\frac{1}{3}$, into the equation: $y - y_1 = m'(x - x_1)$, we obtain:

$$y - 5 = -\frac{1}{3}(x - 2).$$

or

$$x + 3y - 17 = 0.$$

This is the equation of the normal.

Minimum and Maximum Values

If a function f is defined on an interval I, then

a) f is increasing on I if $f(x_1) < f(x_2)$ whenever x_1, x_2 are in I and $x_1 < x_2$.

b) f is decreasing on I if $f(x_1) > f(x_2)$ whenever $x_1 < x_2$ in I.

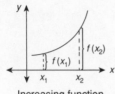
Increasing function

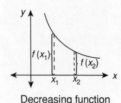
Decreasing function

c) f is constant if $f(x_1) = f(x_2)$ for every x_1, x_2 in I.

Suppose f is defined on an open interval I, and c is a number in I. Then,

a) $f(c)$ is a local maximum value if $f(x) \leq f(c)$ for all x in I.

b) $f(c)$ is a local minimum value if $f(x) \geq f(c)$ for all x in I.

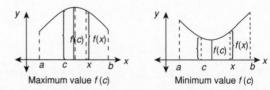
Maximum value $f(c)$ Minimum value $f(c)$

In the figure below in the interval $[a, b]$, the local maxima occur at c_1, c_3, c_5, with an absolute maximum at c_5 and the local minima occur at c_2, c_4.

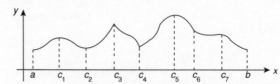

To find Absolute Extrema for functions, first calculate $f(c)$ for each critical number c, then calculate $f(a)$ and $f(b)$. The absolute extrema of f on $[a, b]$ will then be the largest and the smallest of these functional values. If $f(a)$ or $f(b)$ is an extremum we call it an endpoint extremum.

Viewing the derivative as the slope of a curve, there may be points (or critical values) where the curve has a zero derivative. At these values the tangent to the curve is horizontal.

Conversely, if the derivative at a point exists and is not zero, then the point is not a local extrema.

PROBLEM

Find the maxima and minima of the function $f(x) = x^4$.

SOLUTION

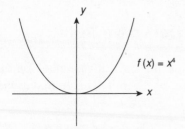

To determine maxima and minima we find $f'(x)$, set it equal to 0, and solve for x to obtain the critical points. We find: $f'(x) = 4x^3 = 0$, therefore $x = 0$ is the critical value. We must now determine whether $x = 0$ is a maximum or minimum value. In this example the Second Derivative Test fails because $f''(x) = 12x^2$ and $f''(0) = 0$. We must, therefore, use the First Derivative Test. We examine $f'(x)$ when $x < 0$, and when $x > 0$. We find that for $x < 0$, $f'(x)$ is negative, and for $x > 0$, $f'(x)$ is positive. Therefore there is a minimum at $(0, 0)$. (See figure.)

PROBLEM

> Locate the maxima and minima of $y = 2x^2 - 8x + 6$.

SOLUTION

To obtain the minima and maxima we find $\dfrac{dy}{dx}$, set it equal to 0 and solve for x. We find:

$$\frac{dy}{dx} = 4x - 8 = 0$$

Therefore, $x = 2$ is the critical point. We now use the Second Derivative Test to determine whether $x = 2$ is a maximum or a minimum. We find $\dfrac{d^2y}{dx^2} = 4$, (positive). The second derivative is positive, hence $x = 2$ is a minimum.

Now substitute $x = 2$ back into the original equation to get the corresponding ordinate.

$y = 2x^2 - 8x + 6 = 2 \cdot 2^2 - 8 \cdot 2 + 6 = 8 - 16 + 6$

$\quad = -2.$

Therefore, the minimum is at $x = 2$, $y = -2$, or $(2, -2)$.

Solving Maxima and Minima Problems

Step 1. Determine which variable is to be maximized or minimized (i.e., the dependent variable y).

Step 2. Find the independent variable x.

Step 3. Write an equation involving x and y. All other variables can be eliminated by substitution.

Step 4. Differentiate with respect to the independent variable.

Step 5. Set the derivative equal to zero to obtain critical values.

Step 6. Determine maxima and minima.

PROBLEM

> Locate the maxima and minima of
>
> $$y = \frac{x^3}{3} - \frac{5x^2}{2} + 6x + 4$$
>
>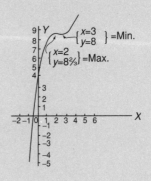

SOLUTION

To find the maxima and minima we find $\dfrac{dy}{dx}$, set it equal to 0, and solve for x, obtaining the critical points. We have:

$$\frac{dy}{dx} = x^2 - 5x + 6 = 0, (x - 2)(x - 3) = 0$$

Therefore,

$x = 3$ and $2.$

We now use the Second Derivative Test to determine whether the critical values are maximum, minimum, or neither. We find:

$$\frac{d^2y}{dx^2} = 2x - 5.$$

For $x = 3$,

$$\frac{d^2y}{dx^2} = 2x - 5 = 2 \cdot 3 - 5 = +(positive),$$

which indicates a minimum.

For $x = 2$,

$$\frac{d^2y}{dx^2} = 2x - 5 = 2 \cdot 2 - 5 = -(negative),$$

which indicates a maximum.

Therefore, we have a minimum at $x = 3$ and a maximum at $x = 2$. We now wish to find the corresponding ordinates. Going back to the original equation, we have:

For $x = 3$,

$$y = \frac{x^3}{3} - \frac{5x^2}{2} + 6x + 4 = \frac{3^3}{3} - \frac{5 \cdot 3^2}{2} + 6 \cdot 3 + 4$$

$$= 9 - \frac{45}{2} + 18 + 4 = 8\frac{1}{2}.$$

For $x = 2$,

$$y = \frac{x^3}{3} - \frac{5x^2}{2} + 6x + 4 = \frac{2^3}{3} - \frac{5 \cdot 2^2}{2} + 6 \cdot 2 + 4$$

$$= \frac{8}{3} - 10 + 12 + 4 = 8\frac{2}{3}.$$

Therefore, the minimum is at $x = 3$, $y = 8\frac{1}{2}$, or $(3, 8\frac{1}{2})$, and the maximum is at $x = 2$, $y = 8\frac{2}{3}$, or $(2, 8\frac{2}{3})$.

Curve Sketching and the Derivative Tests

Using the knowledge we have about local extrema and the following properties of the first and second derivatives of a function, we can gain a better understanding of the graphs (and thereby the nature) of a given function.

A function is said to be smooth on an interval (a, b) if both f' and f'' exist for all $x \in (a, b)$.

The First Derivative Test

Suppose that c is a critical value of a function, f, in an interval (a, b). Then if f is continuous and differentiable, we can say that

a) if $f'(x) > 0$ for all $a < x < c$ and $f'(x) < 0$ for all $c < x < b$, then $f(c)$ is a local maximum.

b) if $f'(x) < 0$ for $a < x < c$ and $f'(x) > 0$ for $c < x < b$, then $f(c)$ is a local minimum.

c) if $f'(x) > 0$ or if $f'(x) < 0$ for all $x \in (a, b)$ then $f(c)$ is not a local extrema.

PROBLEM

Find the maxima and minima of $f(x) = 3x^5 - 5x^3$.

SOLUTION

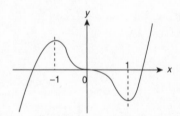

To determine maxima and minima we find $f'(x)$, set it equal to 0, and solve for x, obtaining the critical points. We find:

$$f'(x) = 15x^4 - 15x^2 = 15x^2(x^2 - 1).$$

Therefore, $x = 0, \pm 1$ are the critical points. We must now determine whether the function reaches a maximum, minimum, or neither at each of these values. To do this, we will use the second Derivative Test. Computing the second derivative f'', we have:

$$f''(x) = 60x^3 - 30x = 30(2x^2 - 1).$$

$f''(1) = 30 > 0$. Therefore, $x = 1$ is a relative minimum point, and $x = -1$ is a relative maximum since $f''(-1) = -30 < 0$. Now, $f''(0) = 0$. Therefore the Second Derivative Test indicates a point that is neither maximum nor minimum. This is known as a point of inflection.

For further study of the behavior of f at 0 we must use the First Derivative Test. We examine $f'(x)$ when $-1 < x < 0$ and when $0 < x < 1$. Let us select a representative value from each interval. We will use $x = -\frac{1}{2}$ and $x = \frac{1}{2}$. For $f'\left(-\frac{1}{2}\right)$, we obtain a negative value, and for $f'\left(\frac{1}{2}\right)$, we again obtain a negative value. Because there is no change in sign we conclude that at $x = 0$ there is neither a maximum nor a minimum, as can also be seen from the graph.

Concavity

If a function is differentiable on an open interval containing c, then the graph at this point is

a) concave upward (or convex) if $f''(c) > 0$;

b) concave downward if $f''(c) < 0$.

If a function is concave upward, then f' is increasing as x increases. If the function is concave downward, f' is decreasing as x increases.

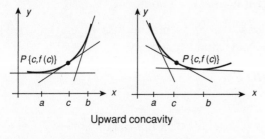

Upward concavity

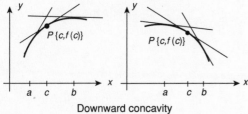

Downward concavity

PROBLEM

Find the intervals of x for which the curve
$$y = 2x^3 - 9x^2 + 12x - 3$$
is concave downward and concave upward.

SOLUTION

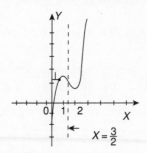

Differentiating twice,
$$\frac{dy}{dx} = 6(x^2 - 3x + 2)$$

and

$$\frac{d^2y}{dx^2} = 6(2x - 3)$$

By setting $\frac{d^2y}{dx^2} = 0$, we have $x = \frac{3}{2}$.
y'' is positive or negative according to $x > \frac{3}{2}$ or $x < \frac{3}{2}$. Hence, the graph is concave downward to the left of $x = \frac{3}{2}$ and concave upward to the right of $x = \frac{3}{2}$.

Points of Inflection

Points that satisfy $f''(x) = 0$ may be positions where concavity changes. These points are called the points of inflection. These are the points at which the curve crosses its tangent line.

PROBLEM

Consider the function $y = (2x - 3)^{\frac{4}{3}}$.

Determine any minimum or maximum point(s).

SOLUTION

Differentiating, $y' = \frac{4}{3}(2x - 3)^{\frac{1}{3}} \cdot 2 = \frac{8}{3}(2x - 3)^{\frac{1}{3}}$

$$= \frac{8(2x - 3)^{\frac{1}{3}}}{3}$$

Now set y' equal to 0. $\dfrac{8(2x-3)^{\frac{1}{3}}}{3} = 0$,

which implies that $(2x-3)^{\frac{1}{3}} = 0$. Thus $2x - 3 = 0$ or $x = \dfrac{3}{2}$.

To determine if the point whose x coordinate is $\dfrac{3}{2}$ represents a maximum or minimum point, we test values of x that are close to $\dfrac{3}{2}$, one higher and one lower.

Use x values of 1 and 2.

When $x = 1$, $y' = \dfrac{8(-1)^{\frac{1}{3}}}{3} = \dfrac{-8}{3}$

When $x = 2$, $y' = \dfrac{8(1)^{\frac{1}{3}}}{3} = \dfrac{8}{3}$

Note that when $x < \dfrac{3}{2}$, y' is negative and when $x > \dfrac{3}{2}$, y' is positive. This implies that the point whose x coordinate is $\dfrac{3}{2}$ represents a minimum point.

The coordinates of this minimum point are $\left(\dfrac{3}{2}, 0\right)$.

To determine the y coordinate, substitute $x = \dfrac{3}{2}$ into the original function. Then $y = \left[2\left(\dfrac{3}{2}\right) - 3\right]^{\frac{4}{3}}$ $= 0^{\frac{4}{3}} = 0$

A general graph of this function would appear as follows.

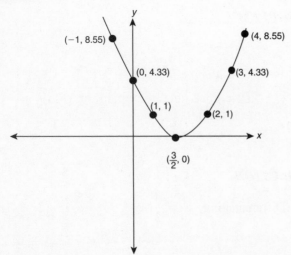

Note that some of the y-coordinate values are approximations.

Graphing a Function by Using the Derivative Tests

The following steps will help us gain a rapid understanding of a function's behavior.

A) Look for some basic properties such as oddness, evenness, periodicity, boundedness, etc.

B) Locate all the zeros by setting $f(x) = 0$.

C) Determine any singularities, $f(x) = \infty$.

D) Set $f'(x)$ equal to zero to find the critical values.

E) Find the points of inflection by setting $f''(x) = 0$.

F) Determine where the curve is concave, $f''(x) < 0$, and where it is convex $f''(x) > 0$.

G) Determine the limiting properties and approximations for large and small $|x|$.

H) Prepare a table of values $x, f(x), f'(x)$, which includes the critical values and the points of inflection.

I) Plot the points found in Step H and draw short tangent lines at each point.

J) Draw the curve making use of the knowledge of concavity and continuity.

PROBLEM

Find the maxima and minima of $y = \dfrac{4}{x^2 - 4}$, and trace the curve.

SOLUTION

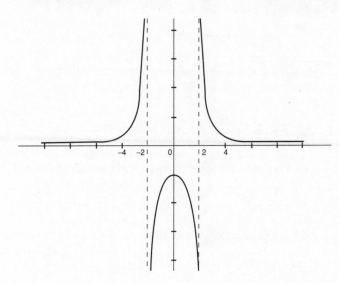

To find the maxima and minima, we determine $\dfrac{dy}{dx}$, equate it to 0, and solve for x, obtaining the critical value. We find:

$$\frac{dy}{dx} = \frac{(x^2 - 4)(0) - 4(2x)}{(x^2 - 4)^2} = -\frac{8x}{(x^2 - 4)^2}.$$

Set $\dfrac{-8x}{(x^2 - 4)^2} = 0$; therefore, $x = 0$. Substituting $x = 0$, into the original equation, $y = -1$. Therefore, the critical point is $(0, -1)$.

To determine whether a maximum, minimum, or neither occurs at this point, we use the First Derivative Test. We examine $\dfrac{dy}{dx}$ at a point less than 0 (use -1), and at a point greater than 0 (use 1). If $\dfrac{dy}{dx}$ changes sign from + to –, a maximum occurs at $x = 0$; from – to +, a minimum occurs and if there is no change in sign, neither a maximum nor a minimum occurs. We find that at $x = -1$, $\dfrac{dy}{dx} = \dfrac{8}{9}$, a positive value, and at $x = 1$, $\dfrac{dy}{dx} = -\dfrac{8}{9}$, a negative value. Therefore, at the point $(0, -1)$, a maximum occurs.

Upon further investigation of the curve: $y = \dfrac{4}{x^2 - 4}$, we observe that for the values $x = 2$ and -2, y is undefined or $y = \pm\infty$. Therefore, the graph of the curve has asymptotes at 2 and -2, as shown in the accompanying graph.

Rectilinear Motion

When an object moves along a straight line, we call the motion rectilinear motion. Distance s, velocity v, and acceleration a, are the chief concerns of the study of motion.

Velocity is the proportion of distance over time.

$$v = \frac{s}{t}$$

$$\text{Average velocity} = \frac{s(t_2) - s(t_1)}{t_2 - t_1}$$

where t_1, t_2 are time instances and $s(t_2) - s(t_1)$ is the displacement of an object.

Instantaneous velocity at time t is defined as

$$v = Ds(t) = \lim_{h \to 0} \frac{s(t + h) - s(t)}{h}$$

We usually write $v(t) = \dfrac{ds}{dt}.$

Acceleration, the rate of change of velocity with respect to time, is

$$a(t) = \frac{dv}{dt}.$$

It follows similarly that

$$a(t) = v'(t) = s''(t).$$

When motion is due to gravitational effects, $g = 32.2$ ft/sec^2 or $g = 9.81$ m/sec^2 is usually substituted for acceleration.

Speed at time t is defined as $|v(t)|$. The speed indicates how fast an object is moving without specifying the direction of motion.

PROBLEM

A rope attached to a boat is being pulled in at a rate of 10 ft/sec. If the water is 20 ft below the level at which the rope is being drawn in, how fast is the boat approaching the wharf when 36 ft of rope are yet to be pulled in?

SOLUTION

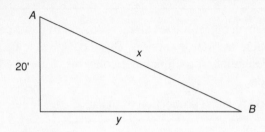

The length AB denotes the rope, and the position of the boat is at B. Since the rope is being drawn in at a rate of 10ft/sec,

$$\frac{dx}{dt} = 10.$$

To find how fast the boat is being towed in when 36 ft of rope are left, $\frac{dy}{dt}$ must be found at $x = 36$.

From the right triangle, $20^2 + y^2 = x^2$, or $y = \sqrt{x^2 - 400}$. Differentiating with respect to t,

$$\frac{dy}{dt} = \frac{dy}{dx} \cdot \frac{dx}{dt} = \frac{1}{2}(x^2 - 400)^{-\frac{1}{2}}(2x)\frac{dx}{dt} = \frac{x\frac{dx}{dt}}{\sqrt{x^2 - 400}}.$$

Substituting the conditions that:

$$\frac{dx}{dt} = -10 \text{ and } x = 36,$$

$$\frac{dy}{dt} = \frac{-360}{\sqrt{896}} = -\frac{45}{\sqrt{14}}.$$

It has now been found that, when there are 36 ft of rope left, the boat is moving in at the rate of:

$$\frac{45}{\sqrt{14}} \text{ ft/sec.}$$

PROBLEM

A boat is being hauled toward a pier at a height of 20 ft above the water level. The rope is drawn in at a rate of 6 ft/sec. Neglecting sag, how fast is the boat approaching the base of the pier when 25 ft of rope remain to be pulled in?

SOLUTION

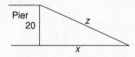

Formulating the given data, we have:

$$\frac{dz}{dt} = 6, z = 25, \text{ and } \frac{dx}{dt} \text{ is to be found.}$$

At any time t, we have, from the Pythagorean Theorem,

$$20^2 + x^2 = z^2$$

By differentiation, we obtain:

$$x\frac{dx}{dt} = z\frac{dz}{dt}$$

When $z = 25$, $x = \sqrt{25^2 - 20^2} = 15$; therefore,

$$15\frac{dx}{dt} = 25(-6)$$

$$\frac{dx}{dt} = -10 \text{ ft/sec}$$

The boat approaches the base at 10 ft/sec.

Rate of Change and Related Rates

Rate of Change

In the last section, we saw how functions of time can be expressed as velocity and acceleration. In general, we can speak about the rate of change of any function with respect to an arbitrary parameter (such as time in the previous section).

For linear functions $f(x) = mx + b$, the rate of change is simply the slope m.

For non-linear functions we define the

1) average rate of change between points c and d to be

$$\frac{f(d) - f(c)}{d - c}$$

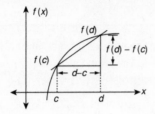

2) instantaneous rate of change of f at point x to be

$$f'(x) = \lim_{h \to 0} \frac{f(x+h) - f(x)}{h}$$

If the limit does not exist, then the rate of change of f at x is not defined.

The form, common to all related rate problems, is as follows:

a) Two variables, x and y, are given. They are functions of time, but the explicit functions are not given.

b) The variables x and y are related to each other by some equation such as $x^2 + y^3 - 2x - 7y^2 + 2 = 0$.

c) An equation that involves the rate of change $\dfrac{dx}{dt}$ and $\dfrac{dy}{dt}$ is obtained by differentiating with respect to t and using the chain rule.

As an illustration, the previous equation leads to

$$2x\frac{dx}{dt} + 3y^2\frac{dy}{dt} - 2\frac{dx}{dt} - 14y\frac{dy}{dt} = 0$$

The derivatives $\dfrac{dx}{dt}$ and $\dfrac{dy}{dt}$ in this equation are called the related rates.

PROBLEM

Compute the average rate of change of $y = f(x) = x^2 - 2$ between $x = 3$ and $x = 4$.

SOLUTION

Average rate of change is defined as:

$$\frac{\Delta y}{\Delta x} \text{ with } \Delta y = f(x + \Delta x) - f(x).$$

Given: $x = 3$, $\Delta x = 4 - 3 = 1$,

$y = f(x) = f(3) = 3^2 - 2 = 7$

For $x = 4$,

$y + \Delta y = f(x + \Delta x) = 4^2 - 2 = 14$

$\Delta y = f(x + \Delta x) - f(x) = f(4) - f(3)$

$\quad = (4^2 - 2) - (3^2 - 2) = 14 - 7 = 7$

$$\frac{\Delta y}{\Delta x} = \frac{7}{1} = \text{the average rate of change.}$$

PROBLEM

Find the rate of change of y with respect to x at the point $x = 5$, if $2y = x^2 + 3x - 1$.

SOLUTION

Rate of change is defined as

$$\lim_{\Delta x \to 0} \frac{\Delta y}{\Delta x} \text{ with}$$

$\Delta y = f(x + \Delta x) - f(x)$.

We have:

$2\Delta y = (x + \Delta x)^2 + 3(x + \Delta x) - 1 - (x^2 + 3x - 1)$

$\quad = x^2 + 2x \cdot \Delta x + (\Delta x)^2 + 3x + 3\Delta x - 1 - x^2 - 3x + 1$

$\quad = 2x \cdot \Delta x + (\Delta x)^2 + 3\Delta x.$

Dividing by Δx,

$$\frac{2\Delta y}{\Delta x} = \frac{2x \cdot \Delta x}{\Delta x} + \frac{(\Delta x)^2}{\Delta x} + \frac{3\Delta x}{\Delta x}$$

$\quad = 2x + \Delta x + 3$

and

$$\frac{\Delta y}{\Delta x} = x + \frac{\Delta x}{2} + \frac{3}{2}.$$

Now,

$$\lim_{\Delta x \to 0} \frac{\Delta y}{\Delta x} = \lim_{\Delta x \to 0} \left(x + \frac{\Delta x}{2} + \frac{3}{2} \right) = x + \frac{3}{2}.$$

For $x = 5$,

$$\lim_{\Delta x \to 0} \frac{\Delta y}{\Delta x} = 5 + \frac{3}{2} = 6\frac{1}{2}$$

This means that the instantaneous rate of change of the function represented by the curve at the point $x = 5$ is $6\frac{1}{2}$.

The function, it is seen, changes $6\frac{1}{2}$ times as fast as the independent variable x at $x = 5$.

The slope of the tangent at $x = 5$ is $6\frac{1}{2}$.

The Definite Integral

Antiderivatives

Definition:

If $F(x)$ is a function whose derivative $F'(x) = f(x)$, then $F(x)$ is called the antiderivative of $f(x)$.

THEOREM:

If $F(x)$ and $G(x)$ are two antiderivatives of $f(x)$, then $F(x) = G(x) + c$, where c is a constant.

Power Rule for Antidifferentiation

Let a be any real number, r any rational number not equal to -1, and c an arbitrary constant.

$$\boxed{\text{If } f(x) = ax^r, \text{ then } F(x) = \frac{a}{r+1}x^{r+1} + c.}$$

THEOREM:

An antiderivative of a sum is the sum of the antiderivatives.

$$\boxed{\frac{d}{dx}(F_1 + F_2) = \frac{d}{dx}(F_1) + \frac{d}{dx}(F_2) = f_1 + f_2}$$

Area

To find the area under the graph of a function f from a to b, we divide the interval $[a, b]$ into n subintervals, all having the same length $(b-a)/n$. This is illustated in the figure.

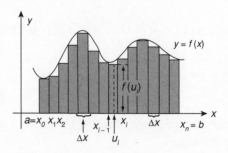

Since f is continuous on each subinterval, f takes on a minimum value at some number u_i in each subinterval.

We can construct a rectangle with one side of length $[x_{i-1} - x_i]$, and the other side of length equal to the minimum distance $f(u_i)$ from the x-axis to the graph of f.

The area of this rectangle is $f(u_i)\Delta x$. The boundary of the region formed by the sum of these rectangles is called the inscribed rectangular polygon.

The area (A) under the graph of f from a to b is

$$A = \lim_{\Delta x \to 0} \sum_{i=1} f(u_i)\Delta x.$$

The area A under the graph may also be obtained by means of circumscribed rectangular polygons.

In the case of the circumscribed rectangular polygons, the maximum value of f on the interval $(x_{i-1}, x_i]$, v_i, is used.

Note that the area obtained using circumscribed rectangular polygons should always be larger than that obtained using inscribed rectangular polygons.

PROBLEM

Determine the area under the curve: $y = f(x) = x^2$ between $x = 2$ and $x = 3$.

SOLUTION

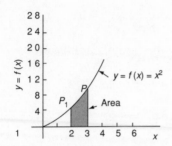

It is given that the area to be evaluated is between $x = 2$ and $x = 3$; therefore, these are the limits of the integral that gives us the required area. Area is equal to the integral of the upper function minus the lower function. From the diagram, it is seen that the required area is between $y = x^2$ as the upper function and $y = 0$ (the x-axis) as the lower function. Therefore, we can write:

$$A = \int_2^3 (x^2 - 0)dx$$

$$= \int_2^3 x^2 dx$$

$$= \frac{x^3}{3}\bigg]_2^3$$

$$A = \frac{3^3}{3} - \frac{2^3}{3} = \frac{19}{3}.$$

Definition of Definite Integral

A partition P of a closed interval $[a, b]$ is any decomposition of $[a, b]$ into subintervals of the form,

$$[x_0, x_1], [x_1, x_2], [x_2, x_3], \ldots , [x_{n-1}, x_n]$$

where n is a positive integer and x_i are numbers such that

$$a = x_0 < x_1 < x_2 < \ldots < x_{n-1} < x_n = b.$$

The length of the subinterval is $\Delta x_i = x_i - x_{i-1}$. The largest of the numbers $\Delta x_1, \Delta x_2 \ldots \Delta x_n$ is called the norm of the partition P and is denoted by $\|P\|$.

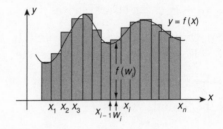

Definition:

Let f be a function that is defined on a closed interval $[a, b]$ and let P be a partition of $[a, b]$. A Riemann Sum of f for P is any expression R_p of the form,

$$R_p = \sum_{i=1}^n f(w_i)\Delta x_i,$$

where w_i is some number in $[x_{i-1}, x_i]$ for $i = 1, 2, \ldots, n$.

Definition:

Let f be a function that is defined on a closed interval $[a, b]$. The definite integral of f from a to b, denoted by

$$\int_a^b f(x)dx \text{ is given by}$$

$$\int_a^b f(x)dx = \lim_{\|P\| \to 0} \sum_i f(w_i)\Delta x_i,$$

provided the limit exists.

THEOREM:

If f is continuous on $[a, b]$, then f is integrable on $[a, b]$; that is, the limit $\int_a^b f(x)dx$ exists.

THEOREM:

If $f(a)$ exists, then $\int_a^b f(x)dx = 0$.

PROBLEM

$$\frac{dy}{dx} = (a - bx)^n. \text{ What is } y = F(x)$$

when $n = 2$?

SOLUTION

$\frac{dy}{dx} = (a - bx)^n$ can be rewritten as $dy = (a - bx)^n dx$.
We can now write: $\int dy = \int (a - bx)^n dx$ or, $y = \int (a-bx)^n dx$. To integrate, we consider the formula:
$\int u^n du = \frac{u^{n+1}}{n+1} + C$, with $u = (a - bx)$ and $du = -bdx$.
Applying the formula, we obtain:

$$y = \int (a - bx)^n dx = -\frac{1}{b} \cdot \frac{(a - bx)^{n+1}}{n+1}$$

$$= -\frac{(a - bx)^{n+1}}{b(n+1)} + C,$$

the integral in the general form.
For $n = 2$,

$$y = \int (a - bx)^2 \cdot dx = -\frac{(a - bx)^3}{3b} + C.$$

PROBLEM

$$\frac{dy}{dx} = (a + bx)^n. \text{ What is } y = F(x) \text{ when}$$
$n = 1, n = 2, \text{ and } n = -2?$

SOLUTION

In solving, we first find the integral in the general form and then substitute and find the integral for $n = 1$, $n = 2$, and $n = -2$.

$\frac{dy}{dx} = (a + bx)^n$ can be rewritten as

$dy = (a + bx)^n dx$. To find the integral, we write:

$\int dy = \int (a + bx)^n dx$, or $y = \int (a + bx)^n dx$.

We now consider the formula:

$$\int u^n du = \frac{u^{n+1}}{n+1} + C, \text{ with } u = (a + bx) \text{ and } du = bdx.$$

Applying the formula, we have:

$$y = \int (a + bx)^n \cdot dx$$

$$= \frac{(a + bx)^{n+1}}{b(n+1)} + C,$$

the integral in the general form.
For $n = 1$,

$$\int (a + bx)^1 dx = \frac{(a + bx)^{1+1}}{b(1+1)} = \frac{(a + bx)^2}{2b} + C.$$

For $n = 2$,

$$\int (a + bx)^2 dx = \frac{(a + bx)^{2+1}}{b(2+1)} = \frac{(a + bx)^3}{3b} + C.$$

For $n = -2$,

$$\int (a + bx)^{-2} \cdot dx = \frac{a + bx^{-2+1}}{b(-2+1)} = \frac{-1}{b(a + bx)} + C.$$

Properties of Definite Integrals

A) If f is integrable on $[a, b]$, and k is any real number, then kf is integrable on $[a, b]$ and

$$\int_a^b kf(x)dx = k \int_a^b f(x)dx.$$

B) If f and g are integrable on $[a, b]$, then $f + g$ is integrable on $[a, b]$ and

$$\int_a^b [f(x) + g(x)]dx = \int_a^b f(x)dx + \int_a^b g(x)dx.$$

C) If $a < c < b$ and f is integrable on both $[a, c]$ and $[c, b]$ then f is integrable on $[a, b]$ and

$$\int_a^b f(x)dx = \int_a^c f(x)dx + \int_c^b f(x)dx.$$

D) If f is integrable on a closed interval and if a, b, and c are any three numbers in the interval, then

$$\int_a^b f(x)dx = \int_a^c f(x)dx + \int_c^b f(x)dx.$$

E) If f is integrable on $[a, b]$ and if $f(x) \geq 0$ for all x in $[a, b]$, then $\int_a^b f(x)dx \geq 0$.

PROBLEM

Evaluate the expression: $\int_2^3 \dfrac{(x+1)dx}{\sqrt{x^2+2x+3}}dx$.

SOLUTION

We can rewrite the given integral as:

$$\int_2^3 (x^2 + 2x + 3)^{\frac{1}{2}}(x+1)dx,$$

and make use of the formula: $\displaystyle\int u^n du = \dfrac{u^{n+1}}{n+1}$.

Let $u = x^2 + 2x + 3$. Then $du = (2x+2)dx$, and $n = -\dfrac{1}{2}$. Applying the formula, we obtain:

$$\int_2^3 \frac{(x+1)dx}{\sqrt{x^2+2x+3}} = \frac{1}{2}\int_2^3 (x^2+2x+3)^{-\frac{1}{2}}2(x+1)dx$$

$$= \frac{1}{2}\left[\frac{(x^2+2x+3)^{\frac{1}{2}}}{\frac{1}{2}}\right]_2^3 = \sqrt{x^2+2x+3}\Big|_2^3.$$

We now evaluate the definite integral between 3 and 2, obtaining:

$$\sqrt{3^2+(2)(3)+3} - \sqrt{2^2+(2)(2)+3} = \sqrt{18} - \sqrt{11}.$$

PROBLEM

Evaluate the expression: $\int_0^2 2x^2\sqrt{x^3+1}dx$.

SOLUTION

We wish to convert the given integral into a form to which we can apply the formula for $\int u^n du$, with $u = (x^3 + 1)$, $du = 3x^2$ and $n = \dfrac{1}{2}$. We obtain:

$$\int_0^2 2x^2\sqrt{x^3+1}dx = \frac{2}{3}\int_0^2 (x^3+1)^{\frac{1}{2}}\left(\frac{3}{2}\cdot 2x^2 dx\right).$$

Applying the formula for $\int u^n du$, we obtain:

$$\frac{2}{3}\left[\frac{(x^3+1)^{\frac{3}{2}}}{\frac{3}{2}}\right]_0^2 = \frac{4}{9}(x^3+1)^{\frac{3}{2}}\Big|_0^2.$$

Evaluating between 2 and 0, we have:

$$\frac{4}{9}(8+1)^{\frac{3}{2}} - \frac{4}{9}(0+1)^{\frac{3}{2}}$$

$$= \frac{4}{9}(27-1)$$

$$= \frac{104}{9}.$$

The Fundamental Theorem of Calculus

The fundamental theorem of calculus establishes the relationship between the indefinite integrals and differentiation by use of the mean value theorem.

Mean Value Theorem for Integrals

If f is continuous on a closed interval $[a, b]$, then there is some number P in the open interval (a, b) such that

$$\int_a^b f(x)dx = f(P)(b-a)$$

To find $f(P)$ we divide both sides of the equation by $(b - a)$, obtaining

$$f(P) = \frac{1}{b-a} \int_a^b f(x)dx.$$

PROBLEM

What is the mean value or mean ordinate of the positive part of the curve $y = 2x - x^2$?

SOLUTION

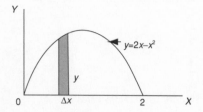

First determine the length of the base to fix the limits of integration for the area by setting y equal to zero, or:

$$0 = 2x - x^2 = x(2 - x).$$

Then, $x_1 = 0$, and $x_2 = 2$.
Now,

$$\bar{y}_x = \frac{1}{x_2 - x_1} \int y \cdot dx$$

$$= \frac{1}{2 - 0} \int_0^2 (2x - x^2)dx$$

$$= \int_0^2 \left(x - \frac{x^2}{2}\right) dx$$

$$= \frac{x^2}{2} - \frac{x^3}{6} \Big|_0^2 = \frac{4}{2} - \frac{8}{6} = \frac{2}{3},$$

the mean ordinate.

The Mean Value Theorem for the integral has a very simple geometric interpretation.

The Mean Value Theorem says that for a continuous function on the closed interval $[a, b]$, there exists a point x_0, where $a < x_0 < b$, such that:

$$f(x_0) = \frac{1}{b-a} \int_a^b f(x)dx.$$

If we multiply both sides by $(b - a)$ we have

$$(b - a)f(x_0) = \int_a^b f(x)dx,$$

which states that the integral from a to b is equal to the area of a rectangle of length $(b - a)$ and height $f(x_0)$. In the diagram below this means that the area in region 1 can be put in region 2, thus forming a rectangle.

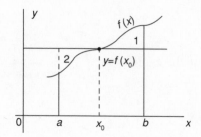

Definition of the Fundamental Theorem

Suppose f is continuous on a closed interval $[a, b]$. Then

a) If the function G is defined by

$$G(x) = \int^x f(t)dt,$$

for all x in $[a, b]$, then G is an antiderivative of f on $[a, b]$.

b) If F is any antiderivative of f, then

$$\int_a^b f(x)dx = F(b) - F(a)$$

PROBLEM

> Find the mean value of the ordinates of the circle $x^2 + y^2 = a^2$ in the first quadrant.
>
> a) With respect to the radius along the x-axis
>
> b) With respect to the arc-length.

SOLUTION

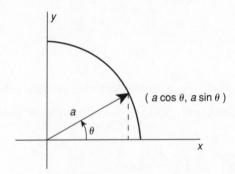

a) Noting that the mean value is defined by:

$$f(x_0) = \frac{1}{b-a} \int_a^b f(x)dx, \text{ where } a < x_0 < b,$$

we have:

$$f(x_0) = \frac{1}{a-0} \int_0^a \sqrt{a^2 - x^2}dx,$$

where $f(x) = y = \pm\sqrt{a^2 - x^2}$. We take $y = \sqrt{a^2 - x^2}$ because we are in the first quadrant. Also, noting from the table of integrals that:

$$\int \sqrt{a^2 - x^2}dx$$

$$= \frac{1}{2}x\sqrt{a^2 - x^2} + \frac{1}{2}a^2 \arcsin \frac{x}{a}\Big|_0^a,$$

we have:

$$f(x_0) = \frac{1}{4}\pi a.$$

b) The coordinates of any point on the circle can be expressed in terms of θ by the following method. For the point in question, drop a perpendicular line to the x-axis. We have a right triangle with hypotenuse of length a.

$$\cos(\theta) = \frac{x}{a},$$

or

$$x = a \cos (\theta). \qquad \sin(\theta) = \frac{y}{a},$$

or

$$y = a \sin (\theta).$$

Now an element of the arc length is $a\Delta\theta$. (Recall that the length of an arc of a circle is equal to $s = r\theta$ where r is the radius and θ the angle in radians.) Therefore, the length of the arc of the circle in the first quadrant is $\frac{1}{2}\pi a$.

By taking the limit, $a\Delta\theta$ becomes $ad\theta$

$$f(\theta) = \frac{1}{\frac{1}{2}\pi a} \int_0^{\frac{\pi}{2}} a \sin\theta(ad\theta)$$

$$= \frac{2a}{\pi} \int_0^{\frac{\pi}{2}} \sin\theta d\theta = \frac{2a}{\pi}\Big[\cos\theta\Big]_0^{\frac{\pi}{2}}$$

$$= \frac{2a}{\pi}(1-0) = \frac{2a}{\pi}.$$

Indefinite Integral

The indefinite integral of $f(x)$, denoted by $\int f(x)dx$, is the most general integral of $f(x)$, that is

$$\int f(x)dx = F(x) + C.$$

$F(x)$ is any function such that $F'(x) = f(x)$. C is an arbitrary constant.

Integration of Formulas

1. $\displaystyle\int x^n dx = \frac{x^{n+1}}{n+1} + C, n \neq -1$

2. $\displaystyle\int \frac{dx}{x} = \ln |x| + C$

3. $\int \dfrac{dx}{x-a} = \ln|x-a| + C$

4. $\int \dfrac{x\,dx}{x^2+a^2} = \dfrac{1}{2}\ln|x^2+a^2| + C$

5. $\int \dfrac{dx}{x^2+a^2} = \dfrac{1}{a}\tan^{-1}\dfrac{x}{a} + C$

6. $\int \dfrac{dx}{(a^2-x^2)^{\frac{1}{2}}} = \sin^{-1}\dfrac{x}{a} + C$

7. $\int \sin ax\,dx = -\dfrac{1}{a}\cos ax + C$

8. $\int \cos ax\,dx = \dfrac{1}{a}\sin ax + C$

9. $\int \sec^2 x\,dx = \tan x + C$

10. $\int e^{ax}\,dx = \dfrac{e^{ax}}{a} + C$

PROBLEM

Integrate the expression: $\int \dfrac{dx}{1+e^x}$.

SOLUTION

We wish to convert the given integral into the form $\int \dfrac{du}{u}$. If we multiply $\dfrac{1}{1+e^x}$ by $\dfrac{e^{-x}}{e^{-x}}$ (which is equal to 1) we obtain:

$$\dfrac{e^{-x}(1)}{e^{-x}(1+e^x)} = \dfrac{e^{-x}}{e^{-x}+e^0} = \dfrac{e^{-x}}{e^{-x}+1}.$$

In integrating this, we apply the formula, $\int \dfrac{du}{u} = \ln|u| + C$, letting $u = e^{-x}+1$. Then $du = -e^{-x}dx$. We obtain:

$$\int \dfrac{e^{-x}}{e^{-x}+1}dx = -\int \dfrac{-e^{-x}\,dx}{e^{-x}+1} = \ln(1+e^{-x}) + C.$$

Algebraic Simplification

Certain apparently complicated integrals can be made simple by algebraic manipulations.

Example: Find $\int \dfrac{x}{x+1}dx$

Write $\dfrac{x}{x+1} = \dfrac{x+1-1}{x+1} = 1 - \dfrac{1}{x+1}$

$$\int \dfrac{x}{x+1}dx = \int dx - \int \dfrac{dx}{x+1} = x - \ln|x+1| + C$$

PROBLEM

Integrate: $\int \dfrac{2x}{x+1}dx$.

SOLUTION

To integrate the given expression we manipulate the integrand to obtain the form $\int \dfrac{du}{u}$. This can be done as follows:

$$\int \dfrac{2x}{x+1}dx = 2\int \dfrac{x}{x+1}dx$$

$$= 2\int \left(\dfrac{x+1}{x+1} - \dfrac{1}{x+1}\right)dx$$

$$= 2\int \left(1 - \dfrac{1}{x+1}\right)dx$$

$$= 2\int dx - 2\int \dfrac{dx}{x+1}.$$

Now, applying the formula $\int \dfrac{du}{u} = \ln u$, we obtain:

$$\int \dfrac{2x}{x+1}dx = 2x - 2\ln(x+1) + C.$$

Substitution of Variables

Suppose $F(x)$ is expressed as a composite function, $F(x) = f(u(x))$,

then $F'(x) = f'(u)\dfrac{du}{dx}$, and $F'(x)dx = f'(u)du$.

Therefore,

$$\int F'(x)dx = \int f'(u)du = f(u) + C$$

$$= f(u(x)) + C = F(x) + C.$$

THEOREM:

Let f and u be functions satisfying the following conditions:

a) f is continuous on a domain including the closed interval $\{x : a \le x \le b\}$.

b) For each point t in the closed interval $\{t : \alpha \le t \le \beta\}$, the value $u(t)$ is a point in $\{x : a \le x \le b\}$.

c) $u(\alpha) = a$, and $u(\beta) = b$.

d) u is continuous on $\{t : \alpha \le t \le \beta\}$.

Then $\displaystyle\int_a^b f(x)dx = \int_\alpha^\beta f(u(t)) \cdot u'(t)dt$.

Example: Evaluate $\displaystyle\int \frac{x}{x^2+a^2}dx$

Let $u = x^2 + a^2$

$du = 2xdx$

$\dfrac{1}{2}du = xdx$

$$\int \frac{x}{x^2+a^2}dx = \frac{1}{2}\int \frac{du}{u} = \frac{1}{2}\ln|u| + C$$

$$= \frac{1}{2}\ln|x^2 + a^2| + C$$

PROBLEM

Evaluate the expression: $\displaystyle\int_0^3 x\sqrt{1+x}\,dx$.

SOLUTION

We wish to convert the given integral into a form to which we can apply the formula for $\int u^n du$. To evaluate the indefinite integral $\int x\sqrt{1+x}\,dx$, we let

$u = \sqrt{1+x}$, $u^2 = 1 + x$, $x = u^2 - 1$, $dx = 2u\,du$

Substituting, we have:

$$\int x\sqrt{1+x}\,dx = \int (u^2 - 1)u(2u\,du)$$

$$= 2\int (u^4 - u^2)du.$$

We can now apply the formula for $\int u^n du$, and we obtain:

$$\frac{2}{5}u^5 - \frac{2}{3}u^3 + C = \frac{2}{5}(1+x)^{\frac{5}{2}} - \frac{2}{3}(1+x)^{\frac{3}{2}} + C,$$

by substitution. Therefore, the definite integral

$$\int_0^3 x\sqrt{1+x}\,dx = \frac{2}{5}(1+x)^{\frac{5}{2}} - \frac{2}{3}(1+x)^{\frac{3}{2}}\Big|_0^3$$

$$= \frac{2}{5}(4)^{\frac{5}{2}} - \frac{2}{3}(4)^{\frac{3}{2}} - \frac{2}{5}(1)^{\frac{5}{2}} + \frac{2}{3}(1)^{\frac{3}{2}}$$

$$= \frac{64}{5} - \frac{16}{3} - \frac{2}{5} + \frac{2}{3}$$

$$= \frac{116}{15}.$$

Change of Variables

Example: Evaluate $\displaystyle\int_0^1 x(1+x)^{\frac{1}{2}}dx$

Let $u = 1+x$, $du = dx$, $x = u - 1$

$$\int_0^1 x(1+x)^{\frac{1}{2}}dx = \int_1^2 (u-1)u^{\frac{1}{2}}du.$$

*Notice the change in the limits from $x(1$ to $0)$ to $u(2$ to $1)$.

$$\int_1^2 (u-1)u^{\frac{1}{2}}du = \int_1^2 \left(u^{\frac{3}{2}} - u^{\frac{1}{2}}\right)du$$

$$= \frac{2}{5}u^{\frac{5}{2}} - \frac{2}{3}u^{\frac{3}{2}}\Big|_1^2$$

$$= \left[\left(\frac{2}{5}\right)\sqrt{32} - \left(\frac{2}{3}\right)\sqrt{8}\right] - \left(\frac{2}{5} - \frac{2}{3}\right)$$

$$= \frac{4\sqrt{2}}{15} + \frac{4}{15} = \frac{4}{15}(\sqrt{2}+1).$$

PROBLEM

Evaluate the expression: $\displaystyle\int_1^2 \frac{x}{(1+2x)^3}dx$.

SOLUTION

This integral is difficult because of the expression $1 + 2x$ in the denominator. Hence, we choose our substitution to eliminate this expression. We let

$u = 1 + 2x$, then $x = \dfrac{u-1}{2}$ and $dx = \dfrac{1}{2}du$.

Now

$u = 3$ when $x = 1$

$u = 5$ when $x = 2$,

giving us new limits. Using substitution, we obtain:

$$\int_1^2 \frac{x}{(1+2x)^3}dx = \int_3^5 \left(\frac{\frac{u-1}{2}}{u^3}\right)\left(\frac{1}{2}\right)du$$

$$= \frac{1}{4}\int_3^5 \left(\frac{1}{u^2} - \frac{1}{u^3}\right)du.$$

We can now use the formula for $\int u^n du$ on both terms of the integrand, obtaining:

$$\frac{1}{4}\left[-\frac{1}{u} + \frac{1}{2u^2}\right]_3^5 = \frac{11}{450}.$$

Integration of Parts

This method is based on the formula

$d(uv) = u\,dv + v\,du$.

The corresponding integration formula,

$uv = \displaystyle\int u\,dv + \int v\,du$, is applied in the form

$$\boxed{\int u\,dv = uv - \int v\,du}$$

This procedure involves the identification of u and dv and their manipulation into the form of the latter equation. v must be easily determined. For a definite integral,

$$\int_a^b u\frac{dv}{dx}dx = uv\Big|_a^b - \int_a^b v\frac{du}{dx}dx.$$

Example: Evaluate $\displaystyle\int x\cos x\,dx$

$u = x \qquad\qquad dv = \cos x\,dx$

$du = dx \qquad\qquad v = \sin x$

$$\int x\cos x\,dx = x\sin x - \int \sin x\,dx$$

$$= x\sin x - (-\cos x) + C$$

$$= x\sin x + \cos x + C$$

PROBLEM

Integrate by parts the expression: $\dfrac{dy}{dx} = x^2 \ln x$.

SOLUTION

$dy = x^2 \ln x \cdot dx$.

$y = \int x^2 \ln x\,dx$.

To integrate by parts we use the equation:

$\int u\,dv = uv - \int v\,du$.

Now, let $u = \ln x$.

Then, $du = \dfrac{1}{x}\cdot dx$.

Let $dv = x^2 \cdot dx$.

Then, $v = \displaystyle\int dv = \int x^2 dx = \frac{x^3}{3}$,

by use of the formula for $\int u^n du$. Substituting into the above equation, we have:

$$y = \int \ln x \cdot x^2 \cdot dx = \frac{x^3}{3}\ \ln x - \int \frac{x^3}{3}\cdot\frac{1}{x}\cdot dx.$$

We can now integrate

$$\int \frac{x^3}{3}\cdot\frac{1}{x}\cdot dx,$$

by using the formula for $\int u^n du$, with $u = x$, $du = dx$, and $n = 2$. Doing this, we obtain.

$$y = \frac{x^3}{3}\ln x - \frac{x^3}{9} + C.$$

Applications of the Integral

Area

If f and g are two continuous functions on the closed interval $[a, b]$, then the area of the region bounded by the graphs of these two functions and the ordinates $x = a$ and $x = b$ is

$$A = \int_a^b [f(x) - g(x)]\,dx.$$

where $f(x) \geq 0$ and $f(x) \geq g(x)$, and $a \leq x \leq b$.

This formula applies whether the curves are above or below the x-axis.

The area below $f(x)$ and above the x-axis is represented by $\int_a^b f(x)$. The area between $g(x)$ and the x-axis is represented by $\int g(x)$.

Example: Find the area of the region bounded by the curves $y = x^2$ and $y = \sqrt{x}$.

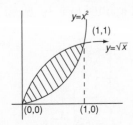

$$\text{Area} = A = \int_0^1 (\sqrt{x} - x^2)\,dx$$

$$= \int_0^1 \sqrt{x}\,dx - \int_0^1 x^2\,dx$$

$$= \left[\frac{2}{3} x^{\frac{3}{2}} - \frac{1}{3} x^3 \right]_0^1$$

$$A = \left[\frac{2}{3} - \frac{1}{3} \right] = \frac{1}{3}$$

PROBLEM

Find the area between the curve: $y = x^3$, and the x-axis, from $x = -2$ to $x = 3$.

SOLUTION

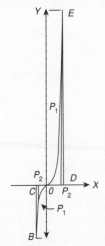

It is generally advantageous to sketch the curve, since parts of the curve may have to be considered separately, particularly when positive and negative limits are given. The desired area is composed of the two parts: *BOC* and *ODE*. To find the total area, we can evaluate each area separately and then add. The area is the integral of the upper function minus the lower function. In the first quadrant, the upper function is the curve $y = x^3$, the lower function is $y = 0$ (the x-axis), and the limits are $x = 0$ and $x = 3$. In the third quadrant, the upper function is $y = 0$, the lower function is the curve $y = x^3$, and the limits are $x = -2$ and $x = 0$. Hence, we can write,

$$A_{\text{total}} = \int_0^3 (x^3 - 0)\,dx + \int_{-2}^0 (0 - x^3)\,dx$$

$$= \int_0^3 x^3\,dx + \int_{-2}^0 -x^3\,dx$$

$$= \left[\frac{x^4}{4} \right]_0^3 + \left[-\frac{x^4}{4} \right]_{-2}^0$$

$$= \frac{81}{4} + \frac{16}{4}$$

$$= 24\frac{1}{4}.$$

Note that refusal to consider this problem in two parts does <u>not</u> give area, but gives "net area" with one area considered positive and the other negative.

PROBLEM

Find the area of the region bounded by the x-axis, the curve: $y = 6x - x^2$ and the vertical lines: $x = 1$ and $x = 4$.

SOLUTION

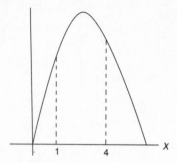

The limits of the integral which give the required area are $x = 1$ and $x = 4$. The function: $y = 6x - x^2$ is above the function $y = 0$ (the x-axis), therefore the area can be found by taking the integral of the upper function minus the lower function, or, $y = 6x - x^2$ minus $y = 0$, from $x = 1$ to $x = 4$. Therefore, we obtain:

$$A = \int_1^4 \left[(6x - x^2) - 0 \right] dx = \left[3x^2 - \frac{x^3}{3} \right]_1^4$$

$$= \frac{80}{3} - \frac{8}{3} = 24.$$

Volume of a Solid of Revolution

If a region is revolved about a line, a solid called a solid of revolution is formed. The solid is generated by the region. The axis of revolution is the line about which the revolution takes place.

There are several methods by which we may obtain the volume of a solid of revolution. We shall now discuss three such methods.

Disk Method

The volume of the solid generated by the revolution of a region about the x-axis is given by the formula

$$V = \pi \int_a^b [f(x)]^2 dx,$$

provided that f is a continuous, nonnegative function on the interval $[a, b]$.

PROBLEM

Find the volume of the solid generated by revolving about the y-axis the region bounded by the parabola: $y^2 = 4x$, the y-axis, and the line $y = 2$.

SOLUTION

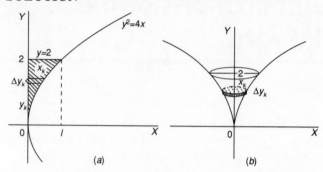

(a)   (b)

An element of volume is the disk generated by rotating a strip: x by dy, about the y-axis. The volume of the disk is: $dV = \pi x^2 dy$.

Hence,

$$V = \pi \int_0^2 x^2 dy$$

$$= \pi \int_0^2 \frac{1}{16} y^4 dy = \frac{2}{5} \pi$$

Shell Method

This method applies to cylindrical shells exemplified by

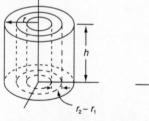

The volume of a cylindrical shell is

$$V = \pi r_2^2 h - \pi r_1^2 h$$
$$= \pi (r_2 + r_1)(r_2 - r_1) h$$
$$= 2\pi \left(\frac{r_2 + r_1}{2} \right)(r_2 - r_1) h$$

where r_1 = inner radius

r_2 = outer radius

h = height

The thickness of the shell is represented by Δr and the average radius of the shell by r, or $r = \dfrac{r_1 + r_2}{2}$ and $\Delta r = r_2 - r_1$. Then the volume of the shell becomes

$$V = 2\pi r h \Delta r$$

Thus,
$$V = 2\pi \int_a^b x f(x)\, dx$$

is the volume of a solid generated by revolving a region about the y-axis. This is illustrated by the figure below.

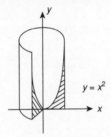

PROBLEM

Find the volume of the solid generated by revolving about the y-axis the region bounded by the parabola $y = -x^2 + 6x - 8$ and the x-axis.

SOLUTION

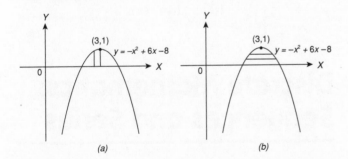

(a) (b)

Method 1. We use the method of cylindrical shells. The curve:

$$y = -x^2 + 6x - 8,$$

cuts the x-axis at $x = 2$ and $x = 4$.

The cylindrical shells are generated by the strip formed by the two lines parallel to the y-axis, at distances x and $x + \Delta x$ from the y-axis, $2 \le x \le 4$, as shown in figure (a). When this strip is revolved about the y-axis, it generates a cylindrical shell of average height y^*, $y \le y^*$ $\le (y^* + \Delta y)$, thickness Δx, and average radius x^*, $x < x^*$ $\le x + \Delta x$. The volume of this element is:

$$\Delta V = 2\pi x^* y^* \Delta x,$$

where $2\pi x^* y^*$ is the surface area. Expressing y in terms of x and passing to the limits, the sum of the volumes of all such cylindrical shells is the integral:

$$\begin{aligned}
V &= 2\pi \int_2^4 x(-x^2 + 6x - 8)\, dx \\
&= 2\pi \int_2^4 (-x^3 + 6x^2 - 8x)\, dx \\
&= 2\pi \left(-\frac{x^4}{4} + 2x^3 - 4x^2 \right)\Bigg|_2^4 \\
&= 2\pi \big((-64 + 128 - 64) - (-4 + 16 - 16) \big) \\
&= 8\pi.
\end{aligned}$$

Method 2. This can also be thought of as the volume comprising a series of concentric washers with variable outer and inner radii, as sectionally shown in figure (b). The variable radii are as follows: Since

$$y = -x^2 + 6x - 8,$$

we solve for x.

To complete the square, we require a 9, so that $x^2 - 6x + 9$ constitutes a perfect square. Rewriting the equation,

$$x^2 - 6x + 9 - 9 + 8 = -y.$$
$$x^2 - 6x + 9 = 1 - y.$$
$$(x - 3)^2 = 1 - y.$$

Therefore,

$$x = 3 \pm \sqrt{1 - y}$$

which shows the washers, y units from the x-axis, have an

inner radius: $x_{in} = 3 - \sqrt{1 - y}$, and an

outer radius: $x_o = 3 + \sqrt{1 - y}$.

(The particular one on the x-axis has $x_{in} = 2$ and $x_o = 4$.)

The volume of this washer with thickness dy is:

$$dV = \pi(x_o^2 - x_{in}^2)\, dy,$$

or $dV = \pi\left[(x_o + x_{in})(x_o - x_{in})\right] dy$.

Substituting the values for x_o and x_{in},

$$dV = \pi\Big(\big((3+\sqrt{1-y})+(3-\sqrt{1-y})\big)\cdot$$
$$\big((3+\sqrt{1-y})-(3-\sqrt{1-y})\big)\Big)\, dy$$
$$= \pi(12\sqrt{1-y})\, dy.$$

Since y varies from 0 to 1, the desired volume is:

$$V = 12\pi\int_0^1 (1-y)^{\frac{1}{2}}\, dy$$

$$= 12\pi\left(-\frac{2}{3}(1-y)^{\frac{3}{2}}\right)\Bigg|_0^1 = 8\pi.$$

Parallel Cross Sections

A cross section of a solid is a region formed by the intersection of a solid by a plane. This is illustrated by the figure below.

If x is a continuous function on the interval $[a, b]$, then the volume of the cross sectional area $A(x)$ is

$$V = \int_a^b A(x)\, dx.$$

PROBLEM

The area bounded by the x axis, $y = 2x$, and $x = 2$, is being rotated about the line $x = 4$. What is the volume of the resulting solid revolution?

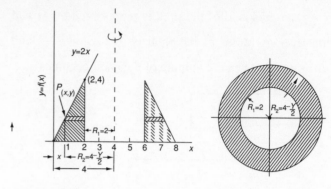

SOLUTION

First, rewrite $y = 2x$ as $x = \dfrac{y}{2}$

$V = \pi \displaystyle\int_a^b (R_2^2 - R_1^2)\, dy,$ where a and b are the limits of y. In this case, $a = 0$ and $b = 4$.

$$R_2 = 4 - \frac{y}{2} = \frac{8-y}{2} \text{ and } R_1 = 4 - 2 = 2$$

$$V = \pi\int_0^4 \left[\left(\frac{8-y}{2}\right)^2 - (2)^2\right] dy$$

$$= \pi\int_0^4 \left(\frac{64 - 16y + y^2}{4} - 4\right) dy$$

$$= \pi\int_0^4 \left(12 - 4y + \frac{1}{4}y^2\right) dy$$

$$\pi\left[12y - 2y^2 + \frac{y^3}{12}\right]_0^4$$

$$= \pi\left[48 - 32 + \frac{64}{12}\right]$$

$$= \pi\left[16 + \frac{16}{3}\right] = \frac{64\pi}{3}$$

Discrete Mathematics: Sequences and Series

A sequence is a function whose domain is the set of all natural numbers. All the sequences described in this section will have a subset in the set of all real numbers as their range. It is common to let a_n represent the nth term of the sequence. For example, if

$$a_n = 10n$$

then the sequence is 10, 20, 30, 40 . . .

The sum of the first n terms of the sequence,

$$a_1, a_2, a_3, \ldots a_n,$$

is indicated by

$$a_1 + a_2 + a_3 + \ldots + a_n,$$

and the sum of these terms is called a series. The Greek letter Σ is used to represent this sum, as indicated below.

$$\sum_{k=1}^{n} a_k = a_1 + a_2 + a_3 + \ldots + a_n$$

For a fixed number a and a fixed number d, the sequence

$$a, a + d, a + 2d, a + 3d, \ldots$$

is called an arithmetic sequence, and the nth term of this sequence is given by

$$a_n = a + (n - 1)d$$

The number a is called the first term and d is called the common difference. The symbol S_n is used to represent the corresponding series and

$$S_n = \sum_{k=1}^{n} a + (k - 1)d$$

or $S_n = n\left(\dfrac{a_1 + a_n}{2}\right)$

A sequence of the form

$$a, ar, ar^2, \ldots$$

is called a geometric sequence, where a is the first term and r is the common ratio. The nth term of such a sequence is

$$a_n = ar^{n-1}$$

The symbol S_n is used to represent the corresponding series and

$$S_n = \frac{a(1 - r^n)}{1 - r}.$$

Expressions of the form

$$a + ar + ar^2 \ldots$$

are called infinite geometric series. When $|r| < 1$, the sum S of the infinite geometric series exists and

$$S = \frac{a}{1 - r}$$

PROBLEM

In an arithmetic sequence, $a_1 = 29$ and $a_8 = 78$. Find the common difference d and the sixth term a_6.

SOLUTION

The nth term in an arithmetic sequence is given by $a_n = a + (n - 1)d$, where a is the initial term and d is the common difference. Using the given information we can first find d.

$$78 = 29 + (8 - 1)d$$
$$78 = 29 + 7d$$
$$49 = 7d$$
$$7 = d$$

Thus the common difference is 7. We may now use this information to obtain a_6.

$$a_6 = 29 + (6 - 1)(7)$$
$$= 29 + 35$$
$$= 64$$

thus the sixth term is 64.

The History of Mathematics

The history of mathematics is as long as the story of human beings on Earth. Humans first cut notches into bones, put knots in a string, shells in a pile of five. They drew on walls and on papyrus. In the early 21st century we use math to explore the cosmos even as we continue to learn more about phenomena of our own planet. Here are some key resources to help you position yourself well for the CSET test itself—and for a long time to come in the classroom.

Requirements

First, here is the requirement for mathematics teacher candidates in the state of California:

Candidates understand the chronological and topical development of mathematics and the contributions of historical figures of various times and cultures. Candidates know important mathematical discoveries and their impact on human society and thought. These discoveries form a historical context for the content contained in the Mathematics Content Standards for California Public Schools (1997) as outlined in the Mathematics Framework for California Public Schools: Kindergarten Through Grade Twelve (1999; numeration systems, algebra, geometry, calculus).

Chronological and Topical Development of Mathematics

(a) Demonstrate understanding of the development of mathematics, its cultural connections, and its contributions to society

(b) Demonstrate understanding of the historical development of mathematics, including the contributions of diverse populations as determined by race, ethnicity, culture, geography, and gender

Preceding information from: *Test Guide, California Subject Examinations for Teachers; MATHEMATICS SUBTEST III; Subtest Description*, © 2002 by the California Commission on Teacher Credentialing and National Evaluation Systems, Inc.

Bibliography

The official CSET website provides a bibliography for the history of mathematics for teacher candidates. We have reproduced it here for your convenience.

Boyer, Carl B. (Revised by Merzbach, Uta C.). *A History of Mathematics*. (2nd edition). New York: John Wiley & Sons. 1991.

Broad coverage from the Greeks to Gödel. Appendix included with chronological table and mathematical developments within a larger historical context.

Courant, Richard, and Robbins, Herbert. *What Is Mathematics? An Elementary Approach to Ideas and Methods*. Oxford: Oxford University Press, 1978.

A classical survey of the whole field of math.

Suzuki, Jeff. *A History of Mathematics*. Upper Saddle River, NJ: Prentice-Hall. 2002.

Emphasis on numeration, notation, mathematical results in their original form and mathematics as an evolving science.

In addition, REA recommends the following resources:

Books

Berlinghoff, William P., Gouvêa, Fernando Q. *Math Through the Ages: A Gentle History for Teachers and Others, Expanded Edition* (Classroom Resource Material). Washington, DC: The Mathematical Association of America: Oxton House Publishing. 2004.

A user friendly and well-organized book.

Struik, Dirk J. *A Concise History of Mathematics* (Paperback), Mineola, NY: Dover Publications, Inc. 1987.

This book focuses on the works of the great mathematicians with clear descriptions. Contains an excellent bibliography with many references to other books in various languages.

Reimer, Luetta, Reimer, Wilbert. *Mathematicians Are People, Too: Stories from the Lives of Great Mathematicians* (Paperback), Dale Seymour Publications. 1990.

This book shows moments of mathematical discovery and dramatizes the lives of important mathematicians.

Websites

A Mathematical Chronology

http://www-groups.dcs.st-and.ac.uk/~history/Chronology/full.html

An extensive listing of the history of math citing events and participants.

Mathematics–Timeline index

http://www.timelineindex.com/content/select/125/912,2,125

A Timeline with instant clicks to desired information on the history of math.

An Integrated Timeline: People, Places, Things

http://jwilson.coe.uga.edu/EMT668/emt668.student.folders/Hix/EMT635/Events.timeline.html

An extensive website with a variety of links to sites of possible interest.

The Mac Tutor History of Mathematics Archive

http://www-history.mcs.st-and.ac.uk/history/

A vast archive of important people and events in the history of math from the University of St. Andrews in Scotland.

The Wonderful World of the History of Mathematics.

http://www.csun.edu/~hcedu037/index.html#1

Sponsored by the History of Mathematics Program at California State University, Northridge. Provides the opportunity to browse, explore, and learn about the history of mathematics.

CSET

Mathematics

Practice Test 1

Subtest I

Answer Sheet

1. Ⓐ Ⓑ Ⓒ Ⓓ

2. Ⓐ Ⓑ Ⓒ Ⓓ

3. Ⓐ Ⓑ Ⓒ Ⓓ

4. Ⓐ Ⓑ Ⓒ Ⓓ

5. Ⓐ Ⓑ Ⓒ Ⓓ

6. Ⓐ Ⓑ Ⓒ Ⓓ

7. Ⓐ Ⓑ Ⓒ Ⓓ

8. Ⓐ Ⓑ Ⓒ Ⓓ

9. Ⓐ Ⓑ Ⓒ Ⓓ

10. Ⓐ Ⓑ Ⓒ Ⓓ

11. Ⓐ Ⓑ Ⓒ Ⓓ

12. Ⓐ Ⓑ Ⓒ Ⓓ

13. Ⓐ Ⓑ Ⓒ Ⓓ

14. Ⓐ Ⓑ Ⓒ Ⓓ

15. Ⓐ Ⓑ Ⓒ Ⓓ

16. Ⓐ Ⓑ Ⓒ Ⓓ

17. Ⓐ Ⓑ Ⓒ Ⓓ

18. Ⓐ Ⓑ Ⓒ Ⓓ

19. Ⓐ Ⓑ Ⓒ Ⓓ

20. Ⓐ Ⓑ Ⓒ Ⓓ

21. Ⓐ Ⓑ Ⓒ Ⓓ

22. Ⓐ Ⓑ Ⓒ Ⓓ

23. Ⓐ Ⓑ Ⓒ Ⓓ

24. Ⓐ Ⓑ Ⓒ Ⓓ

25. Ⓐ Ⓑ Ⓒ Ⓓ

26. Ⓐ Ⓑ Ⓒ Ⓓ

27. Ⓐ Ⓑ Ⓒ Ⓓ

28. Ⓐ Ⓑ Ⓒ Ⓓ

29. Ⓐ Ⓑ Ⓒ Ⓓ

30. Ⓐ Ⓑ Ⓒ Ⓓ

CSET: Mathematics Practice Test 1
Subtest I*
Algebra; Number Theory

TIME: When taking the actual test, you will have one five-hour test session in which to complete the subtest(s) for which you are registered.

> **Directions:** This test consists of two sections: 30 multiple-choice and four constructed-response questions. The constructed-response questions involve written responses.

1.

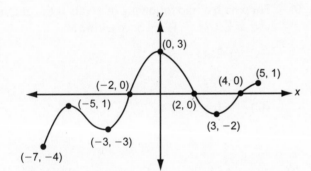

The graph of $g(x)$ is shown above. How many zeros would exist for the graph created by shifting $g(x)$ vertically downward by two units?

(A) 0   (C) 2

(B) 1   (D) 3

2. If $f(x) = |9 - 2x|$, for which values of x will $f(x) < 3$?

(A) $3 < x < 6$

(B) $-3 < x < 6$

(C) $-6 < x < -3$

(D) $-6 < x < 3$

3. The height of an object is given by the equation $z = -16t^2 + 144t$, where z is the distance in feet and t is the time in seconds. After how many seconds will this object reach its maximum height?

(A) 3

(B) 4.5

(C) 7.5

(D) 9

4. If $x = 3 + 2i$ and $y = 1 + 3i$, where $i^2 = -1$, then $\dfrac{x}{y} =$

(A) $\dfrac{9}{10} - \dfrac{2}{3}i.$

(B) $\dfrac{9}{10} - \dfrac{7}{10}i.$

(C) $\dfrac{9}{10} + \dfrac{2}{3}i.$

(D) $3 - \dfrac{7}{10}i.$

*According to the test administrator, Subtest II is always given first in the test session. For further details, visit the official CSET website at http://www.cset.nesinc.com.

5. What is the *least* integer value for n in order that $\left(\frac{2}{3}\right)^n < \left(\frac{1}{2}\right)^3$?

   (A) 6

   (B) 5

   (C) 4

   (D) 3

6. Define the symbol ♠ as follows:

   if $x < y$, $x ♠ y = y^3 - 3x$

   if $x \geq y$, $x ♠ y = x^2 + y^2$

   What is the value of $(2 ♠ 3) ♠ 4$?

   (A) 403

   (B) 425

   (C) 457

   (D) 481

7. A function contains the points $(8, 3)$, $(-1, -3)$, $(-2, 6)$, and $(7, 6)$. Which one of the following *must* be a point belonging to the inverse of this function?

   (A) $(3, -8)$

   (B) $(1, 3)$

   (C) $(-2, 7)$

   (D) $(6, 7)$

8.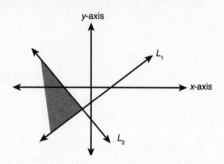

   The shaded region could represent the graphical solution to which pair of inequalities?

   (A) $2x + 3y \geq -6$ (C) $2x + 3y \leq -6$

        $x - y \leq -1$ $x - y \leq 1$

   (B) $2x - 3y \geq 6$ (D) $2x - 3y \leq 6$

        $x + y \geq -1$ $x + y \geq 1$

9. For which of the following intervals is the graph of $y = x^4 - 2x^3 - 12x^2$ concave down?

   (A) $(-2, 1)$

   (B) $(-1, 2)$

   (C) $(-1, -2)$

   (D) $(-\infty, -1)$

10. At the ACE Security Company, each ID badge has 3 letters, which appear consecutively and alphabetically in order, followed by 3 digits from 1 through 7 with no repetition and in any order. How many different ID badges are possible?

    (A) 8918

    (B) 8232

    (C) 5460

    (D) 5040

11. Any Mercenne prime can be written in which form?

    (A) A number of the form $2^n - 1$, where n is composite.

    (B) A number of the form $3^n - 1$, where n is prime.

    (C) A number of the form $2^n - 1$, where n is prime.

    (D) A number of the form $3^n - 1$, where n is composite.

12. Find $A + B$ where $A = \begin{bmatrix} 1 & -2 & 4 \\ 2 & -1 & 3 \end{bmatrix}$,

    $B = \begin{bmatrix} 0 & 2 & -4 \\ 1 & 3 & 1 \end{bmatrix}$

    (A) $\begin{bmatrix} 1 & 0 & 0 \\ 2 & 3 & 4 \end{bmatrix}$ (C) $\begin{bmatrix} 3 & 0 & 4 \\ 1 & 0 & 0 \end{bmatrix}$

    (B) $\begin{bmatrix} 1 & 0 & 0 \\ 3 & 2 & 4 \end{bmatrix}$ (D) $\begin{bmatrix} 3 & 0 & 0 \\ 1 & 2 & 4 \end{bmatrix}$

13. What is the period of the function

    $$f(x) = \left(\frac{1}{2}\right)\left(\sin \frac{2x}{3}\right) + \frac{1}{4}?$$

    (A) 3π

    (B) $\dfrac{3\pi}{2}$

    (C) $\dfrac{4\pi}{3}$

    (D) $\dfrac{2\pi}{3}$

14. In order to evaluate $3^2 - \left(\frac{7}{3}\right) \div \left(\frac{1}{4}\right) + \left(\frac{1}{2}\right)\left(\frac{1}{6}\right)$, for which number would the calculation of its reciprocal be required?

    (A) $\dfrac{7}{3}$

    (B) $\dfrac{1}{2}$

    (C) $\dfrac{1}{4}$

    (D) $\dfrac{1}{6}$

15. If the graph of $px - 4y = 12$ is perpendicular to the graph of $5x + 6y = 24$, what is the value of p?

    (A) 5.4

    (B) 4.8

    (C) 3.75

    (D) 3.33

16. Which functions(s) below is(are) symmetric with respect to the origin?

    I. $f(x) = x^3 - x$

    II. $f(x) = 2x + x^5$

    III. $f(x) = 2x + 4$

    (A) I and II

    (B) I only

    (C) I and III

    (D) II and III

17. Consider the function $f(x) = mnx^2$, where m and n are constants. Which of the following sequences is geometric?

    (A) $f(2), f(6), f(8)$

    (B) $f(1), f(2), f(3)$

    (C) $f(2), f(4), f(8)$

    (D) $f(3), f(5), f(7)$

18. If $f(x) = (x - 2)^2$ and $g(x) = x^2 - 2$, what is the value of $g(f[-2])$?

    (A) 260

    (B) 258

    (C) 256

    (D) 254

19. According to Pierre Fermat's Last Theorem, if x, y, z, and n are positive integers, and $x^n + y^n = z^n$, what are the correct restrictions on n?

    (A) n must be 1

    (B) n must be 1 or 2

    (C) n must be 2

    (D) n must be greater than 2

20. Suppose that P varies directly as the square root of Q and inversely as the cube of R. How does Q vary with P and R?

    (A) Directly as the square root of P and the cube root of R

    (B) Directly as the square of P and the sixth power of R

    (C) Inversely as the square of P and the cube root of R

    (D) Inversely as the square root of P and directly as R

21. What is the domain of the function $\dfrac{(2x^2 + 13x - 15)}{(2x^2 - x - 15)}$?

    (A) All numbers except $-\dfrac{13}{2}$ and 1

    (B) All numbers except $\dfrac{5}{2}$ and -3

    (C) All numbers except $-\dfrac{5}{2}$ and 3

    (D) All numbers except $\dfrac{15}{2}$ and -1

22. Which one of the following matrices represents the product $\begin{bmatrix} 3 & 2 & -1 \\ -2 & 1 & 0 \end{bmatrix} \begin{bmatrix} 1 & -3 \\ 2 & 1 \\ -2 & -1 \end{bmatrix}$?

    (A) $\begin{bmatrix} 5 & 6 \\ 0 & -7 \end{bmatrix}$

    (B) $\begin{bmatrix} 5 & -6 \\ 7 & 0 \end{bmatrix}$

    (C) $\begin{bmatrix} 9 & -6 \\ 0 & 7 \end{bmatrix}$

    (D) $\begin{bmatrix} 9 & 6 \\ -7 & 0 \end{bmatrix}$

23. Which one of the following functions has no horizontal asymptote?

    (A) $f(x) = \dfrac{(3x^2 + x - 7)}{(4x^2 + x + 1)}$

    (B) $f(x) = \dfrac{(x - 4)}{(5x^3 + 3x - 1)}$

    (C) $f(x) = \dfrac{(x^4 + x^3 - x + 3)}{(x^5 - x^4 + 2)}$

    (D) $f(x) = \dfrac{(x^3 + 7x^2 - 2)}{(2x^2 - 5)}$

24. A vector **v** is described by $<5, -12>$. Which of the following describes a vector of length $\frac{1}{2}$ unit in the direction of **v**?

    (A) $\left\langle \frac{5}{26}, -\frac{6}{13} \right\rangle$

    (B) $\left\langle \frac{10}{13}, -\frac{24}{13} \right\rangle$

    (C) $\left\langle \frac{5}{7}, -\frac{12}{7} \right\rangle$

    (D) $\left\langle \frac{5}{2}, -6 \right\rangle$

25. Which one of the following matrices represents the product of $\begin{bmatrix} 2 & 3 & -1 \\ -2 & 1 & 2 \end{bmatrix}$ and $\begin{bmatrix} 1 & 3 \\ 2 & 0 \\ -1 & 2 \end{bmatrix}$?

    (A) $\begin{bmatrix} 9 & -2 \\ 4 & -2 \end{bmatrix}$

    (C) $\begin{bmatrix} 9 & 4 \\ -2 & -2 \end{bmatrix}$

    (B) $\begin{bmatrix} -9 & -4 \\ 2 & 2 \end{bmatrix}$

    (D) $\begin{bmatrix} -9 & 2 \\ -4 & 2 \end{bmatrix}$

26. If $x + y = 8$ and $xy = 6$, then $\frac{1}{x} + \frac{1}{y} =$

    (A) $\frac{1}{8}$

    (C) $\frac{1}{4}$

    (B) $\frac{1}{6}$

    (D) $\frac{4}{3}$

27. Solve the following quadratic equation:

    $2x^2 - 1 = 3x$

    (A) $\frac{3 \pm \sqrt{17}}{2}$

    (C) $\frac{3 \pm \sqrt{17}}{4}$

    (B) $1, \frac{1}{2}$

    (D) $\frac{-3 \pm \sqrt{17}}{4}$

28. The graph of which one of the following equations has no x-intercept?

    (A) $5y = 10$ (C) $2x + 5y = 10$

    (B) $2x = 10$ (D) $5x - 2y = 10$

29. What is the range of the function $f(x) = -x^2 - 3x + 4$?

    (A) All numbers less than or equal to -1.5

    (B) All numbers between -1 and 4, inclusive

    (C) All numbers less than or equal to 6.25

    (D) All numbers between -4 and 1, inclusive

30. For which one of the following linear equations does the change of $+3$ units for the x value correspond to the change of $+4$ units for the associated y value?

    (A) $3x - 4y = 1$ (C) $3x + 4y = 7$

    (B) $4x - 3y = 1$ (D) $4x + 3y = 7$

> **Constructed-response questions 31–34:** For each response you will use up to two pages of the lined pages provided with the CSET test. Please see the sample pages at the end of the book.

31. Let $S = \{a + bi \mid a = 0, 1 \text{ and } b = 0, 1\}$.

    • Decide whether S is closed under each of the following: (a) addition, (b) multiplication. In each case, prove that S is closed or provide a counter-example to show S is not closed.

    • Verify the identity elements for addition and multiplication.

32. Let $f(x) = x^2 + cx + d$, where c, d are real numbers. Suppose $f(x)$ has a real zero at $1 + i\sqrt{2}$.

    • Determine the values of c and d.

    • Determine the y-intercept and the location of the vertex.

33. In 3-dimensional space, let $\alpha_1 = \begin{pmatrix} 1 \\ 2 \\ 1 \end{pmatrix}$, $\alpha_2 = \begin{pmatrix} 1 \\ 0 \\ 2 \end{pmatrix}$ and $\alpha_3 = \begin{pmatrix} 1 \\ 1 \\ 0 \end{pmatrix}$ represent three vectors. Show that the vector $\begin{pmatrix} 2 \\ 1 \\ 5 \end{pmatrix}$ is a linear combination of $\alpha_1, \alpha_2, \alpha_3$.

34. Use the principle of mathematical induction to prove that

$$1 + 3 + 5 + \cdots + (2n - 1) = n^2$$

Answer Key

Q No.	Correct Answer	Q No.	Correct Answer
1.	(C)	18.	(D)
2.	(A)	19.	(B)
3.	(B)	20.	(B)
4.	(B)	21.	(C)
5.	(A)	22.	(C)
6.	(C)	23.	(D)
7.	(D)	24.	(A)
8.	(C)	25.	(C)
9.	(B)	26.	(D)
10.	(D)	27.	(C)
11.	(C)	28.	(A)
12.	(B)	29.	(C)
13.	(A)	30.	(B)
14.	(C)	31.	Constructed-Response
15.	(B)	32.	Constructed-Response
16.	(A)	33.	Constructed-Response
17.	(C)	34.	Constructed-Response

Detailed Explanations of Answers

1. (C)

Real zeros of a function are represented by x-intercepts. Each point of $g(x)$ would have its y value decreased by 2. The only two places where there would be x-intercepts are: a point on $g(x)$ between $(-2, 0)$ and $(0, 3)$; and a point on $g(x)$ between $(0, 3)$ and $(2, 0)$. Note that any point on $g(x)$ between $(4, 0)$ and $(5, 1)$ would lie below the x-axis after the downward shift of 2 units.

2. (A)

If $f(x) < 3$, then $|9 - 2x| < 3$, which means $-3 < 9 - 2x < 3$. Subtracting 9, we get $-12 < -2x < -6$. Now, divide by -2, remembering to reverse the order of inequality, to get $6 > x > 3$, which is equivalent to $3 < x < 6$.

3. (B)

The maximum height of any parabola given in the form $y = Ax^2 + Bx + C$, where A is negative, is given by the y value of the vertex. In this example, z replaces y, and t replaces x. The x value of the vertex is given by $-\dfrac{B}{2A} = -\dfrac{144}{-32} = 4.5$, and this is the required time in seconds.

4. (B)

$$\frac{x}{y} = \frac{3 + 2i}{1 + 3i}$$
$$= \frac{3 + 2i}{1 + 3i} \times \frac{1 - 3i}{1 - 3i}$$
$$= \frac{3 - 9i + 2i - 6i^2}{1^2 - 3^2 i^2}$$
$$= \frac{9 - 7i}{1 + 9}$$
$$= \frac{9}{10} - \frac{7}{10}i$$

5. (A)

$\left(\dfrac{1}{2}\right)^3 = \dfrac{1}{8}$. By substitution, $\left(\dfrac{2}{3}\right)^3 = \dfrac{8}{27}$, $\left(\dfrac{2}{3}\right)^4 = \dfrac{16}{81}$, $\left(\dfrac{2}{3}\right)^5 = \dfrac{32}{243}$, and $\left(\dfrac{2}{3}\right)^6 = \dfrac{64}{729}$. Among these fractions, only $\dfrac{64}{729} < \dfrac{1}{8}$.

6. (C)

Because $2 < 3$, use the equation $2 \spadesuit 3 = 3^3 - (3)(2) = 27 - 6 = 21$. Likewise, because $21 > 4$, $21 \spadesuit 4 = 21^2 + 4^2 = 441 + 16 = 457$.

7. (D)

The inverse of the graph of any function is found by reflecting the graph across the line $y = x$. This means that for any point (x, y) on the original graph, the point (y, x) must be on the inverse graph. The point $(6, 7)$ is a point on the graph of the inverse since $(7, 6)$ is on the graph of the original function.

8. (C)

The equation $2x + 3y = 6$ has a slope of $-\dfrac{2}{3}$, so it must be represented by L_2. Similarly, the equation $x - y = 1$ has a slope of 1, so it must be represented by L_1. The inequality $2x + 3y \leq -6$ can be rewritten as $y \leq \left(-\dfrac{2}{3}\right)x - 2$, so we are looking for a region below L_2. Likewise, the inequality $x - y \leq 1$ can be rewritten as $y \geq x - 1$, so we are also looking for a region above L_1. The given shaded region satisfies both of these requirements.

9. (B)

$$y = x^4 - 2x^3 - 12x^2$$
$$y' = 4x^3 - 6x^2 - 24x$$
$$y'' = 12x^2 - 12x - 24$$
$$= 12(x - 2)(x + 1)$$

```
+ + + + + 0 - - - - - - - - - - - - 0 + + +
          (concave down)
```

10. (D)

The first letter can be any of 24 letters from A through X. Once the first letter is selected, there is only one choice for each of the second letter and the third letter. The reason is because each of the second and third letters must follow the first letter, both alphabetically and in order. For example, if Q is the first letter, then R must be the second letter and S must be the third letter. There are 7 choices for the first digit, 6 choices for the second digit, and 5 choices for the third digit. The number of different ID badges is $(24)(1)(1)(7)(6)(5) = 5040$.

11. (C)

The definition of a Mercenne prime is any number of the form $2^n - 1$, where n is prime.

12. (B)

Using the definition of matrix addition, add the (ij) entry of A to the (ij) entry of B. Thus,

$$A + B = \begin{bmatrix} 1+0 & -2+2 & 4-4 \\ 2+1 & -1+3 & 3+1 \end{bmatrix} = \begin{bmatrix} 1 & 0 & 0 \\ 3 & 2 & 4 \end{bmatrix}$$

13. (A)

The period of a function given by $y = A \sin Bx + C$, where A, B, C are constants is $\dfrac{2\pi}{B} = \dfrac{2\pi}{\left(\frac{2}{3}\right)} = 3\pi$.

14. (C)

The number $\dfrac{7}{3}$ is divided by $\dfrac{1}{4}$, which requires using the reciprocal of $\dfrac{1}{4}$.

15. (B)

The slope of the graph of $5x + 6y = 24$ is $-\dfrac{5}{6}$, so the slope of the graph of $px - 4y = 12$ must be $\dfrac{6}{5}$. In slope-intercept form, this equation is $y = \dfrac{p}{4}x - 3$. Then $\dfrac{6}{5} = \dfrac{p}{4}$. Solving, $p = \dfrac{24}{5} = 4.8$.

16. (A)

A function is symmetric with respect to the origin if replacing x by $-x$ and y by $-y$ produces an equivalent function.

(I) $y = f(x) = x^3 - x$

$(-y) = (-x)^3 - (-x)$

$-y = -x^3 + x$

$y = x^3 - x$

(I) is symmetric.

(II) $y = f(x) = 2x + x^5$

$-y = 2(-x) + (-x)^5$

$-y = -2x - x^5$

$y = 2x + x^5$

(II) is symmetric.

(III) $y = f(x) = 2x + 4$

$-y = 2(-x) + 4$

$-y = -2x + 4$

$y = 2x - 4$

(III) is not symmetric.

17. (C)

Calculate $f(x)$ for the values of the variable given in each option as follows:

(A) $f(2) = 4mn, f(6) = 36mn, f(8) = 64mn$

(B) $f(1) = mn, f(2) = 4mn, f(3) = 9mn$

(C) $f(2) = 4mn, f(4) = 16mn, f(8) = 64mn$

(D) $f(3) = 9mn, f(5) = 25mn, f(7) = 49mn$

Among the options given, only the terms of (C) form a geometric sequence because $\dfrac{16mn}{4mn} = \dfrac{64mn}{16mn}$.

18. (D)

$f(-2) = (-2 - 2)^2 = (-4)^2 = 16$. Then $g(16) = 16^2 - 2 = 256 - 2 = 254$.

19. (B)

The equation $x^n + y^n = z^n$, where x, y, z, and n are positive integers, has solutions only if $n \leq 2$. For $n > 2$, solutions are possible only if at least one of x, y, z is equal to zero.

20. (B)

If k is a nonzero constant, then $P = \dfrac{k\sqrt{Q}}{R^3}$ would represent the given relationship. To solve for Q, multiply both sides by R^3 to get $PR^3 = k\sqrt{Q}$. Divide by k to get $\dfrac{PR^3}{k} = \sqrt{Q}$. Now square both sides to get $\dfrac{(PR^3)^2}{k^2} = (\sqrt{Q})^2$, which can be written as $\dfrac{1}{k^2}(P^2R^6) = Q$. Note that $\dfrac{1}{k^2}$ is simply another constant. Thus, Q varies directly as the square of P and the sixth power of R.

21. (C)

The domain is determined solely by the denominator. If the denominator is not zero, then the function has a real value. Thus, $2x^2 - x - 15 = 0$ will yield the excluded values of x. $2x^2 - x - 15 = (2x + 5)(x - 3)$. Solving $2x + 5 = 0$ yields $x = -\dfrac{5}{2}$. Solving $x - 3 = 0$ yields $x = 3$. These two numbers represent the excluded values of the domain.

22. (C)

The term in the first row, first column is given by $(3)(1) + (2)(2) + (-1)(-2) = 9$. The term in the second row, first column is given by $(-2)(1) + (1)(2) + (0)(-2) = 0$. The term in the first row, second column is given by $(3)(-3) + (2)(1) + (-1)(-1) = -6$. The term in the second row, second column is given by $(-2)(-3) + (1)(1) + (0)(-1) = 7$.

23. (D)

If a rational function $f(x) = \dfrac{P(x)}{Q(x)}$ has no horizontal asymptote, then the degree of $P(x)$ must be greater than the degree of $Q(x)$. In choice (D), the degree of $P(x)$ is 3, whereas the degree of $Q(x)$ is 2. Thus, there is no horizontal asymptote. For choice (A), the degree of $P(x)$ equals the degree of $Q(x)$; its horizontal asymptote is $y = \dfrac{3}{4}$. For each of choices (B) and (C), the degree of $P(x)$ is less than the degree of $Q(x)$; the horizontal asymptote for each of these answer choices is $y = 0$.

24. (A)

$|v| = \sqrt{5^2 + (-12)^2} = \sqrt{169} = 13$. A unit vector in the direction of v is $\left\langle \dfrac{5}{13}, -\dfrac{12}{13} \right\rangle$. Thus, a vector that has a length of $\dfrac{1}{2}$ unit in this direction is $\left\langle \dfrac{5}{26}, -\dfrac{6}{13} \right\rangle$.

25. (C)

The entry in the upper left is $(2)(1) + (3)(2) + (-1)(-1) = 9$. The entry in the upper right is $(2)(3) + (3)(0) + (-1)(2) = 4$. The entry in the lower left is $(-2)(1) + (1)(2) + (2)(-1) = -2$. The entry in the lower right is $(-2)(3) + (1)(0) + (2)(2) = -2$.

26. (D)

$\dfrac{1}{x} + \dfrac{1}{y} = \dfrac{(y + x)}{xy} = \dfrac{8}{6}$, which reduces to $\dfrac{4}{3}$.

27. (C)

It is necessary to first write the quadratic in standard form: $2x^2 - 3x - 1 = 0$. This quadratic does not factor, so it is necessary to use the quadratic formula to find the solutions. The quadratic formula is as follows:

$x = \dfrac{-b \pm \sqrt{b^2 - 4ac}}{2a}$ with $a = 2$, $b = -3$, and $c = -1$.

$x = \dfrac{3 \pm \sqrt{9 - 4(2)(-1)}}{2(2)} = \dfrac{3 \pm \sqrt{17}}{4}$

(A), (B), and (D) all contain errors in the use of the formula or with simplifying.

28. (A)

If a graph of a line has no x-intercept, it must be parallel to the x-axis. This means that the general form of the equation is $y = k$, where k is a constant. The equation $5y = 10$ can be reduced to $y = 2$, so it represents a line that is parallel to the x-axis.

29. (C)

The x-value of the vertex of this parabola is given by $-\dfrac{(-3)}{[(2)(-1)]} = -1.5$. The corresponding y-value $= -(-1.5)^2 - 3(-1.5) + 4 = 6.25$. Since the coefficient of x^2 is negative, this parabola will have its highest point at the vertex, which is $(-1.5, 6.25)$. Thus, the range will be all numbers less than or equal to the y-value of the vertex, which is 6.25.

30. (B)

The slope of any line is represented by the change in y values divided by the corresponding change in x values between any two points on the line. So we need an equation with a slope of $\frac{4}{3}$. By rewriting $4x - 3y = 1$ as $y = \left(\frac{4}{3}\right)(x) - \frac{1}{3}$, the slope is identified as $\frac{4}{3}$. The slopes for answer choices (A), (C), and (D) are $\frac{3}{4}$, $-\frac{3}{4}$, and $-\frac{4}{3}$, respectively.

31.

- (a) Let $a = 1$ and $b = 1$. $(1 + 1i) + (1 + 1i) = 2 + 2i$, so S is not closed under addition.

- (b) Let $a = 1$ and $b = 1$. $(1 + 1i)(1 + 1i) = 1 + 2i + i^2 = 0 + 2i$, so S is not closed under multiplication.

- The identity element for addition is $0 + 0i$, since $(a + bi) + (0 + 0i) = (a + 0) + (b + 0)i = a + bi$.

  The identity element for multiplication is $1 + 0i$, since $(a + bi)$ times $(1 + 0i) = (a)(1) + (a)(0i) + (1)(bi) + (b)(0i) = a + 0 + bi + 0 = a + bi$.

32. For a real-valued function, if $a + bi$ is a zero, so must its conjugate $a - bi$ be a zero.

- Since $1 + i\sqrt{2}$ is a zero, so must $1 - i\sqrt{2}$ be a zero.
  Set
  $$f(x) = 0 = [x - (1 + i\sqrt{2})][x - (1 - i\sqrt{2})]$$
  Then
  $$0 = x^2 - x - ix\sqrt{2} - x + 1 + i\sqrt{2} + ix\sqrt{2} - i\sqrt{2} - (i)^2(2)$$
  $$0 = x^2 - 2x + 3$$
  Note: $-(i^2)(2) = -(-1)(2) = 2$
  Thus, $c = -2$ and $d = 3$

- The y-intercept is $(0, d) = (0, 3)$

  The x value of the vertex is given by $-c/(2)(1) = 1$

  The corresponding $f(x)$ value is $1^2 + (-2)(1) + 3 = 2$, so the vertex is located at $(1, 2)$.

33. To show that $\begin{pmatrix} 2 \\ 1 \\ 5 \end{pmatrix}$ is a linear combination of α_1, α_2, α_3, we must find 3 real numbers a, b, c such that

$$\begin{pmatrix} 2 \\ 1 \\ 5 \end{pmatrix} = a \begin{pmatrix} 1 \\ 2 \\ 1 \end{pmatrix} + b \begin{pmatrix} 1 \\ 0 \\ 2 \end{pmatrix} + c \begin{pmatrix} 1 \\ 1 \\ 0 \end{pmatrix}$$

This is equivalent to solving the following system of equations

(1) $a + b + c = 2$

(2) $2a + c = 1$

(3) $a + 2b = 5$

Subtracting equation (2) from equation (1), we get $-a + b = 1$. Add this equation to equation (3) to get $3b = 6$, so $b = 2$. By substitution into equation (3), $a + (2)(2) = 5$, so $a = 1$. Using equation (1) $1 + 2 + c = 2$, so $c = -1$

Thus, $\begin{pmatrix} 2 \\ 1 \\ 5 \end{pmatrix} = 1 \begin{pmatrix} 1 \\ 2 \\ 1 \end{pmatrix} + 2 \begin{pmatrix} 1 \\ 0 \\ 2 \end{pmatrix} - 1 \begin{pmatrix} 1 \\ 1 \\ 0 \end{pmatrix}$

34. We first prove that the statement is true for $n = 1$, $1 = 1^2$. Next assume that the statement is true for $n = k$, so that $1 + 3 + 5 + ... + (2k - 1) = k^2$

We need to show that the statement is true for $n = k + 1$, which means $1 + 3 + 5 + ... + (2[k + 1] - 1) = (k + 1)^2$

For the equation $1 + 3 + 5 + ... (2k - 1) = k^2$, add $2(k + 1) - 1$ to each side, to get

$$1 + 3 + 5 + ... + (2k - 1) + (2[k + 1] - 1) = k^2 + 2(k + 1) - 1$$

The right side of this last equation simplifies to $k^2 + 2k + 2 - 1 = k^2 + 2k + 1 = (k + 1)^2$.

CSET

Mathematics

Practice Test 1

Subtest II

Answer Sheet

1. Ⓐ Ⓑ Ⓒ Ⓓ   16. Ⓐ Ⓑ Ⓒ Ⓓ

2. Ⓐ Ⓑ Ⓒ Ⓓ   17. Ⓐ Ⓑ Ⓒ Ⓓ

3. Ⓐ Ⓑ Ⓒ Ⓓ   18. Ⓐ Ⓑ Ⓒ Ⓓ

4. Ⓐ Ⓑ Ⓒ Ⓓ   19. Ⓐ Ⓑ Ⓒ Ⓓ

5. Ⓐ Ⓑ Ⓒ Ⓓ   20. Ⓐ Ⓑ Ⓒ Ⓓ

6. Ⓐ Ⓑ Ⓒ Ⓓ   21. Ⓐ Ⓑ Ⓒ Ⓓ

7. Ⓐ Ⓑ Ⓒ Ⓓ   22. Ⓐ Ⓑ Ⓒ Ⓓ

8. Ⓐ Ⓑ Ⓒ Ⓓ   23. Ⓐ Ⓑ Ⓒ Ⓓ

9. Ⓐ Ⓑ Ⓒ Ⓓ   24. Ⓐ Ⓑ Ⓒ Ⓓ

10. Ⓐ Ⓑ Ⓒ Ⓓ   25. Ⓐ Ⓑ Ⓒ Ⓓ

11. Ⓐ Ⓑ Ⓒ Ⓓ   26. Ⓐ Ⓑ Ⓒ Ⓓ

12. Ⓐ Ⓑ Ⓒ Ⓓ   27. Ⓐ Ⓑ Ⓒ Ⓓ

13. Ⓐ Ⓑ Ⓒ Ⓓ   28. Ⓐ Ⓑ Ⓒ Ⓓ

14. Ⓐ Ⓑ Ⓒ Ⓓ   29. Ⓐ Ⓑ Ⓒ Ⓓ

15. Ⓐ Ⓑ Ⓒ Ⓓ   30. Ⓐ Ⓑ Ⓒ Ⓓ

CSET: Mathematics Practice Test 1
Subtest II*
Geometry; Probability and Statistics

TIME: When taking the actual test, you will have one five-hour test session in which to complete the subtest(s) for which you are registered.

<u>Directions:</u> This test consists of two sections: 30 multiple-choice and four constructed-response questions. The constructed-response questions involve written responses.

A calculator will be needed and will be allowed only for Subtest II. You will be required to bring your own graphing calculator. Please check the current version of the CSET registration bulletin for the list of approved models of graphing calculators.

1.

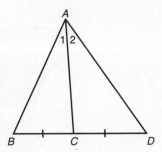

Note: Figure not drawn to scale.

In the figure shown above, $BC = CD$. Which additional information would NOT be sufficient to conclude that $\overline{AC}$ is perpendicular to $\overline{BD}$?

(A) $\angle B \cong \angle D$

(B) $\overline{AC}$ is the shortest distance from point A to $\overline{BD}$.

(C) $AB = AD$

(D) $\angle 1 \cong \angle 2$

2.

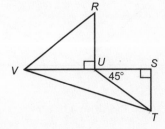

Note: Figure not drawn to scale.

In the figure above, $\overline{RU} = \overline{UV} = \overline{TU}$. If $\overline{RV} = 8$, what is the length of $\overline{TV}$?

(A) 9.66

(B) 10.5

(C) 11.32

(D) 12.0

---

*According to the test administrator, Subtest II is always given first in the test session. For further details, visit the official CSET website at *http://www.cset.nesinc.com.*

3.

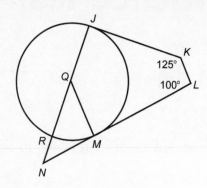

Note: Figure not drawn to scale.

In the figure above, Q is the center of the circle. JK and LM are tangents to the circle. J, Q, N, and R are collinear. Also, L, M, and N are collinear. If $JQ = 6$, what is the length of RN?

(A) $6\sqrt{2} - 6$

(B) $6\sqrt{3} - 6$

(C) $6 - \sqrt{2}$

(D) $6\sqrt{2} - 3$

4.

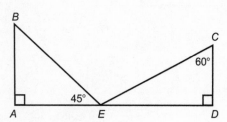

Note: Figure not drawn to scale.

In the figure above, $\overline{BE} = 10$ and $\overline{CE} = 8$. What is the *best* approximation to the length of $\overline{AD}$? (A, E, D are collinear points.)

(A) 12

(B) 13

(C) 14

(D) 15

5.

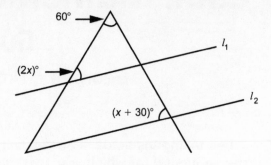

Note: Figure is not drawn to scale.

In the figure above, line l_1 is parallel to line l_2. What is the value of x?

(A) 30

(B) 25

(C) 20

(D) 15

6. In the figure shown, m∡$A = 130°$, m∡$B = 95°$, and m∡$C = 90°$. Point O is the center of a circle with a radius of 12. The area bounded by the polygon $ABCO$ is 30% larger than the shaded area. What is the value of the shaded area?

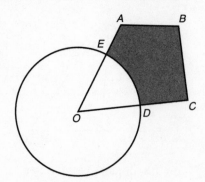

Note: Figure is not drawn to scale.

(A) 18π

(B) 24π

(C) 42π

(D) 60π

7.

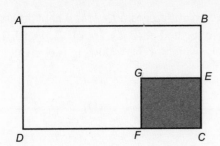

The figure above represents a dartboard in which *ABCD* and *ECFG* are rectangles. $EC = \frac{1}{2}BC$ and $CF = \frac{1}{3}CD$. If a dart is thrown and lands on the dartboard, what is the probability that it lands in the *unshaded* area?

(A) $\frac{1}{6}$

(B) $\frac{1}{5}$

(C) $\frac{3}{5}$

(D) $\frac{5}{6}$

8. In the triangle shown below, cosω is equal to

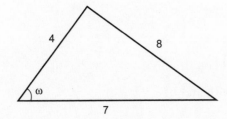

(A) $\frac{1}{56}$.

(B) $\frac{\sqrt{2}}{2}$.

(C) $\frac{1}{28}$.

(D) $\frac{\sqrt{3}}{3}$.

9. The surface area of a cube is exactly the same as the lateral surface area of a cylinder with a radius of $\frac{6}{\pi}$ and a height of 15. What is the best approximation of the volume of the cube?

(A) 135

(B) 150

(C) 165

(D) 180

10. In the accompanying figure of a circle centered about point *O*, the measure of arc *AB* is $\frac{\pi}{5}$ radians. Find ∠*OBA*.

(A) 36°

(B) 144°

(C) 90°

(D) 72°

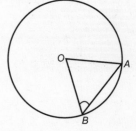

11.

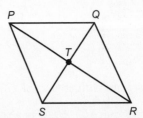

In the figure above, which of the following describes sufficient conditions in order for *PQRS* to be classified as a rhombus?

(A) $\overline{PQ} = \overline{SR}$ and $\overline{PS} = \overline{QR}$

(B) $\overline{SP}$ is parallel to $\overline{QR}$ and $\overline{PQ}$ is parallel to $\overline{RS}$

(C) $\overline{PR}$ and $\overline{QS}$ are perpendicular bisectors of each other

(D) ∢*QPS* ≅ ∢*QRS* and ∢*PSR* ≅ ∢*PQR*

12.

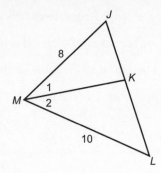

Note: Figure not drawn to scale.

In the figure above, $\angle 1 \cong \angle 2$. If $\overline{JK} = 6$, what is the length of $\overline{KL}$?

(A) 1.5

(C) 7.5

(B) 4.8

(D) 12.8

13. Look at the following figure:

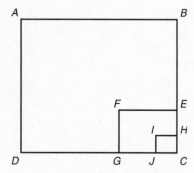

ABCD is a square with area 9. *EFGC* is a square in which $EC = \left(\frac{1}{3}\right)(BC)$. *HIJC* is a square in which $HC = \left(\frac{1}{3}\right)(EC)$. If this pattern is continued so that there are a total of ten squares with a common vertex at *C*, and in which each square lies inside its predecessor, what is the area of the tenth square?

(A) 9^{-12}

(C) 9^{-9}

(B) 9^{-10}

(D) 9^{-8}

14. Given parallelogram *KLMN*, where points *K*, *L*, *M*, *N* are located at (2, 5), (*b*, *c*), (7, 1), (0, 1) respectively, which of the following is equivalent to *c*?

(A) $b - 12$

(C) $2b - 13$

(B) $b + 5$

(D) $2b + 4$

15.

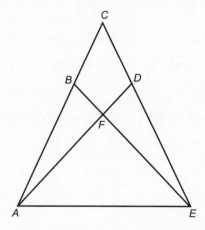

In the figure above, $\overline{AC} = \overline{CE}$ and $\overline{AB} = \overline{DE}$. Which of the following statements must be true?

   I. $\overline{AB} = \overline{FE}$

   II. $\angle CBE \cong \angle CDA$

   III. $\overline{AF} \cong \overline{AE}$

(A) I only

(B) II only

(C) II and III only

(D) I, II, and III

16. Which one of the following geometric figures has neither a horizontal nor vertical line of symmetry?

(A) Isosceles triangle

(B) Parallelogram

(C) Rectangle

(D) Circle

17. Which of the following triangles $A'B'C'$ is the image of triangle ABC that results from reflecting triangle ABC across the y-axis?

(C)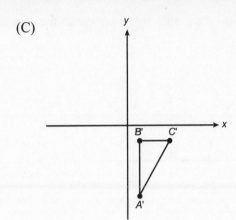

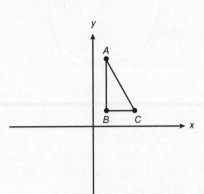

(D)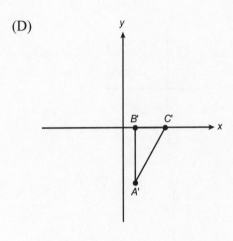

(A)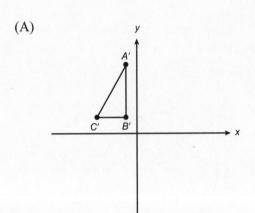

(B)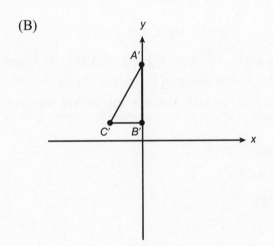

18. Which of the graphs below represents the equation
$$\frac{x^2}{9} - \frac{y^2}{9} = 1?$$

(A)

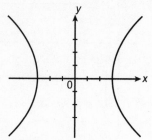

(B)

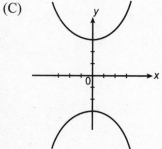

(C)

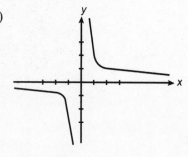

(D)

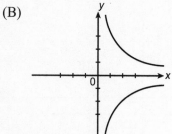

19.

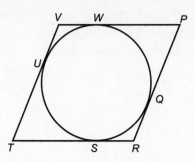

Note: Figure is not drawn to scale.

In the figure above, $\overline{PR}$, $\overline{RT}$, $\overline{TV}$, and $\overline{VP}$ are tangents to the circle at points Q, S, U, and W, respectively. The perimeter of $PRTV$ is 28 and $PW = 4$. Which of the following must be true?

(A) $PR = RT$

(B) $VW = 3$

(C) $PR + TV = 14$

(D) $m\angle P = m\angle T$

20.

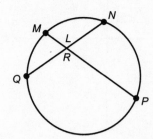

Note: Figure is not drawn to scale.

Chords $\overline{MP}$ and $\overline{NQ}$ intersect at point R, which is not the center of the circle. If $\overset{\frown}{QM} = 50°$ and $\angle MLN = 110°$, what is the degree measure of $\overset{\frown}{NP}$?

(A) 70°

(B) 90°

(C) 105°

(D) 110°

21. The radius of the base of a cone is 2 cm and its total surface area is 70 cm². What is the best approximation, in cm, for its slant height?

    (A) 9.14

    (B) 7.95

    (C) 6.76

    (D) 5.57

22. A sphere and a cylinder have equal volumes. If the height of the cylinder is twice its radius, what ratio represents the cube of the radius of the sphere to the cube of the radius of the cylinder?

    (A) $\dfrac{2}{3}$

    (B) $\dfrac{3}{4}$

    (C) $\dfrac{4}{3}$

    (D) $\dfrac{3}{2}$

23. A sample of drivers involved in motor vehicle accidents was categorized by age. The results appear as:

Age	Number of Accidents
16–25	28
26–35	13
36–45	12
46–55	8
56–65	19
66–75	20

    What is the value of the median age?

    (A) 43

    (B) 46

    (C) 50

    (D) 59

24. The mean weight of 20 people in a room is 130 pounds. Bob and Diane are among these 20 people. If both of them leave the room, the mean weight will decrease by 3%. What is the mean weight, in pounds, for Bob and Diane?

    (A) 162

    (B) 165

    (C) 168

    (D) 171

25. An ice cream parlor claims that 40% of its customers prefer chocolate, 35% prefer vanilla, 15% prefer strawberry, and the remaining 10% prefer other flavors. In an actual survey of 100 people, 49 preferred chocolate, 29 preferred vanilla, 17 preferred strawberry, and the remaining people preferred other flavors. Using the 5% level of significance with the chi-square goodness of fit test, which of the following is completely correct?

    (A) The test chi-square value is 8.13 and the claim should be rejected.

    (B) The test chi-square value is 8.13 and the claim should not be rejected.

    (C) The test chi-square value is 5.82 and the claim should be rejected.

    (D) The test chi-square value is 5.82 and the claim should not be rejected.

26. Which one of the following represents an experiment for which the probability is equal to $\dfrac{1}{221}$?

    (A) Drawing two aces, one at a time, with no replacement, from a deck of 52 cards.

    (B) Drawing two jacks, one at a time, with replacement, from a deck of 52 cards.

    (C) Drawing two slips of paper, numbered 13 and 17, one at a time, with no replacement, from a jar with 17 slips of paper numbered 1 through 17.

    (D) Drawing two slips of paper, numbered 13 and 17, one at a time, with replacement, from a jar with 30 slips of paper numbered 1 through 30.

27. An AP statistics teacher wants to provide her students with a concrete example of a data set that illustrates the normal curve. Select her best choice from the examples below.

   (A) The shoe sizes of the 15 students in her class.

   (B) The weight of all the 17-year-olds in the country.

   (C) The number of times out of 100 tosses that a flipped penny will land on its head.

   (D) The height of the students in the high school.

28. If the probability of a certain team winning is $\frac{3}{4}$, what is the probability that this team will win its first three games and lose the fourth?

   (A) $\frac{3}{256}$ (C) $\frac{27}{256}$

   (B) $\frac{9}{256}$ (D) $\frac{81}{256}$

29. The mean of a group of 20 numbers is 9. If one number is removed, the mean of the remaining numbers is 7. What is the value of the removed number?

   (A) 16   (C) 40

   (B) 25   (D) 47

30. In a group of five women and four men, three people will be randomly chosen. What is the probability that all three people chosen will be women?

   (A) $\frac{3}{5}$ (C) $\frac{125}{729}$

   (B) $\frac{1}{3}$ (D) $\frac{5}{42}$

Constructed-response questions 31–34:
For each response you will use up to two pages of the lined pages provided with the CSET test. Please see the sample pages at the end of the book.

31.

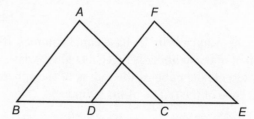

In the diagram shown above, B, D, C, E are collinear points. $\overline{AB}$ is parallel to $\overline{DF}$ and $\overline{AC}$ is parallel to $\overline{EF}$. $BD = CE$. Prove that $AB = FD$.

32.

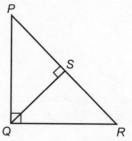

In the diagram shown above, $\overline{PQ}$ is perpendicular to $\overline{QR}$, and $\overline{QS}$ is perpendicular to $\overline{PR}$. $QS = 6$ and $PS = 8$. Determine the length of $\overline{QR}$. Show all work.

33. Find the equation of the curve, in simplified form, traced by a point that moves so that it is always twice as far from (2, 0) as it is from (0, 2).

34. Over the course of many years at Central University, for a course in Economics, the population of scores on a final exam has been normally distributed with a variance of 150. A particular instructor who is teaching Economics this semester wishes to check whether the variance of test scores among the 26 students in her class is significantly greater than that of the university population scores. She notices that the variance for her students' final exam is 210.

   • State the null hypothesis and the alternative hypothesis.

   • Determine the value of the chi-square (χ^2) test statistic for the instructor's sample of test scores.

   • Using the following table of χ^2 values, representing 25 degrees of freedom, determine whether, at the 5% level of significance, the variance for the 26 test scores is significantly higher than that of the university population.

Probability	.10	.05	.025	.01	.005
χ^2 value	34.382	37.652	40.646	44.314	46.928

Answer Key

Q No.	Correct Answer	Q No.	Correct Answer
1.	(D)	18.	(A)
2.	(B)	19.	(C)
3.	(A)	20.	(B)
4.	(C)	21.	(A)
5.	(A)	22.	(D)
6.	(D)	23.	(A)
7.	(D)	24.	(B)
8.	(A)	25.	(D)
9.	(C)	26.	(A)
10.	(D)	27.	(D)
11.	(C)	28.	(C)
12.	(C)	29.	(D)
13.	(D)	30.	(D)
14.	(C)	31.	Constructed-Response
15.	(B)	32.	Constructed-Response
16.	(B)	33.	Constructed-Response
17.	(A)	34.	Constructed-Response

Detailed Explanations of Answers

1.   (D)

If $\angle 1 \cong \angle 2$, the triangles ABC and ACD would have two pairs of congruent sides and a pair of non-inclusive congruent angles. This would be insufficient to prove that these triangles are congruent, which means that we cannot conclude that $\angle ACB \cong \angle ACD$. Thus, we cannot conclude that $\overline{AC}$ is perpendicular to $\overline{BD}$. Answer choice (A) would imply that triangles ABC and ACD are congruent by side-angle-angle, so $\angle ACB \cong \angle ACD$ by corresponding parts. This would imply that $\overline{AC}$ is perpendicular to $\overline{BD}$. Answer choice (B) actually ensures that $\overline{AC}$ is *not* perpendicular to $\overline{BD}$ because $\angle ACB$ would have to be 60° (all angles of an equilateral Δ are 60°). Answer choice (C) would imply that triangles ABC and ACD are congruent by side-side-side, so $\angle ACB \cong \angle ACD$ by corresponding parts. This would imply that $\overline{AC}$ is perpendicular to $\overline{BD}$.

2.   (B)

Triangles RUV and STU are both 45°–45°–90° right triangles. Let $\overline{RU} = \overline{UV} = x$. Because $\overline{RV} = 8$, $x^2 + x^2 = 8^2$. Then $2x^2 = 64$, so $x = \sqrt{32}$. This means that $\overline{UT} = \sqrt{32}$. Let $\overline{ST} = \overline{SU} = y$. Then $y^2 + y^2 = (\sqrt{32})^2 = 32$, so $2y^2 = 32$, $y^2 = 16$, and thus $y = 4$. Now in ΔSTV, $\overline{ST} = 4$ and $\overline{SV} = \overline{UV} + \overline{US} = \sqrt{32} + 4 = 9.657$. Finally, in ΔSTV $\overline{VT}^2 = \overline{SV}^2 + \overline{ST}^2 = 9.657^2 + 4^2 \approx 109.26$. Therefore, $\overline{VT} = \sqrt{109.26} \approx 10.5$.

3.   (A)

$\angle QJK$ and $\angle QML$ are each 90° because tangents to a circle form right angles at points of tangency. In any 5-sided figure, the sum of the interior angles is $(180°)(5-2) = 540°$. So $\angle JQM = 540° - 90° - 90° - 125° - 100° = 135°$; this means that $\angle MQN = 180° - 135° = 45°$. This means that $\angle N = 45°$, by noting that the sum of the angles of ΔQMN is 180°. Because ΔQMN is a 45°–45°–90° right triangle, $\overline{QN} = (\overline{QM})(\sqrt{2}) = 6\sqrt{2}$. Now $\overline{RN} = \overline{QN} - \overline{QR}$, and because $\overline{QR}$ is a radius, $\overline{RN} = 6\sqrt{2} - 6$.

4.   (C)

ΔABE is an isosceles right triangle, so $\overline{AE} = \dfrac{10}{\sqrt{2}} \approx 7.07$. ΔCDE is a right triangle with acute angles of 30° and 60°, so $\overline{ED} = 4\sqrt{3} \approx 6.93$. Thus, $\overline{AD} \approx 7.07 + 6.93 = 14$.

5.   (A)

The third angle in the small triangle, which lies on l_1, has a measure of $(x + 30)°$ because it represents a corresponding angle on l_2. The sum of the angles of any triangle is 180°, so using the three angles of the small triangle, $(2x) + (x + 30) + 60 = 180$; $3x + 90 = 180$, $3x = 90$, so $x = 30$.

6. (D)

The central angle of sector $EOD = 360° − 130° − 95° − 90° = 45°$. Then the area of sector $EOD = \left(\dfrac{45°}{360°}\right)(\pi)(12)^2 = 18\,\pi$. Let x = shaded area. The area of polygon $ABCO = 1.30x$. So $1.30x − x = 18\pi$. Solving, $x = 60\pi$.

7. (D)

Let x = length of BC and y = length of CD. The area of $ABCD$ is xy, and the area of $ECFG = \left(\dfrac{x}{2}\right)\left(\dfrac{y}{3}\right) = \dfrac{xy}{6}$. Thus the unshaded area is $xy − \dfrac{xy}{6} = \left(\dfrac{5}{6}\right)(xy)$. The probability that a dart lands in the unshaded area is $\dfrac{\frac{5}{6}xy}{xy} = \dfrac{5}{6}$.

8. (A)

To solve, we use the law of cosines:

$$c^2 = a^2 + b^2 − 2ab\cos(\text{included angle}).$$

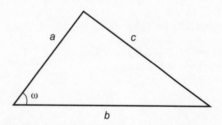

In the figure given, $a = 4$, $b = 7$, $c = 8$, and ω is the included angle.

We solve the law of cosines relation for $\cos\omega$:

$$c^2 = a^2 + b^2 − 2ab\cos\omega.$$

Subtracting a^2 and b^2 from both sides and dividing through by $−2ab$, we obtain:

$$\frac{c^2 − a^2 − b^2}{−2ab} = \cos\omega.$$

Substituting for a, b, and c, we obtain

$$\cos\omega = \frac{8^2 − 4^2 − 7^2}{−2(4)(7)} = \frac{64 − 16 − 49}{−56} = \frac{−1}{−56} = \frac{1}{56}.$$

9. (C)

The surface area of a cube is given by the expression $6s^2$, where s is the length of one side. The lateral surface area of a cylinder is given by the expression $2\pi rh$, where r is the radius and h is the height. Equating these expressions, we get $6s^2 = (2)(\pi)\left(\dfrac{6}{\pi}\right)(15)$. Simplifying, we get $6s^2 = 180$, so $s = \sqrt{30} \approx 5.48$. This means that the volume of the cube is $(5.48)^3 \approx 165$.

10. (D)

From a theorem, we know that a central angle is equal in measurement to the arc it intercepts. The arc measurement is given as

$$m\widehat{AB} = \frac{1}{5}\pi \text{ radians.}$$

Converting this to degrees, we obtain

$$\left(\frac{1}{5}\pi\right)\left(\frac{180}{\pi}\right) = 36°.$$

Note that points A, O, and B form a triangle. Two sides of this triangle are equal to the radius of the circle. Thus, they are equal sides, and $\triangle AOB$ is isosceles (the base angles of an isosceles triangle are equal). The vertex angle is $36°$, and there are $180°$ in a triangle. The relation that is set up is

$$36° + 2\,(\text{base angle}) = 180°.$$

Solving for the base angle:

$$\text{base angle } = \frac{180° − 36°}{2} = 72°.$$

Thus, $\sphericalangle OBA = 72°$.

11. (C)

If $\overline{PR}$ and $\overline{QS}$ are perpendicular bisectors of each other, then all four angles at T are right angles. By using the side-angle-side (SAS) theorem, it can be shown that all four nonoverlapping triangles are congruent to each other. Since corresponding parts of congruent triangles are congruent, $\overline{PQ} = \overline{QR} = \overline{RS} = \overline{SP}$. Thus, $PQRS$ must be a rhombus.

12. (C)

Let x = length of $\overline{KL}$. In any triangle, an angle bisector always divides the side to which it is drawn into two parts whose ratio is equal to the ratio of the two sides forming the angle bisector. So, $\frac{8}{10} = \frac{6}{x}$. Then $8x = 60$, and $x = 7.5$.

13. (D)

The area of the first square $= 9$, the area of the second square $= \left(\frac{1}{9}\right)(9) = 1$. Each subsequent square will have an area equal to $\frac{1}{9}$ of its predecessor. The tenth term is given by $(9)\left(\frac{1}{9}\right)^9 = 9^{-8}$.

14. (C)

The slope of the line segment connecting $(2, 5)$ and $(0, 1)$, which is 2, must equal the slope of the line segment connecting $(7, 1)$ and (b, c). Thus, $2 = \frac{(c - 1)}{(b - 7)}$. This becomes $2b - 14 = c - 1$, so $c = 2b - 13$. Another approach would be to realize that the segment connecting $(0, 1)$ and $(7, 1)$ has a distance of 7 and a slope of zero. This would mean that point (b, c) is really $(2 + 7, 5) = (9, 5)$. This would match the relationship shown in answer choice (C), since $5 = (2)(9) - 13$.

15. (B)

All that is given is $\overline{AC} = \overline{CE}$ and $\overline{AB} = \overline{DE}$. It may be tempting to look at the figure and draw other conclusions (such as "$\triangle ACE$ looks like an equilateral triangle" or "$\overline{BE}$ and $\overline{AD}$ look like angle bisectors"), but not enough information is given for these conclusions. By working with only the information given, we can see that $\triangle ABE$ and $\triangle AED$ are congruent because they have a Side-Angle-Side relationship because $\overline{AC} = \overline{CE}$, $\angle C = \angle C$, and $\overline{BC} = \overline{CD}$ (equals subtracted from equals are equal). Therefore, corresponding angles $\angle CBE \cong \angle CDA$. The other two statements are not necessarily true.

16. (B)

A parallelogram has neither a horizontal nor vertical line of symmetry. Choice (A) is wrong because a perpendicular line from the vertex to the base would be a vertical line of symmetry. Choices (C) and (D) are wrong because a vertical line through the center or horizontal line through the center would be a vertical or horizontal line of symmetry, respectively.

17. (A)

When a figure is reflected across an axis, all points are the same distance from the axis *but* on the other side of it. This is true for choice (A). Choice (B) is incorrect because points A' and B' are not a distance from the y-axis, but on it. Choices (C) and (D) are reflected across the x-axis.

18. (A)

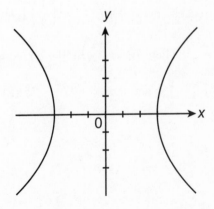

$$\frac{x^2}{9} - \frac{y^2}{9} = 1$$

is an equation of the form:

$$\frac{x^2}{a^2} - \frac{y^2}{b^2} = 1$$

with $a = 3$ and $b = 3$.

Therefore, the graph is a hyperbola. The x-intercepts are found by setting $y = 0$:

$$\frac{x^2}{9} - \frac{0^2}{9} = 1$$
$$x^2 = 9$$
$$x = \pm 3.$$

Thus, the x-intercepts are at $(-3, 0)$ and $(3, 0)$. There are no y-intercepts since for $x = 0$ there are no real values of y satisfying the equation, i.e., no real value of y satisfies $y^2 = -9$.

19. (C)

Given an external point from a circle, two tangents drawn to the circle from that point must be equal. So $PQ = PW$, $QR = RS$, $ST = TU$, $UV = VW$. Then $PQ + QR + TU + UV$ must represent one-half the perimeter of $PRTU$, or 14. By substitution, we get $PR + TV = 14$. Note that $PRTV$ is not any specific kind of quadrilateral.

20. (B)

Because $\angle MLN = 110°$, $\angle MRQ = 70°$. A theorem states that $\angle MRQ = \left(\frac{1}{2}\right)(\widehat{QM} + \widehat{NP})$. Let $\widehat{NP} = x°$. Then $70 = \left(\frac{1}{2}\right)(50 + x)$. Simplifying, $70 = 25 + \left(\frac{1}{2}\right)x$, and thus $x = (70 - 25)(2) = 90$.

21. (A)

The total surface area of a cone is given by the formula $A = \pi rs + \pi r^2$, where r is the radius and s is the slant height. By substitution, $70 = (\pi)(2)(s) + 4\pi$. Solving, $s = \frac{(70 - 4\pi)}{2\pi} \approx 9.14$.

22. (D)

Let R_1 represent the radius of the cylinder, let R_2 represent the radius of the sphere, and let H represent the height of the cylinder. Then $\pi R_1^2 H = \left(\frac{4}{3}\right)\pi R_2^3$. Since $H = 2R_1$, we can rewrite this equation as $(\pi R_1^2)(2R_1) = \left(\frac{4}{3}\right)\pi R_2^3$. Simplifying, we get $2\pi R_1^3 = \left(\frac{4}{3}\right)\pi R_2^3$. Then $\frac{R_2^3}{R_1^3} = \frac{2}{\left(\frac{4}{3}\right)} = \frac{3}{2}$.

23. (A)

The total number of accidents is 100. The median is the $\frac{100}{2} = 50$th number when the numbers are arranged in ascending order. (In this case, we have intervals of numbers instead of just numbers.) The two age intervals 16–25 and 26–35 total 41 accidents. Therefore, we need nine numbers from the next interval age 36–45. Use the lower boundary of this interval 36–45, which is 35.5, and add $\frac{9}{12}$ of the width of the interval (10, which equals $45.5 - 35.5$). Then

$$35.5 + \frac{9}{12}(10) = 43$$

24. (B)

The original total weight of all the people in the room is $(20)(130) = 2600$ pounds. After Bob and Diane leave the room, the mean weight of the remaining 18 people will be $(130)(.97) = 126.1$ pounds. This means that the total weight for these 18 people is $(18)(126.1) \approx 2270$ pounds. Then $2600 - 2270 = 330$ pounds is the total weight for Bob and Diane. Finally, the mean weight for Bob and Diane is $\dfrac{330}{2} = 165$ pounds.

25. (D)

The observed values of the 4 flavors are: 49, 29, 17, and 5.

The expected values of the 4 flavors are: 40, 35, 15, and 10.

Note that the expected values are simply the percents multiplied by the actual number of people, which is 100.

The chi-square value is calculated by the formula $\sum \dfrac{(O_i - E_i)^2}{E_i}$, where each O_i is an observed value and each E_i is an expected value. Then, the chi-square value $= \dfrac{81}{40} + \dfrac{36}{35} + \dfrac{4}{15} + \dfrac{25}{10} \approx 5.82$.
The next step is to locate the critical chi-square value in a table. Here, the number of degrees of freedom is 3. (One less than the number of pairs of data.) At the 5% level of significance, the critical chi-square value is 7.815. Since $5.82 < 7.815$, the claim should not be rejected.

26. (A)

The probability for the experiment in choice (A) is $\left(\dfrac{4}{52}\right)\left(\dfrac{3}{51}\right)$, which reduces to $\dfrac{1}{221}$. For choice (B), the probability would be $\left(\dfrac{4}{52}\right)\left(\dfrac{4}{52}\right) = \dfrac{1}{169}$. For choice

(C), the probability would be $\left(\dfrac{2}{17}\right)\left(\dfrac{1}{16}\right) = \dfrac{1}{136}$. For choice (D), the probability would be $\left(\dfrac{2}{30}\right)\left(\dfrac{2}{30}\right) = \dfrac{1}{225}$.

27. (D)

The students in the statistics class have a reasonable chance at being able to sample a large enough portion of the students at their high school to get a reasonable estimate of the population and the data collected would produce a normal curve under these circumstances. Therefore the choice is concrete and mathematically correct. Choice (A) is incorrect because there are not enough students and the data being collected is unlikely to yield a normal curve over such a small, homogeneous sample. Choice (B) does not work because there is no way to get the data. An internet source may provide a sample but the problem then becomes abstract—a mind exercise. Choice (C) is incorrect because the data collected would not produce a normal curve.

28. (C)

Let's call the event winning A and not winning $\overline{A}$. We want the probability P given by the expression below:

$$P = P(A) \times P(A) \times P(A) \times P(\overline{A})$$
$$= \dfrac{3}{4} \times \dfrac{3}{4} \times \dfrac{3}{4} \times \dfrac{1}{4} = \dfrac{27}{256}$$

29. (D)

The sum of the original group of 20 numbers was $(9)(20) = 180$. The sum of the new group of 19 numbers is $(7)(19) = 133$. The removed number is the difference of 180 and 133 or 47.

30. (D)

The number of combinations of 3 people chosen from 9 is given by $_9C_3 = \dfrac{[(9)(8)(7)]}{[(3)(2)(1)]} = 84$. The number of combinations of 3 women chosen from 5 women is given by $_5C_3 = \dfrac{[(5)(4)(3)]}{[(3)(2)(1)]} = 10$. Thus, the required probability is $\dfrac{10}{84}$, which reduces to $\dfrac{5}{42}$.

31.

Since $\overline{AB}$ is parallel to $\overline{DF}$ and $\overline{BE}$ is a transversal, any pair of corresponding angles, namely $\angle B$ and $\angle FDE$, are congruent. Similarly, since $\overline{AC}$ is parallel to $\overline{EF}$, $\angle E$ and $\angle ACB$ are corresponding angles and so are also congruent. $BC = BD + DC$ and $DE = DC + CE$. Since $BD = CE$, we can conclude that $\overline{BC}$ is congruent to $\overline{DE}$. Now $\triangle ABC$ is congruent to $\triangle FDE$ by the Angle-Side-Angle Theorem. Finally, $AB = FD$ because they are corresponding parts of congruent triangles.

32.

For any right triangle, the altitude to the hypotenuse is the mean proportion between the two segments of the hypotenuse. Thus, $\dfrac{PS}{QS} = \dfrac{QS}{SR}$

By substitution, $\dfrac{8}{6} = \dfrac{6}{SR}$, $8 \cdot SR = 36$, $SR = 4.5$.

Using the Pythagorean Theorem for $\triangle QRS$, $QS^2 + SR^2 = QR^2$, which means $6^2 + 4.5^2 = QR^2$, $56.25 = QR^2$, so $QR = 7.5$.

33.

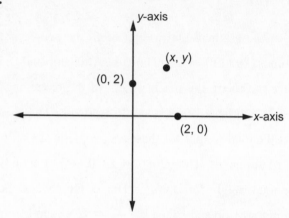

Let (x, y) represent the coordinates of the moving point. Its distance from $(0, 2)$ is represented by $\sqrt{x^2 + (y - 2)^2}$. Its distance from $(2, 0)$ is represented by $\sqrt{(x - 2)^2 + y^2}$. From the given requirements, $\sqrt{(x - 2)^2 + y^2} = 2 \cdot \sqrt{x^2 + (y - 2)^2}$.

Square both sides to get $x^2 - 4x + 4 + y^2 = 4(x^2 + y^2 - 4y + 4)$.

Then $x^2 - 4x + 4 + y^2 = 4x^2 + 4y^2 - 16y + 16$.

Simplifying, $3x^2 + 3y^2 + 4x - 16y + 12 = 0$.

34.

- The null hypothesis (H_0) is that the sample variance is less than or equal to the population variance. This can be expressed as $s^2 \leq \sigma^2$.

The alternate hypothesis (H_1) is that the sample variance is greater than the population variance. This can be expressed as $s^2 > \sigma^2$.

- The χ^2 test statistic is given by the formula

$$\chi^2 = \frac{(n - 1)s^2}{\sigma^2} = \frac{(25)(210)}{150} = 35$$

- Since $35 < 37.652$, which is the critical value at the 5% level of significance, the variance for the sample test scores is not significantly higher than the variance of the population test scores.

CSET

Mathematics

Practice Test 1

Subtest III

Answer Sheet

1. Ⓐ Ⓑ Ⓒ Ⓓ   16. Ⓐ Ⓑ Ⓒ Ⓓ

2. Ⓐ Ⓑ Ⓒ Ⓓ   17. Ⓐ Ⓑ Ⓒ Ⓓ

3. Ⓐ Ⓑ Ⓒ Ⓓ   18. Ⓐ Ⓑ Ⓒ Ⓓ

4. Ⓐ Ⓑ Ⓒ Ⓓ   19. Ⓐ Ⓑ Ⓒ Ⓓ

5. Ⓐ Ⓑ Ⓒ Ⓓ   20. Ⓐ Ⓑ Ⓒ Ⓓ

6. Ⓐ Ⓑ Ⓒ Ⓓ   21. Ⓐ Ⓑ Ⓒ Ⓓ

7. Ⓐ Ⓑ Ⓒ Ⓓ   22. Ⓐ Ⓑ Ⓒ Ⓓ

8. Ⓐ Ⓑ Ⓒ Ⓓ   23. Ⓐ Ⓑ Ⓒ Ⓓ

9. Ⓐ Ⓑ Ⓒ Ⓓ   24. Ⓐ Ⓑ Ⓒ Ⓓ

10. Ⓐ Ⓑ Ⓒ Ⓓ   25. Ⓐ Ⓑ Ⓒ Ⓓ

11. Ⓐ Ⓑ Ⓒ Ⓓ   26. Ⓐ Ⓑ Ⓒ Ⓓ

12. Ⓐ Ⓑ Ⓒ Ⓓ   27. Ⓐ Ⓑ Ⓒ Ⓓ

13. Ⓐ Ⓑ Ⓒ Ⓓ   28. Ⓐ Ⓑ Ⓒ Ⓓ

14. Ⓐ Ⓑ Ⓒ Ⓓ   29. Ⓐ Ⓑ Ⓒ Ⓓ

15. Ⓐ Ⓑ Ⓒ Ⓓ   30. Ⓐ Ⓑ Ⓒ Ⓓ

CSET: Mathematics Practice Test 1
Subtest III
Calculus; History of Mathematics

TIME: When taking the actual test, you will have one five-hour test session in which to complete the subtest(s) for which you are registered.

Directions: This test consists of two sections: 30 multiple-choice and four constructed-response questions. The constructed-response questions involve written responses.

---

1. $\int_1^e x \ln x \, dx = ?$

   (A) e

   (B) $\dfrac{e^2 - 1}{2}$

   (C) $\dfrac{e^2 + 1}{4}$

   (D) $\dfrac{e - 1}{2}$

2. $\lim\limits_{x \to 1} \dfrac{\dfrac{1}{x+1} - \dfrac{1}{2}}{x - 1} =$

   (A) $-\dfrac{1}{4}$

   (B) -1

   (C) $\dfrac{1}{4}$

   (D) 0

3. The area enclosed by the graphs of $y = x^2$ and $y = 2x + 3$ is

   (A) $\dfrac{38}{3}$

   (B) $\dfrac{40}{3}$

   (C) $\dfrac{32}{3}$

   (D) $\dfrac{16}{3}$

4. Given that $\sin(x + y) = 0.9$, $\sin x = 0.3$, and $\cos y = 0.8$, what is the value of $(2)(\sin y)(\cos x)$?

   (A) 0.66

   (B) 0.74

   (C) 1.20

   (D) 1.32

5. An equation of the line normal to the graph of $y = x^4 - 3x^2 + 1$ at the point where $x = 1$ is

    (A) $2x - y + 3 = 0$

    (B) $x - 2y + 3 = 0$

    (C) $2x - y - 3 = 0$

    (D) $x - 2y - 3 = 0$

6. According to the Fundamental Theorem of Calculus, if f is a continuous function on the closed interval $[c, d]$, then $F(x) = \int_{c}^{x} f(t)\, dt$ has what property at every point x in $[c, d]$?

    (A) It may not be defined nor differentiable at a finite number of values of x.

    (B) It is differentiable but may not be defined at each x.

    (C) It is defined and differentiable at each x.

    (D) It is defined but may not be differentiable at each x.

7. If $f(x) = e^{\frac{x^3}{3} - x}$, then $f(x)$

    (A) increases in the interval $(-1, 1)$

    (B) decreases for $|x| > 1$

    (C) increases in the interval $(-1, 1)$ and decreases in the intervals $(-\infty, -1) \cup (1, \infty)$

    (D) increases in the intervals $(-\infty, -1) \cup (1, \infty)$ and decreases in the interval $(-1, 1)$

8. The sum of the first 50 terms of an arithmetic series is 100. If the common difference is 2, what is the first term?

    (A) 47

    (B) 48

    (C) -48

    (D) -47

9. What is the slope of the tangent to the curve $y = x^2 + 11x - 2$ at the point where $x = -3$?

    (A) -44

    (B) -36

    (C) 3

    (D) 5

10. What is the value of $(-1 + i)^{10}$?

    (A) $-\sqrt{2}^{10}$

    (B) $32\,i$

    (C) $-32\,i$

    (D) $\sqrt{2}^{10}$

11. The first term of an infinite geometric series is 1.8. If the sum of this series is 4.5, what is the sum of the first three terms?

    (A) 2.88

    (B) 3.528

    (C) 3.6

    (D) 4.176

12. A person wishes to place nine books on a shelf that has nine slots. There are four math books, two history books, and three English books. In how many ways can these books be arranged so that all books of the same subject are placed together?

    (A) 288   (C) 15,552

    (B) 1,728   (D) 362,880

13. The position function of a particle moving on a coordinate line is given by the equation $s(t) = t^3 + 4t^2 - 2$, where $s(t)$ represents feet and t represents seconds. What is the acceleration of this particle when $t = 5$?

    (A) 18 ft/sec²

    (B) 38 ft/sec²

    (C) 75 ft/sec²

    (D) 115 ft/sec²

14. $(\sin\theta \times \cot\theta)^2 + (\cos\theta \times \tan\theta)^2 =$

(A) 1

(B) $2\cos^2\theta$

(C) $2\sin^2\theta$

(D) $2\cot^2\theta$

15. The area between the line $y = x$ and the curve $y = \dfrac{1}{2}x^2$ is

(A) 1

(B) $\dfrac{1}{2}$

(C) $\dfrac{2}{3}$

(D) $\dfrac{3}{2}$

16. $\sin\left(\dfrac{1}{2}\pi + t\right) =$

(A) $\sin\dfrac{\pi}{2} + \sin t$

(B) $\cos t$

(C) $\sin t$

(D) $\cos 2t$

17. $\lim\limits_{h\to 0} \dfrac{e^{x+h} - e^x}{h}$ equals

(A) 0

(B) e^x

(C) $+\infty$

(D) $-\infty$

18. At what value of x does $f(x) = \dfrac{x^3}{3} - x^2 - 3x + 5$ have a relative minimum?

(A) -1 only

(B) -1 and 3

(C) $+1$ only

(D) 3 only

19. Let a_i, i = 1, 2, 3, ... represent a recursive sequence so that $a_1 = 3$, $a_i = a_{i-1}^2 + 5$. What is the value of $a_3 + a_4$?

(A) 40,205

(B) 40,406

(C) 40,607

(D) 40,808

20. What is the value of $\displaystyle\int_1^{e^2} \dfrac{\ln(x^2)}{x}\,dx$?

(A) $\dfrac{8}{3}$

(B) 2

(C) 0.805

(D) 4

21. If $y = \dfrac{3}{\sin x + \cos x}$ then $\dfrac{dy}{dx} =$

(A) $\dfrac{3(\sin x - \cos x)}{1 + 2\sin x \cos x}$

(B) $\dfrac{6\sin x}{1 + 2\sin x \cos x}$

(C) $\dfrac{3}{\cos x - \sin x}$

(D) $\dfrac{-3}{(\sin x + \cos x)^2}$

22. What is the sum of the infinite series $0.3 + 0.24 + 0.192 + 0.1536 + \ldots$?

(A) 1.5

(B) 1.4

(C) 1.3

(D) 1.2

23. Find $\lim\limits_{x\to 2}\left(\dfrac{x^2 - 5}{x + 3}\right)$

(A) $-\dfrac{1}{3}$

(B) $\dfrac{1}{5}$

(C) $-\dfrac{1}{5}$

(D) $-\dfrac{3}{5}$

24. Consider $f(x) = 10 - x$, where x is defined on the closed interval [2, 8]. For what value of x will $f(x)$ achieve its average (mean) value on this interval?

(A) 8

(B) 6

(C) 4

(D) 2

25. Given that $\dfrac{dy}{dx} + 2y = 3$, and $y(0) = 1$, which of the following is the correct equation?

(A) $y = \left(\dfrac{2}{3}\right)(e^{2x}) + \dfrac{1}{3}$

(B) $y = \left(\dfrac{1}{2}\right)(e^{2x}) + \dfrac{1}{2}$

(C) $y = -\dfrac{1}{2} + \left(\dfrac{3}{2}\right)(e^{-2x})$

(D) $y = \dfrac{3}{2} - \left(\dfrac{1}{2}\right)(e^{-2x})$

26. Integrate the expression:

$\int \ln x \, dx$.

A. $x \ln x - x + C$

B. $- x \ln x + x - C$

C. $x^2 \ln x - x + C$

D. $x \ln x + x + C$

27. The superiority of Babylonian mathematics in 300 B.C. is based on the fact that:

A. The Babylonian number system had no zero.

B. The Babylonians used a positional number system with place-value notation.

C. The Babylonians used only two symbols and combinations of them to represent any number.

D. The Babylonians did not have negative numbers.

28. The following is a list of some of the most famous mathematicians. Place them in chronological order from earliest to latest.

I.   Archimedes

II. Omar Khayyam

III. Florence Nightingale*

IV. Gottfried Leibniz

*Florence Nightingale was a Fellow of the Royal Statistical Society and an honorary member of the American Statistical Association. Through her statistical work, she was able to show that with an improvement of sanitary methods, deaths in municipal and military hospitals would decrease.

A.   I, II, III, IV

B.   II, I, IV, III

C.   I, II, IV, III

D.   IV, II, III, I

29. The following proof that $\sqrt{2}$ is irrational is attributed to Pythagoras and his students in the sixth century B.C.

> Start by assuming $\sqrt{2}$ is rational, equal to some fraction $\dfrac{a}{b}$, reduced to its lowest terms.
>
> $\sqrt{2} = \dfrac{a}{b}$
>
> Then $2 = \dfrac{a^2}{b^2}$
>
> or $a^2 = 2b^2$ (So, a is a multiple of 2, call it $2m$)
>
> Then $4m^2 = 2b^2$
>
> and $2m^2 = b^2$ (So, b is a multiple of 2)
>
> Therefore, both a and b are multiples of 2. But this is impossible, because $\dfrac{a}{b}$ was reduced to its lowest terms. Therefore, $\sqrt{2}$ cannot be expressed as a fraction, which makes $\sqrt{2}$ irrational.

This is an example of what kind of proof?

A. Proof by contradiction

B. Direct proof

C. Mathematical induction

D. Mathematical deduction

30. The Richter scale, which measures the energy released by an earthquake, is based on

A. a direct proportion between energy and damage

B. an indirect proportion between energy and damage

C. a hyperbolic curve

D. a logarithmic scale

> **Constructed-response questions 31–34:** For each response you will use up to two pages of the lined pages provided with the CSET test. Please see the sample pages at the end of the book.

31. Use analytic techniques to find the coordinates of the points of intersection for the graphs of $y = 2 \sin^2 x$ and $y = 1 - \sin x$. The x values are restricted to $0 \le x \le 2\pi$.

32. You are given the function $f(x) = 6x^4 - 8x^3 + 1$

   - Find the coordinates of the inflection points and determine algebraically if the curve is concave up or concave down between these points.

   - Sketch the graph of this function and label the x-intercepts.

33. Find the area of the region bounded by the graphs of $y = x^2 - 2x$ and $y = -x^2 + 3x + 7$. Also identify the coordinates of the points of intersection.

34. Each term in the sequence of numbers attributed to Fibonacci (A.D. 1170–1250) is determined by adding the two preceding terms. So 1, 1, 2, 3, 5, 8, 13, 21, 34, 55, . . . is a Fibonacci sequence. Note that the sum of the first ten numbers in this sequence equals eleven times the seventh term:

$1 + 1 + 2 + 3 + 5 + 8 + 13 + 21 + 34 + 55 = 143 = 11 \times 13$.

Prove that this fact is true for any Fibonacci sequence, no matter what the first two terms are.

Answer Key

Q No.	Correct Answer	Q No.	Correct Answer
1.	(C)	18.	(D)
2.	(A)	19.	(C)
3.	(C)	20.	(D)
4.	(D)	21.	(A)
5.	(D)	22.	(A)
6.	(C)	23.	(C)
7.	(D)	24.	(B)
8.	(D)	25.	(D)
9.	(D)	26.	(A)
10.	(C)	27.	(B)
11.	(B)	28.	(C)
12.	(B)	29.	(A)
13.	(B)	30.	(D)
14.	(A)	31.	Constructed-Response
15.	(C)	32.	Constructed-Response
16.	(B)	33.	Constructed-Response
17.	(B)	34.	Constructed-Response

Detailed Explanations of Answers

1.   (C)

Use integration by parts with

$$u = \ln x \quad \bigg| \quad du = \frac{1}{x}\,dx$$
$$\overline{dv = x \quad \bigg| \quad v = \frac{x^2}{2}}$$

and $\displaystyle \int uv'\,dx = uv - \int u'v\,dx$

$$\int_1^e x \ln x\,dx = \frac{x^2}{2}\ln x - \int_1^e \frac{x}{2}\,dx$$
$$= \left(\frac{x^2}{2}\ln x - \frac{x^2}{4} \right)\bigg|_1^e$$
$$= \frac{e^2 + 1}{4}$$

2.   (A)

$$\lim_{x \to 1} \frac{\dfrac{1}{x+1} - \dfrac{1}{2}}{x - 1}$$

Obtain a common denominator in the main numerator.

$$\lim_{x \to 1} \frac{\dfrac{2 - (x+1)}{2(x+1)}}{x - 1} = \lim_{x \to 1} \frac{1 - x}{2(x+1)(x-1)}$$
$$= \lim_{x \to 1} \frac{-1}{2(x+1)}$$
$$= \frac{-1}{2(1+1)} = -\frac{1}{4}$$

Note: $\dfrac{1-x}{x-1} = -1$ for $x \neq 1$

3.   (C)

First determine where the graphs $y = x^2$ and $y = 2x + 3$ intersect. By substitution,

$$x^2 = 2x + 3$$
$$x^2 - 2x - 3 = 0$$
$$(x - 3)(x + 1) = 0$$
$$x = 3, -1$$
$$A = \int_{-1}^{3} \{(2x+3) - x^2\}\,dx$$
$$= \left(x^2 + 3x - \frac{1}{3}x^3 \right)\bigg|_{-1}^{3}$$
$$= \left[3^2 + 3(3) - \frac{1}{3}(3^3) \right] - \left[(-1)^2 + 3(-1) - \frac{1}{3}(-1)^3 \right]$$
$$= (9 + 9 - 9) - \left(1 - 3 + \frac{1}{3} \right)$$
$$= 9 - \left(-\frac{5}{3} \right) = \frac{32}{3}$$

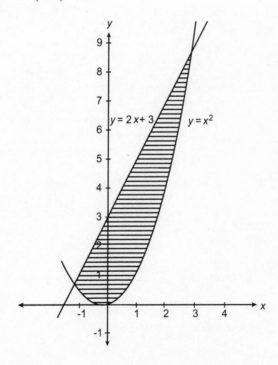

4. (D)

Using the formula $\sin(x + y) = (\sin x)(\cos y) + (\sin y)(\cos x)$, we get $0.9 = (0.3)(0.8) + (\sin y)(\cos x)$. This simplifies to $(\sin y)(\cos x) = 0.66$. Thus, $(2)(\sin y)(\cos x) = 1.32$.

5. (D)

The normal line is the line that is perpendicular to the curve at the given point. Its equation is $y = y_0 + m(x - x_0)$ where (x_0, y_0) is the given point and m is the slope. At the point where $x = 1$,

$$y = x^4 - 3x^2 + 1$$
$$= (1)^4 - 3(1)^2 + 1$$
$$= -1$$

Thus, $(x_0, y_0) = (1, -1)$. The slope m of the normal line is the negative reciprocal of the slope of the tangent line, which is the value of the derivative at the given point;

i.e., $m = \dfrac{-1}{\left.\dfrac{dy}{dx}\right|_{x=1}}$

Since $\dfrac{dy}{dx} = \dfrac{d}{dx}\left(x^4 - 3x^2 + 1\right)$

$$= 4x^3 - 6x,$$

$$m = \frac{-1}{\left(4x^3 - 6x\right)\Big|_{x=1}}$$

$$= \frac{-1}{(4-6)}$$

$$= \frac{-1}{-2}$$

$$= \frac{1}{2}$$

Thus, the equation of the normal line is:

$$y = y_0 + m\left(x - x_0\right)$$
$$y = -1 + \frac{1}{2}(x - 1)$$
$$2y = -2 + (x - 1)$$
$$2y = x - 3$$
$$x - 2y - 3 = 0$$

6. (C)

By definition, since $f(x)$ is continuous on the closed interval $[c, d]$, the integral of $f(x)$ over some interval within $[c, d]$, which is denoted by $F(x)$, must be defined and differentiable at each x.

7. (D)

$$f(x) = e^{\frac{x^3}{3} - x}$$

$$\Rightarrow f'(x) = \left(x^2 - 1\right)e^{\frac{x^3}{3} - x}, \text{ by the chain rule.}$$

We see $f(x) = e^{\frac{x^3}{3} - x} > 0$ for every real number x, and $x^2 - 1 = (x + 1)(x - 1)$

$$\Rightarrow x^2 - 1 < 0 \text{ when } x \in (-1, 1) \text{ and}$$
$$x^2 - 1 > 0 \text{ when } |x| > 1.$$

Hence,

$$f'(x) = (x^2 - 1)\, e^{\frac{x^3}{3} - x} < 0 \text{ for } x \in (-1, 1) \text{ and}$$

$$f'(x) = (x^2 - 1)\, e^{\frac{x^3}{3} - x} > 0 \text{ for } |x| > 1.$$

(D) is the answer.

8. (D)

The sum of n terms in arithmetic series with first term t_1, and common difference d is given by

$$S_n = \frac{n}{2}[2t_1 + (n - 1)d]$$

In this problem $S_n = 100$, $n = 50$, $d = 2$, thus,

$$100 = \frac{50}{2}(2t_1 + (50 - 1)2)$$
$$100 = 25(2t_1 + 98)$$
$$\frac{100}{25} = 2t_1 + 98$$
$$4 = 2t_1 + 98$$
$$2t_1 = 4 - 98 = -94$$
$$t_1 = -\frac{94}{2} = -47$$

9. (D)

The slope of any tangent line to this curve is given by $\dfrac{dy}{dx} = 2x + 11$. Substituting $x = -3$, $\dfrac{dy}{dx} = 5$.

10. (C)

$$-1 + i = \sqrt{2}\left[\cos\left(\frac{3\pi}{4}\right) + i\sin\left(\frac{3\pi}{4}\right)\right].$$

So $(-1 + i)^{10} = \sqrt{2}^{10}\left[\cos\left(\frac{15\pi}{2}\right) + i\sin\left(\frac{15\pi}{2}\right)\right]$

$$= \sqrt{2}^{10}[0 + (i)(-1)]$$

$$= -i\sqrt{2}^{10} = -32i.$$

11. (B)

The formula for the sum of an infinite geometric series is $S = \dfrac{A}{(1 - R)}$, where $A =$ the first term and $R =$ the common ratio. In this example, $A = 1.8$ and R is unknown. By substitution, $4.5 = \dfrac{1.8}{(1 - R)}$. Then $1 - R = \dfrac{1.8}{4.5} = 0.4$. So, $R = 0.6$. The second term must be $(1.8)(0.6) = 1.08$ and the third term must be $(1.08)(0.6) = 0.648$. So, the sum of the first three terms is $1.8 + 1.08 + 0.648 = 3.528$.

12. (B)

The number of ways of arranging all the math books first, all the history books second, and all the English books last is $(4!)(2!)(3!) = 288$. However, there are $(3)(2)(1) = 6$ different ways to arrange the ordering of these three subjects. Thus there are $(6)(288) = 1,728$ ways of arranging the nine books so that all books of the same subject are together.

13. (B)

The acceleration is found by determining the second derivative of this function. The first derivative, denoted at $s'(t)$, is $3t^2 + 8t$. The second derivative, denoted as $s''(t)$, is $6t + 8$. Substituting $t = 5$, we get $(6)(5) + 8 = 38$.

14. (A)

$$(\sin\theta \times \cot\theta)^2 + (\cos\theta\tan\theta)^2$$

$$= \left(\sin\theta\left(\frac{\cos\theta}{\sin\theta}\right)\right)^2 + \left(\cos\theta\left(\frac{\sin\theta}{\cos\theta}\right)\right)^2$$

$$= \cos^2\theta + \sin^2\theta = 1$$

15. (C)

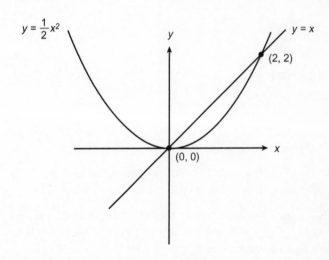

The curve is below the line, so

$$\text{Area} = \int_0^2\left(x - \frac{1}{2}x^2\right)dx = \left(\frac{x^2}{2} - \frac{x^3}{6}\right)\Bigg|_0^2 = 2 - \frac{8}{6} = \frac{2}{3}.$$

16. (B)

$$\sin\left(\frac{\pi}{2}+t\right)=\sin\frac{\pi}{2}\cos t+\cos\frac{\pi}{2}\sin t$$

But $\qquad \sin\frac{\pi}{2}=1$ and $\cos\frac{\pi}{2}=0$

$\therefore \qquad \sin\left(\frac{\pi}{2}+t\right)=\cos t.$

17. (B)

$\displaystyle\lim_{h\to 0}\frac{e^{x+h}-e^x}{h}$ equals the derivative of e^x by using the definition of the derivative

$$f'(x)=\lim_{h\to 0}\frac{f(x+h)-f(x)}{h}.$$

Therefore, for $f(x)=e^x$,

$$\lim_{h\to 0}\frac{e^{x+h}-e^x}{h}=f'(e^x)=e^x$$

18. (D)

$$f'(x)=x^2-2x-3=(x+1)(x-3)$$

$(x+1)(x-3)=0 \Rightarrow x=-1$ and 3 are critical values.

The numbers -1 and 3 divide the x-axis into 3 intervals, from $-\infty$ to -1, -1 to 3, and 3 to $-\infty$.

$f(x)$ has a relative minimum value at $x=x_1$, if and only if $f'(x_1)=0$ and the sign of $f'(x)$ changes from $-$ to $+$ as x increases through x_1.

If $-1 < x < 3$, then $f'(x)=-$

If $x=3$, then $f'(x)=0$

If $x>3$, then $f'(x)=+$

Therefore, $f(3)$ is a relative minimum.

Note that when $x<-1$, $f'(x)=+$. If $x=-1$, $f'(x)=0$. If $-1<x<3$, $f'(x)=-$.

Thus, $f(-1)$ is a relative maximum, not minimum.

19. (C)

$a_2=(a_1)^2+5=9+5=14$, $a_3=(14)^2+5=201$, $a_4=(201)^2+5=40,406$. Then $a_3+a_4=201+40,406=40,607$.

20. (D)

Since $\ln(x^2)=2\ln x$, we have

$$\int_1^{e^2}\frac{\ln(x^2)}{x}dx=2\int_1^{e^2}\frac{\ln x}{x}dx.$$

This integral can be evaluated by using the substitution $u=lnx$. The integrand becomes, u, with $du=\dfrac{dx}{x}$, and the limits of integration change to

$u(1)=\ln 1=0$

$u(e^2)=\ln(e^2)=2.$

We get

$$2\int_0^2 u\,du=u^2\Big|_0^2$$

$$=2^2-0=4$$

21. (A)

$y=\dfrac{3}{\sin x+\cos x}=\dfrac{3}{u}$ where $u=\sin x+\cos x$

So $\dfrac{dy}{dx}=3(-1)u^{-1-1}\dfrac{du}{dx}$ using the derivative of a power and chain rule theorems.

Thus,

$$\frac{dy}{dx}=\frac{-3}{(\sin x+\cos x)^2}(\cos x-\sin x)$$

$$=\frac{3(\sin x-\cos x)}{\sin^2 x+2\sin x\cos x+\cos^2 x}$$

$$\frac{dy}{dx}=\frac{3(\sin x-\cos x)}{1+2\sin x\cos x},$$

using the identity $\sin^2 x+\cos^2 x=1$

22. (A)

The sum of an infinite geometric series is given by the formula $S = \dfrac{A}{(1-R)}$, where A is the first number and R is the ratio. In this example, $A = 0.3$ and $R = \dfrac{0.24}{0.3} = 0.8$. Then $S = \dfrac{0.3}{0.2} = 1.5$.

23. (C)

For the numerator only

$$\lim_{x \to 2} (x^2 - 5) = 4 - 5 = -1$$

For the denominator only

$$\lim_{x \to 2} (x + 3) = 5$$

Therefore,

$$\lim_{x \to 2} \left(\frac{x^2 - 5}{x + 3} \right) = -\frac{1}{5}$$

24. (B)

The average value of

$$f(x) = 1/(10 - 2) \int_2^{10} (10 - x)dx$$

$$\left(\frac{1}{8} \right) \left(10x - \frac{x^2}{2} \right) \Big|_2^{10} = \left(\frac{1}{8} \right) [100 - 50 - 20 + 2]$$

$\left(\dfrac{1}{8} \right) (32) = 4$. Then $4 = 10 - x$, so $x = 6$.

25. (D)

In the standard form $\dfrac{dy}{dx} + [P(x)] [y] = Q(x)$. In this example, $P(x) = 2$ and $Q(x) = 3$. The solution will be given by $y = \dfrac{1}{v(x)} \cdot \int [v(x)][Q(x)]dx$, $v(x) = e^{\int 2dx} = e^{2x}$. Then $y = \dfrac{1}{2e^{2x}} \cdot \int (e^{2x})(3)dx = \left(\dfrac{1}{e^{2x}} \right) \left[\left(\dfrac{3}{2} \right) e^{2x} + C \right] = \dfrac{3}{2} + Ce^{-2x}$ where C is a constant. Since $y(0) = 1$, we can write $1 = \dfrac{3}{2} + Ce^0$. Since $e^0 = 1$, $C = -\dfrac{1}{2}$.

26. (A)

Here we use integration by parts. Then,

$$\int u\,dv = uv - \int v\,du.$$

Let $u = \ln x$, $dv = dx$, $du = 1/x\, dx$, and

$$v = \int dv = \int dx = x.$$

Substituting into the above equation, we obtain:

$$\int \ln x\, dx = (\ln x) x - \int x/x\, dx$$

$$= x \ln x - x + C.$$

27. (B)

Although all answers are true statements for Babylonian mathematics, only the positional notation presented the distinct mathematical advantage that set the Babylonians apart from other civilizations at that time.

28. (C)

Archimedes lived 287–212 B.C.; Omar Khayyam, A.D. 1048–1131; Leibniz, A.D. 1646–1716, and Florence Nightingale, A.D. 1820–1910.

29. (A)

Proof by contradiction assumes the opposite of the desired conclusion and then shows that the assumption must be false and that its opposite (the original conclusion) must be true. A direct proof is straightforward without making any further assumptions. Mathematical induction proves a first statement regarding natural numbers is true and proves it is also true for one other number, and then assumes it is true for all other natural numbers; mathematical deduction draws a conclusion from something already known or assumed.

30. (D)

The Richter scale is logarithmic, so that an earthquake of magnitude 6 has ten times the energy of an earthquake of magnitude 5, and a hundred times the energy of an earthquake of magnitude 4. Although earthquake energy and damage are necessarily related, they are not the basis of the Richter scale. Choice (C) makes no sense.

31.

To find the points of intersection, solve the equation $2\sin^2 x = 1 - \sin x$. Rewriting and factoring, we get $2\sin^2 x + \sin x - 1 = 0$, which becomes $(2\sin x - 1)(\sin x + 1) = 0$.

If $2\sin x - 1 = 0$, then $\sin x = \frac{1}{2}$, which implies that $x = \frac{\pi}{6}$ and $\frac{5\pi}{6}$. If $\sin x + 1 = 0$, then $\sin x = -1$, which implies that $x = \frac{3\pi}{2}$.

To get the corresponding y values, we can substitute these x values into the equation $y = 1 - \sin x$ (Either equation can be used.)

When $x = \frac{\pi}{6}$, $1 - \sin x = 1 - \sin\frac{\pi}{6} = \frac{1}{2}$

When $x = \frac{5\pi}{6}$, $1 - \sin x = 1 - \sin\frac{5\pi}{6} = \frac{1}{2}$

When $x = \frac{3\pi}{2}$, $1 - \sin x = 1 - \sin\frac{3\pi}{2} = 2$

The three points of intersection are therefore

$$\left(\frac{\pi}{6}, \frac{1}{2}\right), \left(\frac{5\pi}{6}, \frac{1}{2}\right), \left(\frac{3\pi}{2}, 2\right)$$

32.

First, find the first derivative of $f(x)$, denoted as $f'(x) = 24x^3 - 24x^2$. Next find the second derivative, denoted as $f''(x) = 72x^2 - 48x$. To find the inflection points, solve the equation $72x^2 - 48x = 0$. This factors as $(24x)(3x - 2) = 0$. Then $24x = 0$ and $3x - 2 = 0$, so $x = 0$ and $x = \frac{2}{3}$. Substitute these values into $f(x)$.

$f(0) : 6(0)^4 - 8(0)^3 + 1 = 1$.

$f\left(\frac{2}{3}\right) = 6\left(\frac{2}{3}\right)^4 - 8\left(\frac{2}{3}\right)^3 + 1 = -\frac{5}{27}$.

This means the points of inflection are $(0, 1)$ and $\left(\frac{2}{3}, -\frac{5}{27}\right)$.

The intervals of the variable x that need to be considered are $(-\infty, 0)$, $\left(0, \frac{2}{3}\right)$, and $\left(\frac{2}{3}, \infty\right)$.

If $x \in (-\infty, 0)$, $3x - 2$ is negative, so $f''(x) = (24) \times$ (negative number) $\times$ (negative number) = positive number, so the curve is concave up.

If $x \in \left(0, \frac{2}{3}\right)$, $3x - 2$ is negative, so $f''(x) = (24x)(3x - 2) = (24) \times$ (positive number) $\times$ (negative number) = negative number, so the curve is concave down.

Finally, if $x \in \left(\frac{2}{3}, \infty\right)$, $3x - 2$ is positive, so $f''(x) = (24) \times$ (positive number) $\times$ (positive number) = positive number. The curve will be concave up.

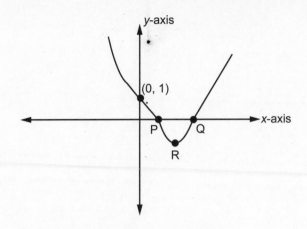

y-axis

(0, 1)

x-axis

P   Q

R

Point Q is approximately $(1.25, 0)$

Point P is approximately $(.61, 0)$

The lowest point of the curve R is approximately $(1, -1)$.

33.

First, determine the points where the curves of these functions intersect. Let $x^2 - 2x = -x^2 + 3x + 7$, which becomes $2x^2 - 5x - 7 = 0$. The left side of this equation factors as $(2x - 7)(x + 1)$. Since $(2x - 7)(x + 1) = 0$, $2x - 7 = 0$ if $x = \dfrac{7}{2}$, and $x + 1 = 0$ if $x = -1$.

This means the x-coordinates of the points of intersection are $x = \dfrac{7}{2}$ and $x = -1$. To find the corresponding y-coordinates, choose either function and substitute the x values of $\dfrac{7}{2}$ and -1. For $y = x^2 - 2x$, using $x = \dfrac{7}{2}$, we get $y = \left(\dfrac{7}{2}\right)^2 - 2\left(\dfrac{7}{2}\right) = \dfrac{21}{4}$, and using $x = -1$, we get $y = (-1)^2 - 2(-1) = 3$. The points of intersection are therefore $\left(\dfrac{7}{2}, \dfrac{21}{4}\right)$ and $(-1, 3)$.

For each x in the interval $\left(-1, \dfrac{7}{2}\right)$, the y values of $y = -x^2 + 3x + 7$ exceed the y values of $y = x^2 - 2x$.

Thus, the area bounded by these two curves is given by

$$\int_{-1}^{\frac{7}{2}} (-x^2 + 3x + 7) - (x^2 - 2x)dx$$

$$= \int_{-1}^{\frac{7}{2}} (-2x^2 + 5x + 7)dx$$

$$= \left[-\dfrac{2}{3}x^3 + \dfrac{5}{2}x^2 + 7x\right]_{-1}^{\frac{7}{2}}$$

$$= \left[-28.58\bar{3} + 30.625 + 24.5\right] - \left[\dfrac{2}{3} + \dfrac{5}{2} - 7\right]$$

$$= 26.541\bar{6} - \left(-3.8\bar{3}\right) = 30.375$$

34.

Suppose the first two terms (arbitrarily chosen) are a and b. Then the first ten terms of the Fibonacci series would be:

$a, b, a + b, a + 2b, 2a + 3b, 3a + 5b, 5a + 8b, 8a + 13b, 13a + 21b, 21a + 34b$.

This sums to $55a + 88b$, which is 11 times the seventh term ($5a + 8b$), no matter what numbers are used for a and b.

4 points for using this type of logic in the answer.

2 points for trying specific numbers several times and "inductively" trying to prove the hypothesis.

0 points otherwise.

CSET

Mathematics

Practice Test 2

Subtest I

Answer Sheet

1. Ⓐ Ⓑ Ⓒ Ⓓ   16. Ⓐ Ⓑ Ⓒ Ⓓ

2. Ⓐ Ⓑ Ⓒ Ⓓ   17. Ⓐ Ⓑ Ⓒ Ⓓ

3. Ⓐ Ⓑ Ⓒ Ⓓ   18. Ⓐ Ⓑ Ⓒ Ⓓ

4. Ⓐ Ⓑ Ⓒ Ⓓ   19. Ⓐ Ⓑ Ⓒ Ⓓ

5. Ⓐ Ⓑ Ⓒ Ⓓ   20. Ⓐ Ⓑ Ⓒ Ⓓ

6. Ⓐ Ⓑ Ⓒ Ⓓ   21. Ⓐ Ⓑ Ⓒ Ⓓ

7. Ⓐ Ⓑ Ⓒ Ⓓ   22. Ⓐ Ⓑ Ⓒ Ⓓ

8. Ⓐ Ⓑ Ⓒ Ⓓ   23. Ⓐ Ⓑ Ⓒ Ⓓ

9. Ⓐ Ⓑ Ⓒ Ⓓ   24. Ⓐ Ⓑ Ⓒ Ⓓ

10. Ⓐ Ⓑ Ⓒ Ⓓ   25. Ⓐ Ⓑ Ⓒ Ⓓ

11. Ⓐ Ⓑ Ⓒ Ⓓ   26. Ⓐ Ⓑ Ⓒ Ⓓ

12. Ⓐ Ⓑ Ⓒ Ⓓ   27. Ⓐ Ⓑ Ⓒ Ⓓ

13. Ⓐ Ⓑ Ⓒ Ⓓ   28. Ⓐ Ⓑ Ⓒ Ⓓ

14. Ⓐ Ⓑ Ⓒ Ⓓ   29. Ⓐ Ⓑ Ⓒ Ⓓ

15. Ⓐ Ⓑ Ⓒ Ⓓ   30. Ⓐ Ⓑ Ⓒ Ⓓ

CSET: Mathematics Practice Test 2
Subtest I*
Algebra; Number Theory

TIME: When taking the actual test, you will have one five-hour test session in which to complete the subtest(s) for which you are registered.

<u>Directions:</u> This test consists of two sections: 30 multiple-choice and four constructed-response questions. The constructed-response questions involve written responses.

---

1. Including 1 and the number itself, how many total positive factors are there for the number $8^3 \cdot 35 \cdot 27^2$?

    (A) 280

    (B) 210

    (C) 168

    (D) 54

2. Let a, b represent positive integers less than 19 for which $19 \equiv a \pmod 3$ and $27 \equiv b \pmod 4$. What is the *maximum* value of $a - b$?

    (A) 18

    (B) 17

    (C) 14

    (D) 13

3. If $(x + 3y)^2 = 100$ and $(3x + y)^2 = 196$, what is the value of $\left(\dfrac{1}{3}\right)(x^2 - y^2)$?

    (A) 3

    (B) 4

    (C) 6

    (D) 9

4. If $\log_3\left(\dfrac{1}{27}\right) = x$ and $y^x = -64$, what is the value of $\log_{\frac{9}{16}} xy$?

    (A) -2

    (B) $-\dfrac{1}{2}$

    (C) $\dfrac{1}{2}$

    (D) 2

---

*According to the test administrator, Subtest II is always given first in the test session. For further details, visit the official CSET website at *http://www.cset.nesinc.com*.

5. Suppose Z varies jointly as W and X. If $Z = 18$ when $W = 9$ and $X = 3$, what is the value of W when $Z = 15$ and $X = \dfrac{1}{3}$?

   (A) 3.5   (C) 30.0

   (B) 10.8   (D) 67.5

6. A polynomial function $g(x)$ of degree 5 has a zero of $2 - i$ and a zero of $4 + i$. What is the maximum number of real zeros for $g(x)$?

   (A) 0   (C) 2

   (B) 1   (D) 3

7. Which one of the following represents a function whose graph has a single vertical asymptote at $x = -3$?

   (A) $\dfrac{(x + 3)}{2x^2 + 5x - 3}$

   (B) $\dfrac{(9x + 1)}{x^3 - 9x}$

   (C) $\dfrac{(3x - 1)}{(x^3 + 3x^2 + 2x + 6)}$

   (D) $\dfrac{(x - 3)}{x^2 + 3x + 9}$

8. If $f(x) = 3x - 5$ and $g(f(x)) = x$, then $g(x) =$

   (A) $\dfrac{x - 5}{3}$.   (C) $\dfrac{2x + 5}{3}$.

   (B) $\dfrac{x + 5}{3}$.   (D) $\dfrac{x + 5}{4}$.

9. If $f(x) = x^3 - x - 1$, then the set of all c for which $f(c) = f(-c)$ is

   (A) {all real numbers}.

   (B) {0}.

   (C) {0, 1}.

   (D) {−1, 0, 1}.

10. Which of the graphs below represents the function $y = 2 + \sin(x - \pi)$?

   (A)
   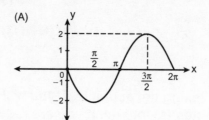

   (B)
   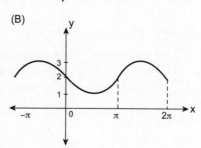

   (C)
   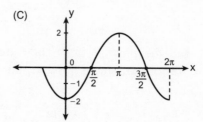

   (D)
   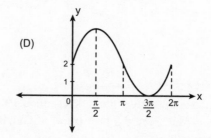

11. If $f(x) = 2x + 4$ and $g(x) = x^2 - 2$, then $(f \circ g)(x)$, where $(f \circ g)(x)$ is a composition of functions, is

   (A) $2x^2 - 8$ (C) $2x^2$

   (B) $2x^2 + 8$ (D) $2x^3 + 4x^2 - 4x - 8$

12. What is the solution for x in the inequality $2x^2 - x - 3 < 0$?

   (A) $-1 < x < \dfrac{3}{2}$ (C) $-\dfrac{3}{2} < x < 1$

   (B) $x > \dfrac{3}{2}$ or $x < -1$ (D) $x > 1$ or $x < -\dfrac{3}{2}$

13. Select the shaded region that graphically represents the conditions $x \geq 0$ and $-3 < y < 3$.

(A)

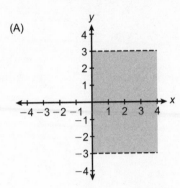

(B)

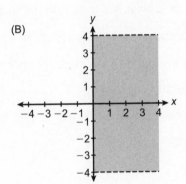

(C)

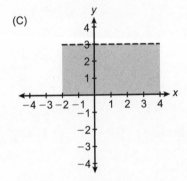

(D)

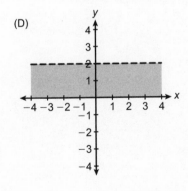

14. What is the range of values for which $|6x - 5| \leq 8$ is satisfied?

(A) $-\dfrac{1}{2} \leq x \leq \dfrac{1}{2}$ (C) $-1 \leq x \leq \dfrac{1}{2}$

(B) $0 \leq x \leq \dfrac{5}{6}$ (D) $-\dfrac{1}{2} \leq x \leq \dfrac{13}{6}$

15. What is the units digit for 4^{891}?

(A) 2   (C) 6

(B) 4   (D) 8

16. The population of bacteria that begins with a count of X and triples every n years is given by the formula $Y = (X)(3^{\frac{t}{n}})$, where t represents the number of years of growth and Y represents the growth after t years. Suppose the bacteria population in the year 1895 was 150, and it grew to 36,450 by the year 1935. In what year was the population equal to 1,350?

(A) 1932   (C) 1911

(B) 1919   (D) 1903

17. In a linear programming problem involving ordered pairs (x, y), the restraints yield feasible solutions in a region where the corner points are $(0, 0)$, $(0, 10)$, $(16, 8)$, and $(40, 0)$. Which one of the following objective functions would *not* have a unique point that corresponds to a maximum P value on this region?

(A) $P = 20x + 70y$ (C) $P = 40x + 100y$

(B) $P = 30x + 90y$ (D) $P = 30x + 350y$

18. If x is divisible by 3 and y is divisible by 6, which of the following *must* be divisible by 4?

(A) $\dfrac{x}{2y}$ (C) $3xy$

(B) $\dfrac{y}{x}$ (D) $8x + 2y$

19. Each point of the graph of $f(x) = (x + 3)^2 - 5$ is moved 4 units in a positive horizontal direction and 6 units in a negative vertical direction. If this new graph is called $g(x)$, which of the following describes $g(x)$?

    (A) $g(x) = (x - 1)^2 - 11$

    (B) $g(x) = (x - 1)^2 + 1$

    (C) $g(x) = (x + 7)^2 - 11$

    (D) $g(x) = (x + 7)^2 + 1$

20. The equation $x^2 + 2x + 7 = 0$ has

    (A) two complex conjugate roots.

    (B) two real rational roots.

    (C) two real equal roots.

    (D) two real irrational roots.

21. What is the equation of the line that is parallel to $6x + 3y = 4$ and has a y-intercept of -6?

    (A) $y = 2x - 6$

    (B) $y = 2x + \dfrac{4}{3}$

    (C) $y = -2x - \dfrac{4}{3}$

    (D) $y = -2x - 6$

22. Which of the following functions has its highest point at $(-1, 5)$?

    (A) $f(x) = -2(x - 1)^2 - 5$

    (B) $f(x) = 2(x + 1)^2 - 5$

    (C) $f(x) = -2(x - 1)^2 + 5$

    (D) $f(x) = -2(x + 1)^2 + 5$

23. If $27^x = 9$ and $2^{x-y} = 64$, then $y =$

    (A) -5

    (B) -3

    (C) $-\dfrac{2}{3}$

    (D) $-\dfrac{16}{3}$

24. Exclusive of the numbers 1 and 1176, how many factors are there for the number 1176?

    (A) 20   (C) 24

    (B) 22   (D) 26

25. Which one of the following has the same value as $-|-8 - (-5)|$?

    (A) $|-8 - 5|$ (C) $-|5 - (-8)|$

    (B) $|-8 - (-5)|$ (D) $-|-8 + 5|$

26. A group of n data, where n is an odd number, is arranged in ascending order. The position of the first quartile is given by $\dfrac{(n + 1)}{4}$, and the position of the third quartile is given by $\dfrac{(3n + 3)}{4}$. If the 66th number is the third quartile, which number is the first quartile?

    (A) 6th (C) 22nd

    (B) 11th (D) 33rd

27. Consider the function $F(x)$ defined as follows:

    $$F(x) = \begin{cases} -x + 3, \text{ if } x < 0 \\ 2x + 3, \text{ if } 0 < x < 3 \\ 3x, \text{ if } x > 3 \end{cases}$$

    What is the value of $F(-3) + F(2) - F(4)$?

    (A) 2   (C) -1

    (B) 1   (D) -2

28. Find the determinant of the matrix A where:

$$A = \begin{bmatrix} 2 & 7 & -3 & 8 & 3 \\ 0 & -3 & 7 & 5 & 1 \\ 0 & 0 & 6 & 7 & 6 \\ 0 & 0 & 0 & 9 & 8 \\ 0 & 0 & 0 & 0 & 4 \end{bmatrix}$$

(A) 90

(B) $-1{,}296$

(C) -1008

(D) -90

29. Let $A = \begin{bmatrix} 2 & 3 & 7 \\ 4 & m & \sqrt{3} \\ 1 & 5 & a \end{bmatrix}$, $B = \begin{bmatrix} \alpha & \beta & \delta \\ \sqrt{5} & 3 & 1 \\ p & q & 4 \end{bmatrix}$

Find $A + B$

(A) $\begin{bmatrix} 2+\alpha & 4+\sqrt{5} & 7+\delta \\ 3+\beta & 1+p & \sqrt{5}+q \\ 7+p & 3+\beta & a+4 \end{bmatrix}$

(B) $\begin{bmatrix} 2+\delta & 3+\alpha & 7+\beta \\ 4+1 & m+1 & \sqrt{3}+\sqrt{5} \\ 1+4 & 5+4 & p+4 \end{bmatrix}$

(C) $\begin{bmatrix} 2+\alpha & 3+\beta & 7+\delta \\ 4+\sqrt{5} & m+3 & \sqrt{3}+1 \\ 1+p & 5+q & a+4 \end{bmatrix}$

(D) $\begin{bmatrix} 2+\alpha & 3+\delta & 7+\beta \\ 4+3 & m+\sqrt{5} & \sqrt{3}+1 \\ 1+q & p+5 & a+4 \end{bmatrix}$

30. Find the determinant of the following matrix:

$$A = \begin{bmatrix} 2 & 0 & 3 & 0 \\ 2 & 1 & 1 & 2 \\ 3 & -1 & 1 & -2 \\ 2 & 1 & -2 & 1 \end{bmatrix}$$

(A) 11

(B) 15

(C) 19

(D) 36

Constructed-response questions 31–34:
For each response you will use up to two pages of the lined pages provided with the CSET test. Please see the sample pages at the end of the book.

31. Let $n \geq 2$ be an integer for which $Z_n = \{$all non-negative integers less than $n\}$. Suppose $x, y \in Z_n$. Define $x \oplus y$ as the least positive remainder when the sum of x and y is divided by n. Define $x * y$ as the least positive remainder when the product of x and y is divided by n.

- What is the value of $3 \oplus 7$ in Z_8?

- What is the value of $4 * 9$ in Z_{10}?

- What is the additive inverse of 5 in Z_{12}?

- What is the multiplicative inverse of 8 in Z_{13}?

32. • Determine the horizontal, vertical, and oblique line asymptotes of the function $f(x) = \dfrac{(x^2 - 3)}{(2x - 4)}$.

• Determine the x and y intercepts of the graph of this function.

33. In 3-dimensional space, let $\alpha_1 = \begin{pmatrix} 1 \\ 2 \\ 4 \end{pmatrix}$, $\alpha_2 = \begin{pmatrix} 1 \\ 0 \\ 0 \end{pmatrix}$, and $\alpha_3 = \begin{pmatrix} 1 \\ 1 \\ 2 \end{pmatrix}$, represent three vectors. Show why the vector $\begin{pmatrix} 5 \\ 6 \\ 9 \end{pmatrix}$ *cannot* be written as a linear combination of α_1, α_2, and, α_3.

34. Use the principle of mathematical induction to prove that:

$$\frac{1}{2^1} + \frac{1}{2^2} + \frac{1}{2^3} + \cdots + \frac{1}{2^n} = 1 - \frac{1}{2^n}$$

for all positive integers n.

Answer Key

Q No.	Correct Answer
1.	(A)
2.	(D)
3.	(B)
4.	(C)
5.	(D)
6.	(B)
7.	(C)
8.	(B)
9.	(D)
10.	(B)
11.	(C)
12.	(A)
13.	(A)
14.	(D)
15.	(B)
16.	(C)
17.	(B)

Q No.	Correct Answer
18.	(D)
19.	(A)
20.	(A)
21.	(D)
22.	(D)
23.	(D)
24.	(B)
25.	(D)
26.	(C)
27.	(B)
28.	(B)
29.	(C)
30.	(A)
31.	Constructed-Response
32.	Constructed-Response
33.	Constructed-Response
34.	Constructed-Response

Detailed Explanations of Answers

1.   (A)

$8^3 = (2^3)^3 = 2^9, 35 = (5)(7), 27^2 = (3^3)^2 = 3^6$. Thus, the original number can be written as $(2^9)(5^1)(7^1)(3^6)$. The total number of factors is found by adding 1 to each exponent of the prime factorization (to include the number itself as a factor, e.g. 8, 35, and 27), and then multiplying. We get $(9 + 1)(1 + 1)(1 + 1)(6 + 1) = 280$.

2.   (D)

The maximum value of $a - b$ can be determined by finding the largest value of a and the smallest value of b. Since $19 - a$ is a multiple of 3 and $a < 19$, the largest value of a is 16. Since $27 - b$ is a multiple of 4 and $b < 19$, the smallest value of b is 3. Finally, $a - b = 16 - 3 = 13$.

3.   (B)

$(x + 3y)^2 = x^2 + 6xy + 9y^2 = 100$. Also, $(3x + y)^2 = 9x^2 + 6xy + y^2 = 196$. By subtraction, $8x^2 - 8y^2 = 96$. Then, $x^2 - y^2 = 12$. Therefore, $\left(\frac{1}{3}\right)(x^2 - y^2) = 4$.

4.   (C)

Since $\log_3\left(\frac{1}{27}\right) = x, 3^x = \frac{1}{27} = 3^{-3}$. So $x = -3$. So $y^x = y^{-3} = \frac{1}{y^3} = -64$, and $\frac{1}{y} = -4$, which means that $y = -\frac{1}{4}$. Let $\log_{\frac{9}{16}} xy = z$. Then, $\log_{\frac{9}{16}}\left(\frac{3}{4}\right) = z$, so $\left(\frac{9}{16}\right)^z = \left(\frac{3}{4}\right)$. But $\left(\frac{9}{16}\right)^z = \left[\left(\frac{3}{4}\right)^2\right]^z = \left(\frac{3}{4}\right)^{2z}$. Therefore, since $\left(\frac{3}{4}\right) = \left(\frac{3}{4}\right)^{2z}$, $2z = 1$, and $z = \frac{1}{2}$.

5.   (D)

Since Z varies jointly as W and Z, $Z = kWX$ for some constant k. By substitution, $18 = (k)(9)(3)$, so $k = \frac{18}{27} = \frac{2}{3}$. Now we know that $Z = \left(\frac{2}{3}\right)WX$. Again, by substitution, $15 = \left(\frac{2}{3}\right)(W)\left(\frac{1}{3}\right)$. Simplifying, $15 = \left(\frac{2}{9}\right)W$, So $W = (15)\left(\frac{9}{2}\right) = 67.5$.

6.   (B)

Since both $2 - i$ and $4 + i$ are zeros of $g(x)$, their conjugates, $2 + i$ and $4 - i$, respectively, must also be zeros of $g(x)$. This means that there are 4 complex zeros of $g(x)$, so there can only be a maximum of 1 real zero because $g(x)$ is of degree 5.

7.   (C)

For polynomial functions, vertical asymptotes are found by setting the denominator equal to zero. Since, $x^3 + 3x^2 + 2x + 6 = (x^2 + 2)(x + 3)$, the vertical asymptotes would be found using the equations $x^2 + 2 = 0$ and $x + 3 = 0$. The first of these equations has no real solution, and the second equation has the solution $x = -3$. Choice (A) is wrong because the denominator factors as $(x + 3)(2x - 1)$, so it has vertical asymptotes of $x = -3$ and $x = \frac{1}{2}$. Choice (B) is wrong because the denominator factors as $(x)(x - 3)(x + 3)$, so it has vertical asymptotes of $x = 0, x = 3$, and $x = -3$. Choice

(D) is wrong because its denominator has no real roots, so it has no vertical asymptotes.

8. (B)

$f(x) = 3x - 5$ and $g(f(x)) = x$

We want to know what value of x (in terms of x) would cause $g(3x - 5)$ to equal x. To distinguish one x from the other, we can represent the x from $3x - 5$ with a y. This will result in:

$$3y - 5 = x$$
$$3y = x + 5$$
$$y = \frac{x + 5}{3}$$
$$g(y) = g(3x - 5) = \frac{3x - 5 + 5}{3} = x$$

Note: $g(x)$ is the inverse of $f(x)$, since $g(f(x)) = f(g(x)) = x$.

9. (D)

$$f(c) = c^3 - c - 1,$$
$$f(-c) = -c^3 + c - 1$$
If $f(c) = f(-c)$, $c^3 = c$
$$\therefore c = -1, 0, \text{ or } 1$$

10. (B)

There are three steps to build this graph.

First Step: Draw the graph $y = \sin x$

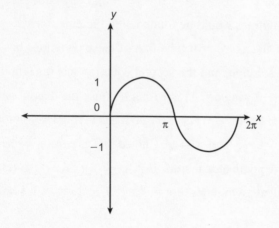

Second Step: Move the graph two units up, because it is $y = \sin(x - \pi) + 2$.

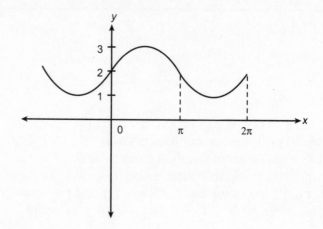

Third Step: Move the graph π units to the right because it is $y = \sin(x - \pi) + 2$.

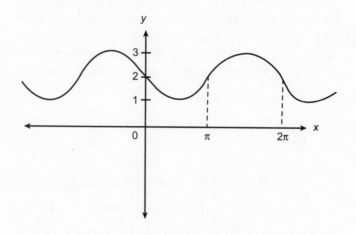

11. (C)

$$(f \circ g)(x) = f(x) \circ g(x) = f(g(x)).$$

This is the definition of the composition of functions. For the functions given in this problem we have

$$f(g(x)) = 2(g(x)) + 4 = 2(x^2 - 2) + 4$$
$$= 2x^2 - 4 + 4 = 2x^2.$$

12. (A)

Factor the left side of the inequality to get $(2x - 3)(x + 1) < 0$. If $2x - 3 > 0$ and $x + 1 < 0$, we get $x > \dfrac{3}{2}$ and $x < -1$, which is impossible. If $2x - 3 < 0$ and $x + 1 > 0$, we have the actual solution of $-1 < x < \dfrac{3}{2}$.

13. (A)

The inequality $x \geq 0$ identifies the region to the right of the y-axis, eliminating choices (C) and (D). The double inequality of $-3 < y < 3$ represents dotted horizontal lines passing through 3 and -3 on the y-axis with the area between the lines shaded. Of the two remaining choices, (A) is the only one that satisfies this constraint.

14. (D)

When given an inequality with an absolute value, recall the definition of absolute value:

$$|x| = \begin{cases} x \text{ if } x \geq 0 \\ -x \text{ if } x < 0 \end{cases}$$

$6x - 5 \leq 8$ if $6x - 5 \geq 0$.

$-6x + 5 \leq 8$ if $6x - 5 < 0$.

If $6x - 5 \leq 8$, then $6x \leq 13$, so $x \leq \dfrac{13}{6}$.

If $-6x + 5 \leq 8$, then $-6x \leq 3$, so $x \geq -\dfrac{1}{2}$.

15. (B)

Note that $4^1 = 4$, $4^2 = 16$, $4^3 = 64$, $4^4 = 216$, $4^5 = 1024$, $4^6 = 4096$, …… Thus, when 4 is raised to an odd exponent, the units digit is 4; when 4 is raised to an even digit, the units digit is 6. Since 891 is odd, 4^{891} has a units digit of 4.

16. (C)

In this example, $X = 150$, $Y = 36{,}450$, and $t = 1935 - 1895 = 40$. Then we have $36{,}450 = (150)\left(3^{\frac{40}{n}}\right)$. Divide both sides by 150 to get $243 = 3^{\frac{40}{n}}$. By inspection, $3^5 = 243$, so $\dfrac{40}{n} = 5$. This leads to $n = 8$, which means that the population triples every 8 years. Now use the equation $1{,}350 = (150)\left(3^{\frac{t}{8}}\right)$. Divide both sides by 150 to get $9 = 3^{\frac{t}{8}}$. This can be written as $3^2 = 3^{\frac{t}{8}}$. Equating exponents, $\dfrac{t}{8} = 2$, so $t = 16$. The required year is then $1895 + 16 = 1911$.

17. (B)

In order for an objective function not to have a unique point that corresponds to a maximum P value, the slope of this function must be the same as one of the lines that form the boundary of this region. The slope of the x-axis is zero and that of the y-axis is undefined. The slope of the line containing (0, 10) and (16, 8) is $-\dfrac{1}{8}$; the slope of the line containing (40, 0) and (16, 8) is $-\dfrac{1}{3}$. The only objective function among these four answer choices with either of these slope values is $P = 30x + 90y$. This objective function has a slope of $-\dfrac{30}{90} = -\dfrac{1}{3}$.

18. (D)

If x is divisible by 3, then $x = 3k_1$, where k_1 is a constant. If y is divisible by 6, then $y = 6k_2$, where k_2 is a constant. Make these substitutions in each answer choice to see whether the result is divisible by 4. Only $8x + 2y = 2(4x + y) = 2(4 \times 3k_1 + 6k_2) = 4(6k_1 + 3k_2)$ can be divided by 4 to yield $6k_1 + 3k_2$. The other choices, (A), (B) and (C) would have coefficients of 0.25, 2 and 54, respectively; none of these numbers is divisible by 4.

19. (A)

For a parabolic function $f(x) = A(x - h)^2 + k$, the vertex is located at (h, k). When this function is moved in a positive horizontal direction, the value of h increases; when the function is moved in a negative vertical direction, the value of k decreases. In this example, the original values of h and k are –3 and –5, respectively. The new value of h is $-3 + 4 = 1$, and the new value of k is $-5 - 6 = -11$. So, the function $g(x) = (x - 1)^2 - 11$.

20. (A)

To solve this quadratic equation, we invoke the quadratic formula:

$$x = \frac{-b \pm \sqrt{b^2 - 4ac}}{2a}$$

The equation is $x^2 + 2x + 7 = 0$.

So $a = 1$, $b = 2$, and $c = 7$.

Substituting into the formula:

$$x = \frac{-2 \pm \sqrt{2^2 - 4(1)(7)}}{2(1)}$$

$$= \frac{-2 \pm \sqrt{4 - 28}}{2} = -1 \pm \sqrt{-6}$$

Since $i = \sqrt{-1}$, $x = -1 \pm i\sqrt{6}$.

These roots are complex conjugates of each other.

21. (D)

We employ the slope intercept form for the equation to be written, since we are given the y-intercept. Our task is then to determine the slope.

We are given the equation of a line parallel to the line whose equation we wish to find. We know that the slopes of two parallel lines are equal. Hence, by finding the slope of the given line, we will also be finding the unknown slope. To find the slope of the given equation

$$6x + 3y = 4$$

we transform the equation $6x + 3y = 4$ into slope intercept form.

$$6x + 3y = 4$$
$$3y = -6x + 4$$
$$y = -\frac{6}{3}x + \frac{4}{3}$$
$$y = -2x + \frac{4}{3}$$

Therefore, the slope of the line we are looking for is –2. The y-intercept is –6. Applying the slope intercept form,

$$y = mx + b,$$

to the unknown line, we obtain

$$y = -2x - 6$$

as the equation of the line.

22. (D)

When a quadratic function is written in the form $f(x) = A(x - h)^2 + k$, the vertex is located at (h, k). This vertex is the highest point, when A is negative, and the lowest point when A is positive. Since we seek a highest point, A must be negative. The values of h and k are -1 and 5, respectively. Thus, $f(x) = A(x - [-1])^2 + 5 = A(x + 1)^2 + 5$. Only choice (D) satisfies all the requirements.

23. (D)

$$27^x = (3^3)^x = 3^{3x}$$
$$9 = 3^2$$

Thus, we have $3^{3x} = 3^2$, which implies $3x = 2$ or $x = \frac{2}{3}$ because the power function is one-to-one, which means that if

$$a^{x_1} = a^{x_2} \text{ then } x_1 = x_2.$$

Now $2^{x-y} = 64 = 2^6$

so $x - y = 6$ or $\frac{2}{3} - y = 6$.

Hence, $y = \frac{2}{3} - 6 = -\frac{16}{3}$.

24. (B)

The number 1176 can be written as $2^3 \cdot 3^1 \cdot 7^2$. The total number of factors is given by the product of the value of the exponents increased by 1, which becomes $(4)(2)(3) = 24$. However, this number includes the factors of 1 and 1176. Remove these two numbers to get 22 factors.

25. (D)

The value of the item in the stem is $-|-8 + 5| = -|-3| = -3$. Answer choice (D) also has a value of -3. The values of answer choices (A), (B), and (C) are 13, 3 and -13, respectively.

26. (C)

If the 66th number is the third quartile, $\dfrac{(3n + 3)}{4} = 66$. Multiplying both sides by 4, $3n + 3 = 264$. Then $3n = 261$, so $n = 87$. The first quartile's position is given by $\dfrac{(87 + 1)}{4} = 22$.

27. (B)

$F(-3) = -(-3) + 3 = 6$. $F(2) = (2)(2) + 3 = 7$. $F(4) = (3)(4) = 12$. $6 + 7 - 12 = 1$.

28. (B)

A is an upper triangular matrix. As we know, if A is an n × n triangular matrix (upper or lower), then det(A) is the product of the entries on the main diagonal.

Hence,

det (A) $= (2) \times (-3) \times (6) \times (9) \times (4) = -1,296$.

29. (C)

Using the definition of matrix addition, add the (ij) entry of A to the (ij) entry of B. Thus,

$$A + B = \begin{bmatrix} 2 & 3 & 7 \\ 4 & m & \sqrt{3} \\ 1 & 5 & a \end{bmatrix} + \begin{bmatrix} \alpha & \beta & \delta \\ \sqrt{5} & 3 & 1 \\ p & q & 4 \end{bmatrix}$$

$$= \begin{bmatrix} 2 + \alpha & 3 + \beta & 7 + \delta \\ 4 + \sqrt{5} & m + 3 & \sqrt{3} + 1 \\ 1 + p & 5 + q & a + 4 \end{bmatrix}$$

30. (A)

Use cofactor expansion.

$$A = \begin{bmatrix} 2 & 0 & 3 & 0 \\ 2 & 1 & 1 & 2 \\ 3 & -1 & 1 & -2 \\ 2 & 1 & -2 & 1 \end{bmatrix}$$

Expanding along the first row:

$$\det(A) = 2 \begin{bmatrix} 1 & 1 & 2 \\ -1 & 1 & -2 \\ 1 & -2 & 1 \end{bmatrix} + 3 \begin{bmatrix} 2 & 1 & 2 \\ 3 & -1 & -2 \\ 2 & 1 & 1 \end{bmatrix}$$

Note that the minors whose multiplying factors were zero have been eliminated. This illustrates the general principle that, when evaluating determinants, expansion along the row (or column) containing the most zeros is the optimal procedure.

Add the second row to the first row for each of the 3 × 3 determinants:

$$\det(A) = 2 \begin{bmatrix} 0 & 2 & 0 \\ -1 & 1 & -2 \\ 1 & -2 & 1 \end{bmatrix} + 3 \begin{bmatrix} 5 & 0 & 0 \\ 3 & -1 & -2 \\ 2 & 1 & 1 \end{bmatrix}$$

Now expand the above determinants by minors using the first row.

$$\det(A) = 2(-2) \begin{bmatrix} -1 & -2 \\ 1 & 1 \end{bmatrix} + 3(5) \begin{bmatrix} -1 & -2 \\ 1 & 1 \end{bmatrix}$$

$$= (-4)(-1 + 2) + (15)(-1 + 2)$$

$$= -4 + 15 = 11$$

31.

- $Z_8 = \{0, 1, 2, 3, \ldots, 7\}$. $3 + 7 = 10$. $10 \div 8 = 1$ with a remainder of 2. Thus, $3 \oplus 7 = 2$.

- $Z_{10} = \{0, 1, 2, 3, \ldots, 9\}$. $(4)(9) = 36$. $36 \div 10 = 3$ with a remainder of 6. Thus, $4 * 9 = 6$.

- $Z_{12} = \{0, 1, 2, 3, \ldots, 11\}$. We note that $x \oplus 0 = x$ for all $x \in Z_{12}$, so 0 is the identity element under $\oplus$. Let p = additive inverse of 5, so that $5 \oplus p = 0$. Since $12 \div 12 = 1$ with a remainder of 0, $5 + p = 12$. This means that $p = 7$.

- $Z_{13} = \{0, 1, 2, 3, \ldots, 12\}$. We note that $x * 1 = x$ for all $x \in Z_{13}$, so 1 is the identity element under $*$. Let q = multiplicative inverse of 8, so that $8 * q = 1$. Try all $q \in Z_{13}$. For $q = 2$, $8 * q \neq 1$, for $q = 3$, $8 * q \neq 1$, for $q = 4$, $8 * q \neq 1$, for $q = 5$, $8 * q = 1$. This means that $q = 5$ is the multiplicative inverse of 8. Note that this results from the fact that $(8)(5) = 40$ and $40 \div 13 = 3$ with a remainder of 1

32.

- Since the highest exponent of the numerator (2) exceeds the highest exponent of the denominator (1), there is no horizontal line asymptote.

The vertical asymptote is found by setting the denominator equal to zero. $2x - 4 = 0$ implies $x = 2$. So $x = 2$ is a vertical line asymptote.

To determine the oblique asymptote, we perform long division on $\frac{(x^2 - 3)}{(2x - 4)}$ to get $\frac{x}{2} + 1 + \frac{1}{2x - 4}$.

As $x \to \infty$, $\frac{1}{2x - 4} \to 0$. Thus $y = \frac{x}{2} + 1$ is an oblique line asymptote.

- The x-intercepts are found by setting $f(x) = 0$. Solving $0 = \frac{(x^2 - 3)}{(2x - 4)}$, or $0 = x^2 - 3$, leads to $x = \pm\sqrt{3}$. Thus, the x-intercepts are $(\pm\sqrt{3}, 0)$.

The y-intercept is found by substituting 0 for x. $f(0) = \frac{(0 - 3)}{(0 - 4)} = \frac{3}{4}$. Thus, the y-intercept is $\left(0, \frac{3}{4}\right)$.

33.

If $\begin{pmatrix} 5 \\ 6 \\ 9 \end{pmatrix}$ could be written as a linear combination of α_1, α_2, and α_3, then there would be three real numbers a, b, c, such that $\begin{pmatrix} 5 \\ 6 \\ 9 \end{pmatrix} = a\begin{pmatrix} 1 \\ 2 \\ 4 \end{pmatrix} + b\begin{pmatrix} 1 \\ 0 \\ 0 \end{pmatrix} + c\begin{pmatrix} 1 \\ 1 \\ 2 \end{pmatrix}$.

This is equivalent to solving the system of equations:

(1) $a + b + c = 5$

(2) $2a + c = 6$

(3) $4a + 2c = 9$

By doubling Equation (2), we get $4a + 2c = 12$. Now subtract Equation (3) to get $0 = 3$. This implies no solution, so $\begin{pmatrix} 5 \\ 6 \\ 9 \end{pmatrix}$ cannot be written as a linear combination of α_1, α_2, and α_3.

34.

We first prove that the statement is true for $n = 1$.

$1 - \frac{1}{2^1} = 1 - \frac{1}{2} = \frac{1}{2^1}$.

Next assume that the statement is true for $n = k$, so that $\frac{1}{2^1} + \frac{1}{2^2} + \frac{1}{2^3} + \cdots + \frac{1}{2^k} = 1 - \frac{1}{2^k}$.

Add $\frac{1}{2^{k+1}}$ to both sides of the last equation to get

$\frac{1}{2^1} + \frac{1}{2^2} + \frac{1}{2^3} + \cdots + \frac{1}{2^k} + \frac{1}{2^{k+1}} = 1 - \frac{1}{2^k} + \frac{1}{2^{k+1}}$.

We now rewrite the right side of this equation as $1 - \frac{2}{2^{k+1}} + \frac{1}{2^{k+1}}$, which becomes $1 - \frac{1}{2^{k+1}}$.

Note: Multiply $\frac{1}{2^k}$ by $\frac{2^1}{2^1}$ and use the law of exponents to express $2^k \cdot 2^1$ as 2^{k+1}.

The proof is complete since assuming that the formula works for $n = k$ implies that the formula works for $n = k + 1$.

CSET

Mathematics

Practice Test 2

Subtest II

Answer Sheet

1. Ⓐ Ⓑ Ⓒ Ⓓ   16. Ⓐ Ⓑ Ⓒ Ⓓ

2. Ⓐ Ⓑ Ⓒ Ⓓ   17. Ⓐ Ⓑ Ⓒ Ⓓ

3. Ⓐ Ⓑ Ⓒ Ⓓ   18. Ⓐ Ⓑ Ⓒ Ⓓ

4. Ⓐ Ⓑ Ⓒ Ⓓ   19. Ⓐ Ⓑ Ⓒ Ⓓ

5. Ⓐ Ⓑ Ⓒ Ⓓ   20. Ⓐ Ⓑ Ⓒ Ⓓ

6. Ⓐ Ⓑ Ⓒ Ⓓ   21. Ⓐ Ⓑ Ⓒ Ⓓ

7. Ⓐ Ⓑ Ⓒ Ⓓ   22. Ⓐ Ⓑ Ⓒ Ⓓ

8. Ⓐ Ⓑ Ⓒ Ⓓ   23. Ⓐ Ⓑ Ⓒ Ⓓ

9. Ⓐ Ⓑ Ⓒ Ⓓ   24. Ⓐ Ⓑ Ⓒ Ⓓ

10. Ⓐ Ⓑ Ⓒ Ⓓ   25. Ⓐ Ⓑ Ⓒ Ⓓ

11. Ⓐ Ⓑ Ⓒ Ⓓ   26. Ⓐ Ⓑ Ⓒ Ⓓ

12. Ⓐ Ⓑ Ⓒ Ⓓ   27. Ⓐ Ⓑ Ⓒ Ⓓ

13. Ⓐ Ⓑ Ⓒ Ⓓ   28. Ⓐ Ⓑ Ⓒ Ⓓ

14. Ⓐ Ⓑ Ⓒ Ⓓ   29. Ⓐ Ⓑ Ⓒ Ⓓ

15. Ⓐ Ⓑ Ⓒ Ⓓ   30. Ⓐ Ⓑ Ⓒ Ⓓ

CSET: Mathematics Practice Test 2
Subtest II*
Geometry; Probability and Statistics

TIME: When taking the actual test, you will have one five-hour test session in which to complete the subtest(s) for which you are registered.

<u>Directions</u>: This test consists of two sections: 30 multiple-choice and four constructed-response questions. The constructed-response questions involve written responses.

A calculator will be needed and will be allowed only for Subtest II. You will be required to bring your own graphing calculator. Please check the current version of the CSET registration bulletin for the list of approved models of graphing calculators.

---

1. Point Q is located at $(2, -3)$. If this point is rotated 90° clockwise about the origin, what will be the new coordinates of Q?

   (A) $(3, 2)$

   (B) $(2, 3)$

   (C) $(-2, -3)$

   (D) $(-3, -2)$

2. A linear translation on a coordinate plane is defined as follows: $(x, y) \rightarrow (x - 4, y + 8)$. If the point $(-7, -1)$ represents the image of a linear translation for point P, what are the coordinates of P?

   (A) $(-11, 7)$

   (B) $(-5, 1)$

   (C) $(-3, -9)$

   (D) $(-1, -7)$

3. What is the area of a circle whose equation is given by $x^2 + 8x + y^2 + 12y + 3 = 0$?

   (A) 98π (C) 49π

   (B) 64π (D) 14π

4. A rectangular piece of metal has an area of 35m^2 and a perimeter of 24 m. Which of the following are possible dimensions of the piece?

   (A) $8\,\text{m} \times 4\,\text{m}$

   (B) $5\,\text{m} \times 7\,\text{m}$

   (C) $35\,\text{m} \times 1\,\text{m}$

   (D) $6\,\text{m} \times 6\,\text{m}$

---

*According to the test administrator, Subtest II is always given first in the test session. For further details, visit the official CSET website at *http://www.cset.nesinc.com.*

5. If the angles of a triangle *ABC* are in the ratio of $3 : 5 : 7$, then the triangle is:

   (A) acute

   (B) right

   (C) isosceles

   (D) obtuse

6. Triangle *ABC* is similar to triangle *ADE*. If the area of triangle *ABC* is 324, the area of triangle *ADE* is 441, and $AC = 36$, what is the length of $\overline{CE}$?

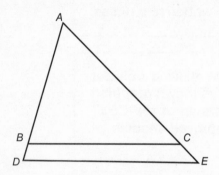

   (A) 3   (C) 9

   (B) 6   (D) 12

7. If the hypotenuse of a right triangle is $x + 1$ and one of the legs is x, then the other leg is

   (A) $\sqrt{2x + 1}$ (C) $\sqrt{x^2 + (x + 1)^2}$

   (B) $\sqrt{2x} + 1$ (D) $\sqrt{2x} - 1$

8.

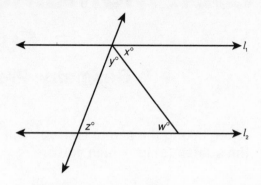

   In the figure shown above, $x° = y°$. Which additional information would be sufficient to conclude that line l_1 is parallel to line l_2?

   (A) $z = 180 - 2x$ (C) $z = 90 - w$

   (B) $w = 180 - y - z$ (D) $w = z - x$

9.

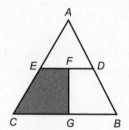

   The figure above represents a dartboard in which $\triangle ABC$ is equilateral, *E* is the midpoint of $\overline{AC}$, *D* is the midpoint if $\overline{AB}$, *F* is the midpoint of $\overline{ED}$, and *G* is the midpoint of $\overline{BC}$. If a dart is thrown and lands on the dartboard, what is the probability that it lands in the shaded area?

   (A) $\dfrac{1}{4}$ (C) $\dfrac{1}{3}$

   (B) $\dfrac{3}{10}$ (D) $\dfrac{3}{8}$

10. If the radius of a sphere is multiplied by 3, then the volume of the sphere is multiplied by

   (A) 3   (C) 9

   (B) 6   (D) 27

11. If m $\overarc{ABC}$ is $\frac{3}{2}\pi$ radians, then y is equal to

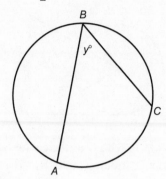

(A) 90° (C) 45°

(B) 72° (D) 36°

12. Which of the following alternatives is correct?

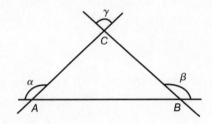

(A) $\alpha + \beta + \gamma = 180°$

(B) $\gamma - \alpha + 180° = \beta$

(C) $\alpha = \beta + \gamma$

(D) $\gamma = \alpha + \beta$

13. A circular region rotated 360° around its diameter as an axis generates a

(A) cube.   (C) cone.

(B) cylinder.   (D) sphere.

14. In the cube $ABCDEFGH$ with side $AB = 2$, what is the length of diagonal AF?

(A) $2\sqrt{6}$

(B) $2\sqrt{5}$

(C) $2\sqrt{3}$

(D) $2\sqrt{2}$

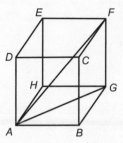

15. In triangle ABC, angle A is a right angle, m $\angle C = 30°$ and the length of BC is 7. What are the lengths of sides AB and AC?

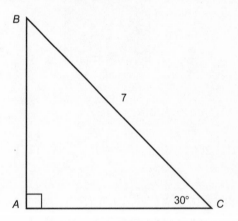

(A) 4.9, 4.9   (C) 3.5, 4.9

(B) 2.0, 6.1   (D) 3.5, 6.1

16.

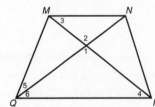

Note: Figure not drawn to scale.

In the figure shown above, $MNPQ$ is an isosceles trapezoid, with $\overline{MN} \parallel \overline{QP}$. Which of the following is *not necessarily* true?

(A) $\angle 3 \cong \angle 4$ (C) $\angle 1 \cong \angle 2$

(B) $\angle 5 \cong \angle 6$ (D) $\angle 4 \cong \angle 6$

17. Let T be a transformation function, $T(x, y) = (3.5x, 6.3y)$. Suppose the vertices of a rectangle of area 5 undergo the transformation $T(x, y)$. What is the area of the transformed rectangle?

    (A) 19.6   (C) 110.25

    (B) 22.05   (D) 259.7

18. What is the area of the shaded portion of the rectangle? The heavy dot represents the center of the semicircle.

    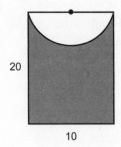

    (A) $200 - 100\pi$ (C) $\dfrac{400 - 25\pi}{2}$

    (B) $200 - 25\pi$ (D) $\dfrac{200 - 25\pi}{2}$

19. For rectangle $PQRS$, point P is located at $(1, 0)$ and point Q is located at $(8, -3)$. What is the slope of $\overline{QR}$?

    (A) $\dfrac{7}{3}$ (C) $-\dfrac{1}{3}$

    (B) $\dfrac{1}{3}$ (D) $-\dfrac{7}{3}$

20. For rhombus $ABCD$, the point A is located at $(-1, 5)$ and the point B is located at $(5, 3)$. Which one of the following could represent the coordinates of point C?

    (A) $(3, -4)$ (C) $(7, -3)$

    (B) $(5, -1)$ (D) $(9, -2)$

21. Look at the following geometric proof.

    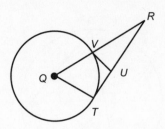

    Given: A circle with Q as the center, $\overline{RT}$ is tangent to the circle at point T, and $\overline{UV}$ is perpendicular to $\overline{RT}$.

    Prove: m $\sphericalangle RVU$ = m $\overset{\frown}{VT}$

Statements	Reasons
1. A circle with Q as the center, $\overline{RT}$ is tangent to the circle at point T, and $\overline{UV}$ is perpendicular to $\overline{RT}$.	1. Given
2. m $\sphericalangle QTR = 90°$	2. A tangent to a circle is perpendicular to a radius at the point of contact.
3. m $\sphericalangle VUR = 90°$	3. Definition of perpendicular lines.
4. $\overline{QT} // \overline{UV}$	4. Two lines perpendicular to the same line are parallel.
5.	5.
6.	6.
7. m $\sphericalangle RVU$ = m $\overset{\frown}{VT}$	7. Substitution.

Which one of the following pairs of statements and reasons would be the MOST APPROPRIATE in Steps 5 and 6?

(A)

Statement	Reason
5. ∡R ≅ ∡R	5. Identity
6. ΔRVU ∽ ΔRQT	6. AAA postulate

(B)

Statement	Reason
5. m ∡Q = m ∡RVU	5. When parallel lines are crossed by a transversal, the corresponding angles are equal.
6. m ∡Q = m $\overparen{VT}$	6. A central angle of a circle has the same measure as its intercepted arc.

(C)

Statement	Reason
5. ∡R ≅ ∡R	5. Identity
6. m ∡Q = m $\overparen{VT}$	6. A central angle of a circle has the same measure as its intercepted arc.

(D)

Statement	Reason
5. m ∡Q = m ∡T	5. Base angles of an isosceles triangle are equal.
6. m ∡Q = m $\overparen{VT}$	6. AAA postulate

22.

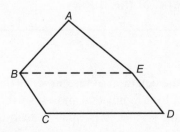

Note: Figure not drawn to scale

In the figure above, *BCDE* is a parallelogram. The distance from point *A* to $\overline{BE}$ is 9 and the distance from point *A* to $\overline{CD}$ is 16.5. If the area of *ABCDE* is 136.8, what is the length of $\overline{CD}$?

(A) 16.55   (C) 8.45

(B) 11.40   (D) 6.50

23. A 7-sided die is rolled twice. The numbers on the die are 1 through 7. What is the probability that the die will show a prime number on the first roll or an even number on the second roll, or both of these results?

(A) $\dfrac{8}{49}$ (C) $\dfrac{37}{49}$

(B) $\dfrac{2}{7}$ (D) $\dfrac{6}{7}$

24. There are 30 slips of paper in a jar. The slips are numbered 1 through 30. An experiment consists of drawing three slips of paper, one at a time, with *no* replacement. If event *E* consists of all outcomes in which the first two numbers drawn are even and the third number is odd, how many outcomes are there in *E*?

(A) 5880   (C) 3150

(B) 3375   (D) 2730

25. Ten people are to be seated in a row with 10 seats in a movie theater. Two of the 10 people do not want to sit in either of the two end seats of this row. In how many accommodating ways can all ten people be seated?

(A) 20,120   (C) 2,257,920

(B) 40,320   (D) 3,628,800

26. Which of the following is the best estimate of the standard deviation for the distribution shown in the diagram below?

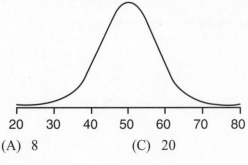

(A) 8   (C) 20

(B) 15   (D) 30

27. The display below shows the cumulative relative frequency histogram of scores from the 20-question math placement examination taken by 40 freshmen upon entering a high school.

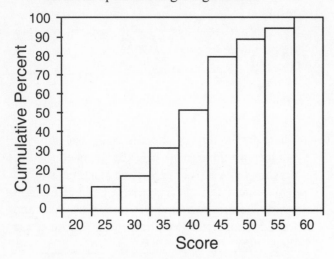

Which of the following is a correct statement based on the information in the display?

(A) The median score is 30.

(B) Most students scored above 50.

(C) No one scored 35 on this test.

(D) There were about equal numbers of students with scores between 50 and 60.

28. The mean number of hours per week that a teenager uses the computer is 10, with a standard deviation of 1.5 hours. Assuming a normal distribution, what is the best approximation to the percent of teenagers who use the computer more than 7.6 hours?

(A) 94.5   (C) 64.5

(B) 75.5   (D) 55.5

29. In order to be accepted into a program at West Point, a person must score in the top 2% of a standardized test on general knowledge. Historically, the mean score for this test is 70, with a standard deviation of 3. What would be the *minimum* integer score on this test in order for a person to be accepted into this program?

(A) 83   (C) 79

(B) 81   (D) 77

30. Look at the following problem:

Lorraine can take any one of three roads to go from city *A* to city *B*, any one of five roads to go from city *B* to city *C*, and any one of six roads to go from city *C* to city *D*. How many different routes are possible for Lorraine to travel from city *A* to city *D*, by way of cities *B* and *C*?

Which of the following would be the *best* way to solve the above problem?

(A) Tree diagram   (C) Frequency curve

(B) Pie graph   (D) Probability table

Constructed-response questions 31–34:
For each response you will use up to two pages of the lined pages provided with the CSET test. Please see the sample pages at the end of the book.

31. Find the equation of the curve, in simplified form, traced by a point that moves so that its distance from the line $y = 2$ is equal to its distance from the point $(4, -2)$. Also, determine what type of curve is traced.

32.

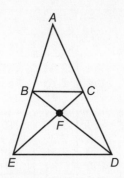

In the diagram shown above, $\overline{AE} = \overline{AD}$. Also, the area of trapezoid *BCDE* is $\dfrac{3}{4}$ of the area of triangle *AED*. Prove that the distance from point *F* to $\overline{DE}$ is twice the distance from point *F* to $\overline{BC}$.

33.

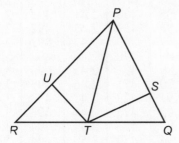

In the diagram above, $\overline{PT}$ is the angle bisector of $\angle RPQ$. $\overline{TS}$ is perpendicular to $\overline{PQ}$ and $\overline{TU}$ is perpendicular to $\overline{PR}$. The area of $\triangle PQR$ is 200 and the area of $\triangle PRT$ is 120. If $\overline{PQ} = 16$, what is the length of $\overline{PR}$? Show all work in your computations.

34. A company that manufactures laundry detergent claims that it uniformly puts 16.4 ounces of detergent into each box that it sells. The Quality Control division checks production of these boxes to ensure that their weights are not statistically different from 16.4 ounces. Suppose that the Quality Control division checks a sample of 49 boxes and finds that the mean weight is 16.37 ounces with a sample standard deviation of .14 ounces.

- State the null hypothesis and the alternative hypothesis.

- Determine the value of the *z*-test statistics for this sample.

- Using the following table of *z*-scores for a normal distribution, determine if, at the 5% level of significance, the mean of the sample of 49 boxes is statistically different from the population mean of 16.4 ounces.

The column under *A* gives the proportion of the area under the entire curve that is between $z = 0$ and a positive value of z.

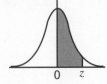

Because the curve is symmetric about the 0-value, the area between $z = 0$ and a *negative* value of z can be found by using the corresponding positive value of *z*.

Area Under the Standard Normal Curve

z	A	z	A	z	A	z	A	z	A	z	A
.00	.000	.56	.212	1.12	.369	1.68	.454	2.24	.487	2.80	.497
.01	.004	.57	.216	1.13	.371	1.69	.454	2.25	.488	2.81	.498
.02	.008	.58	.219	1.14	.373	1.70	.455	2.26	.488	2.82	.498
.03	.012	.59	.222	1.15	.375	1.71	.456	2.27	.488	2.83	.498
.04	.016	.60	.226	1.16	.377	1.72	.457	2.28	.489	2.84	.498
.05	.020	.61	.229	1.17	.379	1.73	.458	2.29	.489	2.85	.498
.06	.024	.62	.232	1.18	.381	1.74	.459	2.30	.489	2.86	.498
.07	.028	.63	.236	1.19	.383	1.75	.460	2.31	.490	2.87	.498
.08	.032	.64	.239	1.20	.385	1.76	.461	2.32	.490	2.88	.498
.09	.036	.65	.242	1.21	.387	1.77	.462	2.33	.490	2.89	.498
.10	.040	.66	.245	1.22	.389	1.78	.462	2.34	.490	2.90	.498
.11	.044	.67	.249	1.23	.391	1.79	.463	2.35	.491	2.91	.498
.12	.048	.68	.252	1.24	.393	1.80	.464	2.36	.491	2.92	.498
.13	.052	.69	.255	1.25	.394	1.81	.465	2.37	.491	2.93	.498
.14	.056	.70	.258	1.26	.396	1.82	.466	2.38	.491	2.94	.498
.15	.060	.71	.261	1.27	.398	1.83	.466	2.39	.492	2.95	.498
.16	.064	.72	.264	1.28	.400	1.84	.467	2.40	.492	2.96	.498
.17	.067	.73	.267	1.29	.401	1.85	.468	2.41	.492	2.97	.499
.18	.071	.74	.270	1.30	.403	1.86	.469	2.42	.492	2.98	.499
.19	.075	.75	.273	1.31	.405	1.87	.469	2.43	.492	2.99	.499
.20	.079	.76	.276	1.32	.407	1.88	.470	2.44	.493	3.00	.499
.21	.083	.77	.279	1.33	.408	1.89	.471	2.45	.493	3.01	.499
.22	.087	.78	.282	1.34	.410	1.90	.471	2.46	.493	3.02	.499
.23	.091	.79	.285	1.35	.411	1.91	.472	2.47	.493	3.03	.499
.24	.095	.80	.288	1.36	.413	1.92	.473	2.48	.493	3.04	.499
.25	.099	.81	.291	1.37	.415	1.93	.473	2.49	.494	3.05	.499
.26	.103	.82	.294	1.38	.416	1.94	.474	2.50	.494	3.06	.499
.27	.106	.83	.297	1.39	.418	1.95	.474	2.51	.494	3.07	.499
.28	.110	.84	.300	1.40	.419	1.96	.475	2.52	.494	3.08	.499
.29	.114	.85	.302	1.41	.421	1.97	.476	2.53	.494	3.09	.499
.30	.118	.86	.305	1.42	.422	1.98	.476	2.54	.494	3.10	.499
.31	.122	.87	.308	1.43	.424	1.99	.477	2.55	.495	3.11	.499
.32	.126	.88	.311	1.44	.425	2.00	.477	2.56	.495	3.12	.499
.33	.129	.89	.313	1.45	.426	2.01	.478	2.57	.495	3.13	.499
.34	.133	.90	.316	1.46	.428	2.02	.478	2.58	.495	3.14	.499
.35	.137	.91	.319	1.47	.429	2.03	.479	2.59	.495	3.15	.499
.36	.141	.92	.321	1.48	.431	2.04	.479	2.60	.495	3.16	.499
.37	.144	.93	.324	1.49	.432	2.05	.480	2.61	.495	3.17	.499
.38	.148	.94	.326	1.50	.433	2.06	.480	2.62	.496	3.18	.499
.39	.152	.95	.329	1.51	.434	2.07	.481	2.63	.496	3.19	.499
.40	.155	.96	.331	1.52	.436	2.08	.481	2.64	.496	3.20	.499
.41	.159	.97	.334	1.53	.437	2.09	.482	2.65	.496	3.21	.499
.42	.163	.98	.336	1.54	.438	2.10	.482	2.66	.496	3.22	.499
.43	.166	.99	.339	1.55	.439	2.11	.483	2.67	.496	3.23	.499
.44	.170	1.00	.341	1.56	.441	2.12	.483	2.68	.496	3.24	.499
.45	.174	1.01	.344	1.57	.442	2.13	.483	2.69	.496	3.25	.499
.46	.177	1.02	.346	1.58	.443	2.14	.484	2.70	.497	3.26	.499
.47	.181	1.03	.348	1.59	.444	2.15	.484	2.71	.497	3.27	.499
.48	.184	1.04	.351	1.60	.445	2.16	.485	2.72	.497	3.28	.499
.49	.188	1.05	.353	1.61	.446	2.17	.485	2.73	.497	3.29	.499
.50	.191	1.06	.355	1.62	.447	2.18	.485	2.74	.497	3.30	.500
.51	.195	1.07	.358	1.63	.448	2.19	.486	2.75	.497	3.31	.500
.52	.198	1.08	.360	1.64	.449	2.20	.486	2.76	.497	3.32	.500
.53	.202	1.09	.362	1.65	.451	2.21	.486	2.77	.497	3.33	.500
.54	.205	1.10	.364	1.66	.452	2.22	.487	2.78	.497	3.34	.500
.55	.209	1.11	.367	1.67	.453	2.23	.487	2.79	.497	3.35	.500

Answer Key

Q No.	Correct Answer	Q No.	Correct Answer
1.	(D)	18.	(C)
2.	(C)	19.	(A)
3.	(C)	20.	(C)
4.	(B)	21.	(B)
5.	(A)	22.	(B)
6.	(B)	23.	(C)
7.	(A)	24.	(C)
8.	(A)	25.	(C)
9.	(D)	26.	(A)
10.	(D)	27.	(D)
11.	(C)	28.	(A)
12.	(B)	29.	(D)
13.	(D)	30.	(A)
14.	(C)	31.	Constructed-Response
15.	(D)	32.	Constructed-Response
16.	(B)	33.	Constructed-Response
17.	(C)	34.	Constructed-Response

Detailed Explanations of Answers

1. (D)

If a point located at (x, y) is rotated 90° clockwise about the origin, its new location is given by $(y, -x)$. Thus, the point $(2, -3)$ becomes $(-3, -2)$.

2. (C)

Since $(-7, -1)$ represents the image of point P, we need to reverse the order for finding each of the coordinates of P. Mathematically, $x - 4 = -7$ and $y + 8 = -1$. Solving, $x = -3$ and $y = -9$.

3. (C)

Rewrite the equation as $(x^2 + 8x + 16) + (y^2 + 12y + 36) = -3 + 16 + 36$. Then, $(x + 4)^2 + (y + 6)^2 = 49$. A circle with this equation will have a center at $(-4, -6)$ and a radius of $\sqrt{49} = 7$. Thus, its area is $(\pi)(7)^2 = 49\pi$.

4. (B)

The perimeter $(P) = (2)(\text{length}) + (2)(\text{width})$. For answer choice (B), the perimeter $= (2)(7) + (2)(5) = 35$ and its area $= (7)(5) = 35$. For answer choice (A), the perimeter $= 24$, but the area $= 32$. For answer choice (C), the area $= 35$ and the perimeter $= 72$. For answer choice (D), the perimeter $= 24$, but the area $= 36$.

5. (A)

The three angles can be represented by $3x$, $5x$, and $7x$. Their sum is 180°, so $3x + 5x + 7x = 180$. Solving, $x = 12$. The values of the three angles are $(3)(12)$, $(5)(12)$, and $(7)(12) = 36°$, $60°$, and $84°$. Since each angle is less than 90°, the triangle is acute.

6. (B)

The ratio of the area of two similar polygons is equal to the square of the ratio of the lengths of any two corresponding sides. Thus:

$$\frac{\text{Area } \Delta ABC}{\text{Area } \Delta ADE} = \left(\frac{AC}{AE}\right)^2$$

$$(AE)^2 = \frac{(AC)^2(\text{Area } \Delta ADE)}{\text{Area } \Delta ABC}$$

$$AE = \sqrt{\frac{(AC)^2(\text{Area } \Delta ADE)}{\text{Area } \Delta ABC}}$$

$$= \sqrt{36^2\left(\frac{441}{324}\right)}$$

Since $441 \div 324 \times 36^2 = 1764$,

$$AE = 42. \text{ Since } AC + CE = AE, \text{ then}$$

$$CE = AE - AC$$

$$= 42 - 36$$

$$= 6$$

7. (A)

If a, b, c are the sides of a right triangle, with c as the hypotenuse, the Pythagorean Theorem states that $a^2 + b^2 = c^2$. Substitute x for a and substitute $x + 1$ for c. Then $x^2 + b^2 = (x + 1)^2$. This simplifies to $x^2 + b^2 = x^2 + 2x + 1$. So $b^2 = 2x + 1$. Finally, taking the square root of each side, $b = \sqrt{2x + 1}$.

8.   (A)

If $z = 180 - (x + y)$, we would have parallel lines, since interior angles of the same side of the transversal would be supplementary. Since $x = y$, the expression $180 - (x + y)$ is equivalent to $180 - 2x$. The statement in answer choice (B) would always be true, whether the lines were parallel or not, since the sum of the angles of any triangle is 180°. The statement in answer choice (C) would be impossible since this would mean that each of x and y equals 90, and the transversal would coincide with line l_1. The statement in answer choice (D) would imply that since $z = w + x = w + y$, $z = 90$. Each of x and y would be the same value less than 90, but would not imply that $l_1 \parallel l_2$.

9.   (D)

Because $\triangle ABC$ is equilateral, $\angle A = \angle B = \angle C = 60°$. If we assign the following numerical values for the lengths of the sides, $\overline{AC} = \overline{AB} = \overline{CB} = 2$, then $\overline{AE} = \overline{AD} = \overline{CG} = \overline{GB} = 1$. In addition, we can find the height of $\triangle ABC$ to be $\sqrt{3}$ when a perpendicular bisector is dropped from A; note that a 30–60–90 triangle is formed. Thus the area of $\triangle ABC = \left(\frac{1}{2}\right)(2)(\sqrt{3}) = \sqrt{3}$. Using the same process we find the area of $\triangle ADE = \left(\frac{1}{2}\right)(1)\left(\frac{\sqrt{3}}{2}\right) = \left(\frac{\sqrt{3}}{4}\right)$. The area of the shaded region, is half the area of $EDBC$, the difference between the areas of the triangle. Subtract the area of $\triangle ADE$ from the area of $\triangle ABC$ and divide by 2:

$$\text{Area}(EFGC) = \frac{\sqrt{3} - \frac{\sqrt{3}}{4}}{2} = \frac{3\sqrt{3}}{4} \div 2 = \frac{3\sqrt{3}}{3}.$$

To find the probability, divide the area of the shaded region by the area of $\triangle ABC$:

$$\frac{3\sqrt{3}}{8} \div \sqrt{3}, \text{ or } \left(\frac{3\sqrt{3}}{8}\right)\left(\frac{1}{\sqrt{3}}\right) = \frac{3}{8}.$$

10.   (D)

The Volume (V) of a sphere $= \left(\frac{4}{3}\right)(\pi)(R^3)$, where R is the radius. If R is increased by a factor of 3, it becomes $3R$ and the new volume is

$$V = \left(\frac{4}{3}\right)(\pi)(3R)^3$$

$$= \left(\frac{4}{3}\right)(\pi)(27)(R^3)$$

which is 27 times the original sphere, no matter what 'R' is.

11.   (C)

From a theorem, we know that the measure of an inscribed angle is equal to half the intercepted arc.

We are told that $m\overset{\frown}{ABC}$ is $\frac{3}{2}\pi$ radians. There are 2π radians in a circle. Therefore, the intercepted arc is the remaining $\frac{\pi}{2}$ radians.

Converting to degrees:

$$\left(\frac{\pi}{2}\right)\left(\frac{180}{\pi}\right) = 90°.$$

Then angle y is half of this:

$$y = \frac{90°}{2} = 45°.$$

12.   (B)

Label the triangle as shown below:

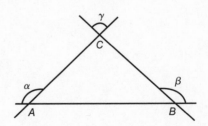

For the interior angles of $\triangle ABC$, the angle at point A is supplementary to α, so that its value is $180 - \alpha$. The angle at point B is supplementary to β, so that its value is $180 - \beta$. The angle at point C is vertical to γ, so that its value is γ. The sum of the interior angles of a triangle is $180°$, so $(180 - \alpha) + (180 - \beta) + \gamma = 180$. Simplifying, $-\alpha + 180 - \beta + \gamma = 0$, which is equivalent to $\gamma - \alpha + 180 = \beta$.

13. (D)

A sphere is formed when a circle is rotated $360°$ about its diameter.

14. (C)

Note that each edge of the cube $= 2$. $\triangle ABG$ is a right triangle, so by using the Pythagorean Theorem, $AB^2 + BG^2 = AG^2$, $2^2 + 2^2 = AG^2$. Simplifying, $8 = AG^2$, so $AG = \sqrt{8}$. $\triangle AFG$ is also a right triangle, so that $AG^2 + FG^2 = AF^2$. By substitution, $(\sqrt{8})^2 + 2^2 = AF^2$. Simplifying, $12 = AF^2$, so $AF = \sqrt{12} = 2\sqrt{3}$.

15. (D)

This is a $30°$, $60°$, $90°$ triangle. The hypotenuse (BC) is twice the length of the shorter leg (AB), and the length of the longer leg (AC) is the length of the shorter leg multiplied by $\sqrt{3}$.

$$2AB = BC$$
$$AB = \frac{BC}{2}$$
$$AB = \frac{7.0}{2} = 3.5$$

and

$$AC = \sqrt{3} \times AB$$
$$= \sqrt{3} \times 3.5$$
$$\sqrt{3} \times 3.5 = 6.1$$

16. (B)

$\angle 5$ and $\angle 6$ together form the base angle at point Q, but they need not be congruent. $\angle 3 \cong \angle 4$, since they are alternate interior angles of parallel lines. $\angle 1 \cong \angle 2$, since they are vertical angles. Triangles MPQ and NQP can be shown to be congruent by side-side-side. (Note that the diagonals of an isosceles trapezoid are congruent.) Then $\angle 4 \cong \angle 6$, since they are corresponding parts of congruent triangles.

17. (C)

The width will be multiplied by 3.5 and the length by 6.3, so the area will be $3.5 \times 6.3 = 22.05$ times the original area. $22.05 \times 5 = 110.25$.

18. (C)

The area of the rectangle $= (20)(10) = 200$. The area of the semicircle $= \left(\frac{1}{2}\right)(\pi)(R^2)$, where R is the radius. Since the diameter $= 10$, the radius $= 5$. Thus the area of the semicircle $= \left(\frac{1}{2}\right)(\pi)(5^2) = \left(\frac{25}{2}\right)(\pi)$. The shaded area is the difference between the area of the rectangle and the area of the semicircle, $200 - \left(\frac{25}{2}\right)(\pi)$, which is equivalent to $= \frac{(400 - 25\pi)}{2}$.

19. (A)

The slope of $\overline{PQ} = \frac{(-3 - 0)}{8 - 1} = -\frac{3}{7}$. Since $\overline{QR}$ is perpendicular to $\overline{PQ}$, its slope must be the negative reciprocal of $-\frac{3}{7}$, which is $\frac{7}{3}$.

20. (C)

The distance of
$\overline{AB} = \sqrt{[(5 - (-1)]^2 + (3 - 5)^2} = \sqrt{36 + 4} = \sqrt{40}$.
Point C must be at a location such that the distance of $\overline{BC}$ is also $\sqrt{40}$. Note that for answer choice (C), the distance of $BC = \sqrt{(7 - 5)^2 + (-3 - 3)^2} = \sqrt{4 + 36} = \sqrt{40}$.
For answer choice (A), the distance would be $\sqrt{53}$. For answer choice (B), the distance would be $\sqrt{16}$. For answer choice (D), the distance would be $\sqrt{41}$.

21. (B)

After establishing that $\overline{QT}$ is parallel to $\overline{UV}$, the next step should be to state that $m \angle Q = m \angle RVU$ because corresponding angles are equal. Then to prove that $m \angle RVU = m \overset{\frown}{VT}$, it is necessary to establish that $m \angle Q = m \overset{\frown}{VT}$. This is done by noting that a central angle's measurement is equal to that of its intercepted arc.

22. (B)

The height of parallelogram $BCDE$ is $16.5 - 9 = 7.5$. If x is the length of CD, then the area of parallelogram $BCDE$ can be represented by $7.5x$. Since $BE = CD$, the area of $\triangle ABE$ can be represented by $\frac{1}{2}(x)(9) = 4.5x$.

Then, $7.5x + 4.5x = 136.8$

Solving, $x = \frac{136.8}{12} = 11.40$.

23. (C)

The prime numbers between 1 and 7, inclusive, are 2, 3, 5, and 7; so the probability of getting a prime number on the first roll is $\frac{4}{7}$. Since the even numbers

are 2, 4, and 6, the probability of getting an even number on the second roll is $\frac{3}{7}$. The probability of getting at least one of these outcomes (and possibly both) is given by $\frac{4}{7} + \frac{3}{7} - \left(\frac{4}{7}\right)\left(\frac{3}{7}\right) = \frac{37}{49}$.

24. (C)

There are 15 even numbers, and since there is no replacement, the number of ways to draw two even numbers is $(15)(14) = 210$. There are also 15 odd numbers available for the third number. Then the number of outcomes in $E = (210)(15) = 3150$.

25. (C)

The number of ways to assign the left-most seat is 8, since two people cannot be seated there. The number of remaining ways to assign the right-most seat is 7, since one person has already been assigned to the left-most seat and the two people who could not be assigned to the left-most seat cannot be assigned to the right-most seat. Since there are no restrictions on the assignment of the remaining 8 seats, there are $8! = (8)(7)(6)(\ldots)(1) = 40,320$ ways of making this seating arrangement. The number of ways to seat all the people $= (8)(8!)(7) = 2,257,920$.

26. (A)

The distribution is symmetric, so the mean is at the peak, around 50. The curve looks very close to that of a normal curve. In a normal distribution density curve, the inflection points are one standard deviation away from the mean. The inflection points appear to be around 42 and 58, making the standard deviation close to 8.

27. (D)

The change in cumulative percentage from 45 to 50 to 55 to 60 is fairly constant, indicating that about the same number of students scored 50, 55, and 60.

Choice A is incorrect. To find the median in a cumulative graph, trace a horizontal line from 50 on the y-axis. We see that here the median is a score of 40. Choice B is incorrect. The height of the bar at score 50 is a cumulative percentage of about 90. This means 90% scored below or at 50. Choice C is wrong. The bars for scores 30 and 35 are not of the same height, so some students must have scored 35.

28. (A)

The standard score, denoted by z, is found by the formula $z = (x - \mu)/\sigma$, where μ is the mean and σ is the standard deviation. Then $z = (7.6 - 10)/1.5 = -1.6$. In the chart of normal distribution values of z, the probability that a z score is greater than -1.6 is .9452, which is approximately 94.5%.

29. (D)

Using the normal distribution, the critical z value is 2.05. The corresponding raw score is $(3)(2.05) + 70 = 76.15$. Since we need a minimum integer score, the correct answer is 77.

30. (A)

Tree diagram

We can illustrate three selections in going from city A to city B, five selections in going from city B to city C, and six selections in going from city C to city D. The actual answer is $(3)(5)(6) = 90$. The diagram would appear as follows:

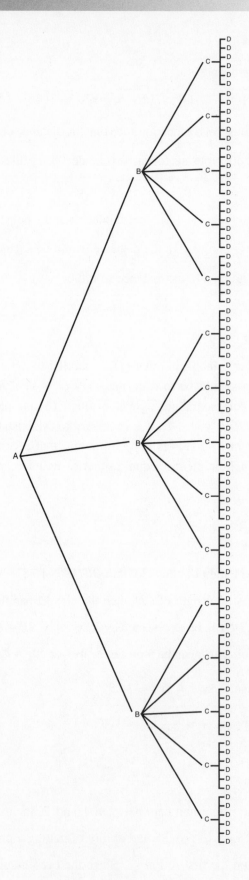

31.

Let (x, y) represent the coordinates of the moving point. Its distance from the line $y = 2$ is given by the length of the perpendicular segment from (x, y) to the line $y = 2$, which is $|2-y|$.

The distance from (x, y) to $(4, -2)$ is given by the expression

$$\sqrt{(x-4)^2 + (y-(-2))^2} = \sqrt{(x-4)^2 + (y+2)^2}$$

Then $|2-y| = \sqrt{(x-4)^2 + (y+2)^2}$

Squaring both sides, $4 - 4y + y^2 = x^2 - 8x + 16 + y^2 + 4y + 4$. Then by cancellation of like terms, $-4y = x^2 - 8x + 16 + 4y$. Further simplification leads to $-8y = x^2 - 8x + 16$, so $y = -\frac{1}{8}(x^2 - 8x + 16)$ or $y = -\frac{1}{8}(x-4)^2$

This curve is a parabola with vertex $(4, 0)$.

32.

Since $BCDE$ is a trapezoid, $\overline{BC}$ is parallel to $\overline{ED}$. $\overline{AE} = \overline{AD}$ implies $\angle AED \cong \angle ADE$. $\angle ABC \cong \angle AED$ and $\angle ACB \cong \angle ADE$, since they are corresponding angles of parallel lines cut by a transversal. We note that $\triangle ABC$ is similar to $\triangle AED$, since all angles of each triangle match up in pairs. The area of $\triangle ABC$ + the area of trapezoid $BCDE$ = the area of $\triangle AED$. We know that the trapezoid represents $\frac{3}{4}$ of the area of $\triangle AED$, so $\triangle ABC$ must be $\frac{1}{4}$ of the area of $\triangle AED$. Furthermore, since the ratio of the areas of the two similar triangles is $\frac{1}{4}$, the ratio of their corresponding sides must be $\frac{1}{2}$.

Then $\overline{BC} = \left(\frac{1}{2}\right)\overline{ED}$. $\angle CED \cong \angle BCE$ and $\angle BDE \cong \angle CBD$, since they are alternate interior angles of parallel lines cut by transversal. We note that $\triangle BCF$ is similar to $\triangle DEF$, since all angles of each triangle match up in pairs. The distances from F to $\overline{BC}$ and to $\overline{ED}$ are

the respective altitudes from F for $\triangle BCF$ and $\triangle DEF$. Since $\overline{BC} = \left(\frac{1}{2}\right)\overline{ED}$, we can conclude that the altitude from F to $\overline{BC}$ is $\frac{1}{2}$ of the altitude from F to $\overline{ED}$. This conclusion is valid because the ratio of corresponding altitudes of similar triangles is equal to the ratio of corresponding sides.

33.

The area of $\triangle PQT$ = Area of $\triangle PQR$ − Area of $\triangle PRT$ = $200 - 120 = 80$. Then $80 = \left(\frac{1}{2}\right)(PQ)(ST) = \left(\frac{1}{2}\right)(16)(ST)$, so $ST = 10$. (Note that the area of any triangle is $\left(\frac{1}{2}\right)$ (base) (altitude to this base).) Since $\overline{PT}$ is the angle bisector of $\angle RPQ$, any point of $\overline{PT}$ is equidistant from $\overline{PR}$ and $\overline{PQ}$. Then $TU = ST = 10$. For $\triangle PRT$, $120 = \left(\frac{1}{2}\right)(10)(PR)$, so $PR = 24$.

34.

- The null hypothesis (H_0) is that the population mean is 16.4 ounces. This can be expressed as: $H_0: \mu = 16.4$.

  The alternative hypothesis (H_1) is that the population mean is not 16.4 ounces. This can be expressed as: $H_1: \mu \neq 16.4$.

- The z-test statistic is given by the formula $z = \frac{(\bar{x} - \mu)}{(s/\sqrt{n})}$, where $\bar{x}$ = sample mean, μ = population mean, s = sample standard deviation, and n = number of items in the sample.
  $$z = \frac{(16.37 - 16.4)}{(.14/\sqrt{49})} = -\frac{.03}{.02} = -1.5$$

- The critical z-score values at the 5% level of significance are ± 1.96. Since $-1.96 < -1.5 < 1.96$, we cannot reject H_0. Thus, the sample mean value of 16.37 ounces is not statistically different from the company's claim of a mean of 16.4 ounces.

CSET

Mathematics

Practice Test 2

Subtest III

Answer Sheet

1. Ⓐ Ⓑ Ⓒ Ⓓ

2. Ⓐ Ⓑ Ⓒ Ⓓ

3. Ⓐ Ⓑ Ⓒ Ⓓ

4. Ⓐ Ⓑ Ⓒ Ⓓ

5. Ⓐ Ⓑ Ⓒ Ⓓ

6. Ⓐ Ⓑ Ⓒ Ⓓ

7. Ⓐ Ⓑ Ⓒ Ⓓ

8. Ⓐ Ⓑ Ⓒ Ⓓ

9. Ⓐ Ⓑ Ⓒ Ⓓ

10. Ⓐ Ⓑ Ⓒ Ⓓ

11. Ⓐ Ⓑ Ⓒ Ⓓ

12. Ⓐ Ⓑ Ⓒ Ⓓ

13. Ⓐ Ⓑ Ⓒ Ⓓ

14. Ⓐ Ⓑ Ⓒ Ⓓ

15. Ⓐ Ⓑ Ⓒ Ⓓ

16. Ⓐ Ⓑ Ⓒ Ⓓ

17. Ⓐ Ⓑ Ⓒ Ⓓ

18. Ⓐ Ⓑ Ⓒ Ⓓ

19. Ⓐ Ⓑ Ⓒ Ⓓ

20. Ⓐ Ⓑ Ⓒ Ⓓ

21. Ⓐ Ⓑ Ⓒ Ⓓ

22. Ⓐ Ⓑ Ⓒ Ⓓ

23. Ⓐ Ⓑ Ⓒ Ⓓ

24. Ⓐ Ⓑ Ⓒ Ⓓ

25. Ⓐ Ⓑ Ⓒ Ⓓ

26. Ⓐ Ⓑ Ⓒ Ⓓ

27. Ⓐ Ⓑ Ⓒ Ⓓ

28. Ⓐ Ⓑ Ⓒ Ⓓ

29. Ⓐ Ⓑ Ⓒ Ⓓ

30. Ⓐ Ⓑ Ⓒ Ⓓ

CSET: Mathematics Practice Test 2
Subtest III
Calculus; History of Mathematics

TIME: When taking the actual test, you will have one five-hour test session in which to complete the subtest(s) for which you are registered.

> <u>Directions:</u> This test consists of two sections: 30 multiple-choice and four constructed-response questions. The constructed-response questions involve written responses.

1.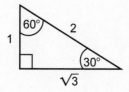

   Evaluate $\cos\left(\sin^{-1}\dfrac{1}{2}\right)$.

   (A) $\dfrac{2}{\sqrt{3}}$ (C) $\dfrac{\sqrt{3}}{2}$

   (B) $\dfrac{1}{2}$ (D) 1

2. $\sec^2\theta - \tan^2\theta =$

   (A) $\cot\theta$ (C) $\tan\theta$

   (B) 1 (D) $\sec^2\theta$

3. In a certain geometric sequence, the third term is 8 and the sixth term is 125. What is the first term?

   (A) .064   (C) 1.28

   (B) .512   (D) 3.2

4. Which one of the following statements is true for the series $\sum_{n=o}^{\infty} \dfrac{x^n}{n!}$?

   (A) It converges for each x value except zero.

   (B) It diverges for each x value.

   (C) It converges for each x value.

   (D) It diverges for each x value except zero.

5.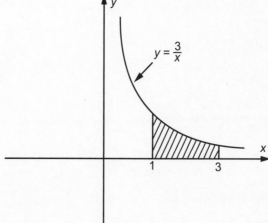

   The figure above shows the graph of $y = \dfrac{3}{x}$. What is the area of the shaded region?

   (A) ln 30   (C) ln 21

   (B) ln 27   (D) ln 18

6. $\int_{-2}^{-1} \sqrt{2}x^{-2}dx =$

   (A) $-\sqrt{2}$

   (B) $-\dfrac{\sqrt{2}}{2}$

   (C) $\dfrac{\sqrt{2}}{2}$

   (D) 1

7. If $f(x) = \pi^3$, then $f'(1) =$

   (A) $\dfrac{\pi^4}{4}$

   (B) π^3

   (C) $3\pi^2$

   (D) 0

8. If $y = \dfrac{1}{\sqrt[3]{e^x}}$, then $y'(1) =$

   (A) $3e^{-\frac{1}{3}}$

   (B) $\dfrac{1}{3}e^{-\frac{1}{3}}$

   (C) $3e^{\frac{1}{3}}$

   (D) $-\dfrac{1}{3}e^{-\frac{1}{3}}$

9. $\lim\limits_{h \to 0} \dfrac{\sin(\pi + h) - \sin \pi}{h} =$

   (A) $-\infty$

   (B) -1

   (C) 0

   (D) 1

10. If $f'(x) = \sin x$ and $f(\pi) = 3$, then $f(x) =$

    (A) $4 + \cos x$

    (B) $3 + \cos x$

    (C) $2 - \cos x$

    (D) $4 - \cos x$

11. If $f(x) = 3^{2x}$, then $f'(x) =$

    (A) $2 \cdot 3^{2x}$

    (B) 6^{2x}

    (C) $9^x (\ln 6)$

    (D) $9^x (\ln 9)$

12. If $y = \left(\sqrt{x} + 1\right)^4$, find $\dfrac{dy}{dx}$.

    (A) $4\left(\sqrt{x} + 1\right)^3$

    (B) $4x\left(\sqrt{x} + 1\right)^3$

    (C) $4\sqrt{x}\left(\sqrt{x} + 1\right)^3$

    (D) $\dfrac{2\left(\sqrt{x} + 1\right)^3}{\sqrt{x}}$

13. $\int_0^{\pi} \sin(3x)dx =$

    (A) $-\dfrac{2}{3}$

    (B) $-\dfrac{1}{3}$

    (C) 0

    (D) $\dfrac{2}{3}$

14.

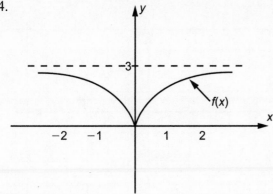

Based on the graph shown above, which of the following is NOT true?

(A) f is continuous at $x = 0$.

(B) $\lim\limits_{x \to 0} f(x) = 0$.

(C) $\lim\limits_{x \to \infty} f(x) = 3$.

(D) f is differentiable at $x = 0$.

15. If $y = xe^x$, then $\dfrac{d^2y}{dx^2} =$

(A) xe^x

(B) $(x + 1)e^x$

(C) $(x + 2)e^x$

(D) $(x + 3)e^x$

16. $\displaystyle\int_{\ln 2}^{\ln 3} e^{3x}\,dx =$

(A) e^4

(B) $e^3 - 1$

(C) $\dfrac{19}{3}$

(D) $\dfrac{15}{8}$

17. $\lim\limits_{x \to \infty} \dfrac{-7x^5 + 3x^3 + 7x - 1}{8x^6 + 2x^4 - 5x^2 + 6} =$

(A) $-\dfrac{7}{8}$

(B) 0

(C) $\dfrac{3}{8}$

(D) $\dfrac{7}{8}$

18. If $f(x) = \sin(\cos x)$, $f'(x) =$

(A) $-\sin x[\cos(\cos x)]$

(B) $2\cos^2(x) - 1$

(C) $-\sin x \cos^2 x$

(D) $\cos x \sin^2 x$

19. $\displaystyle\int_{-2}^{-1} \left|x^3\right|\,dx =$

(A) $-\dfrac{7}{8}$

(B) $\dfrac{1}{3}$

(C) $\dfrac{3}{5}$

(D) $\dfrac{15}{4}$

20. For what value(s) of x will the tangent lines to $f(x) = \ln x$ and $g(x) = 2x^2$ be parallel?

(A) 0

(B) $\dfrac{1}{4}$

(C) $\dfrac{1}{2}$

(D) $\pm\dfrac{1}{2}$

21. If $y = (x^5 - 7)^4$, then $\dfrac{dy}{dx} =$

    (A) $4(x^5 - 7)^3$ (C) $4x^4(x^5 - 7)^3$

    (B) $20x(x^5 - 7)^3$ (D) $20x^4(x^5 - 7)^3$

22. $\displaystyle\int_1^5 3e^{-3x}dx =$

    (A) $e^{-15} - e^{-3}$

    (B) $e^{-12} - e^{-3}$

    (C) e^{-12}

    (D) $e^{-3} - e^{-15}$

23. $\displaystyle\lim_{x \to 2} \dfrac{x - 2}{\sqrt{x - 2}} =$

    (A) $-\sqrt{2}$ (C) 1

    (B) 0 (D) $\sqrt{2}$

24. $\displaystyle\int_0^{\frac{\pi}{3}} 3 \sec x \tan x \, dx =$

    (A) -1 (C) 1

    (B) 0 (D) 3

25.

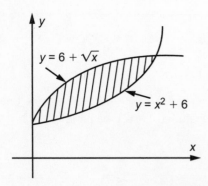

The figure above shows the graphs of $y = x^2 + 6$ and $y = 6 + \sqrt{x}$. What is the shaded area?

    (A) $\dfrac{2}{3}$ (C) $\dfrac{1}{3}$

    (B) $\dfrac{1}{2}$ (D) $\dfrac{1}{4}$

26.

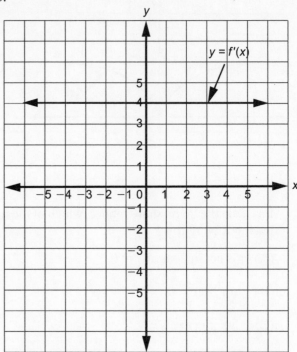

The graph of $y = f'(x)$ is shown above. If $f(0) = 5$, then $f(5) =$

    (A) 5 (C) 15

    (B) 10 (D) 25

27. The Pythagorean Theorem is named for the Greek mathematician Pythagoras, who was responsible for the first written proofs of the theorem around 540 B.C. Which of the following statements about the Pythagorean Theorem is NOT true?

    (A) The theorem dates back to the Babylonians more than 1000 years prior to Pythagoras's time.

    (B) The theorem is irreversible: If the square of any one side of a triangle equals the sum of the squares of the other two sides, the triangle is necessarily a right triangle.

    (C) About 20 different proofs of the Pythagorean Theorem exist.

    (D) Euclid published two proofs of the Pythagorean Theorem.

28. Symbols for plus (+), minus (−), multiplication (×), and equals (=) were developed

    (A) in the 16th century A.D.

    (B) by the Babylonians around 1000 B.C.

    (C) during the Golden Age of Greece in the 5th century B.C.

    (D) by the Chinese around the 2200 B.C.

29. Logarithms were discovered by John Napier in the 17th century A.D. They simplified complicated multiplication and division problems by

    (A) rounding numbers to the nearest 100.

    (B) using exponents to convert such problems to addition and subtraction problems.

    (C) moving decimal points to the same position in all numbers.

    (D) performing all of the multiplication parts of the problems first and then performing the division parts and combining them.

30. Fractals are a fairly recent discovery, dating back to 1875, with extensive discoveries made a century later by Benoit Mandelbrot, who coined the term. Which of the following statements is NOT true about fractals:

    (A) A fractal's detail is not lost as it is magnified.

    (B) Geometric fractals continuously repeat an identical pattern.

    (C) Natural objects that approximate fractals to a degree include mountain ranges, lightning bolts, and coastlines.

    (D) All self-similar objects are fractals.

Constructed-response questions 31–34:
For each response you will use up to two pages of the lined pages provided with the CSET test. Please see the sample pages at the end of the book.

31. Use analytical techniques to find the coordinates of the inflection points and to find the points of local maximum and minimum values for the graph of $f(x) = 2x^4 - 2x^2 + 1$.

32. Find the volume of the solid generated by revolving the region bounded by $f(x) = \sqrt{x}$, the line $y = 1$, and the line x = 9 about the line y = 1.

33. Determine the unit vectors that are tangent and normal, respectively, to the graph of $y = \frac{1}{2}x^3 + \frac{1}{2}$ at the point $\left(2, 4\frac{1}{2}\right)$.

34. Provide reasons for each statement in the following proof that 1 = 2. Explain any errors encountered.

Given $a = b$, $a > 0$, and $b > 0$. Prove that 1 = 2.	
Statement	**Reason**
1. $a, b > 0$	
2. $a = b$	
3. $ab = b^2$	
4. $ab - a^2 = b^2 - a^2$	
5. $a(b - a) = (b + a)(b - a)$	
6. $a = (b + a)$	
7. $a = a + a$	
8. $a = 2a$	
9. Therefore, 1 = 2	

Answer Key

Q No.	Correct Answer	Q No.	Correct Answer
1.	(C)	18.	(A)
2.	(B)	19.	(D)
3.	(C)	20.	(C)
4.	(C)	21.	(D)
5.	(B)	22.	(D)
6.	(C)	23.	(B)
7.	(D)	24.	(D)
8.	(D)	25.	(C)
9.	(B)	26.	(D)
10.	(C)	27.	(C)
11.	(D)	28.	(A)
12.	(D)	29.	(B)
13.	(D)	30.	(D)
14.	(D)	31.	Constructed-Response
15.	(C)	32.	Constructed-Response
16.	(C)	33.	Constructed-Response
17.	(B)	34.	Constructed-Response

Detailed Explanations of Answers

1. (C)

Inverse sine of $\frac{1}{2}$ is the angle whose sin is $\frac{1}{2}$. From our diagram of a $30° - 60° - 90°$ right triangle we observe $\sin 30° = \frac{1}{2}$ so $\sin^{-1}\frac{1}{2} = 30°$. Thus $\cos\left(\sin^{-1}\frac{1}{2}\right) = \cos(30°)$. Consulting our diagram we see $\cos 30° = \frac{\sqrt{3}}{2}$. Therefore $\cos\left(\sin^{-1}\frac{1}{2}\right) = \frac{\sqrt{3}}{2}$.

2. (B)

Given a right triangle, we have:

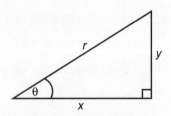

$$\tan\theta = \frac{\text{opposite side}}{\text{adjacent side}} = \frac{y}{x}$$

$$\sec\theta = \frac{1}{\cos\theta} = \frac{\text{hypotenuse}}{\text{adjacent side}} = \frac{r}{x}$$

Substitute these expressions into the identity:

$$\sec^2\theta - \tan^2\theta = \left(\frac{r}{x}\right)^2 - \left(\frac{y}{x}\right)^2$$
$$= \frac{r^2}{x^2} - \frac{y^2}{x^2}$$
$$= \frac{r^2 - y^2}{x^2}$$

By the Pythagorean Theorem, $r^2 = x^2 + y^2$; substitute x^2 for $r^2 - y^2$; since $x^2 + y^2 = r^2$,

$$x^2 = r^2 - y^2.$$

Thus, $\sec^2\theta - \tan^2\theta = \dfrac{x^2}{x^2}$
$$= 1$$

3. (C)

The general formula is $L = (a)(r)^{n-1}$ where L is the nth term, a is the first term, and r is the common ratio between terms. We can then write $8 = (a)(r)^2$ and $125 = (a)(r)^5$. Dividing the second equation by the first equation, we get $r^3 = 15.625$, so $r = 2.5$. The first term can be found by the equation $8 = (a)(2.5)^2 = 6.25a$. Thus $a = \frac{8}{6.25} = 1.28$.

4. (C)

Use the Ratio Test, $|u_{n+1}/u_n| = [x^{n+1}(n+1)!][n!/x^n]$ $= |x|/(n+1)$, which approaches zero for every value of x as $n \to \infty$, so the series converges.

5. **(B)**

$$\text{Area} = \int_1^3 \frac{3}{x}dx = 3\int_1^3 \frac{1}{x}dx = 3\ln|x|\Big|_{x=1}^3$$

$$= 3\ln 3 - 3\ln 1 = 3\ln 3 = \ln 27$$

6. **(C)**

Move the constant outside the integration symbol:

$$\int_{-2}^{-1} \sqrt{2}x^{-2}dx = \sqrt{2}\int_{-2}^{-1} x^{-2}dx$$

Use $\int u^n du = \dfrac{u^{n+1}}{n+1}$;

then $\int x^{-2}dx = \dfrac{x^{-1}}{-1} = -\dfrac{1}{x}$

$$\therefore \sqrt{2}\int_{-2}^{-1} x^{-2}dx = \sqrt{2}\left(-\frac{1}{x}\right)\Big|_{-2}^{-1}$$

Substitute the integration limits:

$$\sqrt{2}\left(-\frac{1}{x}\right)\Big|_{-2}^{-1} = \sqrt{2}\left[\left(\frac{-1}{-1}\right) - \left(\frac{-1}{-2}\right)\right]$$

$$= \sqrt{2}\left[\frac{1}{2}\right] = \frac{\sqrt{2}}{2}$$

7. **(D)**

π is a constant; therefore so is π^3.

$$\frac{d}{dx}[\text{constant}] = 0 \quad \therefore f'(1) = 0$$

8. **(D)**

Rewrite the function in exponential form:

$$f(x) = \frac{1}{\sqrt[3]{e^x}} = e^{-\frac{x}{3}}$$

Use $\dfrac{d}{dx}[e^u] = e^u \dfrac{d}{dx}[u]$ and $\dfrac{d}{dx}[cx] = c$.

$$\therefore f'(x) = \frac{d}{dx}\left[e^{-\frac{x}{3}}\right] = e^{-\frac{x}{3}}\frac{d}{dx}\left[-\frac{x}{3}\right]$$

$$= e^{-\frac{x}{3}}\left(-\frac{1}{3}\right) = -\frac{1}{3}e^{-\frac{x}{3}}$$

Substitute $x = 1$

$$f'(1) = -\frac{1}{3}e^{-\frac{1}{3}}$$

9. **(B)**

$\lim\limits_{h\to 0}\dfrac{f(x+h) - f(x)}{h}$ is the definition of the derivative of $f(x)$.

$\therefore \lim\limits_{h\to 0}\dfrac{\sin(\pi+h) - \sin\pi}{h}$ is the definition of the derivative for $\sin x$ with $x = \pi$.

$$\frac{d}{dx}[\sin x] = \cos x$$

$$\frac{d}{dx}[\sin x]_{x=\pi} = \cos x|_{x=\pi} = \cos\pi = -1$$

10. **(C)**

To get $f(x)$ given $f'(x)$, integrate $f'(x)$:

$$f(x) = \int \sin x\, dx = -\cos x + C$$

Use $f(\pi) = 3$ to calculate the value of C

$$f(\pi) = -\cos\pi + C = 3$$

$$1 + C = 3$$

$$C = 2$$

$$\therefore f(x) = -\cos x + 2 = 2 - \cos x$$

11. **(D)**

$$\frac{d}{dx}[a^u] = a^u\frac{d}{dx}[u]\cdot\ln a$$

$$\therefore \frac{d}{dx}[3^{2x}] = 3^{2x}\frac{d}{dx}[2x]\cdot\ln 3$$

$$= 3^{2x}(2)(\ln 3)$$

$$= 3^{2x}(2\ln 3)$$

Using the log rule that states $\ln a^b = b \ln a$, $\therefore 2 \ln 3 = \ln 3^2 = \ln 9$.

$$\frac{d}{dx}\left(3^{2x}\right) = 3^{2x}(\ln 9)$$
$$= 9^x(\ln 9)$$

12. (D)

Use $\dfrac{d}{dx}(u^n) = nu^{n-1}\dfrac{d}{dx}(u)$.

$$y = \left(x^{\frac{1}{2}} + 1\right)^4$$

$$\frac{dy}{dx} = 4\left(x^{\frac{1}{2}} + 1\right)^3 \frac{d}{dx}\left(x^{\frac{1}{2}} + 1\right)$$

$$= 4\left(x^{\frac{1}{2}} + 1\right)^3 \left(\frac{1}{2}x^{-\frac{1}{2}}\right)$$

$$= \frac{2(\sqrt{x} + 1)^3}{\sqrt{x}}$$

13. (D)

Use $\displaystyle\int_a^b \sin u\, du = -\cos u \Big|_a^b$

Let $u = 3x$ $\therefore du = 3\, dx$, or $dx = \dfrac{1}{3}du$

$$\int_0^\pi \sin(3x)\, dx = \frac{1}{3}\int_0^\pi \sin(3x)3\, dx$$

$$= -\frac{1}{3}\cos(3x)\Big|_0^\pi$$

$$= -\frac{1}{3}[\cos(3\pi) - \cos(0)] = \frac{2}{3}$$

14. (D)

The graph is NOT differentiable at $x = 0$ because $f'(x)$ from the left of zero does not equal $f'(x)$ from the right of zero. It also appears to have a vertical tangent at $x = 0$. $\therefore f'(x)$ is undefined.

15. (C)

Use the product rule to find $\dfrac{dy}{dx}$.

$$y = xe^x$$
$$\frac{dy}{dx} = x(e^x) + e^x(1)$$
$$= xe^x + e^x$$

Take the derivative of $\dfrac{dy}{dx}$ to find $\dfrac{d^2y}{dx^2}$.

$$\frac{dy}{dx} = xe^x + e^x$$
$$\frac{d^2y}{dx^2} = x(e^x) + e^x(1) + e^x$$
$$= xe^x + 2e^x$$
$$= (x + 2)e^x$$

16. (C)

Use $\displaystyle\int_a^b e^u\, du = e^u \Big|_a^b$

Let $u = 3x$ $\therefore du = 3\, dx$, or $dx = \dfrac{1}{3}du$

$$\int_{\ln 2}^{\ln 3} e^{3x}\, dx = \frac{1}{3}\int_{\ln 2}^{\ln 3} e^{3x} \cdot 3\, dx = \frac{1}{3}\int_{x=\ln 2}^{\ln 3} e^u\, du$$

$$= \frac{1}{3}e^u \Big|_{x=\ln 2}^{\ln 3}$$

$$= \frac{1}{3}e^{3x} \Big|_{\ln 2}^{\ln 3}$$

Evaluate the integral.

$$\frac{1}{3}e^{3x} \Big|_{\ln 2}^{\ln 3}$$

$$= \frac{1}{3}\left[e^{3(\ln 3)} - e^{3(\ln 2)}\right]$$

$$= \frac{1}{3}\left[e^{\ln 27} - e^{\ln 8}\right]$$

$$= \frac{1}{3}[27 - 8] = \frac{19}{3}$$

17. (B)

For limits with $x \to \infty$, only the highest powered term in the numerator and the highest powered term in the denominator control the solution.

$$\therefore \lim_{x \to \infty} \frac{-7x^5 + 3x^3 + 7x - 1}{8x^6 + 2x^4 - 5x^2 + 6} \approx \lim_{x \to \infty} \frac{-7x^5}{8x^6}$$

$$= \lim_{x \to \infty} \frac{-7}{8x} = 0$$

18. (A)

This function is of the form $\sin u$, where $u = \cos x$. It is NOT the product of $\sin x$ and $\cos x$.

Use $\dfrac{d}{du}[\sin u] = \cos u \, du$.

Let $u = \cos x$.

$$\frac{d}{dx}[\sin(\cos x)] = \cos(\cos x)\frac{d}{dx}(\cos x)$$

$$= [\cos(\cos x)](-\sin x)$$

$$= -\sin x [\cos(\cos x)]$$

19. (D)

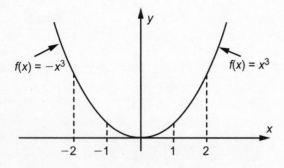

$f(x) = -x^3$ $f(x) = x^3$

It is useful to sketch the graph of $y = |x^3|$

$$\int_{-2}^{-1} \left| x^3 \right| dx = \int_{1}^{2} x^3 dx \quad \text{or} \quad \int_{-2}^{-1} -x^3 dx$$

Use

$$\int_{1}^{2} x^3 dx = \frac{x^4}{4}\bigg|_{1}^{2}$$

$$= \frac{16}{4} - \frac{1}{4} = \frac{15}{4}$$

20. (C)

Find the derivatives of $f(x)$ and $g(x)$. Equate them and solve for x.

$$f'(x) = \frac{1}{x}, \quad g'(x) = 4x$$

$$\frac{1}{x} = 4x$$

$$x^2 = \frac{1}{4}$$

$$\therefore x = \pm\frac{1}{2}$$

However, $\ln\left(-\dfrac{1}{2}\right)$ is not defined, so $x = \dfrac{1}{2}$ only.

21. (D)

Use

$$\frac{d}{dx}[u^n] = nu^{n-1}\frac{d}{dx}[u]$$

$$\frac{d}{dx}(x^5 - 7)^4 = 4(x^5 - 7)^3 \frac{d}{dx}(x^5 - 7)$$

$$= 4(x^5 - 7)^3 \cdot (5x^4)$$

$$= 20x^4(x^5 - 7)^3$$

22. (D)

Use $\displaystyle \int_{u}^{b} e^u du = e^u \bigg|_{a}^{b}$

Let $u = -3x$; then $du = -3dx$

$$\int_{1}^{5} 3e^{-3x} dx = \int_{1}^{5} e^{-3x} \cdot 3dx$$

$$= -\int_{1}^{5} e^{-3x} \cdot (-3dx) = -\int_{x=1}^{5} e^u du$$

$$= -e^u \bigg|_{x=1}^{5} = -e^{-3x} \bigg|_{1}^{5}$$

Evaluate:

$$-e^{-3x}\bigg|_{1}^{5} = -[e^{-3(5)} - e^{-3(1)}]$$

$$= -[e^{-15} - e^{-3}] = e^{-3} - e^{-15}$$

23. (B)

Try plugging in $x = 2$ to see whether you get a numerical answer.

$$\frac{x-2}{\sqrt{x-2}} = \frac{2-2}{\sqrt{2-2}} = \frac{0}{0} \implies \text{this is an indeter-}$$

minate form.

Try rationalizing the denominator.

$$\lim_{x\to 2} \frac{(x-2)}{\sqrt{x-2}} \cdot \frac{\sqrt{x-2}}{\sqrt{x-2}} = \lim_{x\to 2} \frac{(x-2)\sqrt{x-2}}{x-2}$$

$$= \lim_{x\to 2} \sqrt{x-2} = 0$$

24. (D)

Use $\displaystyle\int_a^b \sec x \tan x \, dx = \sec x \Big|_a^b$

$$\int_0^{\frac{\pi}{3}} 3 \sec x \tan x \, dx = 3 \int_0^{\frac{\pi}{3}} \sec x \tan x \, dx = 3 \sec x \Big|_0^{\frac{\pi}{3}}$$

Evaluate:

$$3 \sec x \Big|_0^{\frac{\pi}{3}} = 3 \left[\sec \frac{\pi}{3} - \sec 0 \right] = 3[2-1] = 3.$$

25. (C)

Find the x values where the two graphs cross by setting them equal in each other.

$$x^2 + 6 = 6 + \sqrt{x} \implies x^2 = \sqrt{x} \implies x^4 = x$$

$$x^4 - x = 0 \implies x(x^3 - 1) \therefore x = 0 \text{ and } x = 1.$$

$$\text{Area} = \int_a^b [(\text{top curve}) - (\text{bottom curve})] \, dx$$

$$= \int_0^1 \left[(6 + \sqrt{x}) - (x^2 + 6) \right] dx$$

$$= \int_0^1 (\sqrt{x} - x^2) dx$$

$$= \frac{2}{3} x^{\frac{3}{2}} - \frac{1}{3} x^3 \Big|_0^1 = \frac{1}{3}$$

26. (D)

From the graph, $f'(x) = 4$, which means the slope of $f(x)$ is constant and therefore $f(x)$ is linear.

Given $m = \text{slope} = 4$ and the point $(0, 5)$,

the equation of f is $f(x) = 4x + 5$.

$$f(5) = 4(5) + 5 = 25$$

27. (C)

There are more than 350 known proofs of the Pythagorean Theorem. All the other statements are true.

28. (A)

Although prior civilizations had symbols for mathematical operations, it was not until the 16th century that the symbols we use today were introduced.

29. (B)

A logarithm is simply an exponent. Logarithmic tables tell what exponent of a particular base will yield that number. In base 10, for example, a logarithm of 2 represents 100 because $10^2 = 100$. Since multiplication and division of numbers to the same base is accomplished by adding or subtracting the exponents, complicated problems can be reduced to simply adding or subtracting logarithms from the tables and then converting the logarithm back to a number by using antilog tables. Logs and antilogs are functions on most handheld calculators. All of the other answer choices are false.

30. (D)

Not all self-similar objects are fractals. A prime example is a straight line, which lacks the irregularity condition required of fractals. All of the other answer choices are true.

31.

To find maximum and/or minimum values, we need to find x values for which $f'(x) = 0$. $f'(x) = 8x^3 - 4x = (4x)(2x^2 - 1)$. If $4x = 0$, then $x = 0$. If $2x^2 - 1 = 0$, then $x = \pm\sqrt{\frac{1}{2}} = \pm\frac{\sqrt{2}}{2}$. By substitution, when $x = 0$, $f(x) = 2(0) - 2(0) + 1 = 1$. When $x = \pm\frac{\sqrt{2}}{2}$,

$$f(x) = 2\left(\pm\frac{\sqrt{2}}{2}\right)^4 - 2\left(\pm\frac{\sqrt{2}}{2}\right)^2 + 1 = 2\left(\frac{1}{4}\right) - 2\left(\frac{1}{2}\right) + 1 = \frac{1}{2}.$$ The points under consideration are $(0, 1)$, $\left(\pm\frac{\sqrt{2}}{2}, \frac{1}{2}\right)$.

To determine if these points represent local maximum or minimum values, we compute $f''(x)$ for $x = 0$, $\frac{\sqrt{2}}{2}$, and $-\frac{\sqrt{2}}{2}$. $f''(x) = 24x^2 - 4$, so $f''(0) = -4$, $f''\left(\frac{\sqrt{2}}{2}\right) = f''\left(-\frac{\sqrt{2}}{2}\right) = 8$. Since $f''(0) < 0$, $(0, 1)$ represents a local maximum value. Since $f''\left(\pm\frac{\sqrt{2}}{2}\right) > 0$, $\left(\pm\frac{\sqrt{2}}{2}, \frac{1}{2}\right)$ represent local minimum values.

Inflection points are found by solving $f''(x) = 0$. This means $24x^2 - 4 = 0$, which implies that $x^2 = \frac{1}{6}$. So, $x = \pm\sqrt{\frac{1}{6}} = \pm\frac{\sqrt{6}}{6}$. When $x = \pm\frac{\sqrt{6}}{6}$,

$$f(x) = 2\left(\frac{\sqrt{6}}{6}\right)^4 - 2\left(\frac{\sqrt{6}}{6}\right)^2 + 1 = 2\left(\frac{1}{36}\right) - 2\left(\frac{1}{6}\right) + 1 = \frac{13}{18}.$$ Thus, $\left(\pm\frac{\sqrt{6}}{6}, \frac{13}{18}\right)$ represent the inflection points. These are the points on the graph where concavity changes direction.

32.

Using the disk method, we note that for each x satisfying the inequality $1 \le x \le 9$, the cross-section radius is $\sqrt{x} - 1$. Then the volume

$$= \int_1^9 \pi(\text{radius})^2 dx = \int_1^9 \pi(\sqrt{x} - 1)^2 dx$$

$$= \pi\int_1^9 (x - 2\sqrt{x} + 1)dx = \pi\left[\frac{x^2}{2} - \frac{4}{3}x^{\frac{3}{2}} + x\right]_1^9$$

$$= \pi\left[\left(\frac{81}{2} - 36 + 9\right) - \left(\frac{1}{2} - \frac{4}{3} + 1\right)\right] = \frac{40\pi}{3}$$

33.

We first find $\frac{dy}{dx}$ at $x = 2$. $\frac{dy}{dx} = \frac{3}{2}x^2$, so at $x = 2$, $\frac{dy}{dx} = 6$. The vector $i + 6j$ has a slope of 6, and to find the unit vector u_1, divide $i + 6j$ by its length, which is $\sqrt{1^2 + 6^2} = \sqrt{37}$.

Thus, $u_1 = \frac{1}{\sqrt{37}}i + \frac{6}{\sqrt{37}}j$ is the unit vector tangent to the graph of $y = \frac{1}{2}x^3 + \frac{1}{2}$ at the point $\left(2, 4\frac{1}{2}\right)$.

Next, we find the negative reciprocal of the slope of the tangent line. Since $\frac{dy}{dx} = 6 = $ slope of the tangent line at $\left(2, 4\frac{1}{2}\right)$, $-\frac{1}{6}$ is the slope of the normal line at $\left(2, 4\frac{1}{2}\right)$. The vector $6i - j$ has a slope of $-\frac{1}{6}$, and to find the unit vector u_2, divide $6i - j$ by its length, which is $\sqrt{6^2 + (-1)^2} = \sqrt{37}$.

Thus, $u_2 = \frac{6}{\sqrt{37}}i - \frac{1}{\sqrt{37}}j$ is the unit vector normal to the graph of $y = \frac{1}{2}x^3 + \frac{1}{2}$ at the point $\left(2, 4\frac{1}{2}\right)$.

34.

Possible answers are:

Statement	Reason
1. $a, b > 0$	1. Given
2. $a = b$	2. Given
3. $ab = b^2$	3. Multiply both sides of the equation by b
4. $ab - a^2 = b^2 - a^2$	4. Subtract a^2 from both sides of the equation
5. $a(b - a) = (b + a)(b - a)$	5. Factor $(b - a)$ from each side of the equation
6. $a = (b + a)$	6. Divide both sides of the equation by $b - a$.
7. $a = a + a$	7. Substitute a for b, since $a = b$ is given.
8. $a = 2a$	8. Combine like terms
9. Therefore, $1 = 2$	9. Divide both sides of the equation by a.

The error is in step 6. Since $a = b$ (given), $b - a$ equals zero, and division by zero is not possible.

4 points for stating all of the reasons correctly and finding the error.

3 points for stating all but one reason correctly and finding the error.

2 points for stating all but two reasons correctly and finding the error.

1 point for stating all of the reasons correctly, but not finding the error.

0 for all other answers.

Answer Sheets for Constructed-Response Questions

Use these two page response sheets for each of the constructed-response questions, 31-34, in the six tests. Make copies of the two pages for each question.

Go on to the next page

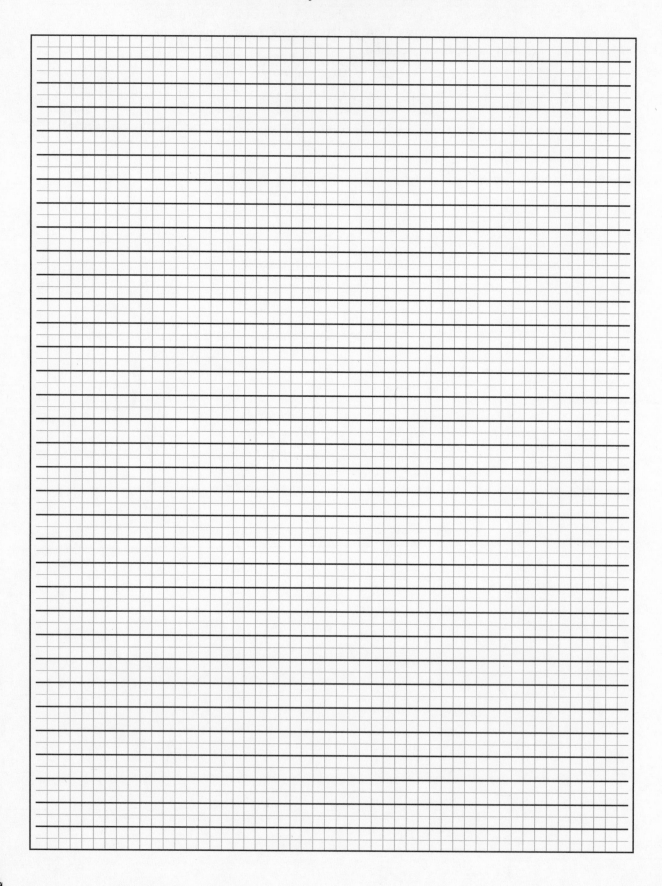

CSET

Mathematics

Index

Index

D

Trinomials, 15, 19
Two-point form, 22, 23

U

Unit circles, 152
Unit vectors, 39
Unknowns, 21, 24, 33

V

Value
    absolute, 36, 37, 74
    intermediate, 166
Variability, 136, 147
    measures of, 142–145
Variables, 15, 16
    change of, 195–196
    conditional inequalities and, 37
    dependent, 45, 148
    differentiating, 181
    graphing, 133–134
    independent, 45, 148
    rate of change, 186–187
    relationship of, 146–147
    substitution of, 194–195
Variance, 144, 147
Variation, 42–43
    of data, 142
    inverse, 43
Vector quantities, 39
Vectors, 39–41
Velocity, 39, 185, 186
Vertex, 73
Vertex angles, 90
Vertical angles, 75, 79–80, 81, 82
Vertical asymptotes, 49–50, 52

Vertical axis, 107
Vertical lines, 22
Vertical tangent, 179
Vertices, 90, 91
Volume
    cube, 104
    cylinder, 104
    cylindrical shell, 198
    rectangular solid, 104
    solid of revolution, 198–200
    sphere, 105

W

Watch, 7
Whole numbers, 11, 12
Wholes, sum-of-parts equality, 80

X

x-coordinate, 107, 153
x-intercept, 22, 50, 111–112

Y

y-coordinate, 107, 153
y-intercept, 22, 50, 111–112

Z

Zero
    constants equal to, 27
    division by, 14, 17
    square of, 14
Zero correlation, 134
Zero matrix, 59
Zero vector, 39
Zeros of a function, 48